Do you want to improve your English conversation?
Do you want to get a higher score on Toeic or Toefl? Then, Study 1250

For Intermediate and High Levels

개정판

Vocabulary 1250 American Style Practical English

by Ok Gyung Kim

한영, 영영, 영한, 중급이상 용

Phrasal Verbs and the Meanings with Examples
for Everyday Practical English
Toeic or Toefl(Idioms Included)

1997 우용출판사
www.choolpansa.com

서문

이 책은 외국에 나가지 않고도 자연스러운 생활영어를 구사할 수 있게 하는 1250개의 어휘들과 실생활에 쓰이는 다양한 예문들이 갖추어져있는 대단히 유익한 책입니다. 유학, 외교, 토익, 토플, 외국회사근무, 또는 무역 등에 관심이 있다면 인내심을 가지고 체계적이고 깊이 있고 포괄적으로 꾸준히 느리게 반복하여가며 공부하는 것이 좋습니다.

영어를 잘 하려면 기본에 충실하십시오. 방법은 단순합니다. 단어. 숙어. 문법을 알아야 독해를 할 수 있고 영작을 할 수 있습니다. 회화라는 것은 상대와 말을 주고받는 것입니다. 말을 주고받기 위해서는 상대의 말을 들을 수 있어야하며 그리고 그에 따라 나의 말을 적절하게 만들어 할 수 있어야겠지요. ***단어, 숙어, 문법, 영작, 듣기, 말하기는 다 연결이 되어 있으며 또한 동시에 이루어져야 합니다.*** 이 단순한 원리를 명심하여 꾸준히 연습하세요.

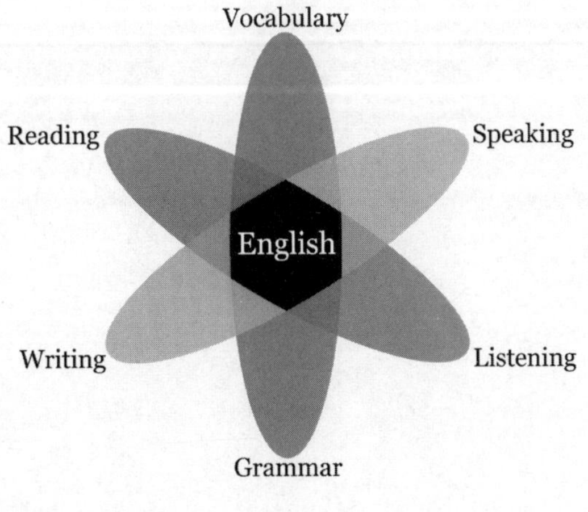

얕은 골짜기를 흐르는 물은 졸졸 소리까지 내며 그 물소리가 요란합니다. 그래서 사람들은 재미있어 합니다. 그러나 깊은 물은 소리 없이 유유히 흐를 뿐입니다. 마치 물이 흐르고 있는지 알 수 조차 없을 정도이며 지루하기까지 합니다. 그러나 그 힘은 시냇물에 견줄 수 없이 막강합니다.

바로 영어를 공부하는 자세도 이와 같습니다. 초급이나 중급정도에서는 시냇물과 같고 고급으로 가는 사람은 깊은 물의 성질을 닮아 야 할 것입니다. 이 책을 옆에 두고 ***조금씩 조금씩 느리게 꾸준히 공부해 나가십시요.*** 반드시 많은 도움이 될 것을 확신합니다.

김옥경

차례 Contents

찾아보기 Index

※ 숫자는 번호순입니다.

ㄱ

ㅇ

ㅊ

ㅎ

영어본문

A

1. Abide (by) (*v.*) – to live up to (a promise), to fulfill (a requirement), to agree to

1) Workers have promised to **abide by** the terms of the agreement they signed last week.
2) Athletes must **abide by** the decision of the referee.
3) I will **abide by** the company's rules and regulations.
4) The football players played the games **abiding by** the rules.

** Abiding (*adj.*) – long-lasting, permanent, enduring

1) She has an **abiding** love for him.
2) He has an **abiding** dream of being a soccer player.

2. About to (*adj.*) – ready to, close to, almost, intending

1) He was **about to** leave the bank when the alarm went off.
2) She is **about to** open her own dry cleaning business.
3) I am **about to** finish my homework.
4) I am not **about to** do anything with him.

3. According to (*prep.*) – as stated or indicated by

1) **According to** the weather forecast, it will rain this afternoon.
2) Proceed **according to** the instructions.
3) Prepare it **according to** the instructions.

** Accordingly (*adj.*) – in a proper way, therefore

1) Students should act **accordingly** in class.
2) The students completed all the course work, and **accordingly** they will receive their grades and should be able to graduate.

4. Account for (*v.*) – to explain, to be responsible for

1) You should **account for** failing the exam.
2) The man makes his wife **account for** every penny she spends.
3) Traffic accidents **account for** many deaths every year.

** Accountable (*adj.*) – responsible, obliged to explain the reason for one's actions

1) The Minister of Environment and the President should be held **accountable** for the destruction of the natural environment.
2) He must be **accountable** for everything he does.

** Answer for (*v.*) – to be held responsible for

1) Everyone must **answer for** their own actions.
2) You cannot **answer for** your brother.

** Answerable (*adj.*) – responsible for, accountable, liable

1) The corrupt politicians, connected with the briberies and unfair practices, should be **answerable** to society and resign from their positions.

5. Against time / Against the clock (*adv.*) – with a rapidly approaching time limit

1) We worked **against** the clock, however, we were able to finish the project on **time**.

2) Deadlines are the reason reporters usually work **against time.**
3) It's stressful to work **against time.**

6. Ahead (*adv.*) – in advance, up forward, to(at) the front

1) I should buy a ticket at least two days **ahead** of the train's departure.
2) Go **ahead.**
3) There is a traffic accident **ahead.**

** Get ahead (*v.*) – to attain success, to advance

1) I work hard to **get ahead.**
2) To **get ahead** at your work, you must work harder.

** Ahead of the game (*adj., adv.*) – ahead, winning

1) Her knowledge of calculus put her **ahead of the game** on the math exam.
2) I would like to be **ahead of the game**, so I preview the next unit before my math class.

** Ahead of time (*adv.*) – before the scheduled or expected time, early

1) The flight from London arrived **ahead of time.**
2) He arrived **ahead of time**, so I was not ready to go out right away.

7. Add up (*v.*) – to come to a correct amount, to make sense

1) These numbers don't **add up.** So you need to check them.
2) His story doesn't **add up** when compared with that of the other witnesses.

**** Add up to** (*v.*) **– to make a total of, to result in**

1) The monthly bills **added up to** $1,400.00.
2) Several days of rain **added up to** flooding in the lowlands.
3) Drinking and driving often **add up to** serious accidents.

8. All at once (*adv.*) – at the same time, all of a sudden

1) She failed the exam because she was trying to do many things **all at once.**
2) **All at once** a man became angry and began yelling obscenities.
3) Usually bad things seem to happen **all at once.**

**** All of a sudden** (*adv.*) **– by a total surprise**

1) He was driving his car, and **all of a sudden** a drunk ran onto the road.

9. All in all (*adv.*) – on the whole, in general, considering everything

1) **All in all**, it was a long but productive day.
2) **All in all**, the movie wasn't as scary as I thought it would be.

10. All in a day's work– something expected (and usually unpleasant)

1) Her job is demanding, but she thinks that the paperwork, the long hours and the demanding customers are **all in a day's work.**
2) It's **all in a day's work**, so make the best of it.

**** All in – exhausted**

1) The soccer players were **all in** when the game was over.
2) After she took care of the customers' complaints on various things, she was **all in.** But it's **all in** a day's work!

11. All kinds of *(adv.)* – various kinds of, plenty of

1) In America, drugstores and pharmacies sell drugs and **all kinds of** other merchandise.
2) The grocery store has **all kinds of** fruit and vegetables.
3) My friends gave me **all kinds of** advice, but I still did what I wanted to do.

12. All of *(adv.)* – fully

1) He couldn't believe he had spent **all of** his vacation working.
2) This is **all of** the money I have now.

13. All over *(adv.)* – everywhere, finished

1) I can't find my keys and I've looked **all over** for them.
2) I have a fever and my body aches **all over.**
3) Their relationship is **all over** now.

14. All the time *(adv.)* – very often, continuously

1) People make mistakes **all the time.**
2) I study **all the time** because I want good grades.

** All the way *(adv.)* – from the beginning to the end, in complete agreement

1) The hikers were exhausted after hiking **all the way** up the mountain.
2) The corporate administration wouldn't go **all the way** in meeting its workers' demands.

** All along *(adv.)* – all the time

1) I knew we could win the election **all along.**

2) She knew **all along** that he was cheating on her.

15. Alongside of (*adv., prep.*) – at the side of, with

1) She walked down the aisle **alongside of** her husband.
2) The boys sat **alongside of** the girls.

16. A lot (of) (*adj., adv.*) – many, much

1) I have **a lot of** things to do this afternoon.
2) I enjoyed the movie **a lot**, but I thought it was a bit long.

** Any number of (*n.*) – many

1) Let's not panic, she could be late for **any number of** reasons.
2) Problems often have **any number of** solutions.

17. Anything but (*adv.*) – the opposite, far from

1) He was **anything but** happy when he was laid off.
2) She didn't get the promotion because she was **anything but** organized.

18. Apple of one's eye (*n.*) – something that is so adored

1) She is the **apple of** her **father's eye**.
2) His son is the **apple of his eye**.

19. Around the clock (*adv.*) – or 24 hours a day

1) The employees worked **around the clock** to complete the job on time.
2) Many convenience stores are open **around the clock**.
3) Some American factories operate **around the clock**.

20. Around the corner (*adv.*) – close by, soon to happen

1) The drugstore is **around the corner** from the library.
2) Spring is just **around the corner.**

21. As best as one can (*adv.*) – in the best way one can

1) I did **as best as I could**, but I don't know what the outcome will be.
2) She always tries to do **as best as she can.**
3) He ran **as best as he could** even though his foot was aching.

22. As far as / so far as (*adv.*) – to the extent that, to the degree that

1) **So far as** I know, next weekend will be sunny.
2) **As far as** I know, the flight will arrive on time.

** As far as ~ goes (*adv.*) – for that matter, actually

1) **As far as** it **goes**, business is booming and we have plenty of new orders.
2) **As far as** the concert **goes**, it was terrible.

23. As follows – listed next

1) The reasons for firing you are **as follows** : First, you are late too often and you don't work well.
2) The list of goods to be shipped is **as follows** : 100 cases of canned fruits, 25 tons of rice, 25 tons of fertilizer and 12 tractors.

24. As for (*prep.*) – speaking of, with regard to, concerning

1) She likes cream and sugar in her coffee, but **as for** me, I like mine black.
2) **As for** money, he likes to spend more than he earns. So sooner or later he will be broke.

25. As good as (*adv.*) – almost the same

1) This watch is **as good as** that one, but it's less expensive.
2) After the chair was repaired, it looked **as good as** new.
3) This is a used one, but it's **as good as** new.

** As much as (*adv.*) – almost the same

1) I have felt **as much** pain **as** you are feeling right now.
2) I care **as much** for you **as** you do for me.
3) I ate **as much as** you did, maybe more.

26. As if / As though (*conj.*) – in the same way one would if, in a way that it would seem to be true or not true

1) My dog often behaves **as if** he knows what goes on.
2) My cat sometimes looks at me **as though** she understands me.

27. As is (*adv.*) – in its present condition, without a guarantee

1) If I were you, I would leave the writing **as is**.
2) Goods bought **as is** cannot be returned.

28. As it were (*adv.*) – so to speak

1) He was a hero among gangsters, **as it were**, until he was caught.
2) Nowadays, young people seem to live, **as it were**, in a different world.

29. As for (*v., informal*) – to cause, to bring upon, to require

1) If you continue to drive without a license, you're **asking for** trouble.
2) He keeps **asking for** trouble by arguing with his boss.

3) The job advertisement **asks for** a resume and a photo.

30. Ask to / Ask over (*v., informal*) – to invite to

1) I **asked** some people **to** my birthday party.
2) I **asked** some of my friends **over** for dinner.

31. As long as / So long as (*conj.*) – considering that

1) **As long as** you return the book tomorrow, there will be no late charge.
2) You may use the computer **as long as** you like.
3) **So long as** you play by the rules, you can play the game with us.

32. As of (*prep.*) – at a specified time or on a certain date

1) **As of** today, I am 25 years old.
2) **As of** today, all employees must use a timecard.
3) My assignment is due **as of** Monday.
4) My new job begins **as of** Monday.

33. As soon as (*conj.*) – immediately after

1) Tell him that I'll return his call **as soon as** the meeting ends.
2) I do my chores **as soon as** I get home from school.

34. As to (*prep.*) – about, on the basis of

1) I doubt she'll get the promotion because there's some doubt **as to** her ability to get the job done.
2) Promotions were given **as to** length of service and productivity.

35. As usual (*adv.*) – in the usual way

1) The factory reopened a week after the fire and its business is **as usual**.

2) He was late, **as usual**, for the meeting.

36. As well (*adv.*) – also, without gain or loss

1) I like apples **as well**.
2) I might **as well** give up now.

** As well as (*conj.*) – also, besides

1) I like rock and roll **as well as** classical music.
2) **As well as** Mary, Nancy is also one of my best friends.

37. As yet (*adv.*) – so far

1) He hasn't returned my phone call **as yet**.
2) We don't know, **as yet**, what university she wants to attend.

38. At all cost / at any cost (*adv.*) – at any expenses, regardless of the cost

1) He wanted to attend an Ivy League school **at all cost**.
2) We want to buy this house **at any cost**.

39. At any rate (*adv.*) – anyhow

1) The movie was a little long, but, **at any rate**, it was interesting.
2) **At any rate**, an agreement was reached, although we disagreed on some issues.

40. At first (*adv.*) – in the beginning

1) I didn't like her **at first**, but now she's one of my best friends.
2) **At first**, it looked like the home team was going to lose the match.

** At first glance (*adj., adv.*) – at first sight

1) They fell in love with the house **at first glance.**
2) **At first glance,** I didn't have much hope for the success of the project.

41. At / From the bottom of one's heart (*adv.*) – deep down in one's heart cost

1) She says that it doesn't matter, but **at the bottom of her heart,** she really wants to have a piano.
2) I thank you for your kindness, **from the bottom of my heart.**
3) **From the bottom of my heart,** I thank you.

** at heart (*adv.*) – basically

1) He isn't very generous, but he's a good man **at heart.**
2) She acts mean, but she's not a bad person **at heart.**

42. At home (*adj., adv.*) – where one lives or came from, comfortable or relaxed

1) I'm sorry, she's not **at home** right now.
2) Come on in and make yourself **at home.**

43. At last (*adv.*) – finally, in the end

1) **At last,** the longest football game in history came to an end.
2) He married his longtime sweetheart, **at last.**

44. At least (*adv.*) – no less than

1) You should study English **at least** an hour a day.
2) Drivers must be **at least** 18 to be eligible to apply for a license.

45. At length *(adv.)* – in detail

1) I wrote a letter describing the incident **at length.**
2) I didn't understand the song until he explained it **at length.**

46. At once *(adv.)* – immediately

1) I need to return this videotape **at once**, otherwise, I have to pay a fine.
2) I must get back to work **at once.**

47. At one time *(adv.)* – at the same time, simultaneously

1) Everything seemed to happen **at one time.**
2) I like to pay all my monthly bills **at one time.**

** At the same time *(adv.)* – at one time, nevertheless, however

1) At the movie theater, two people in front of me stood up **at the same time** and blocked my view.
2) I love him, **at the same time,** I hate him.
3) That was the second time I met him, **at the same time,** I still felt uncomfortable being around him.

** At one *(adv.)* – in harmony, in agreement

1) Walking through the woods made her feel **at one** with nature.
2) The board's opinion was **at one** with his own.
3) Mr. Kim's opinion is **at one** with mine.

48. At present *(adv.)* – now, currently

1) I am unemployed **at present**, but I expect that to change soon.
2) **At present**, the apartment is for rent, but it won't be available for long.

49. At random (*adv.*) – without order or plan

1) The lottery numbers are picked **at random.**
2) The contestants were picked, **at random,** from the telephone directory.

50. At stake (*adv.*) – at risk

1) This is an important game because the district championship is **at stake.**
2) Their relationship is **at stake** because they argue too much.

51. At best / at most (*adv.*) – at the best possibility, the most one can expect

1) He is a competent guitarist **at best**, though not a great one.
2) The new computer is, **at most**, $2,000.00 including a 19" monitor.

52. At the mercy of (*adj.*) – in the power of, at one's mercy

1) Children are often **at the mercy of** unscrupulous adults.
2) The babysitter felt that her sanity was **at the mercy of** the children's moods.

53. At this rate / At that rate (*adv.*) – at a rate of speed or rate of progress

1) If my stocks keep earning **at this rate**, I will be rich soon.
2) If you keep working **at that rate**, you'll never finish the work on time.

54. At times (*adv.*) – not often, once in a while

1) **At times**, she seems moody and depressed.
2) I visit my grandparents on a regular base, and **at times** I bring them small gifts.

55. At work *(adj.)* – working

1) "Where's your mom now?" "She is **at work.**"
2) He is happy when he's **at work.**

56. Back off (*v.*) – to give up, to withdraw a claim, to move backwards

1) Confronted with the evidence, he **backed off** on his claim of innocence.
2) He told the aggressive saleswoman to **back off**.
3) The man **backed off** when my dog barked at him.

** Back out (*v.*) – to withdraw from

1) She **backed out** of her promise to help him buy a new car.
2) In the beginning, they were going to Rome for a vacation, but **backed out** at the last minute.
3) He accepted the job offer, but **backed out** when he found out he's have to take a salary cut.

57. Back up (*v.*) – to move backward, to support, to assist, to copy computer records

1) The driver **backed up**, so the other car could get through.
2) He asked his father to **back** him **up** until business improved.
3) Volunteers **backed up** the regular staff during the emergency.
4) I usually **back up** my work on the computer every afternoon.

** Backup (*n.*) – support, assistance, a copy of computer work

1) The rescue team asked for **backup**.
2) I made the **backups** of my computer work on some floppy diskettes.

58. Bang up (*v.*) – to damage, to injure, to hit

1) She was **banged up** in a motorcycle accident. She banged up her leg.
2) Her car was so **banged up** in the collision that she had to declare it a total loss.

** Bang-up (*adj.*) – very good, successful, great, exciting

1) They did a **bang-up** job on preparing for the party.
2) The football team did a **bang-up** job and won the game.

59. Bark up the wrong tree (*v.*) – to choose a wrong person or action, to make a mistake

1) If you think you can beat me, you're **barking up the wrong tree.**
2) If he thinks she likes him, he's **barking up the wrong tree.**

60. Bear in mind (*v.*) – to keep in mind

1) **Bear in mind** that happiness is the most important thing in life.
2) **Bear** this **in mind** : You must work hard and also have luck to achieve success.

61. Bear with (*v.*) – to have patience with, to endure patiently, to stand

1) She's new on the job, so please **bear with** her when she makes mistakes.
2) I can't **bear with** his vulgar language.
3) Please **bear with** me.

62. Beat around the bush (*v.*) – to avoid the point

1) We talked, but he said nothing important; instead he **beat around the bush.**

2) Quit **beating around the bush**, and just tell me what you want.
3) Don't **beat around the bush.** Just get to the point.

63. Beat down (*v.*) – to conquer, to force down, to lower the price

1) Invaders often try to **beat down** the natives, but are rarely successful.
2) She always **beats** him **down** in front of her friends.
3) She is a great shopper, she always **beats down** the prices.
4) Kim charges $100.00 per hour for his consulting. But Lee can **beat** it **down** easily since he is a good negotiator.

** Beat up (*v.*) – to give a beating

1) The neighborhood bullies **beat up** the new boy.
2) After a night of hard drinking, he felt like he had been **beaten up.**

64. Before long (*adv.*) – soon

1) The semester will be over **before** too **long.**
2) The family was split up during the IMF period, but they were reunited **before long.**

65. Behind bars (*adv.*) – in jail

1) That fellow standing by the door will most likely end up **behind bars.**
2) People who commit crimes often end up **behind bars.**

** Bar exam (*v.*) – an exam for becoming a lawyer

1) A law school graduate must pass the **bar exam** after two years of internship to become a lawyer.

66. Behind the scenes *(adv.)* – unknown to most people, out of sight

1) Our committee worked **behind the scenes** to assist single parents.
2) Most corporate decisions are made **behind the scenes.**

67. Behind the times *(adv.)* – old fashioned, outdated

1) The company's policies concerning female employees are **behind the times.**
2) His political views are **behind the times.**

** Behind time *(adj., adv.)* – late, behind schedule

1) The musicians were late, so the concert was **behind time.**
2) My watch is twenty minutes **behind time.**

68. Beside the point *(adj., adv.)* – off the subject, something different

1) "Its price is **beside the point,**" he said, "The quality isn't what I expected."
2) Winning or losing is **beside the point**, how the game is played is more important.

69. Best bet – best way

1) Your **best bet** is to find any job and get some work experience.
2) Route 24 is probably our **best bet.**

** Make a bet – to bet money

1) He often **makes a bet** on a soccer play with his friends and he sometimes wins.
2) I **made a bet** on the Korean soccer team in the World Cup Games.
3) Many people **make a bet** on horserace.

70. Better late than never (a cliché)
– doing something is better than not doing anything at all, even though it is late

1) She was three hours late and said, "**Better late than never.**"
2) Although I'm middle aged, I want to learn to play an instrument because it's **better late than never.**

71. Beyond question (*adj., adv.*) – very certain, without doubt

1) The unparalleled quality of this stereo system is **beyond question.**
2) His honesty and integrity are **beyond question.**

72. Black-and-white (*adj.*) – having only two sides; one right, the other wrong

1) Reunification is not a **black-and-white** issue. It's much more complicated.
2) Modern problems rarely have a **black-and-white** solution.

73. Black out (*v.*) – to darken, to prevent, to lose consciousness

1) During the war, the country's people had to cover their windows at night to **black out** the city.
2) The repressive government **blacked out** all anti-government news reports.
3) She **blacked out** after she drank too much.

** Blackout (n.) – an electrical stoppage, a temporary loss of consciousness, the act of prohibiting transmission of TV, radio, etc.

1) The storm caused a major **blackout** in the area.
2) Drinking too much alcohol can cause **blackouts.**
3) The government demanded a **blackout** of all foreign media.

74. Blood is thicker than water (a cliché)

1) The mother believed her son's fabricated story in spite of the evidence that it wasn't true because **blood is thicker than water.**
2) The mother stood by her son regardless of the laws he broke since **blood is thicker than water.**

75. Black off (*v.*) – to allow (gas under pressure, steam, air, or anger) to escape

1) Trains used to **blow off** their steam before beginning their run.
2) Accumulated anger is usually **blown off** in a destructive manner.
3) His yelling was a way to **blow off** steam.

** Bottle up (*v.*) – to restrain, to hold in

1) **Bottled up** anger is a leading cause of stress related illnesses.
2) Her unhappy marriage caused her to **bottle up** her feelings.

** Blow up (*v.*) – to explode, to lose one's temper, to fill with air, inflate, to enlarge

1) The latest satellite **blew up** shortly after it was launched.
2) He has a tendency to **blow up** when he gets angry.
3) He **blew up** balloons for his sister's party.
4) Having the picture **blown up** was more expensive than we expected.

76. Blow out (*v.*) – to extinguish, to explode violently, to melt and open an electric circuit

1) The girl **blew out** the candles on her birthday cake.
2) The tire **blew out** while I was driving on the freeway.
3) Our electricity was cut off when the fuse **blew out.**

77. Blow over *(v.)* **– to reach a lower level, to become unimportant after a while**

1) Meteorologists are hoping that the strong typhoon will **blow over** before it reaches land.
2) The latest political scandal **blew over** quickly.

78. Blow the lid off *(v.)* **– to reveal the fact that has been kept as a secret**

1) He threatened to **blow the lid off** the company's secret money dealings.
2) The news reporter's article **blew the lid off** the governmental cover-ups.

79. Brand-new *(adj.)* **– very new, not used**

1) I bought a **brand-new** car, not a used one.
2) It's a **brand-new** television, so it shouldn't need servicing this soon.

80. Break down *(v.)* **– to destroy, to decay, to stop working, to lose control over one's emotions**

1) The bridge was **broken down.**
2) Rocks **break down** and turn into sand over a long period of time.
3) The car **broke down** on the way to Seoul.
4) When her father died, she **broke down** and cried.

** **Breakdown** *(n.)* **– a destruction, a stopping, a collapse of physical and mental health, an analysis or summary consisting of itemized data**

1) A **breakdown** in the tunnel caused a massive traffic jam.
2) She had a nervous **breakdown** when her husband died.
3) This is a **breakdown** on the price of the completed new house.

81. Break even (*v.*) – to have equal gain and loss

1) I lost money on a few stocks, but **broke even** with most of my investments.
2) I barely **broke even** with my investment this time.

** Break-even (*adj.*) – making neither a profit nor a loss

1) This was a **break-even** month, so I didn't manage to save any money.

82. Break in / into (*v.*) – to enter by force, to interrupt, to begin suddenly

1) The burglars **broke into** the store through the rear window.
2) A strange man **broke in** on our conversation while we were talking.
3) The girl **broke into** tears when she heard the sad news.

** Break-in (*n.*) – a forced illegal entry

1) My next door neighbor had a **break-in** last night and their VCR was taken.

83. Break out (*v.*) – to begin showing a skin irritation, to begin suddenly, to escape

1) Her skin began to **break out** because she ate some meat. She is allergic to meat.
2) Sweets make me **break out** with red spots.
3) A riot **broke out** near the American Embassy.
4) A war **broke out** in the Middle East.
5) Three inmates **broke out** of the local prison during the night.

84. Break up (*v.*) – to separate, to end a relationship, to put an end to, to break into pieces

1) He recently **broke up** with his girlfriend, but he still has feelings for her.
2) Did you hear that John and Lilly were going to **break up**?
3) Police moved in quickly and **broke up** the riot before it got out of control.
4) Icebergs are powerful enough to **break up** a strong ship like the Titanic.

** Breakup (*n.*) – the act of breaking up

1) The **breakup** of the earth can be seen through erupting volcanoes.
2) The **breakup** of the family unit continues to worry social organizations.

** Break off (*v.*) – to stop suddenly, to end a relationship

1) We **broke off** our conversation when the phone rang.
2) She **broke off** with her boyfriend last week.

** Break with (*v.*) – to end a membership, to end a relationship

1) His decision to **break with** the company was based on personal reasons.
2) They will **break with** tradition and get married by the sea.

85. Break one's heart (*v.*) – to dishearten, to make very sad

1) It **breaks my heart** to see animals being mistreated.
2) Seeing dying animals in all kinds of useless and cruel testing **broke my heart**.

86. Bring about (*v.*) – to cause to happen

1) Diligence as well as frugality **brought about** his success.
2) I need to **bring about** some changes in my lifestyle.

87. Bring on (*v.*) – to result in

1) Heart disease is often **brought on** by excessive smoking, a lack of exercise and some genetic disorder.
2) Eating too much spicy food **brought on** indigestion.

88. Bring around (*v.*) – to persuade, to make change in thinking

1) Management is opposed to the idea, so we need to find a way to **bring** them **around** to our way of thinking.
2) After a long debate, we finally **brought** them **around** to our side.

89. Bring out (*v.*) – to enhance, to improve, to show, to reveal

1) She always seems to **bring out** the best in others.
2) The band will **bring out** a new album this fall.
3) The public needs to know the truth of the matter ; but the government obviously doesn't want it **brought out** because it will cost them votes.
4) Seasonings can **bring out** the flavor in foods.

90. Bring in (*v.*) – to bring, to earn money, to produce, to give a verdict, to arrive at a verdict

1) The store **brought in** some different styles of dresses.
2) Big department stores compete to **bring in** more customers and their annual sales bring in millions of dollars.
3) A new architect was **brought in** on the building project.
4) The jury **brought in** a verdict of not guilty due to the lack of evidence.
5) The judge arrived at a verdict of "not guilty" for the defendant.

91. Bring off (*v.*) – to succeed in, to accomplish successfully, to make it happen

1) I wasn't sure if I was going to be able to **bring** it **off**.
2) I finally **brought off** the deal.
3) I hope I can **bring off** the deal.

92. Bring to light (*v.*) – to discover from hidden, to expose

1) The incident was **brought to light** after a lengthy cover-up.
2) The writer's most recent work wasn't **brought to light** until after his death.
3) Our research will be **brought to light** next year.

93. Bring up (*v.*) – to raise, to mention

1) She wants to **bring up** her children in a good environment.
2) Several key issues were **brought up** at the meeting.

94. Brush off (*v.*) – to not take seriously, to remove (with a brush)

1) She **brushed off** his advice.
2) I need to **brush** the snow **off** my car.

** Brush-off (*n.*) – an abrupt refusal

1) He tried to say something nice to her, but she just gave him the **brush-off**.

95. Brush up / brush up on (*v.*) – to refresh one knowledge or skill of a certain subject

1) I need to brush up on my Spanish before I go to Spain next summer.
2) I forgot much of the math I learned. I'll brush up on it this semester.

96. Build up (*v.*) – to increase or develop steadily, to improve, to construct by degrees

1) To **build up** your credit, you should make your payments on time.
2) I exercise every day in order to **build up** the strength of my body.
3) This area has been **built up** in recent years.

97. Burn out (*v.*) – to extinguish from a lack of fuel, to be overworked

1) The campfire **burned out** because there wasn't any more wood.
2) I am completely **burned out** after studying for weeks for the exam.
3) I am **burned out** from working too many hours.

98. Burn up (*v.*) – to consume or be consumed completely by fire, to burn completely, to cause to become very angry

1) After she got married, she **burned up** all the letters from her old boyfriends.
2) The bank seized her car when she missed three payments. That really **burned** her **up**.

** Burn down (*v.*) – to burn or cause to burn to the ground

1) One careless smoker can **burn down** an entire forest.
2) The house **burned down** because of faulty electrical wiring.
3) The candle's wick **burned down** very quickly.

** Burn one's bridges (a cliché) – to leave oneself without a way to get out, to damage the relationship

1) Don't **burn your bridges** by arguing with your supervisor.
2) She **burned her bridges** by behaving rudely in front of her friends.

99. Butter up (*v.*) – to try to get a favor by flattery

1) Some students try to **butter up** their teachers for better grades.
2) No matter how much he tried to **butter** her **up**, she wouldn't date him.
3) Sometimes the boss tries to **butter up** his employees by buying them dinner. Of course he wants them to work harder for him.
4) I think you're trying to **butter** me **up**.

** Buy off (*v.*) – to bribe

1) Some lobbyists try to **buy off** politicians with large sums of money.

** Buy out (*v.*) – to buy someone's share to gain all of something

1) He **bought out** all the shares of the company and gained complete control.
2) I want to **buy out** my partner to own the company.

100. By and large (*adv.*) – for the most part, on the whole

1) We have a good relationship, **by and large.**
2) **By and large,** it was a good, but a very expensive trip.
3) He made some small mistakes here and there, but **by and large** he did a good job.

101. By chance (*adv.*) – accidentally

1) Many new vaccines are discovered **by chance.**
2) We met **by chance**, but we got married by choice.
3) Discovery of the new vaccine was **by chance.**

102. By means of (*prep.*) – by using, with the help of

1) They made their way across the river **by means of** a wooden raft.
2) He got across the river **by means of** a small boat.

** **By way of** *(prep.)* **– through, via, as a means of**

1) I flew from Seoul to Cleveland **by way of** San Francisco.
2) What do you suggest we do **by way of** a celebration?

103. By all means *(adv.)* **– certainly**

1) "May I sit here?" "**By all means**, please."
2) **By all means**, you should give her a call.
3) **By all means**, let's meet this week.

** **By no means** *(adv.)* **– certainly not**

1) "Could you let me use your car today?" "**By no means**."
2) I am **by no means** a fool.

104. By word of mouth *(prep.)* **– information passed from person to person by words**

1) The news of the tragic accident quickly has spread around **by word of mouth**.
2) I heard about the story **by word of mouth**.

105. Call down (*v.*) – to scold

1) The dentist **called down** his assistant today because she wasn't careful in treating a patient. Yesterday, he also called her down.

106. Call for (*v.*) – to require, to come and get or pick up

1) The delicate surgical procedure **calls for** precision.
2) This test **calls for** exact timing, otherwise the whole thing will fail.
3) She is supposed to **call for** me to go to a movie, but she hasn't come yet.

** Call on (*v.*) – to request or appeal, to visit, to ask to speak

1) The Mayor **called on** the residents to conserve the electricity and water during summer.
2) I **called on** a friend while I was in Seoul.
3) The Red Cross **calls on** volunteers to donate blood.
4) When his teacher **called on** him, he didn't know the answer.

107. Call it a day (*v.*) – to stop for the day

1) We only played nine holes and then **called it a day**.
2) Let's **call it a day**. We've done enough work for one day.

108. Call off (*v.*) – to cancel

1) We've had to **call off** the picnic because of the approaching rain storm.

2) The wedding was **called off** because they weren't sure whether they were truly in love.

109. Call into question (*v.*) – to raise doubt about

1) His honesty was **called into question** when they discovered there was some money missing from the treasury.

110. Call up (*v.*) – to telephone, to remind, to call for service into court, to draft

1) Please **call** me **up** at six p.m.
2) The pictures **called up** memories of their holiday in Greece.
3) The court **called up** local citizens for jury duty.
4) The government **calls up** young people to serve their country.

** Call to mind (*v.*) – to remind of

1) Your statement **calls to mind** something I've wanted to discuss with you.

111. Come / Bring to the fore (*v.*) – to come or to bring into leadership, to come into the public attention

1) During the war, some great leaders **came to the fore.**
2) Some brilliant young businessmen **came to the fore** during the depression.
3) In recent years, more complicated cellular phones have **come to the fore.**

112. Cancel out (*v.*) – to balance, to get rid of the effect

1) I got an A in Chinese Literature to **cancel out** the D which I got in Human Anatomy.
2) His wealth **canceled out** his lack of a formal education.

113. Can't help but / cannot but *(v.)* **– be compelled to, be unable to resist**

1) When I see cats playing, I **cannot help but** laugh.
2) When he was called up, he **couldn't help but** serve his country.

114. Cannot see the wood for the trees / Can't see the forest for the trees *(v.)* **– be unable to understand the whole, or to value the whole, by focusing only on the small parts**

1) You **can't see the forest for the trees.** Please try to see the big picture instead of seeing only a few small points.

115. Car pool *(n)* **– a plan by a group of people to rotate the use of their cars, such as going to work or school or to a vacation place**

1) It's your week to drive in the **car pool.**
2) **Car-pooling** is economical, though sometimes inconvenient.

116. Care for *(v.)* **– to like, to look after**

1) Would you **care for** another cup of coffee?
2) I don't **care for** rap music.
3) I **care for** my pets.

117. Carrot and stick *(n.)* **– reward and punishment**

1) The company used both a carrot and a stick to negotiate with their employees.

118. Carry away (*v.*) – to arouse

1) I was **carried away** when I heard the sound of the national anthem, and I cried.
2) Most of the people got **carried away** when our football players won in the World Cup Game.

119. Carry a torch (*v.*) – to continue to hold in affection, to sacrifice voluntarily to help someone

1) Even though their relationship has ended, he still **carries a torch** for her.
2) When the man was in deep trouble, some of his followers were willing to **carry a torch** for him.

120. Carry off (*v.*) – to remove, to win or succeed

1) They **carried off** the trash and they got paid for doing it.
2) The athlete hopes to **carry off** a gold medal in the 2004 Athens Olympic Games.

** Carry out (*v.*) – to remove, to fulfil, to accomplish

1) Would you help me **carry out** the groceries?
2) The President must **carry out** the duties of his office.
3) We **carried out** our wedding plans without spending too much money.

** Carryout (*n.*) – take–out food

1) Sometimes, I order at the Chinese **carryout** restaurant.

121. Carry on (*v.*) – to go on with, to continue despite difficulties

1) We've **carried on** our correspondence for over a year.
2) They **carried on** their relationship despite his family's objections.

** Carry through / carry through with (*v.*) – to get done, to accomplish

1) I **carried through** with my plan to get my book published.
2) She had to work full time, but **carried through** with her plan to finish her education.

122. Catch on / catch on to (*v.*) – to understand, to become popular

1) She will soon **catch on to** the duties of her new position.
2) Cellular phones have really **caught on** with the youth market.

123. Catch one's breath (*v.*) – to get back to normal breathing, to rest for a moment

1) I need a minute to **catch my breath.**
2) Would you like to sit down while you **catch your breath?**

124. Catch up (*v.*) – to bring up to date, to come up from behind, to be trapped in a situation, to become involved with (often against one's wishes)

1) I should **catch up** on my correspondence.
2) I've almost **caught up** with my studies.
3) We were **caught up** in a traffic jam and arrived at the opera center an hour late.
4) Nowadays it's rare that a politician is not **caught up** in a scandal.

125. Check in / into (*v.*) – to register, to examine or investigate

1) We can **check in** at the hotel after 10:00 a.m.
2) I am going to **check into** the hotel as soon as I arrive in Sydney.
3) I must **check into** that when I get back to my office.

** Check out (*v.*) – to leave, to test, to borrow, to investigate

1) Can I pay my bill when I **check out?**
2) I need to have my car engine **checked out.**
3) There are some strangers in town. **Check** them **out.**
4) The library is closing in 10 minutes, please **check out** all the books at the front desk.
5) I **checked out** a book for a week.

126. Cheer up (*v.*) – to become cheerful, to make cheerful

1) **Cheer up**, the good times are just around the corner.
2) He thought that taking her to the dance would **cheer** her **up.**

127. Clean off (*v.*) – to clean the surface of

1) My desk needs to be cleaned off. I need to **clean off** my desk.
2) After dinner I usually **clean off** the table, then I wash the dishes.

** Clean out (*v.*) – to deprive completely (as of money), to remove everything from

1) The slumping economy has virtually **cleaned out** the company's treasury.
2) He was **cleaned out** at the horse races.
3) He helped his father **clean out** the garage.

** Clean up (*v.*) – to clean thoroughly, to change one's habits

1) She **cleans up** her bedroom every other weekend.
2) Members of the community got together to **clean up** the neighborhood park.
3) You need to **clean up** your act, or you'll never pass the course.

128. Clear up (*v.*) – to make clear, to heal (particularly a skin condition)

1) The weather is going to **clear up** this afternoon.
2) There's a small problem that we need to **clear up.**
3) My skin rash has all **cleared up.**

129. Climb the walls (*v.*) – to react in frustration or be frustrated

1) She's **climbing the walls** because she lost heavily in the stock market.
2) If the professor had talked for another minute, I would have been **climbing the wall.**
3) I am **climbing the walls** because I am so bored.

** Drive up the wall (*v.*) – to annoy very much, to drive someone crazy

1) Please stop complaining about everything I do. You are **driving** me **up the wall.**
2) The noisy children are **driving** me **up the wall.**

130. Closed-door (*adj.*) – in secret, limited to a few

1) The Appropriations Committee held a **closed-door** meeting to decide the fate of the new missile system.
2) The board of trustees often holds **closed-door** meetings before making an announcement.

131. Close down (*v.*) – to shut down, to stop operating completely

1) The shoe factory **closed down** because making shoes was no longer profitable.
2) Many of the shops on the beach **close down** during the winter.

** **Close out** (*v.*) **– to end, to get rid of all the goods**

1) The company has **closed out** its entire line of furs. They don't plan to carry furs anymore in respect of wildlife.

** **Close-out** (*n.*) **– a sale in which goods are sold at greatly reduced prices to dispose of them quickly**

1) Many shops offer **close-out** sales on Christmas items after the holiday shopping season.
2) A motor company is having a **close-out** sale on last year's models.

132. Coffee break (*n.*) **– a short recess from work to have coffee and to rest**

1) Let's take a quick **coffee break** before the meeting begins.
2) The company gives its employees **coffee breaks** twice a day.

133. Cold feet (*n.*) **– a loss of courage**

1) He was going to ask them for a job, however he got **cold feet**.
2) He wanted to go skydiving, but he got **cold feet** at the last minute.

** **Cold shoulder** (*n.*) **– unfriendly or insignificant treatment**

1) His colleagues started giving him the **cold shoulder**. And it was a sure sign that he was in danger of losing his job.
2) After losing his job, even his closest friends gave him the **cold shoulder**.

134. Come about (*v.*) **– to happen**

1) He wanted to know how his low bank balance had **come about**.
2) He wanted to know how his daughter's expulsion from university had **come about**.

3) I want to know how this incident **came about.**

135. Come across (*v.*) – to find or meet by accident

1) I **came across** my missing credit card while I was moving the bookcase.
2) She **came across** a university friend last week. She hadn't seen him in years.
3) I hope I **come across** my assignment paper. I lost it and it's due tomorrow.

136. Come along (*v.*) – to make progress

1) The doctor said, "She's **coming along** well after her surgery."
2) "How are your classes going?" "They're **coming along** well."

** Come along with (*v.*) – to accompany

1) I'm going to the movies. Do you want to **come along with** me?
2) When the football coach came to Korea, his sweetheart **came along with** him.

137. Come between (*v.*) – to cause a problem

1) He doesn't like to lend money to his friends because he doesn't want it to **come between** them.
2) I don't want money matter to **come between** us.
3) When money problems **came between** them, their relationship was in jeopardy.

138. Come by (*v.*) – to visit, to acquire

1) The neighbors **came by** for a cup of coffee and a chat.
2) Where did you **come by** that beautiful jacket?

**** Come over** *(v.)* **– to come, to occur clearly**

1) **Come over** to my house to study with me.
2) It suddenly **came over** me that I had forgotten all about my appointment.

**** Drop in / drop by / stop by / stop in** *(v.)*
– to make a casual, unannounced, and a short visit

1) I just **dropped in** since I was in the neighborhood.
2) **Stop by** my office when you have a minute.

139. Come out with *(v.)* **– to make known or say something unexpected**

1) The Democratic Party **came out with** a modest economic proposal.
2) Don't say anything unless you can **come out with** the truth.

**** Come up** *(v.)* **– to arise by chance in a discussion, to approach**

1) We were just chatting and suddenly the issue of abortion **came up.**
2) The subject of real estate **came up** while we were talking.
3) A street man **came up** to me and begged for some money.

**** Come up with** *(v.)* **– to provide, to propose**

1) Employees often **come up with** solutions that elude management.
2) She **came up with** a fantastic idea for the spring fashion show.

140. Come through *(v.)* **– to achieve success in spite of difficulties, to do a desired action**

1) The business had a lot of difficulties in the beginning, but it **came through** the tough times and now it's very secure.
2) I was sure that the Korean football team would **come through** and win the games.

3) The publication of my book finally **came through.**

141. Come under (*v.*) – to come under the authority of

1) The small financial firm **came under** one of the major insurance companies.

142. Common ground (*n.*) – shared interests, beliefs, or similar ways

1) Their marriage failed because of a complete lack of **common ground.**
2) The committee's goal is to find areas of **common ground.**
3) Since they could not find any **common ground**, the deal fell through.

143. Cool down / cool off (*v.*) – to become or make calm, to make cool

1) You're too emotional, try to **cool down.**
2) The engine of the car has been overheated. Don't drive until it **cools down.**

** Calm down (*v.*) – to make or become calm

1) You need to **calm down** and think clearly, otherwise you'll fail the exam.
2) Yoga helps me **calm down.**

144. Coop up (*v.*) – to feel confined in a small place

1) I've been **cooped up** in my place doing a final editing of my book for a long while.
2) The rainy days keep me **cooped up** in my small apartment.

145. Count on / upon (*v.*) – to rely on, to depend on

1) You can **count on** me to raise funds for Amnesty International.
2) The team **counts on** him to score points.
3) The Korean team **counted on** the excellent coach, Hiddink.
4) You know you can **count on** me anytime you need my help.

146. Count out (*v.*) – to exclude

1) The incumbent won the election despite being **counted out** by the press.
2) Don't **count** them **out**, the game's not over yet.
3) I don't want to be involved in your plot. **Count** me **out**, please.

** Count in (*v.*) – to include

1) If you need a fourth person for the bridge game, **count** me **in**.
2) We're planning a surprise party for her. Should we **count** you **in**?

147. Cover up (*v.*) – to hide, to conceal

1) The recent money scandal was quickly **covered up**.
2) I don't think that **covering up** a mistake is the best way to handle it.

148. Crack down on (*v.*) – to take strong actions to stop illegal or disapproved activities

1) The police started to **crack down on** drunk driving.
2) The police neglected to **crack down on** forced prostitution and furthermore they condoned it by taking bribes from the owners of bordellos. Then they used a cunning scheme to cover it up.

** **Crackdown** (*n.*) **– a strong action taken to stop illegal or disapproved activities**

1) There was a **crackdown** on illegal gambling casinos.
2) The **crackdown** on forced prostitution has been less successful.

149. Crack up (*v.*) – to break down emotionally

1) He is about to **crack up** with his overloaded responsibilities.
2) The nurse is about to **crack up** with her overloaded responsibilities in the hospital.

** **Crackup** (*n.*) **– a nervous breakdown**

1) With overloaded responsibilities, he finally had a **crackup**.

150. Cross one's fingers (*v.*) – to keep one's fingers crossed hoping for good luck

1) Let's **cross our fingers** and hope the flight isn't cancelled.
2) I'll keep **my fingers crossed** and hope everything turns out all right for you.

151. Cross one's mind (*v.*) – to have sudden and passing thoughts

1) The thought of quitting the job **crossed her mind**.
2) It just **crossed my mind** that we haven't paid you for the work you did.

152. Cross ross off / out (*v.*) – to remove (as from a list), to draw a line through

1) His name was on the list of promotion, but it was **crossed off** at the last minute.
2) I want to **cross out** this sentence because it's redundant.

153. Cut down (*v.*) – to reduce

1) The doctor has advised her to **cut down** on fatty food.
2) **Cut down** on your spending or you'll end up a pauper.

154. Cut in (on) (*v.*) – to interrupt, to move in front of someone or something

1) I didn't want to **cut in** on their conversation, but it was an emergency.
2) The accident occurred when a motorbike suddenly **cut in** the line of traffic.

** Cut off (*v.*) – to stop abruptly, to shut off, to amputate

1) A telecommunication company **cut off** our phone service without notice.
2) He is completely **cut off** from his family.
3) Her insurance has been **cut off** since January.
4) The doctor **cut off** the patient's wounded leg.

** Cut out (*v.*) – to remove, to stop doing something

1) The butcher **cut out** the entrails of the dead chicken.
2) He should **cut out** smoking cigarettes.

** Cut it out (*v.*) – to stop (bad behavior or annoying)

1) I don't like your nagging. Why don't you **cut it out**?

155. Cut up (*v.*) – to cut in small pieces

1) She is **cutting up** some vegetables.

D

156. **Dark horse** (*n.*) – **A contestant who is not well-known and then becomes a winner**

1) To everyone's surprise, the Best Actor Award went to the **dark horse** nominee.

157. **Day after day** (*adv.*) – **everyday, all the time**

1) The swim team practiced **day after day** for the entire summer.
2) I've worked on this project **day after day** without a break.

** **Day and night** (*adv.*) – **continuously, around the clock**

1) Most convenience stores are open, **day and night**, for 365 days a year.
2) The factory operated **day and night** in order to complete the job.

158. **Dates back** (*v.*) – **to have a particular point of origin in the past**

1) The stoneware **dates back** hundreds of years.
2) This pottery **dates back** to the Silla Dynasty.

159. **Deep water** (*n.*) – **a serious problem, difficulty**

1) The President's family is in **deep water** now.
2) Her small lie got her into **deep water** with her parents.
3) Not studying put him in **deep water** when finals arrived.

160. Die out (*v.*) – to disappear slowly, to become extinct

1) The candle burned down and slowly **died out.**
2) Many endangered species have already **died out.**
3) Humanity must prevent endangered species from **dying out.**

161. Dig in (*v.*) – to begin to work hard

1) They **dug in** and worked until the project was finished.
2) I must **dig in** and keep on studying until the exam day.

** Dig out (*v.*) – to get information or to find by searching, to remove or take out by digging

1) **Digging out** the information from the records is difficult.
2) The old dead tree was finally **dug out** of my yard.
3) In Africa, one day, several sweet potato diggers **dug out** a huge diamond accidentally.
4) They had a big job to **dig out** after the snow storm.

162. Do the honors (*v.*) – to act as host or hostess

1) Our boss asked me to **do the honors** and represent our branch office at the company's annual banquet.

163. Do over (*v.*) – to do again, to redo

1) Your assignment has too many errors, so **do** it **over.**
2) I don't like the interior design of my apartment, so I want to **do** it **over.**

164. Double-check (*v.*) – to check again to make sure it is right

1) I think I locked the door, but I should **double-check** it.
2) You should **double-check** your itinerary before going on your trip.

3) Did you **double-check** the oven to make sure it was turned off?
4) She **double-checked** her essay and found several minor errors.
5) I should **double-check** tomorrow's schedule.

165. Double-cross (*v.*) – to betray by doing the opposite of what was agreed on

1) The CIA agent **double-crossed** the government by giving away the country's top secret to the enemy.
2) Don't try to **double-cross** me.

** Double-dealing (*adv., n.*) – treacherous, treachery

1) The **double-dealing** policemen, who received money from the bordellos, are in deep water.

** Double standard (*n.*) – a hypocritical principle which works only for one side

1) It's okay for men to remarry with children, but if it's not okay for women to do so, then, it is a **double standard.**

** Double talk (*n.*) – what is said, thought and acted is different

1) She is full of **double talk.** She says nice things in front of you, but behind your back, she speaks differently.
2) On the phone, she said that she would be glad to see me and I believed it, but it turned out that it was **double talk.**

166. Doubt (*n., v.*) – to distrust, to disbelieve, uncertainty

1) "You think the economy will improve soon? I **doubt** it."

** **Deyond doubt** *(adv.)* **– certainly**

1) It's **beyond doubt** that the economy will improve within a few years.

167. Give the benefit of the doubt *(v.)* **– to believe someone is innocent until proven guilty**

1) Without clear proof you should **give** people **the benefit of the doubt.** Everyone is innocent until proven guilty.
2) She thought the students had cheated but she **gave** them **the benefit of the doubt** and passed them.

168. Double up *(v.)* **– to share a room or any other area meant for one**

1) We had to **double up** our office space to accommodate the new employees.
2) There's only one room available, so we'll have to **double up** for the night.

169. Down-to-earth *(adj.)* **– realistic, practical, sensible**

1) The plan seems to be **down-to-earth**, but is it going to work?
2) He's well liked because of his **down-to-earth** management style.

170. Drag on *(v.)* **– to continue slowly for a long time**

1) The meeting **dragged on** until well into the evening.
2) The hot weather **drags on** and on. Will it never end?

** **Drag out** *(v.)* **– to prolong**

1) I hope this meeting won's be **dragged out**, it usually tends to go on too long.

171. Draw a (the) line (*v.*) – to distinguish, to set a limit to

1) Sometimes, it's not easy to **draw** a clear **line** between moral and immoral.
2) I have to **draw the line** on the amount I spend monthly on entertainment.

172. Dream of (*v.*) – to think or imagine about

1) I often **dream of** having my own business. Maybe I am a dreamer.
2) **Dreaming of** a white Christmas is sweet.

173. Dress up (*v.*) – to dress formally or elegantly

1) Why don't we get **dressed up** for the party on Friday night?
2) You look great when you **dress up**.

174. Drop off (*v.*) – to leave something

1) I need to **drop off** some clothes at the dry cleaner's.
2) Can you **drop** me **off** near the train station?

175. Drop out (*v.*) – to stop attending, to quit

1) Some students **drop out** of college in their freshman year.
2) He **dropped out** of school because of financial difficulties.

** Dropout (*n.*) – One who withdraws from school before graduating

1) He is a high school **dropout** and will have difficulty finding a good job.
2) Our company doesn't hire **dropouts** because they usually lack necessary skills.

176. **Due to** *(prep.)* **– caused by, because of**

1) Many forest fires are **due to** carelessly extinguished fires.
2) The game was called off **due to** rain.

** **Due** *(adj.)* **– required to be paid, submitted, or finished, etc.**

1) My phone bill is **due** today.
2) The amount **due** is $42.95.
3) My homework assignment is **due** next week.

** **Dues** *(n.)* **– a charge or fee for membership**

1) The swimming club **dues** are $120.00 per year.
2) **Dues** should be paid by the fifth of the month.

177. **Dwell on** *(v.)* **– to linger over, to stay on, to not leave something**

1) Don't **dwell on** your mistakes.
2) She is always **dwelling on** her past events.

E

178. Easy come, easy go (cliché) – Something easily earned may easily go

1) As soon as Jim inherited a lot of money, he began to spend it lavishly because it was easy money. **Easy come, easy go.**
2) The money Jim won was spent very quickly. His friend told him it was **easy come, easy go.**

179. Eat one's words (*v.*) – to take back what one has said, to hold back what one wants to say

1) I wanted to complain to my boss, but I **ate my words** instead.
2) He had to **eat his words** in front of his angry boss.
3) She told everybody that she would win the game, but she lost. Now she has to **eat her words.**

180. Edge out (*v.*) – to defeat by a small margin

1) New York **edged out** Toronto in a close game.
2) She was **edged out** of the position by someone with better qualifications.

** to be on edge (*v.*) – to feel apprehensive or nervous

1) He **is on edge** today.
2) I **am** a little **on edge** waiting for my interview result.

181. Eke out (*v.*) – to manage or to make with difficulty

1) Most farmers are barely able to **eke out** a living.
2) Many families are barely **eking out** a living because of the economic crisis.

182. End up (*v.*) – to finish, to come to an end

1) The football match **ended up** with Korea beating Japan 2–0.
2) If he keeps spending more then he earns, he'lll **end up** in bankruptcy court.
3) They **ended up** divorcing.

183. Enjoy oneself (*v.*) – to have a good time, to have a pleasurable time

1) Please **enjoy yourself.**
2) Did you **enjoy yourself** at the party last night?

184. Enough is enough – that's enough

1) I'm tired of your nagging, **enough is enough.**
2) When she asked to borrow more money, in addition to what she had already borrowed, her irate father said, "**Enough is enough.**"

185. Every now and then / Every once in a while (*adv.*) – occasionally

1) We like to eat out **every now and then.**
2) I like to go to a movie **every now and then.**
3) We used to spend a lot of time together, but now we only see each other **every once in a while.**

** **Every so often** (*adv.*) – **occasionally**

1) We used to go there a lot, but now we only go there **every so often.**

186. **Every single** (*adj.*) – **every (usually for emphasis)**

1) I've been working hard **every single** day since last year.
2) I appreciate **every single** thing you've done for me.

** **Every other** (*adj.*) – **on alternate occasions**

1) The milk man comes **every other** day.
2) We do the bulk of our grocery shopping **every other** Saturday.

F

187. Face to face *(adj.)* – directly confronting each other in each other's presence

1) The two boxers stood **face to face** and readied themselves for the bout.
2) I haven't met him **face to face**, but I've heard good things about him.
3) Let's talk **face to face.**

188. Face up to *(v.)* – to accept as real, to confront bravely

1) If he doesn't **face up to** his drinking problem, he won't be able to overcome it.

189. Face value – the value written on, truth of something

1) This rare silver coin has a **face value** of five hundred dollars.
2) I took what he said at **face value**, never thinking he would lie.

190. Fair and square *(adj.)* – honestly

1) We won the game **fair and square.**
2) Let's divide our profit **fair and square.**

** Fair play *(n.)* – honest and right action

1) Sporting events employ referees to insure **fair play.**
2) The lawyers from either party were not interested in **fair play.**

191. Fair-weather friend (*n.*) – a person who is a friend only when one is in good circumstances

1) He's a kind of **fair-weather friend** who's never around when I need help.
2) I'd rather have no friends at all than **fair weather friends.**

192. Flunk out / flunk out of (*v.*) – to be expelled from a school or a course because of a poor grade circumstances

1) Study hard, otherwise you'll **flunk out** of school.
2) They were shocked when their daughter **flunked out** of school.

193. Fall all over (*v.*) – to show too much affection

1) She **falls all over** him in public, but it doesn't embarrass him at all.

194. Fall back on (*v.*) – to turn to for help, to depend on in case of need

1) Everybody should get a good education to **fall back on.**
2) He's an orphan and has no one to **fall back on.**
3) You can always **fall back on** me.
4) It's hard to have to **fall back on** your savings because the interest rates are so low.

** Fall back (*v.*) – to withdraw, to retreat

1) The army had to **fall back** behind the enemy line for safety.
2) The enemy **fell back** under the counterattack.

195. Fall behind / fall behind in (*v.*) – to fail to keep current, to go slower than others

1) She **fell behind** on her credit card payments and needs to get caught up.
2) I need to study because I don't want to **fall behind in** my courses.

196. Fall for (*v.*) – to be infatuated with (or by) or fall in love with, to be taken in by or deceived by

1) He **fell for** her the first time he saw her.
2) He **falls for** every woman he encounters.
3) She told him a lie and he **fell for** it.

** Fall in love (*v.*) – to have a feeling of love

1) We **fell in love** with each other the first time we met.
2) I **fell in love** with him at the first sight.

197. Fall off (*v.*) – to become less, to decline

1) Since the company sales have **fallen off**, there will probably be layoffs.
2) Student registration has **fallen off** sharply this semester.

198. Fall out (*v.*) – to become estranged from

1) They **fell out** after a quarrel over a small matter.
2) She has **fallen out** with her next-door neighbors after an argument.

199. Fall through (*v.*) – to fail to happen

1) My vacation plans **fell through** because I couldn't take the time off.
2) Her plans to go overseas **fell through**.

200. Far cry (*n.*) – something very different

1) Your statement is a **far cry** from the truth.
2) This watch is an imitation Rolex and a **far cry** from what I expected.
3) This movie is a **far cry** from the usual Korean Production.

201. Far-off (*adj.*) – faraway, distant

1) He wants to go to a **far-off** island.
2) To a university freshman, graduation seems **far-off** and somewhat unlikely to ever occur.

202. Fed up / Fed up with (*adj.*) – having had too much of, being sick and tired of

1) He was **fed up** with his wife's nagging.
2) I'm **fed up** with your constant complaints about the way I do things.

203. Feel like ~ing (*v.*) – to be in a mood for doing something

1) I **feel like** getting something to eat.
2) I don't **feel like** studying today.

204. Feel like a million dollars / look like a million dollars (cliché) – to be in the best condition

1) He loves me and it makes me **feel like a million dollars**.
2) You **look like a million dollars** in that new dress.

205. Fifty-fifty (*adj.*) – half for and half against, shared or divided equally

1) Let's split the assets **fifty-fifty**, half to you and half to me.
2) The weather report said that there's a **fifty-fifty** chance of rain today.

206. Fight off (v.) – to battle or act successfully against

1) I'm trying to **fight off** the flu by taking a lot of vitamin C.
2) Our soldiers are bravely **fighting off** the enemy.

** Fight it out – to battle or struggle until one side wins

1) The boxers **fought it out** until only one of them was left standing.
2) In the continuing consumer wars, big companies are **fighting it out**.

207. Figure on (v.) – to plan, to expect

1) We didn't **figure on** having many people at our wedding ceremony anyway.
2) I was **figuring on** a pay raise, but it didn't come through.

208. Figure out (v.) – to find an answer, to solve, to understand

1) Can I ask you for some help **figuring out** this computer program?
2) I can't **figure out** why my internet often goes down.

209. Fill in (v.) – to write words in the blanks, to substitute

1) Please **fill in** the blanks on the application form and put it in that basket.
2) The cook is sick and we need someone to **fill in** right away.

** Fill out (v.) – to complete a form

1) I haven't **filled out** my tax return yet. I should **fill out** the form soon.
2) I **filled out** the registration forms and sent them last week.

210. Fill up (v.) – to make or become completely full

1) I need to **fill up** the gas tank because it's almost empty.

2) (at the gas station) **Fill it up**, please.
3) It's best to add the detergent after the wash tub **fills up**.

211. Find out (*v.*) – to ascertain, to get information about,

1) Did you **find out** what time the movie starts?
2) I **found out** about the scholarship program.

212. Fine feathers do not make fine birds (*proverb.*) – A person who looks nice, talks nice, or wears nice clothing isn't necessarily a nice person.

1) She wears nice clothes, drives a nice car, and smiles a lot, but **fine feathers do not** necessarily **make fine birds**.

213. Finish up (*v.*) – to finish completely, to wrap up

1) I want to **finish up** my work early and go home.
2) He's **finishing up** his homework and then he's going to a movie.

** Finished with (*v.*) – to end a relationship, a task, etc.

1) I am **finished with** him because he never keeps his words.
2) Are you **finished with** the books I loaned you?

** Finished (*adj.*) – ruined, ended, skilled, accomplished, perfect, completely processed

1) He is **finished** as a politician.
2) The company is bankrupt; now it's **finished**.
3) Some final touches are needed to give the furniture a **finished** look.
4) This is a **finished** product.

214. First-class (*adj., adv.*) – of the best quality of service, excellent, first-rate

1) **First-class** passengers are naturally given better service than those in economy class.
2) We stayed at a **first-class** hotel.
3) We sent the gift set you ordered as **first-class** mail.

215. First come, first served – the person who comes first will be served first

1) Reservations are not necessary. Rooms are let on a **first come, first served** basis.
2) The 100 computers were offered on a **first come, first served** basis.

216. Fit in / fit in with (*v.*) – to be suited to, to be adjusted to

1) I think these curtains **fit in** better **with** the color scheme than those.
2) She **fits in** well **with** the other members of the photography club.

217. Fix up / fix up with (*v.*) – to repair, to decorate or furnish, to fix, to supply or provide, to arrange a relationship

1) We **fixed up** a room to use as a study room.
2) I am hungry. I should **fix up** something for myself.
3) I **fixed** him **up with** a job
4) We **fixed** him **up with** a nice girl.

218. Follow through (*v.*) – to finish an action that one started, to complete a task once it is started

1) **Follow through** on your plan before beginning another project.
2) I like to **follow through** on things I started.

** **Follow up** (*v.*) – to make a previous action more effective by doing something extra that adds to it; to carry out, to seek or give more information about

1) Send them your resume and **follow** it **up** in a week or so with a phone call.
2) Good service representatives sell products and then make **follow up** calls.
3) **Follow up** the instruction with a good diagram.
4) We'll **follow up** the story with a review of the activities tomorrow.

219. Fool around (*v.*) – to spend time idly, to play around

1) I don't have time to **fool around**. I have a lot of work to do.
2) Stop **fooling around**, or you will regret it later.
3) Don't **fool around** with a bad crowd or you'll get in trouble.

220. Foot in the door (*n.*) – the first step toward getting something

1) It was a part-time position, but I accepted it as a way of getting my **foot in the door** of the company.
2) This is just a temporary position. But who knows? It can be a **foot in the door**.
3) This is a **foot in the door**-position.

221. For all (*v.*) – in spite of

1) **For all** the soldiers have done for our country, they are not treated right.
2) He has much money and a nice family, but **for all** that, he is not happy.

222. For all the world (*adv.*) – for anything, for any price, at any price

1) I wouldn't change anything about you **for all the world**.

** Forever and ever (*adv.*) – forever, always

1) The memory of this day will be with me **forever and ever.**
2) Things only last **forever and ever** in fairy tales.

** For good (*adv.*) – forever, permanently

1) She's gone **for good** and won't be back.
2) He has finally quit drinking and gambling **for good.**

223. For sure (*adv.*) – without doubt, certainly

1) I know this is real **for sure.**
2) Do you know she'll return **for sure?**

224. For the best (*adj., adv.*) – good, best, luckily, well

1) I'm sorry for him, but it's **for the best** for the rest of the people.
2) Sometimes, bad situations turn out **for the best.**

** For the better (*adj., adv.*) – for something better

1) Reducing his alcohol intake is **for the better.**

** For the worse (*adj., adv.*) – deteriorating

1) He took the new position, but it turned out **for the worse.**
2) The patient's condition changed **for the worse.**
3) When they got married, they vowed to love one another **for better or worse.**

225. Freeze over / freeze up (*v.*) – to become covered with ice, unable to function(because of tension, etc.)

1) When the lake **freezes over**, we go ice skating.
2) Last night, it was so cold that the water pipes **froze up.**
3) He **froze up** in front of the class and couldn't give his speech at all.

** **Freeze out** (*v.*) – to exclude, to force out by unfriendly treatment

1) He wanted to join the exclusive club, but the membership **froze** him **out.**

226. From hand to hand (*adv.*) – From one person to another

1) After their parents died, the children were passed **from hand to hand** until their aunt and uncle were granted permanent custody.
2) Our family shares everything. Even clothing is passed **from hand to hand.**
3) The famous painting was passed **from hand to hand** until I got it.

227. From the bottom of one's heart / With all one's heart (*adv.*) – with deep feeling, with sincerity

1) He loved her **with all his heart.**
2) I thank you **from the bottom of my heart** for all you've done for me.

228. From time to time (*adv.*) – sometimes, occasionally

1) He visits me **from time to time.**
2) He likes to have a glass of wine **from time to time.**

229. From way back (*adj., adv.*) – since a long time ago

1) We know each other **from way back** in high school.
2) We just met, but I feel we've known each other **from way back.**

230. Get across (*v.*) – to convey an idea clearly

1) I explained the matter to them, but I don't think I **got** the message **across.**
2) The professor couldn't **get** the difficult physics theory **across** to the students.
3) I don't know how to **get** my message **across** to you.
4) I barely **got** my ideas **across** to him before he had to leave.

** Get it (*v.*) – to understand, to catch something

1) I explained it as clearly as I could. Did you **get it?**
2) I've got a bad cold. I hope you don't **get it.**
3) Dogs like to play fetch. If you throw a stick, they will **get it.**

231. Get along / get along with (*v.*) – to make progress, to be friends with

1) How are you **getting along** with your studies?
2) I haven't been **getting along** with my boss lately.
3) Even best friends don't always **get along.**
4) Do you **get along** with him?

232. Get around (*v.*) – to go to places, to evade, to become widely known

1) It was difficult to **get around** while her car was in the shop for servicing.
2) Students are creative when it comes to **getting around** doing homework.
3) She knows how to **get around** the rules.

4) Bad news often seems to **get around** more quickly than good news.

233. Get at (*v.*) – to understand, to find a way to, to mean

1) The main theme of the story was hard to **get at.**
2) The truth is often difficult to **get at.**
3) The cat tried everything it could to **get at** the bird.
4) What I'm trying to **get at** is this, we need to talk more often.

234. Get away (*v.*) – to escape, to get free

1) Three prisoners **got away** during last night's riot at the prison.
2) I want to **get away** from everything for a few days to refresh my mind and body.
3) The teenage boy **got away** from his home.

** Get away with (*v.*) – to do without being punished or being caught

1) Criminals may **get away with** their crimes for a while, but sooner or later they pay.
2) The burglars **got away with** a large amount of cash and jewelry.
3) You cannot **get away with** this.

235. Get back at (*v.*) – to revenge

1) Many people feel the need to **get back at** people who insult them.
2) He has **gotten back at** his detractors by becoming successful.
3) He insulted her, so she **got back at** him by fighting with him.

** Get even (*v.*) – to have neither a loss nor a gain, to owe nothing, to take revenge

1) I invested some money in two different stocks. After one month, one went down 10% and the other went up 10%. So I **got even.**

2) After they insulted me at the meeting, I **got even** by discontinuing our business relationship.
3) I will **get even** with her someday.

** break even (*v.*) – to neither win nor lose

1) We finally **broke even** on the deal, and we got back the amount we originally invested in it.

236. Get by / get by with (*v.*) – to survive, to manage, to pass

1) She **gets by** on her social security check.
2) The economy has forced many families to **get by** on less income.
3) The truck pulled over to let the long line of cars **get by.**

237. Get down to (*v.*) – to concentrate on, to turn the attention to, to begin to

1) Let's **get down to** business.
2) Midterms are next week, it's time to **get down to** study.

238. Get a hold of (*v.*) – to see or contact a person

1) I need to **get a hold of** him because I have important news for him.

** Get hold of (*v.*) – to obtain

1) The impending divorce prompted her to **get hold of** as many assets as she could.

239. Get in / get in with (*v.*) – to arrive, to enter, to enter a car, to gain the favor of

1) I'm sorry I missed your call, but I've been out all day and just **got in.**

2) The train **gets in** at about twenty after five.
3) You need to **get in** the car quickly because we've holding up traffic.
4) She really tries to **get in** with her new supervisor.

** **Get on / Get on with** (*v.*) – **to enter a vehicle (a bus, a train, a plane, etc.), to step up and sit on, to advance, to be on friendly terms, to continue (after an interruption)**

1) Passengers! Please **get on** board now. The plane is leaving in a half-hour.
2) He is really **getting on** in the company.
3) How is she **getting on** with her new boyfriend?
4) I must **get on** with my work or I'll never catch up.

240. Get off (*v.*) – to get down or out of, to remove

1) We have to **get off** at the next station.
2) She **got off** the couch and began to prepare dinner.
3) I've **gotten** it **off** my chest, so I feel much better now.

** **Get off easy / Get off with** (*v.*) – **to get away without being punished much, to escape a serious punishment**

1) The thief was captured, but somehow **got off easy**.
2) The disobedient child knew he had **gotten off easy**.
3) The criminal **got off with** a very light sentence.

** **Get off one's back** (*v.*) – **to stop criticizing**

1) You're always criticizing me, now **get off my back** and leave me alone.

241. Get out / Get out of (*v.*) – to leave, to get off, to escape or be released from, to receive a benefit from, to obtain or learn

1) I don't like this place. Let's **get out** of here.
2) What time does she **get out of** class?
3) He **got out of** the car and went into a small shop.
4) Somehow, a bird **got out of** its cage and flew away to get freedom.
5) I don't enjoy this class, but I'm **getting** as much **out of** it as I can.
6) I **got** something new **out of** this seminar.
7) I didn't **get** anything **out of** this deal.

242. Get over / Get over with (*v.*) – to recover from, to overcome, to end something

1) He finally **got over** the painful experience of war.
2) She had hard feelings about not getting the promotion, however, she's **getting over** it and moving on **with** her life.
3) I want to **get over with** this very soon and go on with my life.

243. Get the brush–off (*v.*) – to be treated unkindly, to be ignored

1) I stopped by her house to see her, but I **got the brush–off**.
2) He felt his innovative ideas were given **the brush–off** at the meeting.

244. Get the feel of (*v.*) – to learn about by feeling or handling

1) The computer is an interesting machine. I hope to **get the feel of** it one of these days.
2) It took him a few weeks, but he soon **got the feel of** his new position.
3) **Get the feel of** this silk. It's so soft.

245. Get to (v.) – to begin, to begin by chance, to arrive at, to annoy, to reach a decision

1) I want to go shopping, but I've **got to** consider whether I can afford to spend any more money.
2) We **got to** know each other at a recent social gathering.
3) We **got to** the hotel earlier than we had expected.
4) The practical joke **got to** him, and he became extremely angry.
5) It looks like we've considered all the possibilities; now let's **get to** the point.

** Get to the bottom of (v.) – to find out the real cause of

1) Let's talk about your unhappy feelings and see if we can **get to the bottom of** the problem.

** Get at the heart of (v.) – to find the most important fact, to understand the most important meaning

1) When I study, I try to **get at the heart of** the material.
2) I'm not sure if I **got to the heart of** your story.

246. Get together (v.) – to meet together or gather

1) Would you like to **get together** some time for lunch or dinner?
2) Let's **get together** and discuss your proposal over lunch.

247. Get up (v.) – to get out of bed, to stand up

1) It's 7 o'clock and time to **get up**.
2) He **got up** to let the elderly man have the seat.

248. Give a hard time (*v.*) – to give trouble or a problem, to complain

1) My boss **gave** me a **hard time** today.
2) I did my best, but he still **gave** me a **hard time.**
3) Don't **give** me a **hard time** any more. I had enough.

** Give a pain (*v.*) – to annoy

1) I am disgusted with your behavior and I want you to know it really **gives** me a **pain.**
2) The loud music from next door really **gives** me a **pain.**

249. Give back (*v.*) – to return

1) He wants to stop by for a minute and **give back** the money he borrowed.
2) When can you **give** it **back** to me?

250. Give in / give in to (*v.*) – to yield, to surrender

1) You can't win every argument. Sometimes you have to **give in.**
2) I think that the Middle-East crisis will only be solved when one of the sides **gives in.**

251. Give off (*v.*) – to emit, to send out

1) Some chemical reactions **give off** toxic fumes.
2) Microwave ovens **give off** radioactive rays.
3) Many vehicles **give off** toxic fumes and they pollute the air seriously.

252. Give out (*v.*) – to let something be known, to distribute, to wear out

1) The company has decided to **give out** its press release next Monday.
2) We **gave out** all the chocolate chip and coconut cookies.

3) The engine in my car finally **gave out.**

** Give away (*v.*) – to make a gift of, to reveal a secret

1) When I left Seoul, I **gave away** many of my possessions.
2) One of his staff was caught for **giving away** his company's secrets.

253. Give up / give up on (*v.*) – to stop, to relinquish, to stop hoping for

1) Modern researchers believe it is easier to **give up** drugs than to give up smoking.
2) Her boss didn't ask her to work overtime because he knows she doesn't like to **give up** her weekends.
3) They **gave up on** their dream of buying a new home.
4) The woman **gave up on** her son after he was caught using drugs.

254. Give voice / give voice to (*v.*) – to speak

1) The President **gave voice** to his concern over the recent strikes and the sluggish economy.
2) Nowadays, citizens join organizations to **give voice** on various topics.

255. Go about (*v.*) – to circulate

1) A rumor is **going about** that many schools are having financial difficulties.

** Go around (*v.*) – to circulate, to go from one place to another or one person to another

1) Rumors of their troubled relationship have been **going around** for a while.
2) He **goes around** the countryside preaching sermons.
3) You shouldn't **go around** gossiping.

256. Go ahead (*v.*) – to start or proceed, to go forward without hesitation

1) Can I ask you a question? Sure. **Go ahead.**
2) We can **go ahead** with our project.
3) You **go ahead**, please. I'll catch up to you in a few minutes.

** Go on / go on with (*v.*) – to continue or proceed, to happen

1) I'm sorry I interrupted your conversation, please **go on.**
2) That's quite interesting, **go on** and tell us the rest of the story.
3) What's **going on** here?

257. Go along (*v.*) – to progress or proceed

1) Learning how to use a computer gets easier as I **go along.**
2) Her daily exercises **got** easier as she went **along.**

** Go along with (*v.*) – to agree or act in agreement with, to accompany

1) We like your ideas, but the company can't afford to **go along with** them right now.
2) I am going to Seoul next Saturday. Would you like to **go along with** me?

258. Go off (*v.*) – to leave, to begin ringing, to be discharged or explode, to be shut off suddenly

1) He **went off** in search of fame and fortune.
2) The alarm clock **goes off** at seven o'clock every morning.
3) He didn't know the gun was loaded and it **went off** by accident.
4) The lights **went off** while I was watching TV.

** **Go off with** *(v.)* **– to leave with something or someone without permission**

1) My sister **went off with** my new shoes.

259. Goof off *(v.)* – to fool around, to waste time

1) If he continues to **goof off** at work, he'll probably get fired.
2) We've been working too hard. Let's **goof off** for a while.
3) Children usually **goof off** when their parents are away.

260. Go out *(v.)* – to go outside, to go to public entertainment, to stop working, to move to as in affection or sympathy

1) He just **went out**, but he'll be back in a couple of minutes.
2) Do you want to **go out** this weekend with some of our friends?
3) The factory **went out** of operation two weeks ago due to its financial difficulty.
4) The workers **went out** on strike because they couldn't reach agreement on a new contract.
5) She's a poor widow with young children to feed, so my heart **goes out** to her.

261. Go over *(v.)* – to examine or study carefully or in detail, to visit, to go down

1) Let's **go over** this report again and see if we can get something out of it.
2) They **went over** to London on their summer vacation.
3) Let's **go over** to that new restaurant for dinner.
4) He **went over** the hill and was never heard from again.

262. Go steady (*v.*) – dating the same person exclusively

1) They decided to **go steady.**
2) They **went steady** for a while, but soon realized that they didn't have much in common.

263. Go through (*v.*) – to be approved, to search or examine in detail, to experience or undergo, to pass through a place

1) Her application **went through** the review committee.
2) I **went through** all my books, but I didn't find the one you loaned me.
3) They have **gone through** many difficulties in the past few months.
4) **Go through** that door and you'll see her office on the right.

** Go through with (*v.*) – to complete or pursue to finish, to finish something difficult

1) I was admitted to the doctoral program, but didn't want to **go through with** it because I didn't think it was worth pursuing.
2) We decided to **go through with** our original plan.

264. Go under (*v.*) – to fail or go bankrupt, to sink

1) His business **went under** because of the faltering economy and poor sales.
2) Many ships **went under** in the recent typhoon.

** Go down (*v.*) – to stop functioning, to sink

1) The office computer **went down** today.
2) The real estate prices are **going down.**

** Go up (*v.*) – to increase, to rise

1) Profits have **gone up** a hundred percent since the first of January.
2) The price of rice has **gone up** twice in three months.
3) The temperature is **going up**. It's going to be a real scorcher today.

265. Go with (*v.*) – to match, to go out in the company of

1) That light green jacket **goes with** that blue skirt.
2) His shirt doesn't **go with** his tie.
3) We often **go** to dinner **with** some of our colleagues.

266. The grass is always greener on the other side of the fence (cliché) – People often think what they have is not as good as what other people have

1) He wanted his friend's job very badly, but it turned out to be another case of **the grass being greener on the other side of the fence.**
2) She usually thinks that other people are happier than her. **The grass is always greener on the other side of the fence.**

267. Great oaks grow from little acorns (*proverb*) – Patience is needed, Great people or things often develop from seemingly unimportant beginnings, as does a great oak tree which starts as a small acorn.

1) The life of Thomas Edison is a good example of an **oak growing from an acorn.**

268. Grow on / upon (*v.*) – to become stronger, to become habitual, to be liked by

1) He didn't like her at first, but as time went by she **grew on** him.
2) At first she didn't like the idea, but it **grew on** her.

3) I hope the idea of transferring to our Seoul office will **grow on** you.

269. Grow up *(v.)* – to become mature

1) All their children have **grown up** and moved away from home.
2) The teacher wished her more immature students would **grow up**.
3) Children will soon **grow up** and become adults.

H

270. Hand down (*v.*) – to leave something to one's descendants after death, to deliver or render

1) Her house was **handed down** to her from her parents.
2) Myths and legends are **handed down** from generation to generation.
3) The court **handed down** a verdict of not guilty.

** **Hands down** (*adv.*) – easily

1) We won the game **hands down** by a score of 11–0.
2) He thought the examination would be difficult, but he passed it **hands down.**

271. Hand in hand (*adv.*) – closely linked or associated with, holding hands

1) The two agencies worked **hand in hand** on the project.
2) Some couples were walking **hand in hand** in the park.

272. Hand in (*v.*) – to submit, to turn in

1) When do we **hand in** our final paper?
2) The income tax returns have to be **handed** in by next Friday.

** **Hands out** (*v.*) – to distribute,

1) Professors usually **hand out** a syllabus on the first day of class.
2) The salesperson **handed out** some samples of the new product.

** **Handout** (*n.*) – **something given free, information given out on paper**

1) The beggar sat near the subway entrance seeking **handouts.**
2) He refused all offers of assistance because he saw them as **handouts.**
3) The professor gave us some **handouts** related to our summer project.

273. **Hand over** (*v.*) – **to yield control of, to give or give up**

1) The retiring Supreme Court judge **handed over** his responsibilities to his successor.
2) When he retires, he'll **hand over** the control of the business to his son.
3) You aren't allowed to use notes in the exam. Please **hand** them **over** to me.

274. **Hang around** (*v.*) – **to spend time idly, to loiter, to linger**

1) He usually **hangs around** with a bad crowd that gives him a bad reputation.
2) Since her retirement, she has been **hanging around** the house a lot more.
3) Can you **hang around** here until I get ready to go out so that we can have lunch together?

** **Hangout** (*n.*) – **a place where people gather to drink, eat, or chat casually**

1) The small restaurant on 2nd Street is a popular **hangout** for students.

** **Hangover** (*n.*) – **the unpleasant symptoms from drinking too much**

1) He still has a bad **hangover** because he drank too much last night.

275. Hang in / hang in there (*v.*) – to not give up, to persevere

1) I know you've going through a tough time, but **hang in** there!
2) The job is difficult, but you can do it if you **hang in** a while longer.

** Hang on (*v.*) – to cling tightly to something, to remain on the phone

1) He was laid off over a year ago, but he's still **hanging on** in the hope that his company will rehire him very soon.
2) **Hang on** to the rope until the 119 rescue team arrives.
3) It is always wise to **hang on** to your current job until you find a better one.
4) **Hang on** a moment and I'll put your call through as soon as her line is free.

** Hang up (*v.*) – to end a telephone conversation, to place something on a hook

1) I've got to **hang up** because someone's knocking on the door.
2) I wasn't finished speaking when you **hung up** on me. Don't hang up on me now. I'm not finished speaking yet.
3) Where do you want to **hang up** the picture? / **Hang** it **up** here.

** Hang-up (*n.*) – a fear of something

1) Since her car accident, she's got some **hang-ups** about driving.
2) Since planes crash often, some passengers have **hang-ups** about flying.
3) Many soldiers have **hang-ups** about war.

276. Happy hour (*n.*) – a time in bars or restaurants when cocktails and / or food are served at reduced rates

1) **Happy Hours** at the Oak Tree Lounge are from six to eight p.m.
2) I like their **happy hour** because they always have free chicken wings.

277. Haul away (*v.*) – to carry away

1) The garbage truck **hauls away** garbage on Mondays and recyclable items on Thursdays.
2) The rowdy demonstrators were **hauled away** by the police.

278. Have a ball (*v., slang*) – to have a wonderful time, to have lots of fun

1) The party was actually quite dull, but I **had a ball** anyway.
2) He took the children to the circus and they **had a ball.**

279. Have an eye for (*v.*) – to have good taste in

1) She **has an eye for** color coordination and interior design.
2) You need to develop an ear for music and **an eye for** art work.

** Have an eye on (*v.*) – to watch closely or think about (something wanted) with some degree of intensity

1) Please keep **an eye on** the kids while I do the grocery shopping.
2) He **has** had his **eye on** her for some time.

280. Have been around (*v.*) – to have experience and ability to take care of self, to have been to many places and done many things

1) You and I **have been around** for a long time, so we can take care of ourselves. However, she hasn't been around long enough yet and she's naive, too.
2) I like him because he **has been around** and seems knowledgeable.

281. Have done with / Be done with (v.) – to be through with or finish

1) Have you **done with** the book I loaned you, yet?
2) I **haven't done with** it yet because it's more complicated than I first thought.
3) Let's **be done with** this business and get on with the next matter.

282. Have it out (v.) – to settle a disagreement or an issue by open discussion or fighting, to remove by surgery

1) Since we both have hard feelings for each other, we'd better **have it out.**
2) Let's **have it out** right now and get it over and done with.
3) He **had** his kidney **out** three months ago.

283. Have no use for (v.) – to have no tolerance for, to dislike, to have no need of

1) I **have no use for** people who abuse or mistreat animals.
2) I **have no use for** him because he's not a reliable man.
3) I **have no use for** this chair, so you can take it.

** **Of use – useful**

1) A computer is **of use** in my work.

284. Have on (v.) – to be wearing, to plan

1) She **has on** some old torn jeans and a red T-shirt.
2) You look worried, tell me what you **have on** your mind.

285. Have one's hands full *(v.)* **– to be busy with much work, overwhelmed**

1) We **have our hands full** right now and can't take any more orders.
2) She **has her hands full** trying to work and raise three kids.

286. Have over *(v.)* **– to invite to one's home**

1) Let's **have** them **over** some time for dinner.
2) I'd like to **have** you and your family **over** for the weekend.
3) I want to **have** you **over** this evening, so we can watch the soccer tournament together.

287. Have the courage of one's convictions *(v.)* **– to be courageous to act on one's beliefs**

1) Successful people generally **have the courage of their convictions.**
2) If it weren't for **the courage of his convictions**, he would have given up a long time ago.

288. Have two strikes against one *(v.)* **– to have difficulty in two time in succession, to have something against oneself**

1) He already **has two strikes against him.** First, he was late for the meeting, and then he slammed the door in front of his boss.
2) He'd better be careful because he already **has two strikes against him.**

289. Head above water *(n.)* **– to stay out of financial difficulty**

1) Business is terrible and we've barely keeping our **heads above water.**
2) I work two jobs and yet I can't seem to keep my **head above water.**

290. Heart goes out to – to have sympathy for

1) My **heart goes out to** you because you've been through a lot.
2) Our **hearts went out to** the poor animal that had been hit by a drunk driver.

** Have a heart (*v.*) – to have compassion, to be considerate

1) You should **have a heart** and help that poor man.

291. Heart-to-heart (*adj.*) – personal and sincere, frank

1) I want to have a **heart-to-heart** conversation with him.
2) We had a long **heart-to-heart** conversation and that made things better between us.

292. Help oneself / help oneself to (*v.*) – to serve oneself without asking

1) It's a buffet style luncheon and everyone helps themselves. **Help yourself**, please.
2) I'm going to **help myself to** some more salad and another bowl of soup.
3) Guests at hotels sometimes **help themselves to** extra towels.

293. Help out (*v.*) – to aid someone in a time of need, to help

1) I can **help out** if you have your hands too full with the party.
2) Her parents **helped** her **out** when she bought a new car.
3) He gets a weekly allowance for **helping out** around the house.

294. Hinge on / hinge upon (*v.*) – to depend on, to be decided by

1) Many economists say that Korean economic reform **hinges on** the government's "Big Deal" policy.

2) Our vacation plans **hinge on** our finances.

295. Hit it off *(v.)* – to get along well

1) They **hit it off** and soon became the best of friends.
2) We just **hit it off** well.

296. Hit the ceiling *(v.)* – to go into a rage

1) I **hit the ceiling** when I found out that my lazy co-worker was promoted to a supervisory position.
2) He **hit the ceiling** when he found out how much the repairs would cost.

297. Hit the jackpot *(v.)* – to win a jackpot, to gain sensational success

1) Some lucky person **hit the** $20,000,000 **jackpot** in last night's lottery drawing.
2) The woman screamed with delight when she **hit the jackpot**.

298. Hit the road *(v.)* – to leave especially by car

1) We should **hit the road** before the holiday traffic gets too heavy.
2) Well, it's already 7 o'clock. I'd better **hit the road**. It was nice talking to you. I'll stop by again.

299. Hold back *(v.)* – to restrain, to keep, not to reveal

1) The police cordoned off the crime scene to **hold back** the crowd.
2) Don't let a poor attitude **hold** you **back** from getting ahead in life.
3) He **held back** some of the information as a hedge against losing the account.

300. Hold down *(v.)* – to keep control of, to rule over

1) Autocratic governments **hold down** people through various means.

2) The police were called in and **held down** the boisterous concert crowd.

301. Hold it (*v.*) – to stop someone from doing something, to hold

1) The police caught the burglar and ordered him to **hold it** right there.
2) **Hold it** right there. That's not true.

** Hold on (*v.*) – to wait, to hold, to persevere

1) Can you **hold on** for a minute? I am busy right now.
2) Please **hold on** and I'll transfer your call as soon as her line is free.
3) He **held onto** the safety line as he descended the mountain.

302. Hold in (*v.*) – to keep inside

1) **Holding in** one's feelings is not good for one's health.
2) Don't **hold in** your feelings, find a healthy way to release them.

303. Hold off / hold off on (*v.*) – to delay

1) Would you mind **holding off** your vacation plans for a couple of weeks?
2) **Hold off** on buying a new computer until you shop around.
3) We should **hold off** our wedding plans until we know each other better.

** On hold – postponed, waiting for on the phone

1) The construction plan is **on hold** until the economy gets better.
2) The line is busy now. I'll put you **on hold**.

** Hold over (*v.*) – to postpone, to keep longer than planned

1) Can we **hold** this meeting **over** until next week since we don't have all the information?
2) The concert is going to be **held over** for another week because of public demand.

304. Hold one's head up *(v.)* – to be confident or proud, not to be ashamed

1) You are a good man, **hold your head up** and don't let gossip worry you.

** Keep your chin up *(v.)* – to face trouble with courage

1) I know times are difficult, but **keep your chin up.**
2) I am sorry to hear that you lost your job, but **keep your chin up.** I am sure you'll find another one soon.

305. Horns of a dilemma *(n.)* – one has two choices, but neither is satisfying nor wanted

1) She found herself on the **horns of a dilemma.** If she has a child, she won't be able to pursue her career well; if she pursues her career, she won't be able to raise her child well.

306. Hot air *(n.)* – exaggerated, nonsensical talk with emotion

1) She always threatens to quit, but it's just a lot of **hot air.**
2) He is just full of **hot air.**

307. Hot potato *(n.)* – a question or an issue that raises heated debates and is hard to settle

1) Politics and religion are always **hot potatoes.**
2) The issue of birth control is certainly a **hot potato** for the Catholic Church.

** Hot water *(n.)* – trouble

1) She got herself into **hot water** by talking about religion in public.
2) He is in **hot water** because he missed too many homework assignments.

** **Hot seat** *(n.)* **– a position which is likely to lead to trouble**

1) The mayor of a big city is on the **hot seat.** This is because of the city's phenomenal tax increases.

308. If anything *(adv.)* – instead, rather

1) Sunday is not going to be warm, **if anything**, it will be cool.
2) Cats aren't bad pets, **if anything**, they're pretty good company.

309. If worse comes to worst – if the worst thing happens

1) **If worse comes to** worst, we'll close down the university until the protests subside.
2) **If worse comes to** worst, we'll have to lay off some workers in order to avoid shutting down the factory.

310. Ill at ease *(adj.)* – nervous and uncomfortable

1) Many passengers feel **ill at ease** the first time they fly.
2) The way he was looking at her made her feel **ill at ease.**

311. I tell you what / Tell you what *(informal)* – Here is an idea that I've thought of

1) I know you had your heart set on hiking today, but it's raining. **I tell you what**, let's make some popcorn and watch a movie.
2) The Chinese Restaurant is closed today. **Tell you what**, let's go for Italian today and next time we'll have Chinese.

312. Impose on / Impose upon (*v.*) – to make inconvenient of, to take advantage of, to burden, to place upon

1) I don't want to **impose on** you. But would you mind turning down the volume on your stereo? I'm trying to study.
2) He always **imposes on** us by dropping in for unannounced visits.
3) I don't want to **impose on** you by staying too long.
4) The government **imposes** high taxes **upon** its people.
5) The long hours of work **impose** a great strain **on** me.

313. In addition (*adv.*) – as something extra, besides

1) He treated me to dinner **in addition** to paying for the concert tickets.
2) I'd like to order two more bookcases **in addition** to the one I've already ordered.
3) Please bring me one personal size pizza **in addition** to a family size one.

314. In advance (*adv.*) – ahead of time, in front, before

1) I like to plan my weekly schedule **in advance**.
2) Army scouts go into battle **in advance** of the regular troops.
3) Her ideas were usually **in advance** of those offered by other workers and were generally better ideas, too.

315. In and out (*adv.*) – coming in and going out

1) She has been **in and out** all day and I don't know when she'll return.
2) I'll be **in and out** all day, so if you need to speak to me, call me this evening after seven o'clock.

316. In any case / In any event / At all events (*adv.*) – certainly, anyhow, anyway, no matter what happens

1) We're overstaffed at the moment and aren't hiring, but **in any case**, I'm certain that we can find a place for you in the organization.
2) I can't say for sure when I'll be returning, but **in any event**, I will return by December.

317. In arrears / In arrears on (*adv.*) – the state of being behind in fulfilling payments on an obligation

1) They were evicted because they were three months **in arrears** on their rent.
2) She's **in arrears on** all of her monthly bills including her credit card payments, too.

318. In a sense (*adv.*) – in a way, sort of

1) **In a sense**, I don't want to get a raise because the promotion means I'll have to work additional hours.
2) Breaking up was, **in a sense**, good for their relationship for some reasons.

319. Inasmuch as (*conj.*) – because of the fact that, since, because

1) I'm going to postpone my Hawaiian vacation **inasmuch as** the weather hasn't been as good as we had hoped. In fact, it's been raining everyday.
2) He has changed his mind and is running for reelection **inasmuch as** the politicians have pleaded with him to do so.

320. In behalf of / In one's behalf (*prep.*) – in the interest of, for the benefit of

1) The monument was erected **in behalf of** all those who gave their lives in the cause of Korean independence.
2) Members of the Peace Corp work around the world **in behalf of** the disenfranchised.

** On behalf of / On one's behalf – for, on the part of, in place of

1) Children's Advocates spoke **on behalf of** children everywhere.
2) **On behalf of** my grandmother, I thank each of you for your generosity and kindness.
3) The Prime Minister attended the funeral **on behalf of** the President who is attending the economic summit in Tokyo.

321. In case (*conj.*) – if, if it happens that

1) Let me know where you'll be **in case** I have to work late.
2) I'll take an umbrella with me **in case** it rains.

** In case / Just in case (*adv.*) – if there is need, as a precaution

1) We'd better take some extra cash with us just **in case** there's an emergency.
2) I usually pay by check or credit card, but I'll take some cash with me **just in case** they won't accept a check or a credit card.
3) Please take my phone number **in case** you get lost or delayed.

** In case of (*prep.*) – if there should happen to be, in the event of

1) The doctor said to stop taking the medication in case of drowsiness.
2) **In case of** a fire, please use the stairs to exit the building.

322. In charge (of) (*adj., adv., prep.*) – in authority, to be in control, in a position to care

1) The President leaves the Vice-President **in charge** while he is gone.
2) Dr. Lee is the head surgeon and also **in charge of** the Emergency Room.
3) Who's **in charge of** running the copy machine?

** On the charge of (*prep.*) – on charges of

1) Three men were arrested earlier today **on the charge of** smuggling.
2) The woman was convicted **on charges of** fraud and embezzlement.

323. In circulation / Into circulation (*adj.*) – doing things as usual, to be in circulation

1) The economist hasn't been **in circulation** since he lost his job two years ago.
2) Sources within the company said the new album will be delivered to stores early next week just in time to be put **into circulation** for the holiday season.

324. In common (*adv.*) – shared together, jointly

1) Happy couples usually have a lot of interests **in common.**
2) They have a lot **in common** because they grew up in the same neighborhood, attended the same schools, and chose similar careers.

325. In consequence (*adv.*) – as a result, consequently, therefore

1) He argued with his manager and, **in consequence**, was fired.
2) The annual rainfall was much greater than predicted and **in consequence**, there was severe flooding.

** In consequence of (*prep.*) – because of, as a result of

1) The man was granted a divorce from his wife and given custody of the children, **in consequence** of her abusive character.
2) The student was given a reprimand and a warning **in consequence** of her continued absence.

326. In consideration of (*prep.*) – in view of, because of

1) The award was presented **in consideration** of her service to the community.
2) **In consideration** of all the extra work you've done, I'm quite willing to pay you more than the amount we originally agreed on.

327. In defiance of (*prep.*) – in disobedience to

1) She came home late in defiance of her parent's curfew.
2) The employees went out on strike **in defiance** of the company's no strike policy.

328. In dispute (*adj.*) – in disagreement or argument

1) The role he played in the robbery is **in dispute**.
2) Union leaders, citing recent allegations of fraud and corruption, are **in dispute** of the company's pension plan.

329. In earnest (*adj., adv.*) – seriously, with serious intent, in fact or truth, really

1) She worked **in earnest** towards her goal of becoming a writer.
2) Some of the firemen were working **in earnest** when the roof fell off.
3) I'm not joking. I meant what I said **in earnest**. Either you improve the quality of your work or you'll be fired.

330. In effect (*adj., adv.*) – In fact, actually, in active force, operative

1) What are they saying **in effect**?
2) What they are saying, **in effect**, is the system won't be back online for another week.
3) Studying diligently is, **in effect**, providing insurance for your future.
4) The new law, **in effect** today, allows police to stop and search anyone for any reason.

** In fact (*adv.*) – actually, in truth, as a matter of fact

1) We say that certain things are easy to do; but **in fact** they aren't always easy to do.
2) It appears to be the original; but **in fact** it is a masterfully reproduced copy.

** In force (*adj.*) – in effect, in operation, valid

1) The new drug laws are now **in force** and repeated offenders will be dealt with harshly.
2) The company policy prohibiting employees from accepting part- time employment with a competitor is still **in force.**

331. In evidence (*adj.*) – easily noticeable, present and easily seen

1) It's only early March, but spring is **in evidence** everywhere.
2) Poverty and depression are **in evidence** on almost every street.

332. In favor of (*prep.*) – on the side of, in support of

1) Most workers are **in favor of** accepting the company's latest contract offer.
2) I am **in favor of** a five-day work week.

333. In full swing (*adj.*) – in full operation, at peak activity

1) The pop concert was already **in full swing** when we arrived.
2) After a slow start, the holiday shopping season is now **in full swing.**

334. In general (*adv.*) – generally, for the most part, on the whole

1) **In general**, it is a good program, although it is not as good as they claim (it is) in their brochure.
2) The southwest of the United States, **in general**, is warm and dry.
3) The students in my class are well behaved **in general.**

335. In half (*adv.*) – into halves

1) He cut an apple **in half.**
2) My allowance was cut **in half** because I only did half of my chores.

336. Inhonor of (*prep.*) – as an honor to

1) A reception will be held **in honor of** Professor Kim who is retiring.
2) Children's Day is set aside **in honor of** children.

337. In kind (*adv.*) – to pay with something other than money such as goods, services, food, etc.

1) He cheated on his girlfriend and later she repaid him **in kind.**
2) The Ritz Carlton and The Hyatt Regency offer services that may differ in degree but not **in kind.**

** Kind of – rather

1) It's **kind of** dark in here because a few of the bulbs have burnt out.
2) I **kind of** agree with what you did, but I'm not sure I agree with the method you used.

338. In (the) light of *(adj.)* – considering, in view of

1) We have decided to re-examine the matter **in light of** the new information you recently brought to our attention.
2) **In light of** her dedication to the plight of the homeless, we decided to name a wing of the new hospital after her.

339. In line *(adj.)* – in a line

1) We bought our tickets and then had to stand **in line** before they let us into the theater.

** In line (for) *(adj.)* – in a position in a series, within proper limits

1) Mr. Kim's boss told him that he is next **in line** for a promotion.
2) The government needs to do something to keep prices **in line.**

** In line with *(prep.)* – in accordance with, in agreement with

1) The new proposal is **in line with** the company's general policies.
2) The administrative dean issued the student a warning because his behavior was not **in line with** the university's policies.
3) The company's hiring policies are **in line with** the new federal law.

** On the line – at risk, in a dangerous position, on a telephone line

1) You'd better succeed in the project, otherwise your job will be **on the line.**
2) Mr. Lee is **on the line** and wants to talk to you.

340. In part *(adj.)* – partly, to a certain extent

1) I quit my job, **in part**, because I no longer enjoyed the work and also because the salary was too low.
2) They remodeled their home, **in part**, to increase its resale value.

341. In particular (*adj.*) – specifically, particularly

1) I majored in English Literature, **in particular**, the Romantics.
2) I enjoy vacations, relaxing vacations at the beach **in particular**.
3) He likes to eat; **in particular**, he likes fruit and vegetables.

342. In person (*adv.*) – physically present

1) The principal appeared **in person** at the high school dance.
2) Can I talk to you **in person** about the amount of deductions from my last paycheck?

343. In place (*adv.*) – in the right place, in the usual place

1) Her daughter's room was a mess. Not a thing was **in place**.
2) Put your things **in place**.
3) He's organized. Everything is always **in place**.

** In place of / Instead of (*prep.*) – in lieu of, in the place of

1) They sent us a large pizza with pepperoni **in place of** the medium size one with vegetables I ordered.
2) To everyone's surprise, he married a woman he had just met **instead of** his long time fiancee.

** Out of place (*adj., adv.*) – improper, not in the right place

1) I was the only one wearing a suit, so I felt **out of place**.
2) The enormous sofa looked **out of place** in the tiny living room.

344. In print (*adj.*) – in printed or published form, still offered for sale by a publisher

1) She's longing for the day she'll see her book **in print**.

2) I'm sorry the book is no longer **in print.**
3) There are over six million copies **in print.**

** **Out of print – no longer in print, no longer offered for sale by a publisher**

1) The book is **out of print.**
2) The book you ordered is **out of print.**

345. In private (*adv.*) – confidentially, secretly

1) Can we speak **in private?**
2) The call was of a personal nature, so she took it **in private.**

** **In public (*adv.*) – openly, not secretly, in the presence of others**

1) People act differently **in public** than they do in private.
2) It was the first time they appeared **in public** together since the accident.

346. In question (*adj.*) – under discussion, concerned

1) The person **in question** no longer works for the company.
2) He couldn't have committed the crime because he was out of town on the day **in question.**

347. In reference to / With reference to / In regard to (*prep.*) – in or with respect to, in connection with, about

1) I'm calling **in reference to** the most recent electric bill.
2) He said the deal with H company had fallen through, but **with reference to** the deal with S company, he said it looked good.
3) We had a meeting **in regard to** the team's recent losses.

** **In relation to / With relation to** *(prep.)* **– in connection with, in comparison to, about**

1) The conversation was **in relation to** my future with the company.
2) She chose her major **with relation to** how it would help her future.

** **In respect to / With respect to** *(prep.)* **– in connection with, related to, about**

1) Let's talk about the new law **in respect to** how it will affect people.
2) The management spoke to him **with respect to** his job performance.

348. In return *(adv.)* **– as a return**

1) I gave her a gift and she took me to dinner **in return**.
2) Dick helped me fix my car; **in return**, I invited him to dinner.

349. In and outs *(n.)* **– the details of an activity or process**

1) He knows all the **ins and outs** of the local political situation.
2) The serviceman knew all the **ins and outs** of my computer system.

350. In short order *(adv.)* **– without delay**

1) Tell me what you want done and I'll get it done **in short order**.
2) We did everything he wanted **in short order**.

351. In short supply *(adj.)* **– not enough**

1) Nowadays, honest people seem to be **in short supply**.
2) In some underdeveloped countries, medical supplies and food are in **short supply**.

352. Inside / Inside of *(prep.)* – enclosed within

1) His mother told him to go **inside** and clean his room.
2) The hikers survived the storm by staying **inside of** a cave.

** Inside out *(adj.)* – with the inner surface turned out or reversed

1) She wore her jacket **inside out.**
2) We turned the laundry **inside out** before hanging it on the line.
3) He was so tired that he put his shirt on **inside out.**

353. Insofar as *(adj.)* – to such an extent as, as much as

1) **Insofar as** I can, I will continue to work, despite my age.
2) **Insofar as** he could, he worked on the project in his spare time.

354. In spite of *(prep.)* – despite, notwithstanding

1) The plane landed safely, **in spite of** the heavy fog.
2) **In spite of** the heavy spring rains, they went camping.

** Notwithstanding *(adv., prep.)* – in spite of, in spite of this

1) I'll proceed with my plan **notwithstanding** any objections.
2) The world environmental leaders expressed opposition to the developmental proposal of wet lands, but it was passed by Congress **notwithstanding.**

355. In stock *(adj.)* – available for sale, in present possession, having something ready to sell.

1) If items sell too quickly, it's difficult to keep them **in stock.**
2) The shoes you ordered are now **in stock.**

** **Out of stock** (*adj.*) **- not having available for sale**

1) The advertised computer was **out of stock**, so they gave her a rain-check.
2) Those items are **out of stock** now.

356. In substance (*adv.*) - in the main or basic parts, basically

1) These two stereo systems are the same **in substance**, except for the price.
2) His argument sounds convincing, but generally lacking **in substance**.

357. In terms of (*prep.*) - especially about, in the matter of

1) **In terms of** athletic ability, this year's team is no match for last year's team.
2) **In terms of** recognition, teachers usually don't receive very much.

358. In that (*conj.*) - because, since, for the reason that

1) I like the fall **in that** it is a time when fresh fruits and vegetables are abundant.

359. In the air (*adv.*) - in everyone's thoughts, a general feeling

1) Feelings of anticipation and excitement were **in the air** as the audience awaited the world premiere of the new movie.
2) Now it's April, spring is **in the air**.
3) Christmas is already **in the air**.

** **Up in the air - not settled, undecided**

1) The winner of the recent election is still **up in the air**.
2) Whether she will graduate on time or not is **up in the air**.
3) Those issues are still **up in the air**.

360. In the first place *(adv.)* – in the beginning, at first

1) **In the first place**, I told him that I was engaged.

361. In the least *(adv.)* – even a little

1) I don't understand baseball **in the least.**
2) She is not interested in him **in the least.**

362. In the main *(adv.)* – generally, for the most part, on the whole

1) **In the main**, most people work hard to earn their money.
2) **In the main**, the movie was a box office success.

363. In the nick of time *(adv.)* – just at the critical moment

1) She was just about to leave, and he caught her **in the nick of time.**
2) I finished my homework assignment **in the nick of time.**

364. In the running *(adj., adv.)* – in competition, having a chance to win

1) He's definitely **in the running** for the new management position.
2) There are four students **in the running** for class president.

365. In the saddle *(adj., adv.)* – in a position to order

1) The acting president is **in the saddle**, and things are running well.

366. In the same boat *(adj., adv.)* – in the same situation

1) We need to help one another because all of us are **in the same boat.**
2) With sales down, the prospect of salary cuts are imminent. Even worse, the company has laid off hundreds of its workers. We're all **in the same boat.**

367. In the wake of (*prep.*) – following, right after, as a result of

1) **In the wake of** last week's heavy rains, some of the small dams have been destroyed.
2) Many people were laid off **in the wake of** the economic slump.

368. In time (*adj., adv.*) – not too late, soon enough

1) I got to the airport just **in time** to catch my flight.
2) Traffic was heavy, but I was **in time** for the reception.

369. In touch (*adj.*) – exchanging news, talking or writing, contacting

1) She has promised to keep **in touch** with us while she's away.
2) I keep **in touch** with many of my friends from university.

370. In trust (*adj., adv.*) – in safe care for another

1) The money has been put **in trust** until he reaches twenty-one.
2) The philanthropist put $10,000,000 **in trust** for the scholarship fund.

371. In view of (*adv.*) – taking into account, considering

1) **In view of** his recent performance, the management has decided not to renew his contract.
2) The factory shut down **in view of** the slowing economy and rising labor costs.

372. Invite over (*v.*) – to ask to visit

1) I saw the Smiths and **invited** them **over** for dinner.
2) He **invited** me **over** for Christmas but I'm not sure I can go.

373. Jack up (*v.*) – to lift with a jack, to raise a price

1) The mechanic **jacked up** the car and changed the flat tire.
2) Farmers **jacked up** the price of their crops to combat inflation.

374. Jazz up (*v.*) – to make more lively and exciting

1) The new sofa and coffee table **jazzed up** their living room.
2) The interior renovations certainly **jazzed up** the hotel.
3) The band **jazzed up** the concert with a spectacular light show.

375. Join hands or forces (*v.*) – unite, to get together in a common cause, action, etc.

1) Management and workers **joined forces** to complete the project on time.
2) A number of medical groups have **joined hands** in the fight against AIDS and SARS.

376. Join – to become a member of an organization, to enroll in

1) Do you want to **join** a ski club?
2) No, I don't. I want to **join** a health club.

** Join in (*v.*) – to take part in, to participate, to do something with others

1) Are you going to **join in** the discussion?

2) When the singer got to the song's refrain, members of the audience **joined in**. It was obvious that many of them knew the lyrics by heart.
3) She was more than happy to **join in** the World Wildlife Foundation's annual fund drive.

** **Join up** (*v.*) – to go into military service, to enlist in the armed forces

1) If we go to war, all eligible men will have to **join up**.
2) The college student decided to **join up** after spring semester.

K

377. Keel over (v.) – to tip over, to collapse

1) A strong gale caused the small fishing boat to **keel over.**
2) The conductor was leading the orchestra when he **keeled over** and died.

378. Keep after (v.) – to speak again and again about something, to be persistent with

1) He won't pay me the money he borrowed unless I keep after him.
2) She has to keep after her daughter to study.

379. Keep an eye on (v.) – to watch carefully, not stop paying attention to

1) Would you **keep an eye on** my bag for a minute?
2) I have to run some errands. Would you **keep an eye on** my children for me?

380. Keep at (v.) – to continue, to persevere

1) I have to **keep at** my homework until it's finished.
2) I **kept at** my work until it was done and done right.

381. Keep down (v.) – to control, to keep within limits, to keep from progressing

1) You should learn to **keep** your temper **down.**

2) We try to **keep** costs **down**, but with the economy the way it is, that's difficult.
3) A good student is hard to **keep down.**

382. Keep from (v.) – to prevent oneself from doing something

1) She can't seem to **keep from** talking in class.
2) He can't **keep from** drinking.

** Keep on (v.) – to continue (usually the action in the present participle)

1) We were quite ready to leave, but the speaker **kept on** talking.
2) Her doctor asked her to refrain from eating between meals, but she **kept** right **on** doing it.
3) He **keeps on** harassing her, in spite of a court order prohibiting him from contacting her.
4) The students **kept on** talking after the teacher asked them to stop.

** Keep on with (v.) – to continue with

1) He **kept on with** his research even after the funding was cut.

** Keep up (with) (v.) – to continue something, to stay in condition, to maintain a pace

1) It takes time and effort to **keep up with** an exercise program.
2) You've got to **keep up with** your house payments, otherwise the bank will repossess the house.
3) The recent rains and ensuing crop shortages **kept** prices **up.**
4) You walk so fast that it's hard for me to **keep up with** you.

383. Keep one's chin up (v.) – to face trouble with courage

1) I know times are difficult, but **keep your chin up.**
2) I'm sorry to hear that you lost your job, but **keep your chin up.** And I'm sure you'll find another one soon.

384. Keep one's distance (v.) – to avoid being close or friendly

1) I **keep my distance** because I don't trust them.
2) The fire was so hot that the firefighters were forced to **keep their distance.**

385. Keep track of (v.) – to remain informed about or keep a record of

1) I try to **keep track of** my friends from high school.
2) They move so often that we can hardly **keep track of** them.

** Lose track of (v.) – to fail to keep up with or stay in touch with

1) His speech was so circuitous that I **lost track of** his argument.
2) I've **lost track of** many of the friends I knew when I was a student.

386. Kick around (v.) – to treat roughly, to talk or discuss at leisure, to be laid around

1) Stop **kicking** your younger brother **around.**
2) We **kicked around** the idea of taking a two-week trip to Spain.
3) The possibility of issuing junk bonds has been **kicked around** for a long time. It's not a new idea by any means.

387. Kick off (v.) – in football, to make the kick that begins the game, to begin

1) The leading player **kicked off** to the other team.

2) The campaign was **kicked off** with an interview and a public appearance.

** **Kickoff (with)** *(n)* **– the kicking of a football to start, the beginning of something**

1) It was a nice **kickoff**.
2) The **kickoff** of a new football season is an exciting celebration.

388. Kick oneself *(v.)* – to regret, to feel sorry

1) I am **kicking myself** for making poor choices in the stock market.
2) I **kicked myself** for not having the courage to do it.

389. Kick out *(v.)* – to dismiss, to force to leave, to throw out

1) The boy was **kicked out** of school for beating up his classmate.
2) The landlord **kicked** his tenants **out** for not paying their rent for three months.

390. Kick up *(v.)* – to raise trouble, become aggravated

1) My boss **kicks up** a big fuss over even the smallest mistakes.
2) The old lady's arthritis is **kicking up** again. She is in pain.

391. Kill off *(v.)* – to destroy totally or on a large scale

1) The polluted water released from a local factory **killed off** a large portion of the marine life in the nearby ocean.
2) **Killing off** even one species can upset the balance of Nature.

392. Knock out *(v.)* – to exhaust, to make unconscious

1) The sun and the hard work **knocked** me **out**.
2) The champion **knocked out** the challenger in the first round.

393. Knock it off *(v.)* - to quit or finish

1) They had been arguing for an hour. So I told them to **knock it off.**
2) I am sure I can **knock off** the work within an hour.

394. Know-it-all *(n., adj.)* - a person who behaves or thinks as if s/he knows all about everything

1) I dislike his **know-it-all** attitude and arrogant behavior.
2) She is a real **know-it-all** and it drives me crazy.

395. Know one's way around *(v.)* - to understand how things go in the world, to have experience and skill in some area everything

1) A street-wise person **knows his way around** town without getting into any trouble.
2) She'll do well in her new position because she **knows her way around** the corporate structure.

396. Lay away (*v.*) – to put aside or save for future use, to reserve merchandise until paid for

1) We **lay away** some money every month for our annual trip.
2) Please **lay away** this merchandise for me.

** Layaway (*n., adj.*) – system of making payments, to hold something until it gets paid off

1) Can I use a **layaway** plan to buy this stereo?
2) Please put it on **layaway** for me.

397. Lay in (*v.*) – to get and store (provisions, etc.)

1) The farmer **laid in** six tons of straw so he'd be able to feed his livestock during the cold winter months.
2) We keep an extra freezer to **lay in** food for emergencies.

398. Lay off (*v.*) – to discharge workers, to dismiss from work

1) She was **laid off** last year and hasn't found a new job.
2) Many workers are going to be **laid off** if the economy doesn't improve.

** Layoff (*n.*) – usually a temporary dismissal from employment

1) There are often mass **layoffs** during an economic recession.
2) Financial difficulties led to layoffs, but the company is hoping to rehire many of the **laid off** workers before the end of July.

399. Lay out (v.) – to spread out, to arrange according to a plan, to spend a sum of money

1) The magician **laid out** six cards on the table.
2) Some people believe that their futures have already been **laid out** for them.
3) I am going to **lay out** $10,000 for my wedding.

400. Lead off (v.) – to begin, to go first

1) The band **led off** with one of its older songs and then launched into a medley of their more recent hits.
2) The speaker **led off** with a funny story.

401. Lead on (v.) – to lure someone into something that is not desirable

1) She **led** him **on**, but she denies it.
2) He **led** me **on** and I believed he was honest, but it cost me a lot of money.

402. Lead up to (v.) – to prepare or approach gradually

1) The company is **leading up to** the hiring of younger people and the dismissal of older employees in an effort to revitalize its sales.
2) I knew she was ill, but I didn't see the signs **leading up to** her death.

403. Leave off (v.) – to stop doing something, to leave something on the way somewhere

1) I won't **leave off** my project until I complete it.
2) I always place a marker in the books I read, so I know where I **left off.**
3) He **leaves** his son **off** at a daycare center before going to work.

404. Leave out (*v.*) – to omit, not to include

1) I asked her to edit my work and **leave out** all the unimportant information.
2) I like to **leave out** some less important points when I teach.
3) She was **left out** at the party because no one remembered her.

405. Lend a hand / give a hand (*v.*) – to help, to give assistance

1) My friends came to **lend a hand** when I moved to this apartment.
2) She often **lends a hand** at church socials.
3) Let me **give** you a **hand** with your heavy box.

406. Lend oneself to (*v.*) – to be suitable for

1) Some laws **lend themselves to** various interpretations.

407. Lend out (*v.*) – to lend

1) The bank **lends out** money at reasonable interest rates.
2) He **lent out** his favorite video and never saw it again.

408. Less than (*adv.*) – not, little

1) They were **less than** happy with the results of their exam scores.
2) They were **less than** excited with the news of their daughter's elopement.

** Less than no time (*n.*) – very quickly

1) It seemed like that the party was over in **less than no time**.
2) I can have the copies you need in **less than no time**.

409. Let down (*v.*) – to disappoint, to slow down

1) Please don't **let** me **down**.

2) I trusted her, but she **let** me **down.**
3) We've almost finished, so don't **let down** on the work yet.

** Letdown (*n.*) – a disappointment, discouragement

1) It was such a big **letdown** because he was not offered the job he really wanted.

410. Let go (*v.*) – to allow something to pass as it is, to stop holding something

1) The boys were afraid that she would yell at them for breaking the window, but she just **let** it **go.**
2) He shouldn't continue to **let** himself **go** like this or he'll degenerate in no time.
3) You need to forgive and forget. Why don't you just **let** it **go**? A better life is waiting for you.

411. Let off (*v.*) – to excuse from work or duty, to release with little or no punishment, to explode

1) The students were **let off** easily after they were caught smoking at school.
2) The judge **let** the traffic violator **off** with just a warning.
3) After the angry man **let off** his steam, he felt better.

** Let off steam / Blow off steam (*v.*) – to discharge excessive physical energy or strong negative feelings

1) **Letting off steam** is all right if it's done in a healthy way.
2) The woman jogged to **blow off steam.**

412. Let out (*v.*) – to make leave, to allow to come (go) out

1) Our English teacher **lets** us **out** as soon as the bell rings.
2) On the contrary, our math teacher never **lets** us **out** on time.
3) He **lets** his dog **out** every night to exercise.

** Let the cat out of the bag (*v.*) – to tell or reveal a secret

1) They broke up a week ago and kept it quiet, but one of their friends **let the cat out of the bag** last night.

413. Let up (*v.*) – to become slower or less intense

1) The rain is **letting up** now.
2) The snow has **let up** a little, but there's more on the way.

414. Lick and a promise (*n.*) – a hasty, careless, and unsatisfactory work

1) Nowadays, things are not built to last because many workers do a **lick and a promise** job.
2) I was in such a hurry, I gave the floors just a **lick and a promise.**

415. Lick one's boots (*v.*) – to flatter, to please others like a subordinate

1) Cliché – A wise king doesn't want friends and advisers to **lick his boots.**
2) He's a man who he expects his employees to **lick his boots.**

416. Lie down (*v.*) – to rest in a horizontal position

1) She **lay down** on the bed until her headache was gone.
2) I **lay down** for a brief nap and slept for nearly five hours.

417. Lightning never strikes twice (in the same place) (a cliché) – Luck doesn't come to someone repeatedly.

1) He hit the $1,000,000 jackpot five years ago and has foolishly squandered all of it. He still buys lottery tickets, but I don't think he'll win because **lightning never strikes twice (in the same place).**

418. Light up (v.) – suddenly brightened up, to ignite a cigarette

1) His face **lit up** as his bride to be walked down the aisle.
2) After the reception, the best man **lit up** a cigar.

419. Line up (v.) – to form or get in a line, to arrange, to put in order

1) People **lined up** to buy the tickets.
2) They've **lined up** some good bands for the benefit concert.
3) She **lined up** her family pictures on a bedroom shelf.

420. Give lip service / Pay lip service (v.) – empty words followed by no support or proof

1) Some politicians **give lip service** to community programs, and do little for the community after they are elected.
2) He just **pays lip service** to his girlfriend.
3) Don't believe what she says. It's just **lip service.**

421. Live off (v.) – to live with the means provided by

1) He **lives off** his pension.
2) They **live off** their savings.
3) He **lives off** his friends because he doesn't have either a steady job or savings.

** **Live off the fat of the land** *(v.)* **– to live in comfort without having to work**

1) I'd like to have enough money to retire early and **live off the fat of the land.**
2) Wouldn't it be nice to be able to **live off the fat of the land?**

422. Live on *(v.)* **– to continue to live, to support oneself**

1) The memory of your kind act will **live on** forever in my heart.
2) Many elderly people **live on** a small income.

423. Live up to *(v.)* **– to live in accordance with, to fulfill, to satisfy, not disappoint**

1) I try to **live up to** my ideals.
2) I wasn't born to **live up to** your expectations and you were not born to **live up to** mine, either. But if we can accept one another's differences, then, it'll be beautiful.

424. Long face *(n.)* **– a sad look**

1) Why does she have a **long face** this morning? What's wrong with her?
2) When his father punished him for hitting his sister, the boy put on a **long face** and began to cry.

425. Look after *(v.)* **– to take care of**

1) I am willing to **look after** stray animals.
2) I consider **looking after** stray animals a duty and a pleasure.
3) My parents asked me to **look after** my little brother while they went to the supermarket.
4) **Look after** your grandmother.

426. Look at (v.) – to regard or consider, to examine, to focus, to give attention to

1) You should **look at** the problem objectively.
2) We **look at** things differently when we get older.
3) The doctor **looked at** the patient's medical history.
4) **Look at** that beautiful mockingbird in the oak tree.

** **a mockingbird : a songbird in North America. It has grayish tan feathers. It imitates the songs of other birds.**

427. Look at the world through rose-colored glasses (v.) – to see everything as nice and beautiful, to be very optimistic

1) I often **look at the world through rose-colored glasses.**
2) Many teenagers have a tendency to **look at the world through rose-colored glasses.**

428. Look back (at) (v.) – to think about or remember one's past

1) I sometimes **look back** at my childhood.
2) I try not to **look back**, I'd rather focus on the present and future.

429. Look down on or upon (v.) – to regard with contempt, to consider others as inferior, to show a lack of respect

1) He **looks down on** anyone who is less fortunate than he is.
2) Don't **look down on** me.
3) Some rich people **look down on** the poor as inferior.

430. Look for (v.) – to search for

1) I've been **looking** all over the house **for** my keys.
2) Now that her term in congress has ended, she wants to **look for** a job in the private sector.
3) I am **looking for** a new job.

431. Look forward to (v.) – to anticipate (usually with pleasure)

1) We will **look forward to** seeing you soon.
2) "You must be happy about your upcoming wedding." "Yes, I am **looking forward to** it very much."
3) I am **looking forward to** my trip to Europe this summer.

432. Look in on (v.) – to make a short visit so as to check

1) My friend **looks in on** my mother once in a while.
2) The worried mother **looked in on** the sleeping baby.
3) The nurse **looks in on** the patients once in a while.

433. Look into (v.) – to investigate

1) Please **look into** the matter of the missing documents immediately.
2) I've **looked into** the matter and found out what happened to the documents.
3) The police **looked into** the crime and solved it.

434. Look out (for) (v.) – to be careful, to be alert

1) The sentry was ordered to keep a sharp **look out for** enemy troop movements.
2) **Look out!** There's a car coming!

435. Look over (*v.*) – to examine (often casually)

1) Did you have a chance to **look over** the earnings report?
2) Yes, I **looked** it **over** and added a few comments.

436. Look up (*v.*) – to search for, to locate and call upon

1) Please **look up** Dr. Kim's number for me.
2) I often **look up** words in my dictionary.
3) Going to the class reunion and **looking up** old alumni is fun.

** Look up to (*v.*) – to admire and respect

1) Though the man was only an ordinary person, his son **looked up to** him as if he were the greatest man in the world.
2) Many people **looked up to** the former U.S. President Bill Clinton for his accomplishments.

437. Lose one's heart (to) (*v.*) – to fall in love

1) Before her first date, her mother advised her not to **lose her heart too** quickly.
2) He **lost his heart to** her the first time he saw her.

438. Lose one's temper (*v.*) – to get angry

1) The coach told the player to control his anger and not **lose his temper.**
2) Yes, I **lost my temper**, but only after he continuously provoked me.

439. Lose out (*v.*) – to be defeated

1) We wanted to win the game, but we **lost out** to another team.

** Lose out on (*v.*) – to miss an opportunity

1) He **lost out on** the promotion because of chronic tardiness.

440. Lose track of (*v.*) – to fail to keep in touch, counting, etc.

1) We **lost track of** him and don't know what has become of him.
2) She tried not to **lose track of** her friends from high school, but as the years passed, keeping in touch became more and more difficult.
3) I'm sorry I'm late. I **lost track of** the time while I was playing golf.

441. Luck out (*v.*) – to get lucky, to be fortunate

1) I **lucked out** because the exam was postponed.
2) He felt that he really **lucked out** when he met her.

** In luck (*adj.*) – lucky

1) Going to the airport, the traffic jam was terrible, but I was **in luck** because my flight was delayed an hour.
2) "We're **in luck**," announced the coach, "Their star pitcher has the flu and won't be pitching today."

** Out of luck (*adj.*) – unlucky

1) He wanted to ask her for another chance to save their relationship, but he was **out of luck** and she refused to even speak with him.

442. Mad as a hornet *(adj.)* – extremely angry

1) He was as **mad as a hornet** when he discovered that someone had broken into his car and stolen his cassette player and tapes.
2) She knew her boss would be as **mad as a hornet** because she was more than two hours late and hadn't bothered to call.

443. Make a difference *(v.)* – to change the nature of something or some situation or matter

1) It doesn't make a difference whether you are rich or poor.
2) Painting the house will make a big difference if you decide to sell.

444. Make a fool of *(v.)* – to make someone look foolish

1) He **made a fool of** himself by getting drunk and then behaving belligerently at the company's Christmas party.
2) That woman usually tries to **make a fool of** her husband when they're with other people.

445. Make a hit *(v.)* – to become successful

1) The record company hoped the newly signed band could **make a hit** with their debut album.
2) Her new line of casual wear **made a** big **hit** at the Paris fashion show.

446. Make a mountain out of a molehill / Make a federal case out of nothing / Make a big issue out of nothing (cliché)
– to make something unimportant seem important, to act as if a small thing is a big thing

1) Don't **make a federal case out of nothing**, it's just a small matter.
2) Why do you always have to **make a mountain out of a molehill**? I was only 10 minutes late getting home.

447. Make a practice of (v.) – to make a habit of

1) You've got to **make a practice** of studying more regularly.
2) He **made** it a **practice** to get up early and he was never late for work.

448. Make a virtue of necessity (v.) – to do happily what one has to for an urgent need

1) They lost all their money when the stock market collapsed, but they **made a virtue of necessity** and are well on the way to recovering their losses.

** **Make the best of it (v.) – to do best under unfavorable conditions without complaining**

1) I didn't get into the school I wanted, but the one I'm attending is also a good university and I'm **making the best of it.**
2) He didn't like working at low paying jobs, but he **made the best of them** and worked his way through school. Now he's an attorney.

449. Make ends meet (v.) – just getting by, just to make an income to pay bills, etc.

1) Most people work hard just to **make ends meet**, living from paycheck to paycheck.
2) With the economy the way it is, it's a struggle to **make ends meet.**

450. Make fun of (*v.*) – to laugh at, to tease

1) They **make fun of** him because they think he dresses funny.
2) She scolded him for **making fun of** her in front of her friends.

451. Make hay while the sun shines (a cliché) – You should take advantage of opportunities while they're available, don't waste them

1) We have a very small savings, but I want you to use it for school because we've got to **make hay while the sun is shining.**
2) Land prices are very high now, so we are going to **make hay while the sun shines** and sell some of the land we've been holding onto.

** Make the most of it (*v.*) – to take the full advantage of something

1) The job they offered me isn't the one I wanted, but I'm going to accept their offer and **make the most of it**
2) Too few students **make the most of** the school library facilities.

452. Make light of (*v.*) – to treat as unimportant, to minimize, to play down

1) Don't brag, but don't **make light of** your accomplishments, either.
2) He's a good manager, but he **makes light of** the problems his workers face too often.

** Make much of (*v.*) – to make something seem of more value or more importance than it actually is

1) Newspapers often **make much of** minor stories in their effort to boost their circulation.

453. Make love (v.) – to engage in sexual intercourse

1) The film was banned because the censors felt that it recklessly encouraged our youth to **make love** before they were really ready to accept the responsibilities of their actions.

454. Make off with / Make away with (v.) – to steal

1) The thief **made off with** an undisclosed amount of cash and jewels.
2) The squirrel **made away with** an acorn.

455. Make oneself at home (v.) – to feel comfortable

1) She told her friend to come in and **make himself at home.**
2) I'll be ready in a minute, please **make yourself at home.**

456. Make one's mark (v.) – to establish one's reputation

1) She hoped to **make her mark** as a ballerina.
2) Ernest Hemingway began his career as a journalist, but **made his mark** as a novelist and short-story writer.

457. Make one's way (v.) – to find a path, to work hard to make a living.

1) **Making our way** through the huge crowd wasn't easy.
2) He was an orphan and had to **make his own way** since there was no one to help him.

458. Make out (v.) – to see and identify, to understand, to write out, to fill in by writing, to do well, to get along well, to kiss and embrace

1) The fog was so heavy that the drivers couldn't **make out** the road signs.

2) I can't **make out** the meaning of the third sentence in paragraph two.
3) Before going shopping she usually **makes out** a list.
4) He **made out** the application, but they never offered him the job.
5) How are you **making out** in your physics class?
6) I didn't think she would be a good match for him, but I guess they're **making out** all right.
7) She thought the party was boring because most of the kids spent the evening **making out.**

459. Make over (*n., v.*) – to change or transfer the ownership of, to redo or renew to renovate

1) The old man's property has been **made over** to his son.
2) We're not completely happy with the interior and want to **make it over.**
3) The house needs a complete **make over**, so we'll start with a new paint job.

460. Make sure (*v.*) – to make certain

1) I think she's arriving at 7 o'clock tomorrow morning, but we'd better call the airline and **make sure.**
2) Please **make sure** you turn off the lights and lock the door before you go to bed.

461. Make up (of, for, to) (*v.*) – to construct falsely or fictionally, to constitute of, to compensate for, to satisfy a grievance, to resolve a quarrel, to repeat, to decide, to apply cosmetics tokiss and embrace

1) Just tell me the truth, instead of **making up** another preposterous story.
2) New York City is **made up** of five boroughs and the boroughs are **made up** of many counties.

3) He was absent from school last week and needs to **make up** the work he missed.
4) I know I haven't been generous to you, but I'd like to **make** it **up** to you.
5) I apologize because the quarrel we had was my fault. Let's **make up** and put the past behind us so we can be friends again.
6) I'm too ill to take the exam. Can I **make** it **up** at a later time?
7) I've **made up** my mind to go to France on my summer holiday.
8) She **makes up** her face every morning.

** **Make-up / makeup** *(n.)* **– cosmetics applied, a special exam given to a student who missed or failed a previous one**

1) She should wear a touch of **makeup** because she looks so pale.
2) All the students who missed the final exam were allowed to take a **make-up**.

462. Make waves / Causing waves *(v.)* – to create a disturbance

1) **Making waves** on the job isn't a good idea.
2) If he keeps **causing waves**, he's going to be expelled.

463. Man of his word *(n.)* – a man who keeps his promise

1) My father never says anything he doesn't mean. He's a **man of his word**.
2) We didn't sign the contract yet, but I think he's a **man of his word**. So I'm not too worried about finalizing the deal.

464. Many hands make light work *(proverb)* – working together makes hard work easier

1) It's not going to be easy, but if we all pitch in, we can get the job done on time. Remember the adage, "**Many hands make light work.**"

465. Matter of course (*n.*) – natural, usual way

1) Helping those in need is a **matter of course** to her because she has a generous nature.
2) Keep working diligently and don't worry about your grades. I'm sure you'll do fine. It's just a **matter of course.**

466. Matter of fact (*n.*) – something that can be accepted as true

1) He's been working here for a long time. As a **matter of fact**, he's been here since we opened.
2) "Are they still dating?" "Yes, they are. As a **matter of fact**, they're engaged."

467. Measure up to (*v.*) – to live up to or meet certain standards

1) He never **measured up to** his father's expectations.
2) People are often their own harshest critics and rarely **measure up to** their own standards.

468. Meet with (*v.*) – to meet accidentally, to meet by plan, to experience, to have

1) They were on their honeymoon, but took the time to **meet with** us.
2) In December 1997, many Asian countries **met with** an economic disaster.
3) The fishing boat **met with** disaster in a storm in the Yellow Sea.

** Meet up with (*v.*) – (more informal setting) to meet accidentally, to meet by plan, to meet at a certain place and time, to experience

1) I will **meet up with** you at 7p.m. at that restaurant.
2) I **met up with** him in the hallway.

3) On the way to Seoul, I **met up with** a huge traffic jam.

** Meet (*v.*) – to meet by chance, to meet by plan, to reach a goal or satisfy

1) We **met** heavy traffic as we got on the narrow bridge.
2) I **met** an old friend in a shopping mall whom I hadn't seen in years.
3) I will **meet** you there at 7p.m.
4) Two rivers **meet** here and go into the nearby sea.
5) The government should make an effort to **meet** the needs of their people.
6) The company **met** its sales goal for the year.

469. Melt in one's mouth (*v.*) – to be delicious, to taste good

1) This is so tender and delicious. It just **melts in my mouth.**

470. Mental telepathy (*n*) – Communication by extrasensory perception that cannot be scientifically explained

1) Recent research has documented more than a few interesting cases of **mental telepathy** involving identical twins.
2) I've recently been thinking of an old friend I hadn't seen in many years and received a letter from him this morning. It certainly made me consider the possibility of mental telepathy.

471. Miss out (on) (*v.*) – to fail to gain the benefit or pleasure of something

1) He didn't want to **miss out on** the opportunity to go camping, but the final exam was more important.
2) You **missed out on** a lot of fun by not going on the camping trip.

472. **Mix up** *(v.)* – **to confuse, to mix, to make a mistake, to be con nected**

1) Students sometimes **mix up** the words kitchen and chicken.
2) Would you do me a favor and **mix up** the salad?
3) I listened to what he said, and I was more **mixed up** after he told me his side of the story than I was before we spoke.
4) He's not a bad guy, he was just **mixed up** with the wrong crowd.

473. **Monkey business** *(n.)* – **any unethical, illegitimate, deceitful activity**

1) The police were sure the small shop was a front for illegal gambling, but couldn't prove there was any **monkey business** going on.
2) His mother told him to cut out the monkey business and do his homework.

474. Nail down (*v.*) – to settle, to clinch

1) We've got to **nail down** this contract if we hope to save the company from going into bankruptcy.
2) The team **nailed down** the league championship in the season's final game.
3) The police **nailed down** the drug dealers.

475. Name of the game (*n.*) – something disguised as something else

1) Winning a championship may seem simple, but it isn't. After all is said and done, sometimes winning is the **name of the game.**
2) The matter appears to be a simple incident of bribery, but many believe that government corruption is really the **name of the game.**

476. Natural-born (*adj.*) – born in the country, having an innate ability

1) His parents were naturalized citizens, but he's a **natural-born** citizen.
2) Mozart appears to have been a **natural-born** musical genius.

477. Never mind (*v.*) – to disregard

1) Can you answer the phone for me? **Never mind.** I'll get it myself.

478. Next door (*adj.*) – in, to, or at the adjacent house, apartment, office, etc.

1) They live **next door** to the bakery, just above the pizza place.
2) This is Mrs. Lim. She just moved in **next door.**
3) A new video shop opened right **next door** to the beauty parlor.

** Next–door (*adj.*) – to be adjacent, next to

1) She's my **next–door** neighbor.

479. Nightlife (*n.*) – night time entertainment

1) There's a lot of **nightlife** in any city. Cities thrive on entertainment.
2) When we go on holiday, we enjoy cultural attractions and good **nightlife.**

480. Nip and tuck (*adj., adv.*) – very close, neck and neck

1) The football game was nip and tuck, but the home team eked out a victory in the closing minutes of the game.
2) This year's Indy 500 was really a nip and tuck race.

481. Nip in the bud (*v.*) – to stop the growth in the beginning

1) The principal knew it was normal for teens to get into fights, but he wanted to **nip** the problem **in the bud**, so he suspended them.
2) Smoking and other addictive behaviors are best overcome if they are **nipped in the bud.**

482. Nobody's fool (*n.*) – someone who is smart, and knows what s/he is doing

1) They thought they'd take advantage of the substitute teacher, but he showed them he was **nobody's fool.**

483. No doubt *(adv.)* – a state of certainty

1) He's rich and famous and he has everything a person could want. There's **no doubt** he is very happy.
2) There was **no doubt** in anyone's mind that she deserved to win the prize.

** To be sure *(adv.)* – to know something with certainty

1) The contest is the biggest of his career, but **to be sure** he'll win.
2) She works slowly, **to be sure**, but she's methodical and does a great job.

484. No good *(adj.)* – useless

1) I'm getting rid of my old car because it's **no good.**
2) He's **no good** as a manager because he has no people skills.
3) I tried to negotiate for a higher salary, but it did **no good.**
4) It is **no good** arguing with him because he always thinks he's right.

** Of no avail / To no avail *(adj.)* – useless, unsuccessful

1) Taking the medicine was **of no avail** because I still have a headache.
2) The project was scrapped, so all their hard work was **of no avail.**
3) Her attempts to learn the new computer program were **to no avail.**

485. No longer *(adv.)* – not any longer

1) The person you are looking for **no longer** lives here.
2) The number you are calling is **no longer** in service.
3) I used to eat a lot of sweets, but I **no longer** eat them.
4) I liked him for a long time, but I'm **no longer** interested in him.

486. No matter what / No matter how *(adv.)* – regardless of, in spite of

1) **No matter what** he says, he still loves you.

2) **No matter how** hard he studied, he still failed the exam.

487. No sweat *(adv.)* – easily, without difficulty

1) I'm sure I can finish my job on time, **no sweat.**
2) It's **no sweat,** I can fix your computer.

488. No bad *(adj.)* – good enough

1) I never thought I'd like the taste of this fish, but it's **not bad.**
2) I thought the movie was going to be terrible, but it wasn't **bad.**

489. No for the world *(adv.)* – not for anything

1) I wouldn't hurt your feelings for the world.
2) Not for the world, would I abandon you.

490. Nothing succeeds like success *(proverb)* – Once a person is successful in one area, then she or he is likely to succeed in another area, as well.

1) After his success in the animal food business, he invested in other business ventures and was equally successful. **Nothing succeeds like success.**

491. Not know which way to turn *(v.)* – not know what to do in a difficult situation

1) When she lost her job and didn't have any money to pay her rent, she didn't **know which way to turn.**
2) After being forced to accept early retirement and a meager pension, he truly did **not know which way to turn.**

492. Not the only fish in the sea *(n.)* – not the only person available, one of many

1) I know he is a nice man, but he is **not the only fish in the sea.** I'm sure you'll find someone else.

**** Not the only pebble on the beach *(n.)* – not the only person to be considered or available, one of many**

1) She's **not the only pebble on the beach.** You'll find someone else.

493. No use crying over spilled milk *(proverb)* – to complain or regret something that has already happened

1) They lost the championship game, but there's **no use crying over spilled milk.**
2) I was sure they were going to offer me the position, but they didn't. Oh, well, there's **no use crying over spilt milk.**

**** No use *(n.)* – no gain, no purpose**

1) There's **no use** talking about our past glories because the past is over and done with.
2) It was **no use** asking him to help because he never helps anyone.
3) It's **no use** sending her a letter because her mind is made up.

494. No wonder *(adj.)* – not surprising

1) She's intelligent, personable, and thoroughly professional. It's **no wonder** they were impressed with her.
2) **No wonder** you love this restaurant. The service is excellent and the food is delicious.

495. Oddball (*n.*) – a peculiar or an eccentric person

1) Our neighbor, George, is kind of an **oddball** that keeps odd hours and doesn't associate with anyone.

** Off-center (*adj.*) – odd, not usual

1) He's a little **off-center**, so we never invite him to parties.
2) This picture is a bit **off-center.**

** Off center (*adv.*) – not exactly in the middle

1) The picture frame is **off center**, so we need to adjust it.

496. Of age (*adj.*) – old enough to do something, age which allows one to exercise adult rights and responsibilities

1) She is now **of** driving **age**, so she wants to get her license.
2) You must be at least 21 years **of age** to vote.
3) If you are only twenty, you are not yet **of** voting **age.**

497. Of course (*adv.*) – naturally, surely, without doubt

1) Does he love her? Of course, he loves her.
2) Do you remember me? Yes, of course, I remember you.

498. Off again, on again (*adj.*) – uncertain, not settled

1) They have an **on again, off again** relationship.
2) The rain didn't last all day, but it was **on again, off again**, so the tennis matches were cancelled.

** Off and on / On and off (*adv.*) – sometimes, occasionally, irregularly

1) The electrical power was **off and on** most of the day.
2) We see them **on and off** for dinner or at social gatherings.

499. Off balance (*adj.*) – not in balance

1) The washing machine is **off balance**, so it makes a lot of noise.
2) The tires of my car were **off balance**, so the ride wasn't very comfortable.

500. Off duty (*adj.*) – not working (in a position of responsibility)

1) An **off duty** police officer made the arrest.
2) The doctor is **off duty** today and he's probably playing golf.

** On one's day off – not supposed to work (for general)

1) What do you usually do **on your day off**?
2) **On my day off** I usually spend time working in my garden.
3) I usually go shopping when I have a **day off**.

** On duty (*adj.*) – at one's work or assignment

1) Dr. Sharkis is **on duty** today.
2) He's **on** active **duty** in the Korean Navy.
3) Employees aren't allowed to receive personal phone calls while **on duty** unless it's an emergency.

501. Off one's chest (*adj.*) – tell someone about something that bothers oneself

1) I told my boss that he wasn't treating me fair. It didn't change the way he treated me, but I felt much better after I got it **off my chest.**
2) He listened to her story and let her get it **off her chest.**

502. Off the cuff (*adv.*) – without any preparation

1) He prefers to give speeches **off the cuff.**
2) He gave a presentation of the proposed project **off the cuff.**

** Off–the–cuff (*adj.*) – instantly, immediately and without preparation

1) He is wonderfully talented at giving **off–the–cuff** speeches.
2) He gave a marvelous **off–the–cuff** speech.

503. Off the top of one's head (*adj., adv.*) – without thinking much, just spontaneously

1) She didn't take time to think. She just answered the question **off the top of her head.**
2) He didn't think about what he wrote. He just wrote **off the top of his head.**

** Offhand (*adj., adv.*) / offhanded (*adj.*) – without much thought, without planning or thinking ahead

1) I can't recall it **offhand.**
2) The politician made some **offhand** remarks on a few sensitive issues.

504. Of late *(adv.)* – recently, lately

1) He hasn't been his usual happy-go-lucky self **of late.**
2) The newspaper has been focusing on trivial matters rather than hard news **of late.**

505. Of one's own free will / Of one's own accord *(adv.)* – voluntarily, without outside influence

1) Are you signing the contract **of your own free will?**
2) Yes, I'm signing it **of my own accord.**
3) The decision on a one-year leave of absence was made **of my own accord.**

506. On account of *(prep.)* – for the sake of, by reason of, because of

1) He wants to move to a warmer southern climate **on account of** his health.
2) They emigrated **on account of** the tense political situation in their country.
3) She arrived late **on account of** heavy traffic.

507. On the average *(adv.)* – using the average as a basis of judgment

1) **On the average,** I have my motor oil changed every 3000 miles.
2) **On the average,** I spend $100.00 a month on entertainment.

508. On approval *(adv.)* – a set of criteria one must meet before being allowed credit,

1) She wanted the merchandise delivered immediately, but had to wait because they would only ship them on approval of her credit application.
2) We can issue the credit card on approval of your credit application.
3) We can give you a money-back guarantee on this product if you buy it on approval.

509. On call / At call (*adj.*) – available for use, ready to respond to a summons or command, subject to demand for payment or return without previous notice

1) Dr. Smith is the **on call** surgeon today.
2) The position is an **on call** position, but I accepted it anyway.
3) The man urgently borrowed a large sum of money **on call** from a local bank. Now, the lender wants it back, however, he isn't ready to pay it back.

510. Once and for all (*adv., n.*) – one time only with certainty, conclusively, certainly

1) Let me say, **once and for all**, the answer is "no."
2) Let's get the job finished and be done with it **once and for all.**

511. Once in a while (*adv.*) – now and then, occasionally

1) We go out to dinner with them **once in a while.**
2) I go out, **once in a while**, for coffee with my coworkers.
3) Don't be a stranger. Drop by and see us **once in a while.**

512. On condition that (*conj.*) – if, provided that

1) I'll accept your apology **on condition that** you are sincere.
2) I borrowed some money from the bank **on condition that** I would pay it back within two years at 10% interest.
3) I will gladly cook dinner **on condition that** you wash the dishes.

513. Once edge (*adj.*) – tense, nervous, irritable

1) The unpleasant incident put everyone in the office **on edge.**

2) His unpleasant tone of voice was a dead giveaway that he was still a little **on edge.**

514. On end (*adj.*) – in an upright position, without interruption, continuously

1) He was so angered by her remarks that his hair stood **on end.**
2) She had worked on her homework assignment for hours **on end,** but it remained incomplete.
3) I've been trying to write this article for hours **on end,** but constant interruptions keep me from finishing it.
4) It has been raining for hours **on end.**

515. One of these days (*adv.*) – sometime soon

1) He promised his wife that he would clean out the garage **one of these days.**
2) Let's meet for coffee or a few drinks **one of these days.**

516. On faith (*adv.*) – with trust, confidently

1) You'll have to take his word **on faith** if you want to save your relationship with him.
2) She sold him the car **on** good **faith,** but he never paid her.

517. On guard (*adj.*) – alert, watchful, cautious

1) Be **on guard** when you go to a big city because there are many pickpockets.

** Off guard (*adj.*) – not alert, incautious

1) After a few glasses of wine, he was **off guard** and told her the secret.
2) The runner stole home because the pitcher was caught **off guard.**

518. On hand (*adv.*) – available for use, nearby

1) The secretary keeps extra medical supplies **on hand** in case of emergencies.
2) When I study, I always have a dictionary **on hand.**

519. On one's hands (*adj., adv.*) – in one's care or possession, usually as a responsibility

1) With so much work **on her hands**, she had to postpone her vacation until late July.
2) Those matters are **on his hands** now.

** Off one's hands – out of one's care or possession or responsibility

1) Her son is over 21 and **off her hands.** She's not responsible for his debts. So, he should find a job to pay off his debts.
2) I'm glad the job is finished and finally **off my hands.**

520. On one's honor (*adj.*) – with one's honesty, trusted

1) The students took the exam **on their honor** and no one cheated.

521. On one's mind (*adv.*) – in one's thoughts

1) She was far from home, but her family was still **on her mind.**
2) I argued with my friend more than a month ago, but it is still **on my mind.**
3) What's on your mind? Something must be **on your mind.**

522. On one's own (*adj.*) – a state of independence, or something done independently

1) After the death of his parents, he was **on his own.**

2) I don't have the time to help you with your homework, you're **on your own.**
3) The thought of being **on her own** made her feel uneasy.

523. On the part of / On one's part (*adj.*) – with regard to the one specified

1) The accident was blamed on carelessness **on the part of** the driver.
2) He stole the money, but **on her part**, she didn't report him.

524. On one's shoulders (*adj., adv.*) – as one's responsibility

1) Taking care of her family weighed heavily **on her shoulders.**
2) Much of the success of the company rests **on his shoulders.**

525. On one's toes (*adj.*) – ready to act, alert

1) A good attorney is always **on his toes** and rarely makes mistakes.
2) Our police officers must be **on their toes** when they are on duty.

526. On paper (*adj., adv.*) – in writing or print

1) We managed to get an agreement **on paper.** The contract has been signed.
2) Many prospective employees look good **on paper**, but they often don't measure up to expectations.

527. On purpose (*adv.*) – for a reason, intentionally

1) The police think that fire may have been started **on purpose.**
2) The flagrant foul was no accident, it was done **on purpose.**

528. On record (*adj.*) – publicly known, written down in a record

1) Student misbehavior is noted **on** school **records.**

2) The politician stated his position, **on record**, for the upcoming elections.
3) Many old reports have been lost and are no longer **on record**.

529. On sale *(adj.)* – selling for a special discounted price for a certain period

1) Many items were offered **on sale** for the University's Spring Fundraiser.
2) A designer's dress that usually sells for $1,200.00 went **on sale** for $500.00.

530. On schedule *(adv.)* – as planned or expected

1) Flight KE 460 has landed **on schedule**.
2) The boat for Jeju Island didn't leave **on schedule** because of bad weather.

531. On the air *(adj., adv.)* – being broadcast

1) The golf tournament will be **on the air** this afternoon.
2) The documentary will be **on the air** next Saturday on channel 9.

532. On the contrary *(adv.)* – oppositely, rather

1) He thought he would win the game; **on the contrary**, he lost.
2) People thought she didn't like animals; **on the contrary**, she is an animal's rights advocate.

533. On the face of it *(adv.)* – apparently, as it seems

1) **On the face of it**, his story made sense, but it fell apart under close examination.
2) Her behavior, **on the face of it**, was unexpected under the circumstances.

534. On the go (*adj.*) – active and busy

1) She's the most energetic person I know. She's always **on the go.**
2) His new position includes a lot of travelling and keeps him **on the go.**

535. On the house (*adj.*) – free, as a gift from the management

1) They gave us beverages **on the house** because we waited an hour for our meal.
2) Many restaurants offer soft drinks **on the house** to draw customers.

536. On the line (*adj.*) – immediately available, ready, at stake

1) There is a caller **on the line** for you now.
2) She felt her reputation was **on the line** and it motivated her to do her best work.

** Lay it on the line / Put it on the line (*v.*) – to state clearly, to speak openly without concealing anything, to put or spend

1) I hope you don't mind me **laying it on the line.** Your work is unsatisfactory.
2) I know you have a lot on your mind. Why don't you **lay it on the line?**
3) The company **laid** $1,000,000.00 **on the line** for its employee's health plan.

** On line / Online (*adj.*) – having a connection to a network of computers, immediately available, working properly

1) All banks have **online** systems these days.
2) My computer was down earlier, but it's **online** now.

**** Off-line** *(adj.)* **– not having a connection to a network of computers, not working properly**

1) The internet has been **off-line** all day.
2) At the bank, I couldn't withdraw my money because its computer system was **off-line.**

537. On the lookout for *(adj.)* **– to expect, to watch for something or someone**

1) The agency is always **on the lookout for** new talent.
2) She has a reputation as someone who's always **on the lookout for** a bargain.
3) Police are **on the lookout for** the arsonist who started the recent fires.

538. On the run *(adj., adv.)* **– in a hurry**

1) I'd like to help you, but I'm **on the run**, I've got a meeting.
2) We'd like to invite her to dinner, but she's always **on the run.**

539. On the point of *(prep.)* **– Just about doing something**

1) He was **on the point of** quitting when they finally offered him a promotion.
2) His speech was so poignant that she was **on the point of** crying.

540. On the spot *(adj., adv.)* **– without delay, at once, at the scene of action, in a difficult situation**

1) Her insubordination justified his firing her **on the spot.**
2) Three witnesses and conclusive evidence put the robber **on the spot.**
3) He's **on the spot** because he doesn't have his rent money.

541. On the spur of the moment (*adv.*) – on a sudden impulse

1) She packed and left for a week in Hawaii **on the spur of the moment.**
2) He made the promise **on the spur of the moment** and lived to regret it.

542. On the strength of (*prep.*) – on the basis of

1) The contract was signed **on the strength of** the company's reputation.
2) He opened an art gallery **on the strength of** his experience as an artist.

543. On the way / on one's way (*adj., adv.*) – in the process of coming, going, or travelling, on the route of one's journey

1) I'm **on my way** home and should arrive in about twenty minutes.
2) The buds on the trees are a good sign that spring is **on its way.**
3) I was **on my way** to Cleveland, but ended up in Washington D.C. instead.

544. On time (*adj., adv.*) – according to the scheduled time, at the time arranged

1) As usual, the six o'clock train didn't arrive **on time.**
2) Her date for the evening came **on time,** but she wasn't quite ready.
3) The students complained that the class never started **on time.**

545. On top of (*prep.*) – knowing all about, besides, in addition to, on top of, in control of

1) Modern multimedia allows us to stay **on top of** world news and events.
2) She's been diagnosed with cancer and **on top of** that she lost her job.
3) An apple falling from the tree hit him **on top of** his head.
4) He's putting in extra hours to stay **on top of** his work.

** **On top of the world** (cliché) **– feeling successful, very pleased**

1) When she received an A+ in English, she felt she was **on top of the world.**

546. Open doors (*v.*) – to give an opportunity to start or to join, to begin to open

1) The scholarship fund has **opened doors** for many needy youngsters.
2) The Bistro Restaurant **opened** its **doors** 20 years ago today.

547. Open one's eyes (*v.*) – to see the truth, to realize what is really happening

1) Growing up in the country **opened my eyes** to the beauty of nature.
2) **Open your eyes** and see the truth.

548. Open one's heart (*v.*) – to give love or sympathy, to confide in

1) A little cat opened my heart.
2) The Red Cross is asking citizens to **open their hearts** and do-nate blood.
3) Seeing the orphans **opened her heart** and prompted her to dedicate the rest of her life to improving their lot in life.
4) She pleaded with him to **open his heart** before it was too late.

549. Out of breath (*adj., adv.*) – breathing hard, panting

1) The runners were **out of breath** after running the six-kilometer race.
2) Smokers run **out of breath** more quickly because smoking affects lung capacity.

550. Out of one's character (*adj., adv.*) – not consistent with someone's general character or behavior

1) He studied diligently and cheating seemed **out of character**, nevertheless,

he was caught cheating on the final exam.

** **in character – consistent with someone's general character or behavior**

1) Volunteering her time and energy to assist those in need is one of the fine points in her **character.**

551. Out of hand *(adv.)* – out of control

1) His parents said his behavior is getting **out of hand** and grounding him for two weeks is the punishment they've decided on.
2) Several neighbors called the police to report a fraternity party that was getting **out of hand.**

552. Out of line *(adj.)* – improper, not in a straight line

1) His remarks were **out of line** and the chairperson censured them.
2) Your recent behavior has been **out of line** with school policies. We have no alternative, but to expel you for the remainder of the semester.
3) The kindergarten teacher gave repeated warnings, but the children continued to stray **out of line.**

553. Out of luck *(adj.)* – having bad luck, unlucky

1) I tried to get to the bank before it closed, but I was **out of luck.**
2) The team made it to the semi-finals, but ran **out of luck** in the finals.

554. Out of nowhere *(adv.)* – suddenly and unexpectedly

1) I didn't see any highway patrol. So I drove over the speed limit. Then a highway patrol appeared **out of nowhere** and chased me. So I ended up in a court and was fined $120.

555. Out of order (*adj., adv.*) – not according to rule, not acceptable procedure, not working properly

1) The student's behavior was **out of order**, so he was reprimanded.
2) Young children often say the alphabet **out of order.**
3) I called the company to let them know the coffee machine is **out of order.**

556. Out of print (*adj.*) – no longer offered for sale by a publisher, no longer printed

1) He wrote prolifically and was well read in his time, but today his works are **out of print.**

** in print – in a printed or a published form, offered to be published

1) The author's fans are happy to hear their long awaited sequel is now **in print.**
2) The new edition of the astronomy textbook will soon be **in print.**

557. Out of season (*adv.*) – not at the right or proper time, not available in a particular season

1) Tomatoes are **out of season**, so all we have are hothouse tomatoes.
2) Her attire is **out of season.** It's odd that she continues to wear sweaters in the middle of the summer.

558. Out of the question (*adj.*) – not even thinkable, not to be considered

1) Your request for an additional loan is **out of the question.**
2) For her, failure at anything was **out of the question.** She feels she must succeed in everything.

** **in question – Under discussion, concerned**

1) I made a list of the people **in question**, but I'm not sure whether I added all of those deserving a promotion.

559. Out of the running (*adv.*) – having no chance to win, not among those to be considered

1) She thought she was **out of the running**, but nevertheless she got the position.
2) The horses I bet on are usually **out of the running** at the starting gate.

560. Over one's head (*adj., adv.*) – beyond one's ability to understand or deal with

1) A complete understanding of computers is **over my head.**
2) It's a complex paper and I admit parts of it are **over my head.**
3) I'm sorry but I can't answer that question. The decision came from someone within the company who's **over my head.**

561. **Pack off** (*v.*) – to send away

1) When the parents had finally **packed** the children **off** to summer camp, they breathed a sigh of relief.
2) The boy wanted to stay home for the summer holiday, but his parents **packed** him **off** to Europe.

562. **Pain in the neck** (*n*) – unpleasant, offensive, bothersome or obnoxious person or thing

1) One of my colleagues is a **pain in the neck.**
2) Many students think writing is a **pain in the neck.**

563. **Pair off / Pair up** (*v.*) – to become grouped or separated into pairs, to make a pair of, to become associated with

1) The couples **paired off** for the next dance.
2) The host **paired off** his guests by age and interests.
3) I was **paired off** with him in a tennis doubles match.
4) Lee **paired up** with Kim to work on the project.

564. **Pawn off** (*v.*) – to get rid of by deception

1) The jeweler **pawned off** the ring for far more than it was worth.
2) Her colleagues usually **pawned off** the lion's share of the work on her.

565. Partake (in, of) (*v.*) **– to participate, to take a portion, to share some of the properties**

1) Many people **partake in** the company's annual spring get-together.
2) The guests eagerly **partook in** the celebration.
3) The partygoers **partook in** the cornucopia of food and drink.

566. Part and parcel (*n.*) **– an inseparable part**

1) Working overtime seems to be **part and parcel** of the contract.
2) Injuries are **part and parcel** of being an athlete.

567. Part with (*v.*) **– to give up, to separate from**

1) She was sad to **part with** the friends she had made, but eager to move and begin her new job.
2) **Parting with** her family seems to be a painful experience for her.

568. Pass away (*v.*) **– to die, to slip by or pass, to recede or cease**

1) My grandfather **passed away** at the ripe old age of 98.
2) Time **passes away** much more quickly than we realize.
3) It takes a few hours for the effect of the medication to **pass away**.

569. Pass on (*v.*) **– to give by or as if by inheritance**

1) Genetic traits are **passed on** from one generation to the next.
2) University students often **pass** their textbooks **on** to other students.

570. Pass out (*v.*) **– to distribute, to faint**

1) She was hired to **pass out** the companies' advertising flyers.
2) Please take your exam and **pass** the others **out** to the rest of the class.

3) She **passed out** when she heard the news of her sister's accident.

571. Pass over (*v.*) – to omit or overlook

1) Let's **pass over** this matter for the time being and get to the issue at hand.
2) It seems you **passed over** what I see as the most important point of the film in your review.

572. Pass up (*v.*) – to turn down, to refuse

1) "Would you like some chocolate?" "No, thank you. I'll **pass** it **up** because I'm on a diet."
2) Her job offer was attractive, but she **passed** it **up** and found a better one.

573. Patch up (*v.*) – to settle or smooth over, to mend a hole or repair

1) They have **patched** things **up** to improve their relationship.
2) We should **patch up** the roof before the monsoon season begins.

574. Pave the way (*v.*) – to make the development or progress easier

1) It's not true that a good education **paves the way** to financial success.
2) Her family lineage helped **pave her way** into an Ivy League College.

575. Pay back (*v.*) – to retaliate upon, to get even with

1) He promised them he'd find a way to **pay back** their insults.
2) The entire team was eager to **pay** them **back** for last year's humiliating defeat in the championship game.

576. Pay for (*v.*) – to suffer the consequences of

1) Youth is a time when we make our mistakes and forget about them. Adulthood is the time when we **pay for** our mistakes.
2) If you don't quit smoking now, you'll have to **pay for** it later.

577. Pay up (*v.*) – to pay in full, to pay what is owed

1) We expected to be **paid up** when the work was completed, but not three weeks later!
2) It's wise to make sure your credit cards are **paid up** in full before leaving on an extended holiday.

** Pay off (*v.*) – to pay in full, to pay the wages of and discharge, to make a profit, rewarding

1) The mortgage on my house has been **paid off**, so I don't owe the bank anything.
2) She was finally able to **pay off** her long overdue telephone bill.
3) His investment in a textile mill never **paid off** big, but he was able to make a comfortable living.
4) Improving my English ability was difficult, but it **paid off** when I got a good job that required a high level of English proficiency.

578. Penny wise and (but) pound foolish (*proverb*) – wise or careful in small things, but foolish in important matters

1) He didn't take the time to repair the small rust-spot. Now there's a big hole. He was **penny wise, but pound foolish.**
2) She thought she was getting a bargain buying a used washing machine, but it broke down after a few weeks. She's penny wise and pound foolish.

579. Pep up (*v.*) – to bring energy or liveliness to

1) The coach's half-time speech pepped up the discouraged football team.
2) A good teacher usually peps up whatever class they enter.

** Pep talk – encouraging words

1) After the coach gave a **pep talk**, the team returned to the field and played their best game of the season.
2) Whenever I feel down, my friend helps me out by giving me a **pep talk** that usually makes me feel better.

580. Perk up (*v.*) – to regain or cause to regain one's good spirits or liveliness

1) The listless students **perked up** when their professor announced the class was cancelled.
2) A cup of hot coffee **perks** me **up**.
3) My cat always **perks up** when I give him some catnip.

581. Pick and choose (*v.*) – to choose or select with much care, in a fussy way, or in one's own way

1) His father told him it was time to **pick and choose** a career.
2) Early shoppers **pick and choose** the best of the sale items. Late shoppers get to sift through the remainder.
3) We're in a hurry. You don't have time to **pick and choose**. Just take one and come along.

582. Pick at (*v.*) – to eat in small bites without much appetite, to criticize someone repeatedly in small ways

1) He is a picky eater and he **picks at** any food.

2) She's quitting because her supervisor **picks at** every small mistake she makes.

** Pick on – to tease, to annoy continually

1) The student told his teacher that the other students were **picking on** him.
2) He gets **picked on** by many of his classmates because he's a slow learner.

583. Pick out (*v.*) – to choose, to select

1) She was pleased that her boyfriend **picked out** a beautiful dress for her birthday.
2) He **picked out** the dress and bought it at Say Department Store.

584. Pick up (*v.*) – to lift up, to take on, to get on the way, to receive, to learn quickly without much effort, to improve

1) He **picked up** the heavy box.
2) The school bus stopped to **pick up** the students.
3) I am **picking up** my suit from the dry cleaner on the way home.
4) The control tower **picked up** a distress signal from flight 713.
5) It is easier for children to **pick up** a foreign language.
6) He's behind, but he's sure he can **pick up** his course work quickly.

585. Pin down (*v.*) – to explain or establish precisely, to determine the cause, significance or meaning of, to cause to make a response or commitment

1) Using modern techniques, the archeologist **pinned down** the age of a fossil.
2) She doesn't like her job, but she can't **pin down** the reason.

3) I want a raise, but it's too early to **pin** my boss **down** to discuss the matter.

** On pins and needles (*n.*) – in a state of anxiety or suspense

1) She's been **on pins and needles** since she applied for the job.
2) The students were **on pins and needles** while they awaited the exam results.

586. Pitter-patter (*n., adj., adv.*) – the sound of a rapid beats or light taps, with a series of quick heart beats.

1) My heart goes **pitter-patter** when spring comes around.
2) Her heart went **pitter-patter** when he asked her to marry him.

587. Play down (*v.*) – to minimize the importance of

1) The salesman **played down** the weak points of the car and emphasized the good points.
2) He is a wise man and always **plays down** his ability and knowledge.

** Play up (*v.*) – to emphasize or publicize with some exaggeration

1) The newspaper review **played up** the writer's artistic talents.
2) He likes to **play up** the fact that he is popular with the girls.

** Play up to (*v.*) – to try to win the favor of someone by flattery

1) She has been **playing up to** her boss to get a raise.
2) He **plays up to** women's vanities and then takes advantage of them.

588. Play havoc with / Raise havoc with *(v.)*
– to make or cause a great disturbance, to damage badly

1) The torrential rains **played havoc with** the area's electricity.
2) The researcher's unethical treatment of animals **raised havoc** among those in the animal rights community.

589. Play hooky *(v.)* **– to be absent from school without permission**

1) The principal warned the three students to stop playing hooky.
2) If they don't stop playing hooky, they won't graduate.

590. Play on / upon *(v.)* **– to take advantage of (someone's feelings or hopes) for one's own purpose, to have an affect on, to influence**

1) Some people like to **play on** the fears of others.
2) The speech **played upon** the young man's political ambition.

591. Play politics *(v.)* **– to handle people cleverly or cunningly for one's own advantage**

1) She **plays politics** to get what she wants.
2) Presidential candidates play politics in key districts for many years prior to the general elections.

592. Play it safe *(v.)* **– to avoid loss or danger for the sake of safety**

1) He'd rather **play it safe** in the stock market than take unnecessary risks and lose everything.
2) I like to **play it safe**, so I never put all my eggs in one basket.

593. **Plow back** (*v.*) – to reinvest earnings in one's business

1) He promised the employees he would **plow back** 50% of the company's profits and offer them stock options.

594. **Plow into** (*v.*) – to run into with great force, to undertake with great energy or enthusiasm

1) A motorcycle **plowed into** a bush.
2) He **plowed into** his work and finished it by midnight.

** **Plug away** (*v.*) – to persist, to work hard steadily

1) The boy **plugged away** at the difficult math problem until he was rewarded with the right answer and a feeling of accomplishment.
2) The construction workers kept **plugging away** and completed the building earlier than anyone expected they would.

595. **Plug in / into** (*v.*) – to connect into the socket of an electrical device

1) If you want the iron to heat up, you must **plug** it **in**.
2) I **plugged** the cord **into** the socket, but it didn't work.

596. **Plunge into** (*v.*) – to thrust or throw oneself or place forcefully into something, to cause to enter suddenly, to enter violently into a situation

1) She **plunged into** her work as if it were the last opportunity she'd have to complete the book.
2) As the diver **plunged into** the water completing a perfect dive, the crowd applauded.
3) The man who lost his job committed suicide by jumping from the bridge and **plunging into** the icy water.

4) The assassination of the king **plunged** the two countries **into** a state of war.

597. Point out (*v.*) – to bring to notice, to make known as by showing

1) Very few people appreciate having their faults **pointed out.**
2) The tour guide **pointed out** the historical sites and other points of interest.

598. Poles apart (*adj.*) – completely different

1) Some newly married couples discover that they are **poles apart** in many ways.
2) Their personalities and their outlooks on life were **poles apart.**

599. Polish off (*v.*) – to finish or dispose quickly and easily

1) The boy **polished off** his dinner so he could go out and play with his friends.
2) I **polished off** my homework and then went to a movie.

600. Possessed of (*adj.*) – having or owning

1) He was a witty man and was **possessed of** a great mind.
2) My younger brother is **possessed of** great potential.
3) We moved in and took **possession of** the house as of 31 May, 2003.

601. Pot calling the kettle black (cliché) – used when a person accusing someone else of a fault, shares the same fault

1) Their argument began when the mayor accused the police chief of incompetence and the police chief replied that it was a case of the **pot calling the kettle black.**

602. Press one's luck / Push one's luck (v.) – to push something in spite of odds against it

1) Prudent people don't **press their luck** too far.
2) The teacher told the unruly students not to **push their luck.**

603. Prevail on / upon (v.) – to persuade successfully

1) He **prevailed upon** me to believe he was powerful and wealthy as well as sincere.
2) The lawyer's arguments **prevailed upon** the jury and they found his client innocent.

604. Prey on / upon (v.) – to feed by seizing as prey, to take unfair advantage of as by swindling, to bring a harmful effect

1) Owls **prey on** mice.
2) The young and the defenseless members of our society are the most likely to be **preyed upon.**

605. Pride (oneself) on (v.) – to be proud of

1) We often **pride ourselves on** our achievements.
2) You should **pride yourself on** your talent.

** Take pride in – to be proud of

1) I **take pride in** my ability to write.
2) Parents often **take pride in** their children's talents.

606. Promise the moon (v.) – to promise something impossible

1) He **promised** her **the moon** and the stars, but she was sorely disappointed.

2) I can't **promise** you **the moon**, but I will support you completely.

607. Pull in / pull into (v.) – to arrive

1) The train **pulled into** the station five minutes behind schedule.
2) He is **pulling** the car **in** the driveway as we speak.

608. Pull off (v.) – to do or accomplish something in spite of difficulties

1) The cellist was pleasantly surprised when he managed to **pull off** the contract with the Seoul Symphony Orchestra.
2) Three robbers **pulled off** a daring daylight robbery of the local bank.

609. Pull (oneself) together (v.) – to regain one's composure or self-control

1) Try to **pull yourself together**.
2) He lost his job and then the bank foreclosed on his home, but things are getting better and he is slowly but surely **pulling himself together**.

** Pull through (v.) – to recover from illness or misfortune, to regain one's self-control

1) A loan from a family friend **pulled** us **through** our financial difficulties.
2) The operation was a complete success and the patient will surely **pull through**.
3) The company has to **pull through** these difficult times and look forward.

** Pull together (v.) – to cooperate

1) We must **pull together** to succeed in this project.
2) We all need to **pull together** to do this job.

610. Pull over (v.) – to stop a vehicle on the side of a road

1) A highway patrolman **pulled** her **over** for speeding.
2) The driver **pulled over** and opened the hood of his car.

** Pull up (v.) – to come to a stop

1) John **pulled up** in front of the building in a new sports car.
2) The driver slowed down and **pulled up** to the curb.
3) I was sitting in the parking lot when he **pulled up** alongside me.

611. Puppy love (n.) – new love, especially between young people

1) **Puppy love** is nice, but it usually fades as quickly as it begins.

612. Pure and simple (adj.) – simply stated

1) Paying your bills, **pure and simple**, is your problem.
2) My life's goal, **pure and simple**, is to be an environmental protectionist.

613. Push around (v.) – to give harassment or unfair treatment, to be bossy with

1) No one understands why he lets his wife **push** him **around**.
2) His mother told him to stop **pushing** his younger brother **around**.
3) Stop **pushing** me **around**.

614. Put all one's eggs in one basket (v.) – to put all one's efforts, hopes, or money into one thing

1) I won't invest all my money in one company, because that would be like **putting all my eggs in one basket**.
2) **Putting all your eggs in one basket** is risky and limits your chances to make a profit.

615. Put an end to (v.) – to stop, to end

1) She advocates **putting an end to** corporal punishment in the school system.
2) The police have steeped up their vigilance in order to **put an end to** gang related violence.

616. Put away (v.) – to put in a proper place, to place in confinement

1) **Put away** your books and school supplies after you've finished using them.
2) His lawyer told him he'd be **put away** for two years.

** Put away / Put aside (v.) – to save, to lay aside

1) Every month, without exception, I **put away** some money for my future.
2) You should **put aside** some money every time you get paid.

617. Put down (v.) – to set aside, to suppress, to make fun of

1) Why don't you **put down** your bag?
2) The National Guard had to be called in to **put down** the student riots.
3) The fight began when one of the boys **put down** the other.

618. Put off (v.) – to repel someone, to postpone or procrastinate

1) Her taciturn disposition **puts** people **off**, but she's really not a bad person.
2) Don't be **put off** by the difficulty of learning English. Continue to study and you will be successful.
3) Her fiance keeps **putting off** their wedding date, but she's sure he'll marry her someday.
4) She kept **putting off** studying until it was too late.

619. Put on (*v.*) – to wear, to set on the stove, to activate, to pretend

1) If you don't **put on** a warm coat, you'll be cold. The temperature is quite low.
2) Please **put** the kettle **on** for tea.
3) He **put on** the brakes, but the car continued to roll down the hill.
4) She always **puts on** an air of superiority.

620. Put out (*v.*) – to extinguish, to turn off, to annoy

1) It took several hours for the firefighters to **put out** the fire.
2) Please **put** the light **out** before you go to bed.
3) I was really **put out** when I had to wait for two hours at the doctor's office.

621. Put two and two together (*v.*) – to reason from the known facts

1) She **put two and two together** and figured out that her son wanted his diaper changed.
2) He finally **put two and two together** and realized he'd never pass the course unless he studied.

622. Put through (*v.*) – to complete successfully, to connect by phone

1) The proposal shouldn't be difficult to **put through**. We can do it if we put our heads together.
2) The family has ample savings to **put** both their children **through** university.
3) Can you **put** this call **through** to the admissions office?

623. Put up (*v.*) – to build, to raise, to accommodate or offer (as for sale)

1) We are planning to **put up** a new garage.

2) The robbers wore ski masks and told us to **put** our hands **up**.
3) You don't need to go to a hotel. We can **put** you **up** in the spare bedroom.
4) When their business went bankrupt, they **put** their home **up** for sale.

** **Put up with** (*v.*) **– to be patient with, to endure, to bear, to tolerate**

1) He refused to **put up with** his son's decadent lifestyle.
2) As long as we continue to **put up with** environmental pollution, our wildlife will continue to die off.
3) He divorced his wife because he could no longer **put up with** her incessant nagging.

624. Put words into one's mouth (*v.*)
– to speak for another person without permission or the right to do so

1) Don't **put words in her mouth**. She can speak for herself.
2) He became annoyed when the salesman kept **putting words in his mouth**.

Q

625. Quite a (*adj.*) – unusual, remarkable

1) **Quite** a large crowd had gathered for the annual flower festival.
2) It is **quite an** exhibition for a newly discovered artist.
3) Her students think she is **quite a** good teacher.

626. Quite a few (*adj., n.*) – a large number, many

1) The storm destroyed many homes and left **quite a few** people isolated.
2) We still have **quite a few** miles to go before we reach Seoul.
3) **Quite a few** people came to the party last night.
4) There are still **quite a few** things left to sell.

627. Quite a bit (a little, a few) (*adj., n.*) – a large amount

1) I still have **quite a bit** of work to complete before I can go home.
2) We had **quite a bit** of snow last night.

628. Rain check (*n.*) – a promise to get an invitation or an item at another time, between people or between a customer and a business

1) I have a cold and can't make your dinner invitation. Can I take a **rain check**?
2) The store manager offered the disappointed customers a **rain check** and promised to contact them when the item was restocked.

629. Rain out (*v.*) – to force the postponement of an outdoor event because of rain

1) The annual company picnic was **rained out**.
2) Yesterday's ball game was **rained out**.

630. Rainy day (*n.*) – a future time of need

1) I've been saving money for a **rainy day**.
2) She puts some money aside for a **rainy day**.
3) Squirrels gather acorns for **rainy days**.

631. Reach out (*v.*) – to make an effort in order to achieve a relationship or understanding

1) You should **reach out** if you want to find people who can be your friends.

632. Reckon with *(v.)* – to take into account, to consider something as one of the things to change a situation

1) Farmers must **reckon with** the weather and plant a variety of crops.

** be reckoned with – not to be ignored, important

1) He doesn't look like an important person, however he is a big businessman who should **be reckoned with.**
2) Teenagers today are a group to **be reckoned with.**

633. Refine *(v.)* – to improve, to make better

1) He needs to **refine** his knowledge of English grammar and vocabulary before attempting to take the advanced placement test.
2) The professor asked her to **refine** her outline before handing it in.

634. Relative to *(prep.)* – about, related to

1) That issue is **relative to** morality.
2) Supply is **relative to** demand.
3) The meaning of "expensive or cheap" is **relative to** a person's income.

635. Rent out *(v.)* – to rent to someone

1) I have three bedrooms and I want to **rent out** one of the rooms.
2) The house they wanted to rent had already been **rented out.**

636. Ride on *(v.)* – to depend on

1) The outcome of the election **rides on** her popularity with the voters.

637. Ride for a fall (*v.*) – doing something risky

1) The businessman built a very luxurious home and is spending faster than he earns. He is **riding for a fall.**
2) He has borrowed too much money from the bank for his home. He is **riding for a fall.**

638. Ride out (*v.*) – to survive successfully, to endure

1) The small sailboat had **ridden out** the storm and returned to the marina without serious damage.
2) Astute politicians know how capricious the public is and are willing to **ride out** most scandals.

639. Get rid of (*v.*) – to remove something

1) I want to **get rid of** this old chair and get a new one.
2) We finally redecorated our home and **got rid of** the ugly living room furniture.

** to be rid of (*v.*) – to be free of

1) She thought she **was rid of** her math professor but she was shocked to see his name again on her summer schedule.

640. Right along (*adv.*) – without trouble or delay

1) In spite of turbulence, the plane flew **right along** and landed on schedule.

** Right away (*adv.*) – immediately, without delay

1) If we want to reach the summit before nightfall, we'd better start **right away.**

2) We'll be there in about half-hour, if we leave **right away.**
3) The people who have been affected by the flood need help **right away.**

641. Ring up (*v.*) – to record a sale on a cash register

1) I'll **ring up** your purchase as soon as I finish with this customer.
2) The clerk **rang up** the merchandise and said I owed 25,950 won.

642. Rip into (*v.*) – to attack or scold violently

1) A tiger **ripped into** a zookeeper as the horrified crowd looked on.
2) Her boss **ripped into** her for being late three times in one week.

** Rip off (*v.*) – to steal or take something without giving a fair price

1) He had been **ripping off** the store for months until he was finally caught red-handed.
2) Some tourists visiting Korea have complained about being **ripped off** by unscrupulous salespeople.

** Rip-off (*n.*) – an act of stealing

1) The prices are so high, it's almost a **rip-off.**

643. Rip up (*v.*) – to tear into pieces

1) His letter made her so angry that she **ripped** it **up.**
2) The homework was so poorly done that the teacher **ripped** it **up** and threw it into the wastebasket.

644. Rise up (*v.*) – to rebel against

1) When freedom is denied, the people will eventually **rise up.**

2) The workers were exhorted to **rise up** and defend their right to have a union.

** Give rise to (*v.*) – to be a cause of, to lead to

1) The development of the computer chip **gave rise to** the information age.
2) Shipbuilding **gave rise to** many other industries.

645. Rob the cradle (*v.*) – to marry or have a sexual relationship with a person who is much younger

1) Nowadays, some men really **rob the cradle** by engaging in sexual relationship with teenagers.
2) He really **robbed the cradle** when he chose her for his wife.

646. Roll in (*v.*) – to arrive in large numbers

1) Tickets went on sale and according to the latest tallies the money is **rolling in.**
2) They did all they could and then sat back and watched the election results **roll in.**

647. Roll back (*v.*) – to reduce prices to a previous level

1) The administration hopes to **roll back** prices while maintaining present wages.
2) In an attempt to bring in new business, the travel company **rolled back** its prices to compete with those offered in the 1980's.

648. Roll up (*v.*) – to roll something up or to amass

1) After the party, we had to **roll up** the rug and take it to the dry cleaner.

2) The company asked its workers to **roll up** their sleeves and get the job done.
3) He **rolled up** a huge fortune by collecting and selling stamps.

649. Rough up (*v.*) – to harm physically, to beat up, to damage

1) On his way home from school, Lee was grabbed and **roughed up** by a couple of bullies from the local high school.
2) The boxer **roughed up** his opponent in the first three rounds and won on a T.K.O in the forth round.

** A diamond in the rough – in a natural or unrefined state

1) She is like **a diamond in the rough.** She has great potential.
2) The early computers can now be seen as **diamonds in the rough.**

650. Round off / round out (*v.*) – to bring to the nearest whole number, to finish nicely, to make round

1) The average score on the examination was 87.69. **Rounded off,** the average score was 88.
2) We **rounded off** dinner with delicious strawberry shortcake.
3) I'd like to have someone **round off** the sharp edges of the dining room table.

** Round up (*v.*) – to herd together, to seek out and bring together, to raise a number to the next highest one

1) It's getting dark. We need to **round up** our gear and get the tent pitched before nightfall.
2) Let's **round** everyone **up** and get ready to go home.
3) 87.69 **rounded up** is 88.

651. Rub down (*v.*) – to massage

1) Some people go to a masseuse or a masseur for a **rub down.**
2) The therapist **rubbed down** my back to relax the muscle.

652. Rule on (*v.*) – to make a decision in law, to sentence

1) The jury asked the judge to **rule on** some of the issues in dispute. So the judge arrived at a verdict of "not guilty" for the defendant.
2) The Supreme Court recently passed its **ruling on** a huge tobacco case.

** Rule out (*v.*) – to exclude, to remove from consideration

1) A jury must **rule out** the unproven evidence before reaching a verdict. Therefore, the jury arrived at a verdict of "not guilty" for the defendant.
2) The suggestions of the employees should not be **ruled out** when decisions are being made.

653. Run across / Run into (*v.*) – to meet or find by chance

1) I **ran across** Mary at the shopping mall and was surprised because I didn't know she was back in town.
2) Kim and I **run into** each other all the time because we work in the same building.

654. Run after (*v.*) – to chase after

1) He's a hound who likes to **run after** women.
2) The boy **ran after** the ball as fast as he could.

655. Run a risk / Take a risk (*v.*) – to put oneself in danger

1) I don't want to **take a risk**, so I always wear a life jacket when I'm on a boat because I can't swim.

2) Don't **take the risk** of damaging your eyes, wear safety goggles.
3) I try not to put all my eggs in one basket because I don't want to **take a risk.**

646. Run around (*v.*) – to go here and there for pleasure and company

1) I have a lot to do and don't have time to **run around** doing errands for her.
2) Right now he likes to **run around** with his friends, but he'll settle down after he's married.

657. Run a temperature (*v.*) – to have a fever

1) Call the doctor immediately. The baby is **running a high temperature.**

658. Run away from (*v.*) – to flee or escape from

1) After **running away from** home three times, the boy was placed in a home for runaways.
2) The girls screamed and **ran away from** the boys who were chasing them with water balloons.

** Run away with (*v.*) – to steal or take and run away, to elope, to win easily

1) She took money and documents from the safe and **ran away with** them.
2) They **ran away** and got married before anyone could stop them.
3) The dark horse nominee **ran away with** a top award.

659. Run down (*v.*) – to slow down and stop, to criticize, to get into poor condition, to chase until exhausted, to knock down or hit

1) The battery in the alarm clock **ran down.**

2) He left his parking lights on and the battery in his car **ran down.**
3) It is better to praise people rather than **run** them **down** if you want them to do a good job.
4) The small farmhouse is completely **run down.**
5) A dog **ran down** a rabbit.
6) The motorcyclist almost **ran down** a pedestrian.

** Run-down (*adj.*) – old and decayed, needing to be repaired

1) The city must find the funds to renovate its **run-down** tenements.
2) Running a marathon made John feel **run-down** and tired.
3) The old **run-down** house on our street is finally being renovated.
4) This is one of the **run-down** areas in Seoul, so the government is planning to build a new town in this area.

660. Run for (*v.*) – to campaign for public office

1) The senator announced he would **run for** reelection.
2) She is **running for** the state legislature.

661. Run off (*v.*) – to make copies on a machine, to leave hurriedly, to make someone leave, to drain

1) We **ran off** three thousand copies of the flyer and distributed them.
2) The boys who were fighting **ran off** as soon as they saw a policeman.
3) The reservoir depends on the water that **runs off** the mountain.

662. Run out (of) (*v.*) – to deplete the supply, to come to an end, to become used up

1) Please pick up some more toilet paper, we've **run out of** it.
2) He usually **runs out of** money before payday.
3) We'd better stop at the next gas station. We've **running out of** gas.
4) We **ran out of** gas on the free way and had to contact road service.

** **Run through** (*v.*) – to use or spend rapidly

1) The widow **ran through** her inheritance within a few years.
2) The students **ran through** their assignment in record time. It was definitely too easy.

663. Run over (*v.*) – to ride over, to review quickly, to flow over

1) **Running over** a squirrel was a terrible experience.
2) The drunk driver **ran over** a pedestrian and sped off.
3) Students were standing in the hallway **running over** their notes before taking the final exam.
4) She forgot to turn off the water and it **ran over** the sink and onto the floor.

664. Run short (*v.*) – to not have enough, to be not enough in quantity

1) She was **running short** and asked me to lend her some money until payday.
2) We were having a great time until we realized we were **running short** of money.

665. Run out on (*v.*) – to desert

1) She **ran out on** her child.
2) He **ran out on** his family.

666. Run up (*v.*) – to increase rapidly, to raise or hoist

1) She **ran up** her credit card and left the bills for her poor husband to pay.
2) They **ran up** the telephone bill and the service was finally cut off.
3) OPEC is **running up** the price of crude oil.
4) On national holidays, it is seen as patriotic to **run up** the flag.

667. Safe and sound *(adv.)* – safe and not damaged, not hurt

1) The fragile package was delivered **safe and sound**.
2) Her parents were worried until she arrived home **safe and sound**.
3) David returned home from his trip abroad **safe and sound**.

668. Save face *(v.)* – to save reputation or dignity

1) I like to give a person the chance to **save face**.
2) Giving someone the opportunity to **save face** is often a good way to earn their respect.

669. Save one's breath *(v.)* – not talk because it will do no good

1) He's stubborn and won't change his mind, so **save your breath**.

670. Save up *(v.)* – to save, to accumulate for future use

1) They are **saving up** to buy a home, so they hardly ever go out on holiday.
2) She **saves up** all the rubber bands and paperclips she finds around the office.

671. Savings account *(n.)* – an account for savings in a bank

1) He recently opened a **savings account** with a local Bank.

**** Checking account** *(n.)* **– an account for checking**

1) I'd like to close my savings account and put the funds into my **checking account.**

672. Scare away / Scare off *(v.)* – to frighten away

1) The barking dog **scared away** the deliveryman.
2) In the beginning of their relationship, he liked her, but has been gradually **scared off** by her overbearing behavior.

673. Scratch one's back *(v.)* – to do something good for someone in the hope that the other party will do the same

1) If you help me with my homework, I'll pay for the movie: You **scratch my back** and I'll scratch yours.

**** From scratch** *(adv.)* **– with left over fresh cooking ingredients, from almost nothing**

1) She likes to cook **from scratch.**
2) He started his business **from scratch.**

674. Screen out *(v.)* – to eliminate by a process of purification, etc., to eliminate by a test, interview, etc.

1) The Department of Natural Resources **screens out** impurities in the water, so the water is safe to drink.
2) The company is **screening out** applicants through short lists and interviews.

675. Search one's heart / Search one's soul *(v.)* **– to try to discover the truth or reason for one's behavior or desire, etc.**

1) He **searched his soul** trying to find a way to accommodate both his parents's wishes and his own desires.
2) I've been **searching my soul** trying to find what I really want in my life.

676. Second thought *(n.)* **– a change in one's way of thinking after further thought**

1) She wanted to take summer classes, but on the **second thought**, she decided to take the summer off and relax.
2) I decided to go to Hawaii, but I am having **second thoughts** and Bali seems more exotic.

677. See about *(v.)* **– to find out about, to pay attention to**

1) She was angry at being passed over for the promotion, but her boss told her to continue to work hard and he would **see** what he could do **about** it.
2) We called in a plumber to **see about** the broken water pipes.
3) The director of human resources promised to **see about** my transfer to the head office within the next few days.

678. See daylight *(v.)* **– a result or success is near**

1) We've been working on this project for a few years and finally we are starting to **see daylight.**
2) I've been writing this book since 1998, and I am sure now that I'll **see daylight** by the end of 2003.

679. See off (*v.*) – to escort to or attend a place of departure, to watch someone depart

1) We are coming to the airport to **see** you **off**.
2) He drove her to the train station and waited to **see** her **off**.

680. See through (*v.*) – to understand the true nature of, to stand by or support a person in a time of difficulty, to accomplish, fulfill, or finish

1) His excuse for missing the exam was so bad that a child could **see through** it.
2) Her family and friends **saw** her **through** the difficult times, so she'd like to repay their kindness.
3) The project is much larger than I had anticipated, but I'll **see** it **through**.

681. Sell off (*v.*) – to get rid of by selling, often at a lower price than a usual price

1) I **sold off** all my household appliances before returning to Korea.
2) He's **selling off** his blue chip stocks and reinvesting in real estate.

** Sell out (*v.*) – to completely sell all of something, to betray for a reward

1) The men's suits in the spring sale **sold out** faster than expected.
2) The store is **sold out** of the Christmas items.
3) The union **sold out** its members in the last round of bargaining.

682. Send back (*v.*) – to return

1) She **sent back** the merchandise because it was not what she had ordered.

2) I bought a gold necklace through a home shopping TV channel. But I'll **send** it **back** because it's not what I want.

683. Send for (*v.*) – to order something to be brought or delivered, to request a person to come

1) I **sent for** a pair of Nike tennis shoes from the catalogue.
2) I **sent for** a taxi about ten minutes ago.
3) He **sent for** the doctor because his wife was very ill.

684. Send out (*v.*) – to send, to mail or distribute

1) These packages need to be **sent out** with today's mail.
2) Our university language school **sends out** a lot of advertising brochures.
3) Some customers prefer to pick up their credit card in person, but most are **sent out** by mail.

** Send over (*v.*) – to send a short distance by a special messenger

1) We called the delivery service and asked them to **send** someone **over** as soon as possible to deliver these packages.
2) He couldn't keep our dinner date, so he **sent** some flowers **over** to my home.
3) U.N. troops were **sent over** to the Sarajevo to act as a peacekeeping force.

685. Send up (*v.*) – to send to prison, to cause to rise

1) The defendant was found guilty and **sent up** for five to seven years.
2) The survivors from their wrecked ship reached a small island and **sent up** a flare.

686. Serve up (*v.*) – to prepare and serve

1) The soup and salad are to be **served up** before the main course.
2) The cook **served up** a very delicious meal.

687. Set about (*v.*) – to begin

1) He couldn't **set about** putting the machine together because he couldn't understand the instructions.
2) She **set about** learning computers five years ago and has made remarkable progress.

** Set in (*v.*) – to begin, to develop

1) The storm **set in** before they could reach the summit.
2) A strong wind **set in** before the small fishing boat could reach port.
3) Night **sets in** earlier in winter than it does in summer.
4) The suddenness with which his illness has **set in** shocked his family.

688. Set against (*v.*) – to disapprove or oppose strongly

1) She is **set against** her daughter's marriage because her fiance is a heavy drinker.
2) I am dead **set against** going to that meeting because it's going to be too controversial.

** Set (*adj.*) – decided, determined, ready, prepared

1) I'm **set** on going to a graduate school to study further.

689. Set aside (*v.*) – to put aside for future use, to pay no attention

1) Father **sets aside** some money each month for my college education.
2) The original plan was temporarily **set aside** because the new business venture was too important to be neglected.

690. Set back (*v.*) – to slow down the process of, to hinder, to cost

1) The heavy rains **set back** the scheduled remodeling plans.
2) His lack of real work experience **set** him **back**, but his eagerness and ability helped him overcome all obstacles.
3) Remodeling their house **set** them **back** more than $175,000.

691. Set down (*v.*) – to put in writing, to put something down, to attribute

1) They decided to **set down** all of the points they agreed on and meet again at a later time.
2) He **set** the book **down** on the desk.
3) I didn't get the position I wanted and **set** it **down** to my lack of experience.

692. Set fire to (*v.*) – to start a fire, to catch fire

1) An arsonist **set fire** to three video shops within the last month.
2) The flames leaped from the burning building and **set fire** to the neighboring buildings.

693. Set forth (*v.*) – to express, propose, or present, to start a trip

1) The company's new fiscal policy was **set forth** at its bimonthly meeting.
2) The President has ordered his aides to **set forth** on a new campaign to stamp out corruption.
3) They **set forth** on their trip to Mexico.

694. Set off (*v.*) – to cause to explode, to make more apparent by contrast, to accentuate, to distinguish

1) Every year, on August 15th, many people **set off** firecrackers in celebration of our nation's independence.
2) No one has claimed responsibility for the bomb that was **set off** last

week in Dublin.

3) The blouse she wore **set off** the color of her eyes.
4) The gray walls were **set off** by the addition of lush green carpeting.
5) The burgundy drapes really **set off** the ivory wall and white trimming.

695. Set on / upon *(v.)* – to direct to attack or attack

1) The owner of the house **set** his dog **on** the intruder.
2) Israeli troops were **set upon** by angry Palestinians early last night in Gaza.

696. Set one's heart on *(v.)* – to want very much

1) She had **her heart set on** going to Europe, but her poor grades forced her to cancel her trip.
2) He doesn't know it yet, but his girlfriend has **her heart set on** a large sapphire and diamond wedding ring.

697. Set out *(v.)* – to put in a known place, to plant, to explain

1) I always **set out** a dish of food for stray cats.
2) She **sets out** tomato seedlings every summer.
3) His staff had to **set out** all the facts before he would come to a decision.

698. Set up *(v.)* – to arrange or assemble, to found or establish, to place in a position of authority, to provide with the necessary means or money

1) Her nightly chore was to **set up** the dinner table and put out the china.
2) The school **set up** a special program to assist business majors in finding employment after graduation.
3) I want to **set up** a publishing company.
4) He **set** himself **up** in business and made an enormous amount of money.
5) His family helped **set** him **up** in the restaurant business.

699. Settle down (*v.*) **– to begin living a more orderly life, to become calm**

1) They hope to **settle down** in a quiet family oriented area.
2) Most people tend to **settle down** after they get married.
3) The students **settled down** as soon as the teacher walked into the classroom.

700. Settle for (*v.*) **– to accept something or someone even though not satisfied.**

1) He wanted $100.00 for the bike, but **settled for** $65.00
2) She had dreamed of marrying a multimillionaire, but **settled for** a millionaire.
3) I wanted to find a better job, but I **settled** for the present one.

701. Settle on / upon (*v.*) **– to reach a decision**

1) The First Merit Corporation has recently had a lot of corporate policy changes, but they've finally **settled on** new policies that are believed to carry them into the next decade.
2) The issue of how to combine the assets of the two banks was **settled upon** at last week's meeting.

702. Settle up (*v.*) **– to pay money owed or resolve a dispute**

1) Let's **settle up** quickly and get out of here, or we'll be late for the concert.
2) The settlement calls for them to **settle up** their ongoing dispute over the fundraising irregularities.

**** Settle with** (*v.*) **– to reach an agreement, to pay**

1) He has agreed to **settle** his dispute **with** the company in return for a fair share of the profits from ticket sales.

2) She needs to **settle** her account immediately **with** the bank, or service will be discontinued.

703. Shake down (*v.*) – to extort money from

1) The police officers were caught trying to **shake down** business owners in the area.
2) The Mafia has often been accused of **shaking down** small business owners or destroying their businesses.

704. Shake off (*v.*) – to get rid of

1) The spy knew some people were following him and he tried to **shake** them **off**, but to no avail.
2) She wants to get rid of the stalker, but she doesn't know how to **shake** him **off**.

705. Shake up (*v.*) – to disturb

1) The grisly crime **shook up** the entire community.
2) The news of forced layoffs and early retirement **shook up** the entire staff.

706. Shape up (*v.*) – to improve one's behavior or performance

1) After midterms, her teacher told her to **shape up** or she would fail the course.
2) His father told him to **shape up** or find another place to live.
3) My body is in such bad shape, I really need to **shape up**.

707. Ship out (*v.*) – to ship to another location

1) We are planning to **ship out** all the merchandise soon.
2) If the packages are **shipped out** today, they'll arrive in three days.

708. Shoot for (*v.*) – to try to achieve a goal

1) He **shot for** a June opening, but didn't make it.
2) They're **shooting for** the 1st place prize in the dance contest.

709. Shoot off (*v.*) – to shoot, to set off

1) The army has decided to **shoot off** the new missile before August 2002.
2) Revelers **shot off** firecrackers in celebration of Independence Day.

710. Show into / out (*v.*) – to guide or escort someone entering or leaving

1) I will **show** you **into** the house.
2) I will **show** you **out.**

711. Show off (*v.*) – to display or behave in an ostentatious or conspicuous manner

1) He should be studying, but he's busy **showing off** his new car to his friends.
2) She is ostentatious and jumps at every opportunity to **show off** her wealth.

712. Show up (*v.*) – to arrive, to come, to appear, to reveal

1) Just for once, everybody **showed up** on time.
2) The band **showed up** more than an hour late for their concert.
3) When she didn't **show up** for dinner, her family began to worry.
4) Many book-keeping inaccuracies **showed up** during the routine inspection.

713. Shrug off (*v.*) **– to minimize the importance of, to act as if s/he doesn't care**

1) She **shrugged off** her disappointment over not being promoted and kept on working, sure she would get the next one.
2) His family and friends made several suggestions, but he just **shrugged** them **off**.

714. Shut down (*v.*) **– to stop operating, to halt operation of**

1) The company **shut down** the mill until the labor dispute was resolved.
2) The company **shuts down** for two weeks every summer.

715. Shut off (*v.*) **– to turn off**

1) Please make sure you **shut off** the television before you go to sleep.
2) The water shortage probably means the Water Company will **shut off** the water on alternate weekends.

716. Shut out (*v.*) **– to exclude, to keep someone or something from entering**

1) She felt her coworkers had completely **shut** her **out** at the weekly meeting
2) We closed all the windows in an effort to **shut out** the noise.

717. Shy away from (*v.*) **– to avoid or move away from something with fear or disgust**

1) The students **shied away from** the new teacher's questions.
2) Kittens usually **shy away from** strangers.

718. Sick and tired of (*adj.*) – irritated, or annoyed by something repeated or continued too long very unpleasantly

1) I am **sick and tired of** answering the phone all day.
2) I am **sick and tired of** listening to her complaints.

719. Side by side (*adv.*) – next to each other

1) Their houses are **side by side** on 1st Street.
2) They always sit **side by side** in the classroom.
3) The dresses were displayed **side by side** in the window.
4) They played **side by side** all afternoon.

720. Side with (*v.*) – to align oneself with

1) She **sides with** him whether he's right or wrong.
2) He thanked his boss for **siding with** him in his request for a leave of absence.

** Side against (*v.*) – to align oneself against

1) Many of the people she considered friends **sided against** her.
2) It was unusual to see workers take the side of management and **side against** the labor union.

721. Sign in (*v.*) – to sign a register or log on entering

1) Students taking the exam must **sign in** when they enter the test site.
2) Beginning Monday, staff must **sign in** when they come to work.

** Sign out (*v.*) – to sign a register or log on leaving

1) Employees must sign in when they arrive and **sign out** when they finish their shift.

722. Sign off (*v.*) – a broadcasting term, to stop transmitting or to complete one's on air presentation

1) The station **signs off** at the same time every night.
2) The newscaster always **signs off** by saying, "Have a good night."

723. Sign on (*v.*) – to sign an agreement to work, or do volunteer work

1) If you are interested in a summer job, you must **sign on** now.
2) Many celebrities have **signed on** to help flood victims.

** Sign up (*v.*) – to sign one's name to an agreement

1) He **signed up** for the Navy last week.
2) The university is hoping more students will **sign up** for their summer intensive courses.

724. Sign over (*v.*) – to give legally by signing one's name

1) He **signed over** the deed of his house.
2) She will **sign** her property **over** to her adopted son when he is old enough.

725. Sit back (*v.*) – to relax, to stand away from

1) After I retire, I am going to **sit back** and enjoy life.
2) I couldn't believe she just **sat back** and let her kids do whatever they wanted to do.

726. Sit in (on) (*v.*) – to participate or attend in, to be included usually as an observer

1) He was asked to **sit in on** the finance meeting because he is an expert in corporate fundraising.

2) The new teacher asked if she could **sit in on** one of the principal's classes.

** **Sit on** (*v.*) **– to be a member of**

1) The twelve people who **sat on** the jury had found the defendant guilty.
2) He's retired, but he still **sits on** the board of trustees.

727. Size up (*v.*) – to make an estimate of, to meet certain specifications

1) The counselor **sized up** the problem only after he had spoken with all the individuals involved in the dispute.
2) He needed some additional time to **size up** the situation.
3) The thought that the interviewer was **sizing** her **up** made her feel uncomfortable.

728. Skeleton in the closet (*n.*) – a shameful secret which is kept hidden

1) Almost everyone has at least one **skeleton in the closet.**

729. Sketch out (*v.*) – to make an outline

1) His boss asked him to **sketch out** a rough draft of the proposal before they meet with the rest of the team.
2) The architect **sketched out** a plan of the proposed building project.

730. Skin and bones (*n.*) – very thin and undernourished state

1) Photographs of the famine stricken country showed horrific scenes of children who were little more than **skin and bones.**
2) The cat is healthy now, but it was near starvation and merely **skin and bones** when I found it.

731. Skin-deep *(adj.)* – superficial, shallow

1) He claims to have studied world history, but his knowledge is only **skin-deep.**
2) She pretends to be my friend, but her friendship is only **skin-deep.**
3) Her beauty is only **skin deep.**

732. Skip out (on) – to leave without permission

1) The girl **skipped out** of school because she wanted to meet her friend.

** Skip over *(v.)* – to omit

1) Our teacher **skipped over** Chapter 3 of the textbook because it didn't look interesting.

733. Slap down *(v.)* – to refuse roughly, to stop someone in a lower position from speaking

1) She brought her complaint to her supervisor, but it was **slapped down** immediately.
2) Management **slapped down** their employees' suggestion of a pay raise.

** Slap in the face *(n., v.)* – an insult, a disappointment, to insult or embarrass

1) Her refusal to return my phone calls was a **slap in the face.**
2) He felt his demotion was a **slap in the face.**
3) Your public insult felt like a **slap in the face.**

734. Sleep a wink *(v.)* – to get a moment's sleep

1) He was so concerned about his project that he didn't **sleep a wink** last night.

735. Sleep on it *(v.)* **– to consider something overnight before deciding**

1) I'd like to join the club, but I'm not sure whether I have the time. Let me **sleep on it** and I'll give you an answer tomorrow.
2) I appreciate your invitation, but let me **sleep on it** and I'll get back to you tomorrow.

736. Slip away *(v.)* **– to pass unnoticed**

1) When I'm busy, time seems to **slip away**.
2) Before they were aware of it, a month of their vacation had already **slipped away**.

** **Slip out** *(v.)* **– to leave quietly without being noticed**

1) We were tired and **slipped out** of the party early.
2) She **slipped out** of the house after supper to meet her friends.

737. Slip of the tongue *(n.)* **– utterance of something by mistake**

1) He didn't mean to reveal the secret, it was just a **slip of the tongue**.
2) Try not to make any **slips of the tongue** during your speech.

** **Slip up** *(v.)* **– to make a mistake or an error**

1) The bank teller must have **slipped up** when she was counting the money because her till was short more than $200.00.
2) I did all right on the exam, but I **slipped up** on the last question.

738. Slow down *(v.)* **– to go slowly or cause to go more slowly**

1) **Slow down**! There's no need to hurry.
2) He's busy as usual, but one of these days he'll **slow down**.

3) The factory **slowed down** its production of the item because its demand was down.

739. Smash up (*v.*) – to wreck completely

1) His car was **smashed up** in the accident.
2) The drunk driver drove into a wall and **smashed up** his car.

740. Smooth over (*v.*) – to make a troubled situation seem better.

1) The government is trying to **smooth over** the scandal.
2) He is good at **smoothing over** disputes between management and labor.

741. Snap out of it (*v.*) – to recover quickly from a bad mood, depression or illness, etc.

1) She **snapped out of** her gloomy mood as soon as she got married.
2) When he first heard the test results he was depressed, but he soon **snapped out of it** and got back to studying.

742. Snap up (*v.*) – to take quickly and eagerly

1) The customers **snapped up** all the Christmas items we had on sale.
2) The children **snapped up** all of the cookies before she had even put the tray on the table.

743. Sneak up on (*v.*) – to approach or move stealthily

1) He **sneaked up on** her and she screamed because it startled her.

** Sneak into / onto (*v.*) – to enter a place stealthily without being noticed

1) A few students were late and **sneaked into** the classroom through

the backdoor.

2) Two young men were caught trying to **sneak onto** the ferry without paying.

744. Snowed in *(v.)* – to be trapped by heavy snow

1) They were **snowed in** for three days because of heavy blizzard.

745. So far, so good – up until now things have gone well.

1) We were worried about her ability to make the grade as a businesswoman, but **so far, so good.**
2) All of the signs point to an improved economy, and **so far, so good.**

746. Only so many *(adj.)* – a limited number of

1) There are **only so many** things I can accomplish in a day.
2) They can **only** issue **so many** copies of each card under the terms of their agreement with Major League Baseball.
3) I can do **only so many** things in a day.

** Only so much *(adj.)* – a limited amount (of)

1) I have **only so much** time to do so many things.
2) I have **only so much** money to spend on home improvement, the rest of the money needs to go towards other things.

747. Something (else) *(adj.)* – something or someone very unusual, far beyond average

1) That new hairdo she got is really **something else!**
2) Yes, she's really **something else!**
3) The new Corvette sport cars are **something else!**

** Something else again – something different

1) Borrowing the book is one thing, but taking it without permission is **something else again.**

748. So–so (*adj.*) – neither good nor bad

1) The movie was **so–so.**
2) The food was quite good, but the service was **so–so.**

749. So that (*conj.*) – in order that, so, as a result of that

1) I am going to make a few phone calls to realtors **so that** I can find a home.
2) A meeting was called, **so that** we could discuss the issue.
3) I stayed in bed most of the day **so that** I would feel better for the party.

** So as to (*prep.*) – in order to

1) Send packages early **so as to** be sure they arrive on time.
2) I want to save as much as I can, **so as to** take a trip overseas.

** So ~ that – used with an adjective or an adverb.

1) She is **so** pretty **that** everyone notices her.
2) The subway train was **so** crowded **that** I could barely squeeze in.
3) He did **so** well on the test **that** he made the Dean's List.

750. Sort out (*v.*) – to arrange or sort by classification

1) His job is **sorting out** the mail.
2) **Sort out** these letters by alphabetical order.

751. Sought after *(adj.)* – in demand

1) Her first film was so successful that now she's much **sought after.**
2) Old and rare coins are **sought after** by collectors because of their value.
3) Classic furniture is always **sought after.**

752. Sound off *(v.)* – to speak in a loud, or complaining way

1) The students **sounded off** when they received their poor grades.

753. Sound out *(v.)* – to try to find out how the other person feels or thinks cautiously

1) She **sounded out** the boss about a week off, but decided against making the request.
2) The meeting is to **sound out** the members about raising dues.

754. Space out *(v.)* – to have gaps

1) She's a good student, but sometimes she is **spaced out.**
2) I like to **space** things **out** instead of trying to do everything at once.

755. Speak for *(v.)* – to speak on behalf of, to claim

1) I am here today to **speak for** the rights of all living creatures, including animals.
2) You don't need to **speak for** me, I can speak for myself.
3) A man asked her to dance, but she said she was already **spoken for.**

756. Speak of the devil and he appears *(proverb.)* – Used when people are talking about a person and the person shows up unexpectedly.

1) **Speaking of the devil,** here comes Jim and we were just talking about him.

757. Speak out (*v.*) – to protest, to talk freely, to make one's opinions known

1) The oppressed will never better their lot until they **speak out.**
2) Nowadays, labor often **speaks out** to the administration.

** Speak up (*v.*) – to speak in a loud voice

1) Please **speak up**, so everyone can hear you.

** Speak well for (*v.*) – to be good evidence

1) The paper he wrote **speaks well for** his alma mater.
2) His recent letter **speaks well for** a possible reconciliation.

758. Speed up (*v.*) – to go faster, to make go faster

1) We'd better **speed up** the work pace or we'll have to work this weekend to get the job completed.
2) The company made a decision to **speed up** its production.

759. Spell out (*v.*) – to make clear and understandable, to read slowly letter by letter, to write out in full

1) The teacher **spelled out** the whole procedure.
2) She **spelled** her name **out** loud, "N-a-n-c-y."
3) **Spell out** your full name, please.

760. Split off (*v.*) – to divide, to separate

1) We **split off** some decayed branches and used them for firewood.
2) The management's decision to **split off** the sales department from the main office was not well received.

** **Split up** (*v.*) – to split into pieces, to separate

1) They **split up** the work and finished it faster.
2) They're going to **split up** because they don't get along well.

761. **Spread out** (*v.*) – to extend over a large area or time

1) She **spread out** a cloth and placed the peppers on it.
2) We **spread out** the workload to give everyone a fair share.
3) The use of cell phones has **spread out** all over the country.

762. **Spring up** (*v.*) – to appear or emerge suddenly

1) The IT businesses seemed to **spring up** overnight.
2) Civil rights organizations have **sprung up** throughout the country.

763. **Spruce up** (*v.*) – to make neat or improve the appearance of

1) She has a large wardrobe and always **spruces** herself **up**.
2) When we expect company, we always **spruce up** the house.

764. **Square off** (*v.*) – to get into a fighting position

1) The two boys had just **squared off** when the teacher arrived.

765. **Square with** (*v.*) – to agree or conform

1) Her story doesn't **square with** the facts.

766. **A square peg in a round hole** – Someone who does not fit

1) She quit her job because she felt like **a square peg in a round hole**.

767. Square up (*v.*) – to settle debts, to make even

1) After I **square up** my debts, I'm going to take a long vacation.
2) Last time you paid for lunch, so today I'll pay. I'd like to **square up.**

768. Stack up (*v.*) – to pile one thing on another, to add up

1) His boss asked him to stay late and help **stack up** the boxes that would be shipped out on the next truck.
2) I've fallen behind on my payments and the bills have **stacked up.**

769. Stamp out (*v.*) – to suppress, to destroy or put out by stamping, to make an impression in something by pressing down on it

1) Customs officials are trying to **stamp out** the importation and sale of endangered species.
2) Despots, like Hitler and Stalin, were unsuccessful in their bids to **stamp out** democracy.
3) We **stamped out** the campfire and then doused it with water.
4) The mint is **stamping out** more Nobel Peace Prize commemorative coins to meet public demands.

770. Stand a chance (*v.*) – to have a possibility or hope of succeeding

1) She didn't think she **stood a chance** of being elected to Congress.
2) Unless you buckle down and begin to study, you don't **stand a chance** of passing the course.

771. Stand by (*v.*) – to be loyal to, to wait until needed or called

1) She had a party in honor of the friends who **stood by** her when she was in dire straits.

2) Passengers should **stand by** at the gate and have their seats confirmed.

** **Stand up for** (*v.*) **– to be loyal to or side with, to support**

1) She always **stands up** for her brother.
2) Whenever people blamed him, she **stood up** for him.
3) We must encourage people to **stand up** for their inalienable rights.

772. Stand for (*v.*) **– to put up with, to bear, or represent in a symbolic or shortened form**

1) I won't **stand for** students fighting in the classroom.
2) The $ symbol **stands for** dollar or dollars.

773. Stand off (*v.*) **– to withstand, to repel, to prevent an attack**

1) The allies **stood off** a fierce enemy attack.
2) The enemy attacked our country, but our army **stood** the enemy **off**.

** **Standoffish** (*adj.*) **– unfriendly, aloof**

1) She's nice, but a little **standoffish**.

774. Stand on (*v.*) **– to insist on, to have one's position in the opinion of others**

1) He **stood on** his Constitutional Right to have an attorney.
2) The voters wanted to know where the Presidential candidate **stands on** the issue of abortion.

** **Stand one's ground** (*v.*) **– to defend one's beliefs, to hold out against attack or criticism**

1) He **stood his ground** when everyone criticized him.

2) Our soldiers **stood their ground** when the enemy attacked.

** Stand on one's own feet *(v.)* – to be independent, to depend on oneself

1) Her parents told her they weren't going to pay her bills any longer because it was time for her to **stand on her own feet.**
2) When she turned 18, she got a job and began **standing on her own feet.**

775. Stand out *(v.)* – to be noticeable, to continue to oppose, to be prominent, outstanding

1) When compared with similar products on the market, our products **stand out.**
2) Even after an agreement was reached, the dissatisfaction of some workers **stood out.**
3) The team played well, but their center really **stood out.**

776. Stand up to *(v.)* – to face with courage

1) His friends told him to **stand up to** the bully and they would support him.
2) She stood up for her belief that all living creatures deserve to be treated with respect.

777. Start out *(v.)* – to begin a career or life, to begin to go

1) He **started out** as a newspaper boy and now he owns the newspaper.
2) I wanted to see them before they went on holiday, but they had already **started out** when I arrived at their house.

** Start up *(v.)* – to get something started, to start operating

1) Despite the cold weather, the engine **started up** on the first try.

2) School is out for the summer and will **start up** again in September.

778. Stay away (*v.*) – not to go near

1) Play in the yard, but **stay away** from the garden.
2) If you want to lose weight, **stay away** from snacks.
3) He told the young man to **stay away** from his daughter.

779. Stay over (*v.*) – to stay in a place for an additional period of time

1) We **stayed over** for an extra two days at their house when we visited them.
2) They enjoyed their trip so much that they decided to **stay over** for another week.

780. Stay put (*v.*) – not leave or move

1) When he called his mother to let her know he was going to walk home, she told him to **stay put** and she would pick him up.
2) In a rain or a snowstorm, it is always wise to **stay put** instead of driving on the highway.
3) It's hard to find a new job. **Stay put** where you are now.

781. Stay up (*v.*) – to stay without going to bed

1) She's like a night owl and likes to **stay up** late.
2) We watched television last night, but we didn't **stay up** too late.

782. Steamed up (*adj.*) – (usually a negative feeling) to be excited or angry at someone or something

1) He's a nice guy, but he often gets **steamed up** over small matters.
2) He got **steamed up** when he found out his computer wasn't working.

** **Worked up** (*adj.*) **– excited, angry, or worried**

1) Don't get all **worked up**, everything will probably turn out all right.
2) He's all **worked up** because he got blamed for something he didn't do.

** **Fired up** (*adj.*) **– (usually a positive and competitive feeling) to be excited or eager to do something**

1) The coach's encouraging half-time speech got the team all **fired up** to win the game.

** **Run out of steam – to lose the physical energy**

1) He's working too many hours, and he's beginning to **run out of steam**.
2) The fighters punched each other hoping the other would **run out of steam** first.

783. **Step aside** (*v.*) **– to move to aside, to give in**

1) The usher asked the people waiting in line to **step aside** so that those already holding tickets could enter the theater.
2) He willingly **stepped aside** because he felt the other candidate had a better chance of winning the election.

784. **Step down** (*v.*) **– to resign from a high post, to come down from a higher place to a lower**

1) The president was forced to **step down** before completing his term.
2) His reasons for **stepping down** were health related.

** **Step up** (*v.*) **– to rise to a higher position, to increase, to go from a lower to a higher place**

1) Her promotion was certainly a **step up** and moved her closer to her

goal of becoming vice-president of the company.
2) We **stepped up** production to stay ahead of demand.
3) You have to **step up** to enter the kitchen.

785. Step in (v.) – to intervene, to enter for a moment

1) He **stepped in** to stop the fight before someone got hurt.
2) Would you **step in** my office for a minute? I'd like to speak with you.

** Step out (v.) – to go outside for a short time

1) His secretary said he had just **stepped out** for a minute.
2) He just **stepped out** for a cup of coffee.

** Step into (v.) – to take or gain without any difficulty, to enter

1) She was fortunate to **step into** such a good position so quickly.
2) He **stepped into** a good position in his father's company as soon as he graduated from college.
3) The supervisor asked me to **step into** his office for a minute.

786. Stick around (v.) – to remain in the same place or stay nearby

1) I'll be finished in a few minutes. Can you **stick around**?
2) She had nothing else to do, so she **stuck around** waiting for her friends to finish shopping.

787. Stick by (v.) – to remain faithful

1) When people get married, they vow to **stick by** one another for better or worse.
2) Good friends are those who **stick by** you during difficult times.

788. Stick one's neck out (v.) – to take a risk

1) Her credit is terrible, but he **stuck out his neck** and loaned her $10,000.
2) He really **stuck his neck out** when he supported the President on the controversial policy, but it paid off in the end.

789. Stick out (v.) – to be prominent or obvious, to stand out

1) He's extremely tall and has colored his long curly hair blue, so he **sticks out** in any crowd.
2) The green car certainly **sticks out** in any parking lot.

790. Stick to (v.) – to persist

1) Once she begins a job she **sticks to** it until it's finished.
2) People don't seem to **stick to** the old customs any more.

** Stick with (v.) – to continue doing something (usually a difficult task), to stay with

1) Getting through college is difficult, but **stick with** it. The rewards are great.
2) Although many of his friends didn't like her, he **stuck with** her.
3) He divorced his wife and is **stuck with** paying child support until his children turn eighteen.

791. Stir up (v.) – to arouse, to incite

1) He was fired because he was always trying to **stir** things **up**.
2) His girlfriend's elopement **stirred** him **up** because he didn't know she was seeing someone else.

792. Stock up on (v.) – to put or lay in a supply of

1) People who live in rural areas usually **stock up on** food for the winter.

** **Store up** (*v.*) **– to put aside for future use**

1) Squirrels **store up** acorns and walnuts to eat during the winter.
2) We use our pantry to **store up** staple food and other items.

793. Stop off / over (*v.*) – to make a short stop on the way to somewhere, to stay or visit briefly

1) On our way home to Korea we **stopped off** in Hawaii.
2) He **stopped off** to have a beer with some friends after finishing work.
3) She called her parents-in-law and asked them to **stop over** for coffee and dessert after dinner.

794. Stow away (*v.*) – to put away in a proper place, to be a stow away

1) We've **stowed away** our Christmas decorations until next year.
2) The refugee **stowed away** on the ship hoping not to be caught.

** **A stowaway** (*n.*) **– a person who hides on a ship, train, etc. to get a free ride**

1) During the flight from Rome to Chicago, the flight crew discovered **a stowaway.** They turned him over to Customs officials when the flight landed at O' Hare Airport.

795. Straight away (*adv.*) – immediately, without hesitation

1) His father told him to come home **straight away.**
2) He seldom beats around the bush, so he came to the point **straight away.**

796. Straighten out *(v.)* **– to solve problems, to restore, to reform, to correct**

1) We need to **straighten out** something between us.
2) They thought a military academy would help **straighten out** their unruly son.

**** Straighten up** *(v.)* **– to correct, to behave better, to make neat or orderly**

1) You'd better **straighten up** from this new year.
2) This closet is cluttered and it needs to be **straightened up**.

797. Stretch the point *(v.)* **– to make an exception, to lie**

1) He **stretches the point** whenever he thinks it will be to his benefit.
2) "Don't **stretch the point**. Just tell the truth."

798. Stretch out *(v.)* **– to become lengthened or widened**

1) After a hard day's work, it feels good to **stretch out** and take a quick nap before dinner.
2) Students usually try to **stretch out** their ten-minute break and usually end up taking a fifteen-minute break.

799. Strike it rich *(v.)* **– to gain a sudden wealth**

1) He **struck it rich** by finding an oil well.
2) Her dream was to **strike it rich** by winning a lottery.

800. Strike out (at) *(v.)* **– to hit indiscriminately**

1) He **strikes out at** those around him when he's angry.

** **Strike out** *(v.)* **– to eliminate, to cross out**

1) Her editor asked her to **strike out** several awkward phrases.
2) So she **struck** them **out**.

801. **Strike up** *(v.)* **– to play music vigorously, to bring about, to begin**

1) The band **struck up** the national anthem as the ceremonies got under way.
2) We met at the university and immediately **struck up** a lifelong friendship.

802. **String along** *(v.)* **– to deceive, to keep someone waiting or dangling, to follow along or cooperate**

1) She loved him but he **strung** her **along** although he had no intention of marrying her.
2) My decision is as follows: give me a new contract or release me, don't **string** me **along**.
3) Although they didn't agree with his plan, they decided to **string along** and see what developed.

** **Pull strings** *(v.)* **– to use one's influence or power in order to gain an advantage**

1) Mr. Shin told her that he could **pull strings** if she wanted the position.
2) He can **pull strings** for you.

803. **Strip** *(v.)* **– to undress, to rob or plunder, or to remove by stripping**

1) The **stripper** danced across the stage.
2) The civil war **stripped** the country of its most valuable asset, people.
3) The carpenters **stripped** off the old varnish, sanded the cabinet, and then varnished it again.

804. Subject to *(adj.)* **– under the control or authority of, to be prone or liable**

1) Employees who joined the company after June 1, 1995 are **subject to** the new retirement policy.
2) All fees and service charges are **subject to** change without notice.
3) Southeast Asia is **subject to** typhoons during the monsoon season.

805. Sum up *(v.)* **– to summarize**

1) The lecture can be **summed up** in a few brief sentences.
2) My boss asked me to write a letter **summing up** the main points of our discussion.

806. Summon up *(v.)* **– to gather, to arouse, to rouse, to call forth**

1) When she finally **summoned up** enough courage to sing, most of the audience had already left for home.
2) Gifted speakers generally consider it an easy task to **summon up** passion in their listeners.

807. Sure enough *(adv.)* **– as expected**

1) Her boyfriend promised to marry her, and **sure enough**, he proposed.
2) The weather forecast was for a stormy weekend, and **sure enough**, the weekend brought gusty winds and heavy rains.

808. Survival of the fittest *(n.)* **– the idea that often those species best able to adapt survive and those unable to adapt die out**

1) The natural world is a good place and a clear example of **survival of the fittest.**

2) Life in our increasingly competitive world is another example of **survival of the fittest.**

809. Swallow one's pride (*v.*) – to bear humbly or tolerate

1) When he was demoted, he decided to **swallow his pride** and continue working for the company.

** Swallow ones's words (*v.*) – to retract words one has uttered

1) They said he would never reach the major in the Air Force, but he did and they were forced to **swallow their words.**
2) Her harshest critics had to **swallow their words** when she won a Grammy Award.

** Swallow ones's feelings (*v.*) – to suppress one's feelings

1) When he first received the university's rejection letter he was devastated, but after a few weeks he was able to **swallow his feelings** and get on with his life.

810. Swallow up (*v.*) – to destroy or consume

1) A large conglomerate **swallowed up** the small company.
2) She said she didn't like large crowds because she always felt as if she were being **swallowed up.**

811. Swear by (*v.*) – to name something in taking an oath, as a pledge of truth or honesty, to have great confidence in

1) He **swore by** all that he held holy that he would be faithful.
2) When a new President is **sworn** in, he takes what is called an oath of office.

3) She likes that brand so much that she **swears by** it.

** **Swear in** (*v.*) – **to administer a legal or official oath to, to have someone swear to do one's duty**

1) The President **swore in** the Chief Justice of the Supreme Court.
2) Shortly after the jury was **sworn in**, one of the jurors was excused because of illness.

812. Swear off (*v.*) – to pledge to give up something

1) She **swore off** smoking after she got pregnant.
2) He **swore off** drinking many times, nevertheless he continues to drink.

813. Sweep off one's feet (*v.*) – to cause very strong feeling and excitement

1) She was **swept off her feet** by his attractive appearance.
2) She gets easily **swept off her feet** by handsome men.

814. Swim with the stream – to go along with the majority

1) He disagreed with the proposed plan, but decided that **swimming with the stream** was his best option if he wanted to stay with the firm.

** **Swim against the stream or current – to go opposite from the majority**

1) People generally go with the flow rather than attempt **swimming against the stream** of public opinion.

815. Tag along *(v.)* – to follow closely (often when not wanted)

1) I don't have anything to do. Do you mind if I **tag along** with you when you go shopping?
2) When I go for a walk, my dog won't stay home because he always **tags along** behind me.

816. Take a chance *(v.)* – to take a risk

1) She decided to leave home and **take a chance** on finding a job in the city.
2) She usually doesn't help strangers, but she **took a chance** this time.

817. Take advantage of *(v.)* – to use a person unfairly for one's own advantage, to make good use of

1) He is generous and some people **take advantage of** his generosity.
2) The students **took advantage of** the new library.

818. Take after *(v.)* – to resemble, to chase

1) He **takes after** his father in his physical appearance and mannerisms.
2) The dog **took after** a squirrel.

819. Take apart *(v.)* – to dismantle, to criticize severely

1) My brother likes to **take** radios and watches **apart**.
2) The student's main argument was quickly **taken apart** by the professor.

820. Take at one's word (*v.*) – to believe what someone says

1) She **took** him **at his word** when he said he'd never lie to her again.

821. Take back (*v.*) – to return, to withdraw

1) I **took back** a pair of slacks and got a refund.
2) The fight began when one of the boys refused to **take back** what he had said about the other boy.

822. Take care of (*v.*) – to look after, to do what is needed to, to solve,

1) He **took care of** the baby while his wife went shopping.
2) It's difficult to contact her because she works and **takes care of** her mother.
3) We need to **take care of** the bills before we go on vacation.

** Take care (*v.*) – to heed or beware, to be careful about

1) He was late so often that his boss told him he'd better **take care** or he'd be out of a job.

823. Take charge (*v.*) – to lead, to take control or responsibility

1) He was promoted and will take **charge of** the department as of January 1, 2004.
2) While her mother was away, she took **charge of** the house.

824. Take down (*v.*) – to put in writing, to bring from a higher place to a lower place, to dismantle

1) He **took down** my phone number.
2) We decided not to **take** the Christmas Tree **down** for another week.
3) Let's **take down** the old tree house and build a new one in its place.

825. Take effect (*v.*) – to produce a change, to become lawfully operative

1) The doctor told him that the medication would **take effect** immediately.
2) The new policy will **take effect** as of the first working day of next month.

826. Take exception (*v.*) – to be displeased, to object to, to take issue with

1) She's contentious and **takes exception** to anything anyone says.
2) He didn't have a valid reason to **take exception** to my comments.

827. Take for (*v.*) – to suppose someone to be something other than they are (often mistakenly)

1) The policeman **took** the man with a moustache **for** a drug dealer.
2) I **took** the tall woman **for** a teacher.

828. Take for granted (*v.*) – to accept without a realization of importance of

1) It upset him that people **took** his generosity **for granted.**
2) Many people **take** their parents **for granted** until it is too late.
3) We, humans, **take** Nature **for granted.**

829. Take heart (*v.*) – to take courage or confidence

1) **Take heart!** You can do it if you really work hard.
2) It **took heart** for herto return to school and study computer science at the age of 60.

830. Take in (v.) – to include or comprise, to grant admittance to, to deceive, to trick, o provide a shelter

1) The United Kingdom **takes in** England, Scotland, Wales, and Ireland.
2) Last summer, Lotte World **took in** over 100,000,000 visitors.
3) She **takes in** stray animals and feeds them.
4) The insurance company **took** people **in** on their product.

831. Take in stride (v.) – to accept everything as it is and move on

1) After years of arguing with his boss, he has learned to **take** things **in stride.**
2) He doesn't get upset when he fails because he has learned to **take** things **in stride.**
3) You must **take** things **in stride** or you will feel depressed and angry all of the time.

832. Take into account (v.) – to consider with other matters in a decision

1) We didn't **take** the traffic **into account** and we were late for the opera.
2) The trip will cost about $6,000.00 when you **take** everything **into account.**

** Take into consideration (v.) – to consider

1) We thought the new house would be completed earlier than it was because we failed to **take** human error **into consideration.**
2) We must **take** the icy road **into consideration** and allow more time to get to the airport.

** Take under consideration (v.) – to think seriously

1) A company offered me a better position and I need to **take it under consideration.**

833. Take it (v.) – to endure, to get the impression

1) The other kids are picking on him and he can't **take it** anymore.
2) It was said as a joke, but she **took it** personally.

** **Take it out on (v.) – to abuse by venting one's anger or frustration**

1) When she's angry, she **takes it out on** her children.

** **Take it or leave it (v.) – accept someone or something as it is or refuse it**

1) The team told him it was their final offer and he could either **take it or leave it.**

834. Take it easy (v.) – to avoid hard work, to go or act gently

1) She's been working too hard, so her boss told her to **take it easy.**
2) If you're not feeling well you should **take it easy.**
3) Her husband was usually too strict with the children, so she asked him to **take it easy** with them.

835. Take liberties with (v.) – to behave in a way that offends by being overly friendly, to make changes in too much freely, to use someone's property without permission

1) The man regretted **taking liberties with** the young female secretary.
2) The editor was accused of **taking liberties with** the author's writing.
3) The girl **took liberties** of using her roommate's personal property.

836. Take notice of (*v.*) – to pay attention to

1) Because of poor planning and promotion, the public **took** little **notice** of the event.
2) She is stunning and people immediately **take notice of** her.

837. Take off (*v.*) – to remove one's clothing, to rise up, to leave, to take time from

1) When you enter a temple, you must **take off** your shoes.
2) Sales really **took off** after an extensive advertising campaign.
3) The flight was due to **take off** at 4:05, but heavy rains delayed its departure.
4) He **took** some time **off** and went to Hawaii.

838. Take on (*v.*) – to hire, to undertake

1) The booming economy has caused the company to **take on** 1,000 new employees.
2) She couldn't **take on** the project because she already had too many things to do.

839. Take one's time (*v.*) – not to hurry

1) His mother **told** him to take **his time** and not to rush through his homework assignments.
2) Those who **take their time** usually make fewer mistakes.

840. Take out (*v.*) – to remove or extract, to escort as on a date

1) He **took** the meat **out** of the freezer before leaving for work, so it would have ample time to thaw.
2) The cookies are ready to be **taken out** of the oven.
3) His mother asked him to **take out** the garbage after dinner.

4) He **takes** her **out** once in a while, but they're just friends.

841. Take over (*v.*) – to control the management of

1) New management **took over**, so employees are expecting a lot of changes.
2) When he retired, his son **took over** the business.

842. Take place (*v.*) – to happen, to occur

1) The event will **take place** at the Palace Theater.
2) The accident **took place** at the four-way intersection.

843. Take steps (*v.*) – to take action to make change, to begin to make plans or arrangements

1) The company is **taking** the necessary **steps** to upgrade its products.
2) He promised to **take steps** to improve his job performance.

844. Take to (*v.*) – to become fond of, to proceed with something as if it has become habitual

1) He **took to** her immediately.
2) She didn't think she'd like swimming, but she **took to** it like a fish.

845. Take the law into one's own hands (*v.*) – to punish or to take revenge without reference to a court

1) Police arrived before the mob **took the law into its own hands.**
2) Vigilantes are people who **take the law into their own hands.**

846. Take to heart (*v.*) – to be deeply affected or troubled by something

1) She **took** her friend's death **to heart.**

2) He often **takes** things said in anger **to heart.**

847. Take turns (v.) – to do or take part in something one after another

1) We **took turns** driving on the highways.
2) We **take turns** washing the dinner dishes.

848. Take up (v.) – to develop an interest, to begin with, to shorten, to use up or occupy

1) She **took up** jogging last year and has become an avid runner.
2) We'll **take up** the matter of sick days at the next staff meeting.
3) These slacks need to be **taken up** an inch.
4) That sofa **takes up** too much space.

** Take up with (v.) – to develop a friendship with

1) Since he has **taken up with** her, he ignores his other friends.
2) His behavior has changed since he **took up with** that crowd.

849. Take back (v.) – to reply rudely, to respond in a disrespectful way

1) Her parents punished her for **talking back** to her teacher.
2) He was dismissed because he **talked back** to his supervisor.

850. Talk down (to) (v.) – to depreciate, to address someone in a condescending manner

1) She **talks down to** me and is disdainful of my work.
2) He's not well liked because he **talks down to** everyone.

851. Talk into (*v.*) – to persuade

1) I didn't want to go to the dance, but he **talked** me **into** going.
2) You **talked** her **into** skipping classes.

** Talk out of (*v.*) – to dissuade someone from doing something

1) I **talked** him **out of** gambling.
2) We **talked** him **out of** fighting his friends.
3) They hope to **talk** her **out of** getting married until she completes her studies.

852. Talk out (*v.*) – to resolve by discussing thoroughly

1) We have a lot of problems, but we've trying to **talk** them **out**.
2) If you have a problem with me, let's **talk** it **out**.

** Level with (*v., informal*) – to be frank and open, to tell frankly and completely

1) The negotiators **leveled with** each other in the meeting to resolve the problem.
2) The boy's father wants his son to be a football player, but he doesn't like to be an athlete. The boy should **level with** his father.
3) He finally **leveled with** his wife that he lost quite a sum of money in stocks and nothing left in his savings.

853. Talk over (*v.*) – to discuss something in depth.

1) I like to **talk over** my decisions before I act on them.
2) She's busy, but she can **talk** it **over** with you later.

854. Tear down *(v.)* – to demolish, to destroy or criticize severely

1) They're going to **tear down** the old building and build a new one on the existing site.
2) He was their hero, but when his new film flopped at the box office the studio **tore** him **down.**

** Tear up *(v.)* – to tear or rip into small pieces

1) She read the letter and then **tore** it **up.**
2) She **tore** it **up** because its contents upset her.

855. Tell off *(v.)* – to criticize or scold sharply

1) The boss lost his temper and **told** her **off.**
2) She deserves to be **told off** because she gave us terrible service.

856. Think about *(v.)* – to examine, to consider or reflect on

1) My brother is **thinking about** going overseas.
2) My girlfriend asked me to **think about** lending her my camera.
3) He told his daughter to go to her room and **think about** her behavior.

** Think of *(v.)* – to consider a matter, to recall, to imagine, or suggest

1) Our family is **thinking of** moving to a smaller city.
2) I can't **think of** her name.
3) I can't even **think of** what life would be like without great art, music, or literature.
4) Can you **think of** a good place to go for dinner?

857. Think better of *(v.)* – to reconsider and make a better decision about

1) He was going to quit his job, but **thought better of it.**
2) She thought of stealing the money, but **thought better of it.**

858. Think nothing of *(v.)* – to regard as routine or usual

1) Her roommate **thinks nothing of** playing loud music late at night.
2) He **thinks nothing of** borrowing things and keeping them

859. Think over *(v.)* – to think carefully before coming to a decision

1) Take your time and **think** it **over** before you give your final answer.
2) I've already **thought** it **over** and I've decided to accept the position.

** Think twice *(v.)* – to reconsider or think carefully

1) They asked their son to **think twice** before quitting school.
2) **Think twice** before you borrow money from a loan shark.

860. Throw away *(v.)* – to discard, to waste as useless

1) Don't **throw away** these magazines, as I haven't read them yet.
2) He **threw away** his money at the racetrack.
3) He **threw away** his money on drinking and philandering.

** Throw out *(v.)* – to discard, to reject, to force to leave

1) She **threw out** her old shoes and bought new ones.
2) The boss **threw out** the idea before the meeting.
3) He was **thrown out** of school for setting off the fire alarm.

861. Throw up (*v.*) – to regurgitate, to vomit

1) After heavy drinking, the student **threw up.**

862. Tide over (*v.*) – to support through a difficult period

1) If you could lend me $25.00, it would **tide** me **over** until payday.

863. Tie down (*v.*) – to lash down, to restrict the freedom of, to limit or confine

1) The boys put their camping gear on top of the van and then **tied** it **down.**
2) She's **tied down** with her studies and rarely goes out.

** Tie up (*v.*) – to stop the movement of, or to prevent from doing something, to have money invested that cannot be used

1) The accident **tied up** traffic for more than two hours.
2) She's **tied up** in meetings all morning, but she's free after lunch.
3) His money is **tied up** in a trust fund until he's twenty-five.

864. Tie in (with) (*v.*) – to have a connection with

1) They're releasing the film which was **tied in** with the book.
2) The suspect's confession **tied in** with the evidence.

865. Tighten up (*v.*) – to make tighter

1) After we finish putting the bookcase together, we'll **tighten up** the screws.
2) The wheels may need to be **tightened up** more.

866. Time and again / Time after time (*adv.*) – repeatedly

1) I've asked her **time and again** not to slam the door when she leaves, but she still does it.
2) The elderly patients tend to be forgetful and need to be told **time after time** to take their medication.

867. The time is ripe (*v.*) – An auspicious time has arrived to do something

1) She says that she'll get married when **the time is ripe.**
2) The legislators believe that **the time is ripe** for this piece of legislation.

868. Tip off (*v.*) – to provide advance or inside information to

1) The police were **tipped off** and were waiting for the robbers when they entered the bank.
2) A friend **tipped** me **off** by telling me that a job would soon be opening up in her office.

869. To-be / To be (*adj.*) – about to become, that is going to be

1) She hugged her mother-in-law-**to-be.**
2) He has always believed that what is **to be**, will be.

870. To be sure (*adv.*) – with certainty

1) **To be sure**, we'll win the tournament.
2) The new system went online without a glitch, but you can **be sure** that there will be some problems down the road.

871. To blame (*adj.*) – responsible, to be blamed

1) They wanted to know who was **to blame** for the broken lamp.

2) As it turned out, John, their youngest, was **to blame.**

872. To date *(adj., adv.)* – until now, up to the present time

1) **To date**, less than ten students have registered for the class.
2) The university hasn't sent out registration materials **to date.**
3) **To date**, the data from our experiments is inconclusive.

** Up to date – in line with the current knowledge, modern methods, or recent styles

1) The research was based on the most **up to date** information.
2) The police promised to keep the family **up to date** on any progress they made in their ongoing investigation.

** Out of date – no longer current or useful, no longer in style

1) Her report was flawed because she had used **out of date** data.
2) Torn jeans and maxi-skirts are **out of date.**

873. Tone down *(v.)* – to make more moderate, to soften

1) She was asked to **tone down** and behave more professionally.
2) After **toning down** some inflammatory statements, he sent the letter.
3) She **toned down** the colors in her apartment.

** Tone up *(v.)* – to make stronger, healthier, brighter or more vigorous

1) He lifts weights twice a week to **tone up.**
2) A good decorator can **tone up** even the drabbest apartment.

874. Too bad *(adj.)* **– regrettable, unfortunate**

1) It's **too bad** Tom was laid off, he was an asset to the company.
2) It's **too bad** that the company is losing so many quality people.

875. Top off *(v.)* **– to complete or add a finishing touch**

1) We had salad for dinner and **topped** it **off** with ice cream sundaes.
2) They went to Australia on their holiday and **topped** it **off** with three days in Singapore on their way home.

876. Toss off *(v.)* **– to perform in a quick, easy, and casual manner, to drink quickly, to make or say easily without thinking hard**

1) She is so skilled at her job, she is able to **toss off** any problem that arises.
2) We **tossed off** a couple of margarita and then went to dinner.
3) His reputation as a speaker is based on his ability to **toss off** a witty remark whenever the audience appears to be getting restless.

877. To the best of one's knowledge – to the extent of one's knowledge

1) **To the best of my knowledge**, she is single.
2) He's an honest and sincere man, **to the best of my knowledge.**

878. To the fore *(adj., adv.)* **– in or to the front, forward, out into notice**

1) During our meeting, several key issues were brought **to the fore.**
2) His ability as a brilliant strategist came **to the fore** during the war.

879. To the good *(adv.)* – for the best, to one's benefit

1) We never made it to Seoul, but that was all **to the good** because we got home early and had a few days rest before returning to work.
2) After she sold the flowers, she was $80.00 **to the good.**

880. To the letter *(adv.)* – exactly, with attention to every detail

1) He followed her instructions **to the letter.**
2) The judge swore to perform her duties **to the letter** of the law.

881. To the wall *(adv.)* – in a trap or corner from which there seems to be no escape

1) His failing business drove him **to the wall.**
2) Her back was **to the wall**, but she's been in that position before and was certain she would find a way to succeed once again.
3) Losing her home due to her financial difficulty drove her **to the wall.**

882. Touch off *(v.)* – to cause a fire or explosion, to cause or start

1) Smoking in bed **touched off** the fire.
2) A disagreement with the general manager touched off the coach's decision to resign.

883. Touch on *(v.)* – to mention briefly

1) He **touched** lightly **on** the subject of pay raises and then went on to other topics.
2) Despite the banner headline on anti-abortion, the article barely **touched on** the issue of abortion.

884. Touch up (*v.*) **– to improve by making minor changes or additions, to paint over imperfections**

1) The apartment wasn't in too bad of a condition, it just needed a little **touching up.**
2) You should **touch up** those rust spots on your car before they get any worse.

885. Track down (*v.*) **– to locate by trailing or searching diligently**

1) The police hope to **track down** the rapist before he strikes again.
2) She spent nearly the whole day at the library before she was able to **track down** the information she needed for her research paper.

886. Trade in (*v.*) **– to give something old or used as a partial payment on a new purchase**

1) He's going to **trade in** his old computer for a newer model.
2) The car dealer tried to talk me into **trading in** my old car when I showed interest in buying a new one.

887. Trade on (*v.*) **– to use to the greatest possible advantage, to exploit**

1) The politician **traded on** his grandfather's reputation to win the election
2) The professor is **trading on** his reputation because he hasn't published anything in more than ten years.

888. Trial and error (*n.*) **– a way of solving problems by trying various possible ways until the best solution is found.**

1) Most scientists solve their problems by **trial and error.**
2) John solved his algebra problem by the method of **trial and error.**

3) Parents learn how to raise their children by **trial and error.**

889. Trick or treat *(n.)* **– a phrase said by children on Halloween when going from door to door asking for goodies and then playing tricks when goodies are not given – custom**

1) The children went out "**trick or treat**" on Halloween.
2) They knocked at people's doors yelling "**trick or treat.**"

890. Trip up *(v.)* **– to cause to stumble, fall, or to make a mistake**

1) The would-be purse-snatcher was **tripped up** by an off-duty policeman who was jogging nearby.
2) Quite a few of the students were **tripped up** on the exam by tricky questions.

891. Try on *(v.)* **– to put on to see the appearance or if it fits**

1) She's **tried on** several coats, but she hasn't found one she likes.
2) I'd like to **try on** this skirt to see how it looks on me.

892. Try out (for) *(v.)* **– to take or undergo a test in an attempt to qualify, to test by trial**

1) Companies **try out** hundreds of designs before they decide on one they will market.
2) She **tried out** pottery, but didn't like it much.
3) He **tried out for** the swim team but he wasn't chosen.

893. Tune in *(v.)* **– to adjust a radio or television to get a particular broadcast**

1) **Tune in** to Channel 9 to watch the drama "Wang Gun."

2) I adjusted the antenna on my radio, now I can **tune in** to Cool FM on 98.6.

894. Tune up *(v.)* **– to adjust a musical instrument to a desired key or sound, to adjust many parts of a machine so as to put it into proper conditions, to prepare oneself for a specified activity**

1) The band was just **tuning up** when we arrived at the club.
2) She took her car in for a **tune-up**.
3) You really need to **tune up** your skills before the final exam.

895. Turn away *(v.)* **– to send away, to reject**

1) She couldn't **turn away** her daughter.
2) At a bar, the customer was **turned away** because he had already had too many drinks.

896. Turn down *(v.)* **– to reject or refuse to accept, to reduce the loudness, brightness, or heat, etc.**

1) Management has **turned down** my request for a raise.
2) We called our neighbor and asked her to **turn down** her stereo because she had it turned up too loud.
3) **Turn down** the heat, it's too warm.

** **Turn up** *(v.)* **– to discover or be found by chance, to appear unexpectedly, to increase the volume**

1) I was going through some boxes and the credit cards which I thought I had lost **turned up**.
2) Our research **turned up** new information.
3) Please **turn up** the volume, I can't hear what they're saying.

897. Turn in *(v.)* **– to hand in, to give over, to return, to deliver or give information about, to go to bed**

1) You must **turn in** all assignments by the last week of the semester.
2) Tell Joe that he needs to **turn in** the videotape by Saturday.
3) An informer **turned** him **in** for the reward.
4) I'm tired, so I'm going to **turn in** early tonight.

898. Turn off *(v.)* **– to stop the operation or flow of, to leave by making a turn, to disgust, repel, or bore**

1) You forgot to **turn off** the heater, so I **turned** it **off**.
2) We should **turn off** at the next exit.
3) People who claim never to be wrong **turn** me **off**.

** **Turn on** *(n, v.)* **– to begin the operation, flow, activity, etc., to put on a light, to arouse the pleasant senses, to be very interested in**

1) The hallway light **turns on** and off automatically.
2) Please **turn on** the air conditioner.
3) Please **turn on** Channel 30.
4) He's very attractive and she gets **turned on** every time she sees him.
5) The astronomy course was such a **turn on** that I considered changing my major.

899. Turn of the century *(n.)* **– the time between the end of one century and the beginning of the next century**

1) The **turn of the century** is usually a time of strife and turmoil.
2) Automobiles were introduced at the **turn of the 19th century.**

900. Turn one's back on (v.) – to refuse to help

1) I thought he was my friend, but he **turned his back on** me when I needed help.
2) I will not **turn my back on** you when you need my help.

901. Turn one's stomach (v.) – to make one feel sick

1) The strong odor emanating from the room **turned his stomach.**
2) The accident was so horrible that it **turned her stomach.**

902. Turn out (v.) – to shut off, to produce or create, to result or end up, to attend or assemble as for a public event, to be found to be, to evict or eject, to turn inside out or empty

1) Please **turn out** the lights before you come to bed.
2) The new printer **turns out** sixty pages a minute.
3) Many workers have been displaced because robots are now used to **turn out** automobiles.
4) I don't know how the project will **turn out**, but I'll give it my best.
5) Thousands of people **turned out** for the rock concert.
6) The rumor that she was divorced **turned out** to be false.
7) The former tenants were **turned out** because they didn't pay the rent.
8) He **turned out** his pockets looking for the missing car keys.

903. Turn over (v.) – to rotate, overturn or shift position, to think about, to transfer to another

1) The engine won't **turn over** because the battery is dead.
2) Take a few days to **turn** the offer **over** in your mind before coming to a decision.
3) The defendant was **turned over** to state correction officers after his conviction.

**** Turnover** *(n)* **– the act of turning over, the number of workers hired to replace those who have left, a small pastry made with a filling, usually apple**

1) The **turnover** rate for teachers is pretty high in this district.
2) These apple **turnovers** are delicious.

904. Turn to *(v.)* **– to apply, appeal, or resort to something or someone for support, information, etc. to begin work, to refer to a specified page in a book, etc.**

1) The refugees **turned to** the Chinese Government for assistance, but were returned to North Korea instead of being granted asylum.
2) Please **turn to** the page 24 of the text.

905. Underage (*adj.*) **– below legal age**

1) He's **underage** and isn't allowed to buy alcoholic beverages.
2) He can't get a driver's license because he's **underage.**

906. Under arrest (*adj.*) **– held by the police or held in legal custody**

1) The woman was placed **under arrest** for shoplifting.

907. Under fire (*adj.*) **– under attack, blame, or accusations**

1) The troops came **under** heavy **fire** and were forced to retreat.
2) Japan has been **under fire** for refusing to correct their textbooks.
3) The new law came **under fire** before it was even enacted.

908. Under the table (*adv.*) **– in secret**

1) He earned a modest salary, but became rich through bribes received **under the table.**
2) She gave him some money **under the table.**

909. Up against (*adj.*) **– confronted with**

1) The plan to consolidate the two companies has come **up against** many difficulties.
2) John is **up against** the wall because he's going to lose his job.

910. Up front *(adj.)* – very honest, open

1) The Service Company was **up front** about their maintenance fees.
2) The mayor was **up front** about his political convictions and policies.

911. Ups and downs *(n.)* – good and bad periods

1) Everyone goes through periods of **ups and downs.**
2) A successful life has more **ups than downs.**

912. Up to *(prep.)* – dependent upon, occupied with, prepared for

1) The position is yours if you want it. It's really **up to** you.
2) Hearing a loud bang, the mother wondered what they were **up to.**
3) Although she had no proof, she was sure her neighbor was **up to** no good.
4) He's out of the hospital and feels he'll be **up to** returning to work in a week or two.

913. Use up *(v.)* – to consume completely

1) She **used up** all the butter making the cake and forgot to get more for tomorrow's breakfast.
2) He **used up** all his energy playing volleyball and now he doesn't want to go dancing.
3) We **used up** all the shampoo, so we have to buy more.

914. Vote (*v.*) – to vote

1) The Democratic Party is calling on every registered **voter** to vote in the upcoming election.

** Vote for (*v.*) – to vote in favor of

1) The voters **voted for** the tax increase by a margin of 2 – 1.

** Vote against (*v.*) – to vote to oppose

1) The school board **voted against** the proposal to hire more teachers.

915. Vote down (*v.*) – to defeat or to reject by vote

1) The proposed amendment was **voted down**, seven to three.
2) The Congressional Committee **voted down** the proposal to increase imports.

916. Vote in (*v.*) – to elect

1) He was **voted in** by a narrow margin, and yet we're happy with the way he's handling his job.
2) Mr. Kim was **voted in** at the annual shareholders meeting.

W

917. Wait on (v.) – to serve or attend as a waiter, waitress, sales clerk, etc.

1) They wanted to know why they hadn't been **waited on** yet because some other customers that had arrived after them were already being served.
2) She has a part-time job **waiting on** tables.

918. Wake up (v.) – to awake, to arouse conscious interest in

1) I usually **wake up** at about six o'clock.
2) He **woke up** late and missed his first class.
3) The speaker was so inspirational that it **woke up** many of his listeners to the plight of refugees.

919. Walk away from (v.) – to leave or abandon, to survive with little or no injury from an accident

1) I cannot respect anyone who **walks away from** raising their young children.
2) She was lucky to **walk away from** the accident without a scratch.

** Walk away with / walk off with (v.) – to steal and take away, to gain through an act of personal excellence

1) The thief must have **walked away with** the watch while I was helping another customer.
2) The Russian team **walked off with** the gold medal.

920. Walk of life (*n.*) – social class or occupation, ways of living

1) People from all **walks of life** attended the conference.
2) They objected to the wedding because their daughter and the man she wants to marry come from different **walks of life**.

921. Walk out (*v.*) – to go on strike, to leave suddenly, to desert

1) The teachers **walked out** in a move to get the district to listen to their demands for an increase in salary and other benefits.
2) When his promotion was denied, he just **walked out** of the office without saying a word.
3) She **walked out** on her three children and never returned.

922. Walk over / Walk all over (*v.*) – someone who controls or manipulates another person without respect or concern

1) I don't know why she lets him **walk** all **over** her.
2) He's such a wimp. He lets his wife **walk all over** him.

923. Warm up (*v.*) – to make or become warm or warmer, to become ready for action by exercising or practicing

1) The weather is going to **warm up** toward the end of the week.
2) I **warmed up** some soup for dinner.
3) Athletes **warm up** before their performance.

924. Wash out (*v.*) – to remove by washing or by the action of water

1) This shirt has a coffee stain that needs to be washed out.
2) Blueberry stains won't wash out.
3) Heavy rains washed out the corn field.

925. Waste away *(v.)* **– to become gradually thinner, weaker, feebler**

1) After his wife died, he just seemed to **waste away** with grief.

926. Waste one's breath *(v.)* **– no use to talk, to speak with no result**

1) Don't **waste your breath** talking to her, she doesn't accept advice.
2) You're **wasting your breath.** She's not going to change her mind.

927. Watch out *(v.)* **– use caution, or be alert**

1) **Watch out** for deer when driving on that road at night.
2) When you cross the street, **watch out** for traffic.

928. Water down *(v.)* **– to weaken or reduce the force of, to make less potent**

1) He thought it was the best article he had ever written until the editor **watered** it **down** to appease the newspaper's owner.
2) These drinks taste like they're **watered down.**

929. Ways and means *(n.)* **– methods and resources to do something, especially for defraying expenses**

1) He was selected to serve on the **ways and means** committee.
2) He has neither the **ways** nor the **means** to travel.

930. Wear down *(v.)* **– to decay as a result of use or friction, ruin**

1) Erosion **wore down** mountains over the years.
2) Teaching children is rewarding, but it can certainly **wear** you **down.**

** Wear out *(v.)* – to use or be used until useless, to exhaust or tireout

1) She wore her favorite jeans until they **wore out.**
2) He **wears out** two pairs of running shoes every three months or so.
3) I had a rough day and I'm **worn out.**
4) The long hike **wore** me **out.**
5) The students in her class are so active that they're **wearing** her **out.**

931. Wear off *(v.)* – to disappear gradually, to diminish by degrees

1) They've only been married for six months and their love is already beginning to **wear off.**
2) The names carved in the headstones **wore off** a long time ago.

932. Weed out *(v.)* – to get rid of what is not wanted

1) This weekend, I'll **weed out** my old clothes.
2) We need to **weed out** harmful Internet sites to protect children.

933. Weigh down *(v.)* – to burden or oppress

1) The heavy overnight snow **weighed down** the evergreens.
2) The Olympic coverage was **weighed down** by commercials.
3) The truck was **weighed down** with a heavy load of tiles.
4) The employees feel **weighed down** by the pending bankruptcy of the company.

934. What have you / What not *(n.)* – any of various other things that might also be mentioned

1) I introduced myself and told them my name, where I was from, why I was here and **what have you.**
2) We have to buy milk, bread, butter and **what not.**

935. What if – what would happen if, suppose that

1) **What** would you do **if** you were to find $1,000,000?
2) He wondered **what** would happen **if** he couldn't find a job after graduation.
3) So, **what if** I didn't go on this business trip?

936. A while ago *(adv.)* – a few minutes ago, not long ago

1) I saw him, although it was **a while ago.**
2) I left my dictionary here **a while ago** and now it's gone.

** A while back *(adv.)* – several weeks or months ago

1) She worked here **a while back**, but we haven't heard from her since she left.
2) I went fishing there **a while back** and was disappointed at the amount of pollution.

937. Wide of the mark *(adj., adv.)* – located away from a desired goal, deviated from something specified, not true

1) Her first two shots were **wide of the mark.**
2) His comments on the budget crisis were **wide of the mark.**

** Wide-awake *(adj.)* – completely awake

1) Someone called me at 3 a.m. After I hung up the phone, I wanted to go back to sleep but I couldn't because I was **wide-awake.**

938. Win out (over) *(v.)* – to succeed or prevail

1) Hard work and diligence will usually **win out over** smooth talk.

**** Win one's way** *(adj.)* **– to succeed in life**

1) He **won his way** into her heart because he has a great sense of humor and a gentle nature.

939. Win over *(v.)* **– to persuade to be on one's side**

1) He **won** her **over** just by being himself.
2) His clear presentation and strong arguments finally **won** them **over**.

940. Wind up *(v.)* **– to come to an end, finish, to tighten**

1) The movie **winds up** with the typical happy ending.
2) I'll **wind up** what I'm doing and join you at the restaurant in about a half hour.
3) He woke up late because he's forgot to **wind up** his alarm clock.

941. Wipe off *(v.)* **– to remove from the surface by wiping**

1) This table needs to be **wiped off**.
2) **Wipe off** the television screen.

**** Wipe out** *(v.)* **– to remove, erase or wipe by rubbing, to destroy**

1) She sprayed the stain remover on and then **wiped out** the stain.
2) The tornado **wiped out** dozens of homes at a local resort.
3) Today's confrontation **wiped out** any possibility of a quick end to the hostilities.

942. Within reason *(adj., adv.)* **– moderate, within the limit of good sense**

1) The company is willing, **within reason**, to accommodate the demands of striking workers.
2) Her father promised to buy her any car she wanted, **within reason**.

943. With good grace (adv.) – graciously, kindly and politely

1) They always acted **with good grace**, even when things didn't go their way.
2) My late grandmother used to treat people **with good grace.**

** With bad grace (adv.) – disgracefully

1) The team embarrassed its coach by taking the latest lost with **bad grace.**

944. With no strings attached (adv.) – without any condition attached

1) He said he wanted to help her fix her car and that he would do it **with no strings attached.**
2) I will help you finish this project **with no strings attached.**

945. With open arms (adv.) – gladly, eagerly

1) After a long separation, her family welcomed her home **with open arms.**
2) I know we broke up, but if you want to get back together I'll greet you **with open arms.**

946. Without fail (adv.) – certainly

1) They paid their mortgage every month for 30 years **without fail.**
2) He promised his teacher that from now on he'd be on time for class **without fail.**

947. With the best (of) (adv.) – as well as, as good as

1) He can play basketball **with the best of** them.
2) She speaks English **with the best of** native speakers.

948. Word for word (*adv.*) – without changing a word, in exactly the same words

1) The reporter wrote down what was said **word for word.**
2) I remember what you said **word for word.**

949. Worked up (*adj.*) – excited, angry, or worried

1) His wife gets all **worked up** whenever he comes home a few hours late.
2) He was all **worked up** because he failed the test, however we reminded him that it wasn't the end of the world.

950. Work off (*v.*) – to get rid of something

1) She constantly exercises to **work off** excess weight.
2) He has **worked off** his anger and he is calm now.
3) Jogging is an excellent way to **work off** unwanted pounds.

951. Work on (*v.*) – to affect, to have an effect on, to persuade

1) Since his retirement, he keeps busy **working on** a variety of small community projects.
2) The President is **working on** perceived fence sitters in an effort to get his tax reform initiatives through the finance committee.

952. Work out (*v.*) – to develop, to prove successful or suitable, to exercise

1) After months of wrangling, an agreement was finally **worked out.**
2) The administration **worked out** a new schedule that will benefit all employees.
3) The government has been trying to **work out** a new approach to overhauling the national business system since last year.
4) I see her **working out** at the gym every now and then.

953. **Wrapped up in** (*adj.*) – thinking only in something

1) I'm sorry I haven't called you, as I've been **wrapped up in** searching for a job.
2) He is **wrapped up in** his final project and rarely has time to go out.
3) She's **wrapped up in** herself and doesn't think of anyone else.

** **Wrap up** (*v.*) – to wrap, to end, to dress warmly

1) Please **wrap** this **up**, it's a gift.
2) I should be able to **wrap up** my work in an hour or so and go home.
3) Be sure to **wrap up** today. It's freezing outside.

954. **Write down** (*v.*) – to put in writing

1) She **wrote down** the address and phone number in her phonebook.
2) I just bought a dictaphone, so now I just dictate and my secretary **writes** everything **down**.

** **Write off** (*v.*) – to cancel as a loss, to offset

1) Western nations are considering **writing off** all existing Third World loans.
2) He filed for bankruptcy hoping to **write off** his debts.

** **Write out** (*v.*) – to write in full

1) Please **write out** your full name on the application form.

** **Write up** (*v.*) – to write a report or description of

1) Reporters were busy **writing up** the articles for their newspapers when the new fire began.
2) The scientist **wrote up** the results of his experiment.
3) I was asked to **write up** a summary of the lecture.

Y

955. Year-around / Year-round (*adj.*) – operating all year, yearlong

1) Indoor rinks have turned ice skating into a **year-around** sport.
2) Athletes may play their sport only in season, although they get the **year-round** training.

** Yearlong (*adj.*) – asting throughout the year

1) A **yearlong** drought was a major factor in starting the massive forest fire.
2) It seems as if school is becoming a **yearlong** institution for many of today's students.

956. Year-end (*adj.*) – made or occurring at the end of the year

1) Employees who work in the company's accounting office have to work this weekend compiling **year-end** reports.
2) A **year-end** upsurge in the price of oil has had a disastrous effect on low-income families.
3) Many people tend to overly drink at the annual **year-end** party and many of them drive home while they are intoxicated.

957. Yearn for (*v.*) – to be filled with longing

1) She **yearns for** a nice companion; someone who will bring joy to her lonely life.
2) He yearns for a European vacation and it's his greatest yearning.

958. Yield (*v.*) – to reveal

1) Through scientific discovery, the cosmos, little by little, has begun to **yield** its secrets.
2) The excavation of the king's tomb **yielded** important information about life during the period of his reign.

본문해석

A

1. Abide (by)(*v.*) – (약속, 협정, 결의, 규칙 등을) 지키다. 따르다.

1) 노동자들은 자신들이 지난 주에 서명한 협정을 준수하겠다고 약속했다.
2) 선수들은 심판의 결정에 따라야만 한다.
3) 저는 회사의 규정과 규칙을 준수하겠습니다.
4) 축구 선수들은 규칙을 지키면서 경기를 했다.

** Abiding (*adj.*) – 영원한, 불변의

1) 그녀는 그에 대한 불변의 사랑을 가지고 있다.
2) 그는 축구선수가 되겠다는 불변의 꿈을 가지고 있다.

2. About to (*adj.*) – 막 ~하려던 참의, 거의 준비가 된, ~할 작정인

1) 경보가 울렸을 때 그는 막 은행을 떠나려던 참이었다.
2) 그녀는 세탁사업을 시작할 준비가 거의 다 되었다.
3) 나는 숙제를 거의 끝내었다.
4) 나는 그와 어떤 일도 하지 않으려는 참이다.

3. According to (*prep.*) – ~에 의하면, ~에 의해서

1) 일기예보에 따르면 오늘 오후에는 비가 올 것이다.
2) 지시에 따라서 계속 진행해라.
3) 지시에 따라서 그것을 준비해라.

** Accordingly (*adv.*) – 따라서, 그에 맞게

1) 학생들은 수업 중에 적절히 행동해야 한다.
2) 학생들은 모든 교육과정을 마쳤으며 그에 따라서 성적을 받고 졸업을 할 수 있을 것이다.

4. Account for (*v.*) – 설명하다, 책임 또는 원인이 되다.

1) 너는 시험에 떨어진 이유를 설명해야만 한다.
2) 그 남자는 아내가 쓴 1원까지 설명하도록 만든다.
3) 교통사고가 매년 많은 사람들의 죽음에 책임이 있다.

** Accountable (*adj.*) – 책임 있는, 자신의 행동에 대해 해명할 의무가 있는

1) 환경부 장관과 대통령에게 자연 환경 파괴에 대한 책임을 물어야 한다.

2) 그는 그가 한 모든 일에 책임을 져야 한다.

**** Answer for (*v.*) – 책임지다.**

1) 모든 사람들은 그 자신들의 행동에 대해서 책임을 져야만 한다.
2) 너는 너의 동생을 책임질 수 없다.

**** Answerable (*adj.*) – 책임있는**

1) 뇌물과 불공정한 행위에 연루된 부패 정치인들은 사회에 대한 책임을 져야하고 그들의 직위들로부터 사임하여야 한다.

5. Against time / Against the clock (*adv.*) – 시간을 다투어, 기한에 임박해서

1) 우리는 시간을 다투어 일했으나, 시간에 맞추어 과제를 끝마칠 수 있었다.
2) 기사 마감시간이 기자들이 보통 시간을 다투어 일하는 이유이다.
3) 기한에 임박해서 일하는 것은 긴장이 많이 된다.

6. Ahead (*adv.*) – 미리, 전에, 앞에

1) 나는 최소한 기차출발 이틀 전에는 표를 사야만 한다.
2) 계속하세요.
3) 앞쪽에 교통사고가 났다.

**** Get ahead (*v.*) – 성공하다. 승진하다.**

1) 나는 성공하기 위해 열심히 일한다.
2) 너의 직장에서 승진하기 위해서, 너는 더 열심히 일해야만 한다.

**** Ahead of the game (*adj., adv.*) – 앞서는, 유리한**

1) 미적분에 대한 그녀의 지식은 그녀가 수학시험에서 앞서게 만들었다.
2) 나는 앞서고 싶다. 그래서 수학시간 전에 미리 다음 장을 예습한다.

**** Ahead of time (*adv.*) – 예정시간보다 일찍**

1) 런던에서 오는 비행기는 예정보다 일찍 도착하였다.
2) 그는 예정보다 일찍 도착했다, 그래서 나는 당장 나갈 준비가 되어있지 않았다.

7. Add up (*v.*) (계산, 이치 등이) – 맞다.

1) 이 숫자들은 계산이 맞지 않는다. 그래서 너는 그것들을 확인해 볼 필요가 있다.
2) 그의 이야기는 다른 증인들의 이야기와 비교했을 때 조리가 맞지 않는다.

**** Add up to (*v.*) – 총계 하다. 결과를 가져오다. 의미하다.**

1) 매달 나오는 청구서 총계가 $1,400 이 되었다.
2) 몇 일간의 비가 저지대에 홍수를 가져왔다.
3) 음주운전은 종종 심각한 사고를 초래한다.

8. All at once (*adv.*) **– 동시에, 갑자기**

1) 그녀는 동시에 여러 가지 일을 하려고 했기 때문에 시험에서 떨어졌다.
2) 갑자기 한 남자가 화를 내어 욕설을 하기 시작했다.
3) 대개 나쁜 일들은 동시에 발생하는 것 같다.

**** All of a sudden** (*adv.*) **– 갑자기**

1) 그가 차를 운전하고 있었다. 그리고 갑자기 한 술취한 사람이 길로 뛰어들어 왔다.

9. All in all (*adv.*) **– 전반적으로**

1) 전반적으로, 오늘은 힘든 날이었지만 생산적인 날이었다.
2) 전반적으로, 그 영화는 내가 생각했던 것만큼 무섭지는 않았다.

10. All in a day's work – 예상되는 일상적인 일들 (대개 부정적인 의미로)

1) 그녀의 일은 벅찬 일이지만, 그녀는 문서처리, 오랜 노동시간과 요구 많은 소비자들을 일상적인 일들로 생각한다.
2) 그것은 모두 일상적인 일들이야. 그러니 순응해서 잘 해라.

**** All in – 매우 피곤한**

1) 경기가 끝났을 때, 축구 선수들은 매우 피곤해 있었다.
2) 다양한 것들에 대한 소비자들의 불만을 해결한 후 그녀는 매우 피곤했다. 그러나 그것은 일상적인 일이다.

11. All kinds of (*adj.*) **– 여러 종류의, 많은**

1) 미국에서는, 잡화점과 약국에서 약과 다양한 종류의 다른 상품들을 판다.
2) 식료품점에 많은 종류의 과일과 채소들이 있다.
3) 나의 친구들은 내게 많은 충고를 했지만, 나는 여전히 내가 하고 싶은 것들을 했다.

12. All of (*adj.*) **– 전부**

1) 그는 휴가 전부를 일하는데 써버렸다는 것을 믿을 수가 없었다.
2) 이것이 지금 내가 가진 돈의 전부이다.

13. All over (*adv.*) **– 도처에, 여러 곳에, 끝난**

1) 나는 나의 열쇠들을 찾을 수가 없다. 그리고 나는 여러 곳을 찾아보았다.
2) 나는 열이 나고 온몸이 아프다.
3) 그들의 관계는 이제 끝났다.

14. All the time (*adv.*) **– 매우 종종, 항상**

1) 사람들은 매우 종종 실수를 한다.
2) 나는 좋은 점수를 원하기 때문에 늘 공부를 한다.

** All the way (*adv.*) – 처음부터 끝까지, 완전히 동의하는

1) 등산객들은 정상에 오른 다음에 기진맥진했다.
2) 그 회사의 경영진들은 회의에서 노동자들의 요구에 완전히 동의하지는 않을 것이다.

** All along (*adv.*) – 줄곧, 항상

1) 나는 그가 선거에서 이길 것이라는 것을 줄곧 알았다.
2) 그녀는 그가 그녀를 속인다는 것을 항상 알았다.

15. Alongside of (*adv., prep.*) – ~와 접하여 나란히, ~와 함께

1) 그녀는 남편과 나란히 복도를 걸었다.
2) 소년들이 소녀들과 함께 앉았다.

16. A lot (of) (*adj., adv.*) – 많은

1) 나는 오늘 오후에 할 일이 많다.
2) 나는 그 영화를 매우 재미있게 보았지만, 내 생각에 조금 긴 것 같았다.

** Any number of (*n.*) – 많은

1) 겁먹지 말자, 그녀는 많은 이유 때문에 늦을 수도 있다.
2) 문제들은 종종 많은 해법을 가지고 있다.

17. Anything but (*adv.*) – 반대로

1) 그는 그가 임시로 해고되었을 때 결코 행복하지 않았다.
2) 그녀는 체계적으로 준비성이 없어 승진 하지 못했다.

18. Apple of one's eye (*n.*) – 무척 사랑스러운 것

1) 그녀는 그녀의 아버지에게 무척 사랑스러운 존재이다.
2) 그는 아들을 매우 끔찍이 사랑한다.

19. Around the clock (*adv.*) – (24시간 동안) 하루 종일 계속해서

1) 직원들은 일을 제시간에 끝내기 위해서 하루 종일 일을 했다.
2) 많은 편의점들은 하루 종일 문을 연다.
3) 어떤 미국 공장들은 하루 종일 조업을 한다.

20. Around the corner (*adv.*) – 가까이, 곧 다가올

1) 그 약국은 도서관에서 가까운 곳에 위치해있다.
2) 봄이 곧 다가올 것이다.

21. As best as one can (*adv.*) – 할 수 있는 한 최대로, 최선을 다해

1) 나는 최선을 다했다, 그러나 결과가 어떻게 나올지는 모르겠다.

2) 그녀는 항상 최선을 다한다.
3) 그는 다리가 아픔에도 불구하고 그가 할 수 있는 한 최선을 다해 달렸다.

22. As far as / so far as (*adv.*) – ~하는 한

1) 내가 아는 한 다음 주는 맑을 것이다.
2) 내가 아는 한 그 비행기는 정시에 도착할 것이다.

** As far as … goes (*adv.*) – 그 점에 관해서는, 사실은

1) 사실 사업이 성황 중이고 새 주문을 많이 받았다.
2) 콘서트에 대해 말하자면, 그것은 아주 형편없었다.

23. As follows – 다음과 같은

1) 당신을 해고하는 이유는 다음과 같다; 첫째, 당신은 지각이 잦고 일도 잘하지 못 한다.
2) 선적될 물건의 목록은 다음과 같다. 통조림 과일 100상자, 쌀25톤, 비료25톤과 12대의 트랙터이다.

24. As for (*prep.*) – ~에 대해 말한다면, ~에 관해서는

1) 그녀는 커피에 설탕과 프림을 넣는 것을 좋아하지만, 나에 대해 말한다면, 나는 블랙커피를 좋아한다.
2) 돈에 대해 말한다면, 그는 버는 것 보다는 쓰는 것을 좋아한다. 그래서 그는 머지않아 파산할 것이다.

25. As good as (*adv.*) – 거의 같은

1) 이 시계는 저 것과 성능은 거의 같지만 덜 비싸다.
2) 그 의자는 수리 후, 거의 새것과 같이 보였다.
3) 이것은 중고품이지만, 거의 새것과 다름이 없다.

** As much as (*adv.*) – 거의 같이, 같은 양으로

1) 나는 네가 지금 느끼는 것과 거의 같은 고통을 느껴 왔다.
2) 나는 네가 나를 생각하는 만큼 너를 생각한다.
3) 나는 네가 먹은 만큼 먹었다. 아마 더 먹었을 지도 모른다.

26. As if / As though (*conj.*) – 마치 ~처럼

1) 나의 개는 종종 무슨 일이 일어나고 있는 지 아는 것처럼 행동한다.
2) 내 고양이는 종종 나를 이해하는 것처럼 나를 바라본다.

27. As is (*adv.*) – 그대로, 보장 없이

1) 내가 만약에 너라면, 그 글을 그대로 놓아둘 것이다.
2) 보증 없이 산 물건은 반품할 수 없다.

28. As it were (*adv.*) **– 말하자면**

1) 그가 잡히기 전까지 그는, 말하자면, 갱들의 영웅이었다.
2) 요즘에는, 말하자면, 젊은이들은 다른 세계에 살고 있는 것 같다.

29. Ask for (*v., informal*) **– 문제를 자초하다. 요구하다.**

1) 만약 네가 운전면허 없이 계속 차를 운전한다면, 너는 화를 자초하는 것이다.
2) 그는 상사와 말다툼을 함으로써 화를 계속 자초한다.
3) 그 일자리 광고는 이력서와 사진을 요구한다.

30. Ask to / Ask over (*v., informal*) **– 초대하다.**

1) 나는 내 생일 잔치에 몇몇을 초대했다.
2) 나는 내 친구들 중 몇 명을 저녁 식사에 초대했다.

31. As long as / So long as (*conj.*) **– ~을 고려한다면, ~하는 한**

1) 내일까지 책을 반납하면, 연체료는 없습니다.
2) 당신은 원하는 대로 컴퓨터를 사용해도 좋습니다.
3) 당신이 규칙에 따라 플레이한다면, 우리와 함께 게임을 할 수 있다.

32. As of (*prep.*) **– (지정된 시간이나 날짜)~로써, ~까지, ~에**

1) 나는 오늘로써 25살 이다.
2) 오늘로써 모든 직원들은 근무시간 기록카드를 사용해야만 한다.
3) 나의 과제는 목요일까지이다.
4) 내 새로운 일은 월요일에 시작이다.

33. As soon as (*conj.*) **– ~하자마자, 즉시**

1) 회의가 끝나자마자 그의 전화와 관련해 내가 전화한다고 그에게 말해라.
2) 나는 학교가 끝나고 집에 오자마자 집안일을 한다.

34. As to (*prep.*) **– ~에 관해서, ~에 기본하여**

1) 그녀의 업무 수행능력에 약간의 불신이 있기 때문에 나는 그녀가 승진할 수 있을지 의심한다.
2) 승진은 근무연수와 근무성과를 기본으로 하여 주어진다.

35. As usual (*adv.*) **– 평소와 같이**

1) 그 공장은 화재 후 일주일 만에 다시 문을 열었고 평소와 같이 일을 한다.
2) 그는 회의에 여느 때와 같이 지각했다.

36. As well (*adv.*) **– 또한, 역시, 손익 없이**

1) 나는 사과도 좋아한다.

2) 나는 손익 없이 지금 포기할지도 몰라.

** As well as (*conj.*) – ~뿐만 아니라, 게다가

1) 나는 고전음악뿐만 아니라 락음악도 좋아한다.
2) 메리뿐만 아니라 낸시도 나의 가장 친한 친구들 중 한명이다.

37. As yet (*adv.*) – 아직

1) 그는 아직 내게 전화하지 않았다.
2) 우리는 아직 그녀가 어떤 대학에 다니고 싶어 하는지 모른다.

38. At all cost / at any cost (*adv.*) – 어떠한 대가를 치르더라도 꼭

1) 그는 꼭 북동부 명문대학에 다니고 싶어 했다.
2) 우리는 어떤 대가를 치루더라도 이 집을 사고 싶다.

39. At any rate (*adv.*) – 하여튼

1) 그 영화는 조금 길었지만, 어쨌든 재미있었다.
2) 우리는 비록 몇몇 쟁점들에 대해서 동의하지 않았지만, 어쨌든 합의 안에 도달했다.

40. At first (*adv.*) – 처음에, 시작할 때

1) 나는 처음에는 그녀를 좋아하지 않았지만, 지금은 내 가장 친한 친구들 중의 하나이다.
2) 처음에는 홈팀이 경기에 지는 것처럼 보였다.

** At first glance (*adj., adv.*) – 첫눈에

1) 그들은 첫눈에 그 집에 반했다.
2) 나는 첫눈에 그 과제의 성공에 대해 별로 희망이 없었다.

41. At / From the bottom of one's heart (*adv.*) – 마음 깊은 곳에

1) 그녀는 그것은 중요하지 않다고 말하지만, 마음 깊은 곳에서는, 정말로 피아노를 가지고 싶어 한다.
2) 진심으로 당신의 친절에 대해서 감사드립니다.
3) 진심으로 감사합니다.

** at heart (*adv.*) – 근본적으로, 마음으로는

1) 그는 별로 관대하지는 않지만, 근본은 착한 사람이다.
2) 그녀는 비열하게 행동하지만, 근본이 나쁜 사람은 아니다.

42. At home (*adj., adv.*) – 집에, 편안히

1) 죄송합니다만, 그녀는 지금 집에 없습니다.
2) 들어오셔서 편하게 계시기 바랍니다.

43. At last (*adv.*) **- 드디어, 마침내, 결국**

1) 마침내, 역사상 가장 길었던 축구 경기가 끝났다.
2) 그는 마침내 오래된 애인과 결혼했다.

44. At least (*adv.*) **- 적어도, ~보다 적지 않은**

1) 적어도 하루에 한 시간은 영어 공부를 해야만 한다.
2) 운전면허 시험 신청자격이 되기 위해서 운전자는 적어도 18살이 되어야만 한다.

45. At length (*adv.*) **- 자세히, 충분히**

1) 나는 그 사건을 자세히 설명하는 편지를 썼다.
2) 나는 그가 자세히 설명해 주기 전에는 그 노래를 이해하지 못했다.

46. At once (*adv.*) **- 즉시, 지체하지 않고**

1) 나는 이 비디오테이프를 즉시 반납해야 한다. 그렇지 않으면 벌금을 물어야 한다.
2) 나는 지금 즉시 일하러 돌아가야 한다.

47. At one time (*adv.*) **- 한꺼번에, 한번에**

1) 모든 일이 한꺼번에 일어나는 것 같았다.
2) 나는 매월 나오는 모든 청구서들을 한 번에 지불하기를 좋아한다.

**** At the same time** (*adv.*) **- 동시에, 그럼에도, 그러나**

1) 영화관에서, 내 앞에 앉았던 두 사람이 동시에 일어나서 내 시야를 가렸다.
2) 나는 그를 사랑한다. 동시에 그를 증오한다.
3) 그것이 내가 그를 두 번째 만난 것이었다. 그럼에도 나는 여전히 불편했다.

**** At one** (*adj.*) **- 조화로운, 동의 또는 합의 하는**

1) 숲 속으로 산책하는 것이 그녀를 자연과 동화되는 느낌을 갖도록 하였다.
2) 위원회의 의견은 그 자신의 의견과 같았다.
3) 김선생의 의견은 나의 의견과 같다.

48. At present (*adv.*) **- 현재**

1) 나는 지금 현재는 실업상태 이지만, 조만간 바뀌기를 희망한다.
2) 현재는 이 아파트는 임대로 내어 놓았지만, 오래지 않아 나갈 것이다.

49. At random (*adv.*) **- (계획, 순서 없이) 무작위로**

1) 복권 번호는 무작위로 선택된다.
2) 그 경쟁자들은 전화번호부에서 무작위로 선발되었다.

50. At stake (*adj.*) **– ~이 걸린, 문제가 있는, 위험에 처한**

1) 이 게임은 지역 우승컵이 걸린 중요한 경기이다.

2) 그들은 말다툼을 너무 많이 하기 때문에 그들의 관계는 위험에 처해 있다.

51. At best / at most – 기껏해야, 최대한

1) 그는 위대한 연주자는 아니지만 그래도 유능한 기타연주자 이다.

2) 그 새 컴퓨터는 19인치 모니터를 포함해서 최대한으로 잡아 2000불이다.

52. At the mercy of (*adj.*) **– ~의 손에 달려있는**

1) 어린이들은 종종 철칙도 없는 부정직한 어른들의 손에 달려있다.

2) 보모는 그녀 자신의 온전한 정신이 아이들의 기분에 달려 있는 것을 느꼈다.

53. At this rate / At that rate (*adv.*) **– 이(그)와 같은 속도로**

1) 만약 내 주식이 이 같은 속도로 계속 돈을 번다면, 나는 머지않아 부자가 될 것이다.

2) 만약 그런 속도로 계속 일을 한다면, 너는 결코 제시간에 일을 끝낼 수 없을 것이다.

54. At times (*adv.*) **– 이따금**

1) 이따금, 그녀는 우울해 하거나 풀이 죽어 보인다.

2) 나는 정기적으로 조부모님을 방문한다. 그리고 이따금 조그마한 선물을 가져간다.

55. At work (*adj.*) **– 직장에서 일하고 있는 중, 근무중**

1) "어머니 지금 어디 계시니?" "지금 직장에 계십니다."

2) 그는 일할 때 행복을 느낀다.

B

56. Back off (*v.*) – 포기하다, 물러서다.

1) 증거에 직면했을 때, 그는 그의 무죄주장을 포기했다.
2) 그는 과격한 판매여성에게 물러서라고 말했다.
3) 그 사람은 나의 개가 짖었을 때, 뒤로 물러섰다.

** Back out (*v.*) – 지키지 못하다. 취소하다. 그만두다.

1) 그녀는 그에게 새 차를 사도록 도와준다는 약속을 지키지 못했다.
2) 처음에 그들은 로마로 여행 갈 예정이었으나, 마지막 순간에 취소하였다.
3) 그는 채용제의에 승낙했으나, 연봉이 감소된다는 것을 알았을 때, 그만두었다.

57. Back up (*v.*) – 뒤로 움직이다. 지원하다. 보조하다. 컴퓨터 기록을 복사/저장하다.

1) 그 기사가 뒤로 물러났다, 그래서 다른 차가 지나갈 수 있었다.
2) 그는 아버지께 사업이 나아질 때까지 지원을 해달라고 요청했다.
3) 비상시에 자원봉사자들이 정규 직원들을 지원했다.
4) 나는 보통 나의 작업을 컴퓨터에 저장한다.

** Backup (*n.*) – 지원, 보조, 컴퓨터 작업의 복사본

1) 구조팀이 지원을 요청했다.
2) 나는 디스켓 몇 장에다 내 컴퓨터의 작업의 복사본을 만들었다.

58. Bang up (*v.*) – 세게 부딪쳐 엉망으로 만들다.

1) 그녀는 오토바이 사고에서 크게 다쳤다. 특히 그녀의 다리를 다쳤다.
2) 그녀의 차는 충돌에서 너무 크게 망가져서 완전손실로 보고해야 했다.

** Bang-up (*adj.*) – 매우 뛰어난, 성공적인, 신나는

1) 그들은 파티 준비를 매우 잘해 놓았다.
2) 그 축구팀은 경기를 매우 잘 하였고 게임에서 이겼다.

59. Bark up the wrong tree (*v.*) – 사람이나 액션을 잘못 선택하다. 실수하다.

1) 만약에 네가 나를 이길 수 있다고 생각한다면, 그것은 잘못 본 것이다.
2) 만약 그가 그녀가 자기를 사랑한다고 생각한다면 그것은 착각하고 있는 것이다.

60. Bear in mind (*v.*) – 명심하다.

1) 행복이 인생에서 가장 중요한 것이라는 것을 명심해라.
2) 성공하기 위해서는 열심히 일을 해야 한다. 또한 운도 따라야 한다는 것을 명심해라.

61. Bear with (*v.*) – 인내심을 가지다. 참다.

1) 그녀는 그 일이 처음이니, 그녀가 실수를 하더라도 부디 인내심을 가지기 바란다.
2) 나는 그의 상스러운 말을 참을 수가 없다.
3) 저에게 인내심을 가져주세요.

62. Beat around the bush (*v.*) – 요점을 말하지 않고 변죽만 울리다.

1) 우리는 대화를 했지만 그는 아무런 중요한 말도 하지 않고 대신에 빙빙 돌리기만 했다.
2) 그만 둘러대고 원하는 것을 말해라.
3) 빙빙 돌려 말하지 말고, 요점으로 들어가라.

63. Beat down (*v.*) – 정복하다. 이기다. 누르다. (가격 경쟁에서) 값을 내리다.

1) 침략자들은 종종 원주민들에게 이기려고 시도하지만, 거의 성공하지 못한다.
2) 그녀는 항상 그녀의 친구들 앞에서 그를 깎아 내린다.
3) 그녀는 대단한 구매자이다. 그녀는 항상 가격을 깎는다.
4) 김씨는 상담의 대가로 매 시간 $100을 받는다. 그러나 이씨는 훌륭한 협상자이기 때문에 쉽게 깎을 수 있다.

** Beat up (*v.*) – 두들겨 패다

1) 골목대장들이 새로 온 녀석을 두들겨 팼다.
2) 하루 밤새 심하게 술을 마신 후, 그는 마치 두들겨 맞은 듯한 느낌을 받았다.

64. Before long (*adv.*) –오래지 않아, 얼마 안 있어

1) 학기는 오래지 않아 끝이 날 것이다.
2) 그 가족은 IMF 동안에 헤어졌지만, 오래지 않아 다시 결합했다.

65. Behind bars (*adv.*) – 교도소에

1) 저 문 옆에 서있는 녀석은 결국 교도소에 갇히게 될 것이다.
2) 범죄를 저지르는 사람들은 종종 교도소에 갇힌다.

** Bar exam (*n.*) – 변호사 시험

1) 법학대학 졸업생들은 변호사가 되기 위해서 2년간의 수습사원기간 후에 시험을 통과해야 한다.

66. Behind the scenes (*adv.*) – 외부에 알려지지 않게, 내밀히

1) 우리 위원회는 편부 편모를 보조하기 위해서 외부에 알려지지 않게 일했다.

2) 대부분의 기업의 결정들은 내밀히 이루어진다.

67. Behind the times (*adj.*) **- 구식의, 시대에 뒤진**

1) 그 회사의 여자 직원들에 관한 정책은 시대에 뒤쳐져 있다.
2) 그의 정치적 소견은 구식이다.

** Behind time (*adj., adv.*) - 늦게, 예정보다 늦게

1) 음악가들이 늦게 도착해서, 음악회가 제시간보다 늦어졌다.
2) 내 시계는 20분 늦다.

68. Beside the point (*adj., adv.*) **- 요점을 벗어난, 다른**

1) "그것의 가격이 문제가 아니다."라고 그가 말했다. "품질이 내가 기대했던 것과 다르다."
2) 이기고 지는 것은 중요하지 않다. 게임을 어떻게 하는가가 중요한 것이다.

69. Best bet - 가장 안전하고 가장 좋은 방법

1) 너에게 가장 좋은 대책은 일단 아무 일이나 잡고 근무 경력을 쌓는 것이다.
2) 24번 도로가 아마 우리에게 최선의 선택일 것이다.

** Make a bet - 돈을 걸다.

1) 그는 종종 친구들과 축구 경기에 내기를 걸고 가끔은 그가 내기에서 이긴다.
2) 나는 월드컵 경기에서 한국 팀에게 돈을 걸었다.
3) 많은 사람들이 경마에 돈을 건다.

70. Better late than never (a cliché) - 늦게라도 하는 것이 아주 하지 않는 것보다는 낫다(속담).

1) 그녀는 세 시간이나 늦었다. 그리고는 "안 오는 것 보다는 낫다 "하고 말했다.
2) 비록 내가 중년의 나이이기는 하지만, 나는 악기를 연주하는 것을 배우고 싶다. 왜냐하면 늦더라도 안 하는 것보다는 낫기 때문이다.

71. Beyond question (*adj., adv.*) **- 틀림없는, 의심할 여지가 없는**

1) 이 전축의 뛰어난 음질은 틀림없다.
2) 그의 정직성과 성실성은 의심할 여지가 없다.

72. Black-and-white (*adj.*) **- 이면만 있는, 오직 옳고 그름 만으로 나누어지는**

1) 통일은 흑백논리의 문제가 아니다. 그것은 훨씬 더 복잡하다.
2) 현대적인 문제들은 흑백논리로 풀 수 있는 것이 거의 없다.

73. Black out (*v.*) **- 어둡게 하다. 금지하다. 의식을 잃다.**

1) 전쟁 동안에는, 국민들은 밤에 도시를 어둡게 하기 위해 창문을 덮어야만 했다.

2) 억압적인 정부는 반정부 신문의 모든 기사를 금지시켰다.

3) 그녀는 술을 너무 많이 마신 후 의식을 잃었다.

**** Blackout (*n.*) – 전기 공급 중단, 일시적인 의식 불명, 방송금지**

1) 폭풍우가 이 지역 일대에 큰 정전을 야기했다.

2) 너무 많은 술을 마시는 것은 의식불명을 일으킬 수 있다.

3) 정부는 모든 외신의 방송금지를 요구했다.

74. Blood is thicker than water (a cliché) – 피는 물보다 진하다.

1) 그 어머니는 아들의 꾸며낸 이야기가 거짓이라는 증거가 있음에도 피는 물보다 진하기 때문에 그것을 믿었다.

2) 그 어머니는 아들이 법들을 어겼음에 상관없이 피는 물보다 진하기 때문에 그녀의 아들의 편을 들었다.

75. Blow off (*v.*) – (압축된 가스, 증기, 공기, 또는 노여움 등을) 내뿜다.

1) 기차는 출발하기 전에 증기를 뿜어내곤 했다.

2) 축적화 된 화는 대개는 파괴적인 양상으로 나타난다.

3) 그가 소리를 지르는 것은 화를 표출하는 한 방법이다.

**** Bottle up (*v.*) – (출구 없이) 억제하다.**

1) 억제된 화는 스트레스와 연관된 병의 대표적인 원인이다.

2) 그녀의 불행한 결혼은 그녀에게 감정을 안으로 억제하도록 만들었다.

**** Blow up (*v.*) – 폭발하다. 화내다. 공기 주입으로 부풀리다. 확대하다.**

1) 최근의 인공위성이 발사되자마자 폭발했다.

2) 그는 화가 나면 엄청 성질을 부리는 경향이 있다.

3) 그는 여동생의 파티를 위해 풍선을 불었다.

4) 그림을 확대하는 것은 우리가 예상했던 것 보다 훨씬 더 비쌌다.

76. Blow out (*v.*) – 끄다. 갑자기 터지다. 전기배선이 녹아서 터지다.

1) 그 소녀는 생일 케이크 위의 촛불을 껐다.

2) 내가 고속도로를 달리는 동안 자동차의 타이어가 터졌다.

3) 퓨즈가 녹아 내렸을 때, 전기가 나갔다.

77. Blow over (*v.*) – 잠잠해지다. 한동안 후 중요하지 않게되다.

1) 기상학자들은 그 강한 태풍이 육지에 도달하기 전에 잠잠해지기를 희망하고 있다.

2) 최근의 정치적 추문은 빨리 잊혀졌다.

78. Blow the lid off (*v.*) **- 비밀로 감추어온 사실을 폭로하다.**

1) 그는 회사의 불법 자금거래 사실을 폭로하겠다고 협박했다.

2) 그 신문기자의 기사는 정부의 비밀을 폭로했다.

79. Brand-new (*adj.*) **- 아주 새 것의**

1) 나는 중고가 아니라 새 자동차를 샀다.

2) 그것은 새 TV 이다. 그래서 이렇게 빨리 수리를 받아야 할 필요가 있어서는 안 된다.

80. Break down (*v.*) **- 파괴, 부식, 분해 또는 고장나다. 감정의 자제를 못하다.**

1) 그 다리가 무너졌다.

2) 바위들은 오랜 시간에 걸쳐 부식되어 모래가 된다.

3) 차가 서울로 가는 도중에 고장이 났다.

4) 그녀의 아버지가 돌아가자, 그녀는 감정을 주체하지 못하고 울었다.

** Breakdown (*v.*) - 파괴, 정지, 육체적 정신적 붕괴, 항목화 된 자료의 분석이나 요점

1) 터널 안에서의 고장은 엄청난 교통대란을 초래했다.

2) 그녀의 남편이 죽었을 때 그녀는 신경쇠약에 걸렸다.

3) 이것은 완성된 새 집의 항목화 된 가격 분석이다.

81. Break even (*v.*) **- 이득과 손실이 비기다.**

1) 나는 두세 주식에서 돈을 잃었지만, 나의 대부분의 투자는 본전이었다.

2) 나는 이번 나의 투자에서 가까스로 본전이다.

** Break-even (*adj.*) - 본전인

1) 이번 달은 겨우 본전이다. 나는 조금도 저금을 할 수 없었다.

82. Break in / into (*v.*) **- 무력으로 침입하다. 끼어들다. 갑자기 ~하기 시작하다.**

1) 강도들은 뒷창을 이용하여 가게로 침입했다.

2) 어떤 이상한 사람이 우리가 대화하는 도중에 갑자기 말참견을 하였다.

3) 그 소녀는 슬픈 소식을 듣자마자 갑자기 울기 시작했다.

** Break-in (*n.*) - 무력을 사용한 불법침입

1) 내 바로 옆집에 지난 밤에 도둑이 들어서 VCR을 도둑맞았다.

83. Break out (*v.*) **- 피부염이 생기다. 갑자기 일어나다. 탈출하다.**

1) 고기를 먹었기 때문에 그녀에게 피부염이 생기기 시작했다. 그녀는 고기에 알레르기 반응을 보인다.

2) 단것은 내게 붉은 반점의 피부염이 생기도록 한다.

3) 미국 대사관 근처에서 갑자기 폭동이 일어났다.
4) 중동에서 갑자기 전쟁이 일어났다.
5) 밤사이 지역 교도소의 수감자 세 명이 탈출했다.

84. Break up (*v.*) – 헤어지다, 관계를 끝내다. 끝내다. 부수다.

1) 그는 최근에 여자 친구와 헤어졌지만, 여전히 그녀를 사랑한다.
2) John과 Lilly가 곧 헤어질 것이라는 이야기를 들었니?
3) 경찰이 재빨리 진입해서 폭동이 통제 불능의 상태가 되기 전에 진압하였다.
4) 빙산은 타이타닉과 같은 튼튼한 배를 부술 수 있을 만큼 충분히 강력하다.

**** Breakup (*n.*) – 갈라짐, 헤어짐**

1) 화산폭발을 통해서 땅이 갈라지는 것을 볼 수 있다.
2) 가정의 파괴는 계속적으로 복지단체들을 걱정하게 한다.

**** Break off (*v.*) – 갑자기 중지하다. 관계를 끝내다.**

1) 전화벨이 울렸을 때 우리는 갑자기 대화를 중단했다.
2) 그녀는 지난 주에 남자친구와 헤어졌다.

**** Break with (*v.*) – 멤버쉽을 끝내다. 관계를 끝내다.**

1) 그 회사와 관계를 끝내기로 한 그의 결정은 개인적인 사유에 있다.
2) 그들은 전통을 깨고 바다 옆에서 결혼할 것이다.

85. Break one's heart (*v.*) – 깊게 상심 시키다. 슬프게 하다.

1) 동물들이 학대 받는 것을 보면 나의 마음이 슬프다.
2) 쓸모없고 잔인한 모든 종류의 실험으로 죽어가는 동물을 보는 것은 나를 몹시 슬프게 했다.

86. Bring about (*v.*) – ~을 가져오다. ~을 야기하다.

1) 검소뿐만이 아니라 부지런함은 그에게 성공을 가져다 주었다.
2) 나는 내 생활방식에 약간 변화를 주어야 할 필요가 있다.

87. Bring on (*v.*) – ~의 결과를 가져오다.

1) 심장질환은 종종 과도한 흡연, 운동 부족과 유전적 장애 때문에 야기된다.
2) 매운 음식의 과다 섭취가 소화불량을 초래했다.

88. Bring around (*v.*) – 설득하다. 생각을 바꾸게 하다.

1) 경영진은 그 생각에 반대한다. 그래서 우리는 그들을 우리가 생각하는 식으로 설득할 방법을 찾아야한다.
2) 오랜 시간의 토론 후에, 우리는 마침내 그들을 우리 편으로 설득했다.

89. Bring out (*v.*) (가치등을) - 높이다. 끌어내다. 보여주다. 드러내다.

1) 그녀는 항상 다른 사람들에서 최선을 끌어내는 것 같다.
2) 그 밴드는 이번 가을 새로운 음반을 발표할 것이다.
3) 대중들은 그 사건에 관한 진실을 알기를 원하지만, 정부는 그것이 표를 떨어뜨릴 것이기 때문에 분명히 그것을 드러내지 않기를 원한다.
4) 조미료는 음식에 맛을 줄 수 있다.

90. Bring in (*v.*) - 들여오다. 돈을 벌어들이다. 생산하다. 평결하다.

1) 그 가게는 약간의 다른 스타일의 옷을 들여왔다.
2) 대형백화점들은 더 많은 고객들을 유치하기위해 경쟁한다. 그리고 그들의 연간 매출은 수백만 달러를 벌어들인다.
3) 그 빌딩 프로젝트에 새로운 건축사가 투입되었다.
4) 배심원은 증거 부족으로 인해서 무죄를 평결했다.
5) 판사는 피고에게 무죄를 선고했다.

91. Bring off (*v.*) - 성공적으로 완수하다.

1) 나는 내가 그것에 성공할 수 있을 지 확신하지 못했다.
2) 나는 결국 그 거래를 성사시켰다.
3) 나는 그 거래를 성사시킬 수 있기를 바란다.

92. Bring to light (*v.*) - 발굴해 내다. 드러내다. 알려지다.

1) 오랜 시간의 은폐 후에 그 사건의 진상이 알려졌다.
2) 그 작가의 가장 최신작품은 그의 죽음 후에야 알려졌다.
3) 우리의 연구는 내년에 발표될 것이다.

93. Bring up (*v.*) - 양육하다, 언급하다.

1) 그녀는 좋은 환경에서 자녀를 양육하길 원한다.
2) 그 회의에서 몇몇의 중요한 쟁점들이 언급되었다.

94. Brush off (*v.*) - 가벼이 여기다. 털다.

1) 그녀는 그의 충고를 가벼이 여겼다.
2) 나는 내 차에 쌓인 눈을 치워야 한다.

** Brush-off (*n.*) - 퉁명스러운 거절

1) 그는 그녀에게 친절하게 말하려고 노력했으나, 그녀는 퉁명스럽게 거절했다.

95. Brush up / brush up on (*v.*) - 어느 특정 분야에 대한 지식이나 기억 기술 등을 새로이 하다.

1) 내가 내년 여름에 스페인에 가기 전에 내 스페인어 실력을 새롭게 해야 할 필요가 있다.
2) 나는 내가 배웠던 수학을 많이 잊었다. 이번 학기에 다시 공부하여 기억을 되살릴 것이다.

96. Build up (*v.*) – 꾸준히 증가 시키다. 향상 시키다. 점진적으로 건축을 하다.

1) 신용을 향상시키기 위해서 너는 제때에 납부금을 내야만 한다.
2) 내 건강을 증진시키기 위해 나는 매일 운동을 한다.
3) 이 지역은 최근 몇 년 간 점진적으로 개발이 되어왔다.

97. Burn out (*v.*) – 연료부족으로 타는 것이 중단되다. 지치다. 과로하다.

1) 나무가 더 없었기 때문에 캠프파이어가 꺼졌다.
2) 나는 시험공부를 몇 주 간 한 뒤 완전히 지쳤다.
3) 나는 일을 너무 오랜 시간하기 때문에 과로한다.

98. Burn up (*v.*) – 완전히 태워 없애다. 완전히 타다. 성나게 하다.

1) 결혼 후 그녀는 옛 남자친구들이 보낸 편지를 모두 불태워 버렸다.
2) 그녀가 세 번 지불금을 못 내자 그 은행은 그녀의 차를 압류해 버렸다. 그것은 그녀를 매우 화나게 했다.

** Burn down (*v.*) – 다 태워 없애다.

1) 한 사람의 부주의한 흡연자가 온 숲을 다 태워 버릴 수 있다.
2) 그 집은 전기 선 이상으로 다 타버렸다.
3) 그 초의 심지는 매우 빨리 탔다.

** Burn one's bridges (a clich) (속담) – 나갈 길이 없는 처지에 자신을 두다. 관계를 나쁘게 하다. 어려운 처지에 있게 되다.

1) 관리자와 다툼으로 인해 어려운 처지에 놓이지 말아라.
2) 그녀는 친구들 앞에서 무례하게 행동했기 때문에 관계를 나쁘게 만들었다.

99. Butter up (*v.*) – 아첨하여 이득을 얻으려고 하다.

1) 어떤 학생들은 점수를 잘 맞기 위해서 선생님에게 아첨을 한다.
2) 그가 아무리 그녀에게 아첨을 했어도 그녀는 그와 데이트 하지 않았을 것이다.
3) 종종 사장은 사원들에게 저녁을 사줌으로써 그들에게 잘 보이려고 한다. 이는 물론 그들이 더 열심히 일하기를 원하기 때문이다.
4) 나는 네가 아첨을 하려고 한다고 생각한다.

** Buy off (*v.*) – 뇌물로 매수하다.

1) 어떤 로비스트들은 많은 돈을 가지고 정치인들을 매수하려고 시도한다.

** Buy out (*v.*) – ~의 전부를 얻기 위해 누군가의 몫을 사들이다.

1) 그는 그 회사의 지분의 전부를 사들였고, 완전히 회사를 장악했다.
2) 나는 그 회사를 소유하기 위해서 내 동업자의 지분을 사길 원한다.

100. By and large (*adv.*) – 대체적으로, 전체적으로

1) 우리는 대체적으로 좋은 관계를 가지고 있다.
2) 대체적으로 그 여행은 좋았지만, 너무 비쌌다.
3) 그는 여기저기에서 약간의 작은 실수들을 했지만, 전체적으로 일을 잘했다.

101. By chance (*adv.*) – 우연히

1) 많은 새로운 백신들이 우연히 발견된다.
2) 우리는 우연히 만났지만 원해서 결혼했다.
3) 새 백신의 발견은 우연이었다.

102. By means of (*prep.*) – ~을 사용하여, ~의 도움으로

1) 그들은 나무 구명뗏목을 사용하여 강을 건넜다.
2) 그는 작은 보트를 사용하여 강을 건넜다.

**** By way of (*prep.*) – ~을 경유하여, ~의 방법 또는 수단으로**

1) 나는 서울에서 샌프란시스코를 경유하여 클리블랜드까지 비행기를 타고 갔다.
2) 우리가 기념을 하기 위해서 무엇을 하도록 제안하겠니?

103. By all means (*adv.*) – 네, 물론이죠. 틀림없이

1) "제가 여기 앉아도 될까요?" "물론이죠."
2) 너는 틀림없이 그녀에게 전화를 걸어야만 한다.
3) 이번 주에 꼭 만나자.

**** By no means (*adv.*) – 결코 ~이 아닌, 전혀 아닌**

1) "제가 오늘 당신 차를 사용해도 될까요?" "결코 안 된다."
2) 나는 결코 바보가 아니다.

104. By word of mouth (*prep.*) – 사람들의 입에서 입으로

1) 비극적 사고에 대한 소식이 사람들의 입에서 입으로 빨리 퍼졌다.
2) 나는 그 이야기를 사람들로 부터 전해 들었다.

C

105. Call down (*v.*) – 야단치다.

1) 오늘 그 치과의사는 그의 조수가 환자를 조심해서 다루지 않았기 때문에 야단을 쳤다. 어제도 또한 그녀를 야단쳤다.

106. Call for (*v.*) – 요구하다. 필요로 하다. 와서 가지고 가다. 데리러(오)가다.

1) 섬세한 수술 과정은 정밀함을 필요로 한다.
2) 이 실험은 정확한 시간조절을 필요로 한다. 그렇지 않으면 모든 것이 실패로 돌아갈 것이다.
3) 그녀는 영화 보러 가기 위해서 나를 데리러 와야 하지만, 아직까지 오지 않았다.

** Call on (*v.*) – 요청하다. 호소하다. 방문하다. 발언을 요청하다.

1) 시장은 시민들에게 여름동안 물과 전기를 절약해 줄 것을 요청했다.
2) 나는 내가 서울에 있는 동안 친구를 방문했다.
3) 적십자사는 헌혈을 하라고 자원자들에게 호소한다.
4) 그의 선생님이 질문을 했을 때, 그는 답을 몰랐다.

107. Call it a day (*v.*) – 오늘은 이만하다. 중지하다.

1) 우리는 단지 아홉 홀만 치고 그만했다.
2) 오늘은 이만하자, 우리는 하루 일은 충분히 했다.

108. Call off (*v.*) – 취소하다.

1) 다가오는 폭풍우 때문에 우리는 소풍을 취소해야만 했다.
2) 그들은 정말로 사랑하는지 확신이 서지 않았기 때문에 그 결혼식은 취소되었다.

109. Call into question (*v.*) – 의구심을 갖다.

1) 회사의 계좌에서 얼마간의 돈이 없어진 것을 그들이 발견했을 때, 그들은 그의 정직성에 의구심을 가졌다.

110. Call up (*v.*) – 전화하다. 생각나게 하다. 소환 또는 징집하다.

1) 저녁 여섯시에 전화해라.
2) 그 사진들은 그리스에서의 휴가에 대한 기억들을 떠올리게 한다.
3) 법원은 지역 주민들을 배심원 의무를 하게 하기위해 불렀다.
4) 정부는 젊은이들을 징집했다.

** Call to mind (*v.*) – 생각나게 하다.

1) 너의 말은 내가 너와 논의 하고 싶어 했던 것을 생각나게 한다.

111. Come / Bring to the fore (*v.*) 지도자의 위치에 서다. 표면화 되다. 대중에 파고들다.

1) 그 전쟁 중에, 약간의 훌륭한 지도자들이 등장했다.
2) 약간의 뛰어난 젊은 사업가들이 불황기 중에 등장했다.
3) 최근 몇 년간에 더욱 복잡한 휴대폰들이 등장했다.

112. Cancel out (*v.*) – 균형을 맞추다. 상쇄시키다.

1) 나는 인체 해부학에서 받은 "D"를 상쇄시킬 수 있도록 중국 문학에서는 "A"를 받았다.
2) 그의 부는 그가 정식 교육을 별로 받지 못한 것을 상쇄시켰다.

113. Can't help but / cannot but (*v.*) – ~하지 않을 수 없다. ~하는 수 밖에 없다.

1) 고양이들이 놀고 있는 것을 볼 때, 나는 웃지 않을 수 없다.
2) 그가 병역에 소집되었을 때, 그는 나라에 봉사를 하지 않을 수 없었다.

114. Cannot see the wood for the trees / Can't see the forest for the trees – (*v.*) 나무는 보고 숲을 못 본다. 작은 부분에 집중하느라 전체를 이해하거나 또는 그 전체의 가치를 알지 못하다.

1) 너는 나무를 보느라고 숲은 보지 못하는 구나. 두세 개의 작은 부분만을 보는 대신에 큰 그림을 보려고 노력해보라.

115. Car pool (*n.*) – (일하러 가거나, 학교 가거나, 휴가 갈 때) 사람들이 교대로 차를 이용하는 것. 카풀

1) 이번 주는 네가 카풀에서 운전할 차례다.
2) 카풀을 하는 것은 종종 불편하기는 하지만 경제적이다.

116. Care for (*v.*) – 좋아하다. 돌보다.

1) 커피 한잔 더 하시겠어요?
2) 나는 랩 음악을 좋아하지 않는다.
3) 나는 내 애완동물들을 돌본다.

117. Carrot and stick (*n.*) – 보상과 벌(당근과 채찍)

1) 그 회사는 사원들과 협상을 하는데 당근과 채찍을 둘다 사용했다.

118. Carry away (*v.*) – 감정이 북 받치다. ~에 넋을 잃다.

1) 나는 국가가 연주되는 것을 들었을 때, 감정이 북 받쳐서 울었다.

2) 우리 선수들이 월드컵 경기에서 이겼을 때, 대부분의 사람들은 감격해서 울었다.

119. Carry a torch (*v.*) – 계속해서 애정을 품다. 대단한 충성심을 보이다. 다른 사람을 돕기 위해 자발적으로 희생하다. 총대를 매다.

1) 그들의 관계가 끝났음에도 불구하고, 그는 여전히 그녀를 대단히 좋아한다.
2) 그 사람이 심각한 곤경에 빠졌을 때, 그의 추종자 몇 명은 기꺼이 그를 위해 희생을 하려했다.

120. Carry off (*v.*) – 들어내다. 수상하다.

1) 그들은 쓰레기를 들어내 치웠고, 그 일을 한 돈을 지불 받았다.
2) 그 선수는 2004년의 아테네 올림픽에서 금메달을 받길 희망한다.

**** Carry out (*v.*) – 들어내다. 실행하다. 성취하다.**

1) 내가 식료품을 밖으로 운반하는 것을 도와 주시겠습니까?
2) 대통령은 그의 공식적인 의무를 수행해야만 한다.
3) 우리는 돈을 너무 많이 쓰지 않으면서 우리의 결혼 계획을 수행했다.

**** Carryout (*n.*) – 가지고 나가는 음식**

1) 가끔 나는 음식을 싸서 주는 중국 식당에서 음식 주문을 한다.

121. Carry on (*v.*) – 계속하다. 어려움에도 불구하고 계속하다.

1) 우리는 일년 넘게 계속 편지 왕래를 했다.
2) 그들은 그의 가족의 반대에도 불구하고 그들의 관계를 계속 유지했다.

**** Carry through / carry through with (*v.*) – 끝까지 해내다. 성취하다.**

1) 나는 내 책을 출판하려는 나의 계획을 끝까지 성취했다.
2) 그녀는 전일제로 근무해야 했지만, 그녀의 교육을 끝마치려는 계획을 성취했다.

122. Catch on / catch on to (*v.*) – 이해하다. 인기 있다. 눈길을 끌다.

1) 그녀는 곧 그녀의 새 직책의 직무에 대해서 이해할 것이다.
2) 휴대폰은 젊은 층을 위한 시장에서 정말로 인기를 끌었다.

123. Catch one's breath (*v.*) – 정상적인 호흡 상태로 돌아가다. 잠깐 숨을 돌리다.

1) 나는 숨 돌릴 시간이 필요하다.
2) 잠깐 숨 돌리는 동안 앉으시겠어요?

124. Catch up (*v.*) – 뒤따라 잡다. ~의 상태에 빠지다. 연관이 되다(종종 본인 의사에 반하여)

1) 나는 내게 온 편지들에 밀리지 않도록 답장을 해야 되겠다.
2) 나는 공부해야 할 것을 거의 따라 잡았다.

3) 우리는 교통 체증에 빠져서, 오페라 극장에 한 시간 늦게 도착했다.

4) 최근에 정치인이 스캔들에 빠지지 않는 것은 매우 드물다.

125. Check in / into (*v.*) – (숙박부나 출근 카드 등에) 기재하다. 조사하다.

1) 오전 10시 이후에 호텔에 투숙할 수 있다.

2) 나는 시드니에 도착하자마자 그 호텔에 투숙할 것이다.

3) 나는 사무실에 돌아가자마자 그것을 조사해야만 한다.

** Check out (*v.*) – (퇴근시나 숙박시설에서 떠날 때) 떠나다, 점검하다. 빌리다.

1) 퇴실 할 때 요금을 내어도 됩니까?

2) 나는 내 차의 엔진을 점검할 필요가 있다.

3) 마을 안에 몇몇 수상한 사람들이 있다. 그들을 확인해 보라.

4) 도서관이 10분후에 문을 닫으니 모든 책은 앞에서 대출하시기 바랍니다.

5) 나는 일주일간 책을 대출했다.

126. Cheer up (*v.*) – 기운 내다. 기운 내게 하다.

1) 기운 내, 곧 좋은 시기가 곧 올 거야.

2) 그는 그녀를 댄스파티에 데리고 가는 것이 그녀를 기운 내게 할 것이라고 생각했다.

127. Clean off (*v.*) – 표면을 치우다.

1) 내 책상 위가 치워져야 될 필요가 있다. 나는 내 책상위를 치워야 할 필요가 있다.

2) 나는 대개 저녁을 먹은 뒤, 탁자를 치우고, 설거지를 한다.

** Clean out (*v.*) – 완전히 빼앗다 / 고갈시키다. (안의 것을) 깨끗이 청소해 내다.

1) 경기 침체는 사실상 그 회사의 재정을 고갈시켰다.

2) 그는 경마에서 완전히 빈털터리가 되었다.

3) 그는 아버지가 차고를 깨끗이 청소하는 것을 도왔다.

** Clean up (*v.*) – 구석구석 깨끗이 청소하다. (주로 나쁜) 습관을 바꾸다.

1) 그녀는 매 2주말마다 침실을 깨끗이 청소한다.

2) 그 지역 구성원들은 동네 공원을 청소하기 위해 모였다.

3) 너는 너의 행위를 고쳐야한다. 그렇지 않으면 너는 그 과목을 패스할 수가 없다.

128. Clear up (*v.*) – 분명히 하다. 개이다. (상처 부위 등이) 낫다.

1) 날씨가 오늘 오후에는 갤 예정이다.

2) 우리가 분명히 해 두어야 할 작은 문제가 있다.

3) 내 피부의 발진은 모두 깨끗이 나았다.

129. Climb the walls (*v.*) - (불안, 당황 등으로) 어찌할 바를 모르다. 미치다. 도망 가고 싶을 정도다.

1) 그녀는 주식시장에서 돈을 많이 잃었기 때문에 어쩔 줄을 몰라하고 있다.
2) 만약 그 교수님이 일분만 더 말했다면, 나는 미쳐버렸을 것이다.
3) 심심해서 미칠 지경이다.

**** Drive up the wall** (*v.*) - 매우 화나게 하다. 다른 사람을 미치도록 몰다.

1) 내가 하는 모든 일에 대해서 제발 그만 불평해라. 너는 나를 미치도록 만든다.
2) 그 시끄러운 아이들은 나를 미치게 만들고 있다.

130. Closed-door (*adj.*) - 비밀적인, 아주 제한적인

1) 예산위원회는 새로운 미사일 체계의 운명을 결정할 비밀회의를 개최했다.
2) 이사회는 성명을 발표하기 전에 종종 비밀회의들을 한다.

131. Close down (*v.*) - 폐쇄하다. 완전히 가동을 중지하다.

1) 신발을 만드는 것이 더 이상 이익을 내지 못했기 때문에 그 신발회사는 가동을 중지했다.
2) 해변에 있는 많은 상점들은 겨울동안에는 문을 닫는다.

**** Close out** (*v.*) - 끝내다. (상품 등을) 다 처분해 버리다.

1) 그 회사는 모피 전제품의 취급을 끝냈다. 그들은 야생동물을 소중히 여겨 앞으로는 더 이상 모피종류를 취급하지 않을 계획이다.

**** Close-out** (*n.*) - 재고 정리, 다 팔아 치우기 위해 대폭 할인 된 가격으로 상품을 파는 것

1) 휴가의 쇼핑 기간이 끝나면 많은 상점들은 크리스마스 용품들을 재고 정리로 내어 놓는다.
2) 한 자동차 회사가 작년 모델의 재고 정리 할인을 하고 있다.

132. Coffee break (*n.*) - 일 하다가 잠깐 쉬거나 커피를 마시기 위한 짧은 휴식, 커피 휴식시간

1) 회의를 시작하기 전에 잠깐 커피 휴식시간을 가집시다.
2) 그 회사는 직원들에게 하루에 두 번 커피휴식 시간을 준다.

133. Cold feet (*n.*) - 용기를 잃음

1) 그는 그들에게 일자리를 부탁할 예정이었지만, 용기를 잃었다.
2) 그는 스카이다이빙을 하고 싶어 했지만, 마지막 순간에 용기를 잃었다.

**** Cold shoulder** (*n.*) - 불친절하고 하찮은 대우

1) 그의 회사 동료들이 그를 불친절하고 하찮게 취급하기 시작했다. 그것은 그가 그의 직업을 잃을 위험에 처해 있다는 명백한 신호였다.

2) 그가 일자리를 잃은 후, 그의 가장 친한 친구마저도 그를 냉대했다.

134. Come about (*v.*) – 발생하다

1) 그는 그의 은행계좌에 잔고가 적은 이유를 알고 싶어했다.
2) 그는 딸이 대학에서 제적당하게 된 이유를 알고 싶어었다.
3) 나는 이 사건이 어떻게 발생한 것인지 알고 싶다.

135. Come across (*v.*) – 우연히 발견하다. 우연히 만나다.

1) 나는 책장을 옮기다가 내가 잃어버린 신용카드를 우연히 발견했다.
2) 그녀는 지난주에 대학친구를 우연히 만났다. 그녀는 그를 수년 동안이나 보지 못했다.
3) 나는 내 과제물을 찾기를 바란다. 나는 그것을 잃었고 내일이 기한이다.

136. Come along (*v.*) – 진전 향상하다.

1) 의사는 "그녀는 수술 뒤에 상태가 좋아지고 있다"라고 말했다.
2) "수업들은 어떻게 잘 받고 있나?" "점차 나아지고 있습니다."

** Come along with (*v.*) – 동반, 동행하다.

1) 나는 영화보러 갈 예정이다. 너도 같이 갈래?
2) 그 축구 감독이 한국에 왔을 때, 그의 애인도 같이 왔다.

137. Come between (*v.*) – 문제를 일으키다.

1) 그는 돈이 친구들과의 사이에 문제를 일으키는 것을 원치 않기 때문에 그들에게 돈을 빌려주는 것을 좋아하지 않는다.
2) 나는 우리 사이에 돈 문제가 끼이는 것을 원하지 않는다.
3) 그들 사이에 돈 문제가 일어났을 때, 그들의 관계는 심각해졌다.

138. Come by (*v.*) – (사전 약속 없이) 방문하다. 얻다.

1) 이웃들이 커피를 마시고 잡담을 하려고 들렀다.
2) 너는 그 아름다운 재킷을 어디서 샀니?

** Come over (*v.*) – 오다. 분명하게 떠오르다.

1) 나하고 같이 공부하게 우리 집에 와라.
2) 내가 약속에 대해서 까마득히 잊고 있었다는 것이 갑자기 생각났다.

** Drop in / drop by / stop by / stop in (*v.*) – 잠깐 들르다. (대개 사전 약속없이)

1) 동네에 왔기 때문에 그냥 들렀어.
2) 잠깐 시간 나면 내 사무실에 들러라.

139. Come out with (*v.*) - (생각, 계획 등을)발표하다. 가지고 오다.

1) 민주당은 적당한 경제 제안을 내어 놓았다.
2) 진실을 말할 것이 아니면 아무것도 말하지 말아라.

**** Come up (*v.*) - 토의 중에 우연히 어떤 생각이나 화제가 오르다. 접근하다.**

1) 우리는 단지 잡담을 하고 있었는데 갑자기 낙태에 관한 문제가 떠올랐다.
2) 우리가 이야기 하는 동안 부동산에 관한 주제가 떠올랐다.
3) 한 걸인이 내게 다가 와서 돈을 구걸했다.

**** Come up with (*v.*) - 제공하다. 제안하다.**

1) 노동자들은 종종 경영진을 교묘하게 피해나가는 해결책을 제안한다.
2) 그녀는 봄 패션쇼에 대한 아주 환상적인 제안을 했다.

140. Come through (*v.*) - (어려움에도 불구하고) 성공하다. 원했던 것을 잘 해내다.

1) 그 사업은 초기에 많은 어려움이 있었지만, 지금은 그런 어려운 시절을 잘 견디고 매우 견실하다.
2) 나는 한국 축구팀이 어려움을 잘 이겨내고 경기에서 이길 것이라는 것을 확신했다.
3) 내 책의 출판이 어려움에도 불구하고 결국 이루어졌다.

141. Come under (*v.*) - 편입되다. 영향력을 받다.

1) 그 작은 금융회사가 큰 보험 회사들 중 한곳에 편입되었다.

142. Common ground (*n.*) - 공통점, 함께하는 흥미, 믿음, 또는 비슷한 일

1) 그들은 공통점이 거의 없기 때문에 결혼 생활이 파경에 이르렀다.
2) 그 위원회의 목적은 공통영역을 찾는 것이다.
3) 그들은 어떠한 공통점도 찾아내지 못했기 때문에 그 거래는 실패했다.

143. Cool down / cool off (*v.*) - 진정하다.

1) 너는 너무 감정적이다. 진정하려고 노력해라.
2) 그 차의 엔진은 과열되었다. 그 엔진이 식을 때까지 운전하지 마라.

**** Calm down (*v.*) - (노여움 흥분 등을) 가라 앉히다.**

1) 너는 흥분을 가라앉히고 잘 생각해야만 한다. 그렇지 않으면 시험에서 떨어질 것이다.
2) 요가는 내가 마음을 진정시키는데 도움을 준다.

144. Coop up (*v.*) - 비좁은 곳에 갇히거나 그런 느낌을 갖다.

1) 나는 내 책의 마지막 수정을 하느라 오랜 시간동안 내 방안에 갇혀 지냈다.
2) 비오는 날들이 나를 내 조그만 아파트에 가두어 놓았다.

145. Count on / upon (*v.*) - 믿다. 의지하다. 신용하다.

1) 국제 사면회의 기금 모금은 내게 의지해도 좋습니다.
2) 그 팀은 점수를 내는데 그에게 의지한다.
3) 한국 팀은 훌륭한 감독인 히딩크에게 의지 했었다.
4) 너는 내 도움이 필요할 때면 언제나 나에게 의지 할 수 있다는 것을 알잖아.

146. Count out (*v.*) - 제외하다

1) 현직자가 언론기관에 의해서 제외되었음에도 불구하고 선거에서 이겼다.
2) 그들을 제외시키지 마라, 아직 경기가 끝난 것은 아니다.
3) 나는 너의 계략에 동참하고 싶지 않다. 제발 나는 제외시켜줘.

** Count in (*v.*) - 포함하다.

1) 브리지 게임에 네 번째 사람이 필요하거든 나를 좀 끼어줘.
2) 우리는 그녀를 위한 깜짝 파티를 준비 중이다. 너도 끼워주어야 하나?

147. Cover up (*v.*) - 은폐하다.

1) 최근의 돈에 대한 추문은 재빨리 덮어졌다.
2) 나는 실수를 덮어두는 것이 그것을 처리 하는 최선의 방법이라고는 생각하지 않는다.

148. Crack down on (*v.*) - 불법적 또는 불허된 행위들을 중지시키기 위해 강력한 행동을 취하다. 단속하다.

1) 경찰은 음주운전에 대해서 강력하게 처리하기 시작했다.
2) 경찰은 강요된 매춘에 대해서 태만했고 게다가 유곽 업주들로부터 뇌물을 받고 그것을 묵인하였다. 그리고 그것을 은폐시키기 위해서 교활한 계획까지 사용했다.

** Crackdown (*n.*) - 단속, 강경조치

1) 불법적인 도박을 하는 카지노들에 대해서 단속이 있었다.
2) 강요된 매춘에 대한 단속은 별로 실효를 거두지 못해왔다.

149. Crack up (*v.*) - 정신적으로, 신체적으로 쇠약해지다.

1) 그는 과중된 책임들로 인해서 정신적, 신체적으로 몹시 지칠 지경이다.
2) 그 간호사는 병원에서의 그녀의 과중한 업무로 인해 거의 지칠 정도이다.

** Crackup (*n.*) - 신경쇠약

1) 과중된 책임 때문에 그는 결국 신경쇠약이 되었다.

150. Cross one's fingers (*v.*) - (두 손가락을 꼬아) 행운을 빌다.

1) 우리 모두 행운을 빌어서, 우리의 비행이 취소되지 않기를 희망하자.

2) 나는 내 손가락을 꼬아 행운을 빌어서, 너를 위하여 모든 일이 잘 되길 바란다.

151. Cross one's mind (*v.*) – 문득 생각이 나다.

1) 그녀는 문득 직장을 그만두고 싶은 생각이 났다.
2) 당신이 한 일에 대해서 급료를 지불하지 않은 것이 문득 생각이 났다.

152. Cross off / out (*v.*) – (목록에서) 제외시키다. 선을 그어 지우다.

1) 그의 이름은 승진자 명단에 있었으나, 마지막 순간에 제외 되었다.
2) 이 문장은 불필요한 중복이기 때문에 선을 그어 지우고 싶다.

153. Cut down (*v.*) – 감소하다. 줄이다.

1) 의사는 그녀에게 기름진 음식을 줄이라고 충고했다.
2) 씀씀이를 줄이지 않으면 너는 거지가 되고 말 것이다.

154. Cut in (*v.*) – 끼어들다. ~의 앞으로 움직이다.

1) 나는 그들의 대화에 끼어들고 싶지 않았지만, 그것은 긴급 상황이었다.
2) 그 사고는 오토바이가 갑자기 차선을 끼어들면서 발생했다.

**** Cut off (*v.*) – 갑자기 중단하다. 단절하다. 절단하다.**

1) 전화회사가 통고도 없이 전화를 끊어버렸다.
2) 그는 가족으로부터 완전히 단절 되었다.
3) 그녀의 보험은 1월 이후로 중단되었다.
4) 의사는 그 환자의 부상당한 다리를 절단했다.

**** Cut out (*v.*) – 제거하다. 중지하다.**

1) 그 푸주한은 죽은 닭의 내장을 제거했다.
2) 그는 담배피우는 것을 중지해야 한다.

**** Cut it out (*v.*) – 중지하다. (나쁜 행위 또는 귀찮게 하는것)**

1) 나는 너의 잔소리가 싫다. 그만 좀 해.

155. Cut up (*v.*) – 작은 조각으로 자르다.

1) 그녀는 채소를 잘게 자르고 있다.

D

156. Dark horse (*n.*) **– 잘 알려지지 않은 경쟁자 (그러나 최후의 승자가 될 가능성을 가진).**

1) 모든 사람들이 놀랍게도, 최우수 남자 연기상은 잘 알려지지 않은 후보자에게 돌아갔다.

157. Day after day (*adv.*) **– 매일, 한결같이**

1) 그 수영 팀은 여름 내내 매일매일 연습을 했다.
2) 나는 이 과제에 휴식 없이 하루도 빠짐없이 일을 했다.

**** Day and night** (*adv.*) **– (밤낮으로) 계속해서**

1) 대부분의 편의점들은 밤낮으로 계속 1년 365일 문을 연다.
2) 그 공장은 작업을 완성하기 위해 밤낮으로 쉬지 않고 가동했다.

158. Dates back (*v.*) **– 거슬러 오르다.**

1) 석기시대는 수백 년을 거슬러 올라간다.
2) 이 도자기는 신라 왕조까지 거슬러 올라간다.

159. Deep water (*n.*) **– 심각한 문제, 곤경**

1) 대통령가가 지금 곤경에 처해 있다.
2) 그녀의 작은 거짓말은 그녀의 부모님과 심각한 문제에 빠지게 했다.
3) 공부를 하지 않은 것이 기말고사에 이르러서 그를 곤경에 빠뜨렸다.

160. Die out (*v.*) **– 서서히 사라지다. 죽다.**

1) 그 초는 다 타버렸고, 서서히 꺼졌다.
2) 많은 멸종위기의 종들이 이미 사라져 버렸다.
3) 인류는 멸종위기의 종들이 사라져 가는 것을 막아야만 한다.

161. Dig in (*v.*) **– 열심히 일하기 시작하다.**

1) 그들은 열심히 일하기 시작해서 그 과제가 끝날 때까지 계속했다.
2) 나는 열심히 공부하기 시작해서 시험 날까지 계속해야만 한다.

**** Dig out** (*v.*) **– 정보를 알아내다. 캐내다.**

1) 기록에서 정보를 찾아내는 것은 어렵다.

2) 그 오래된 고목이 마침내 내 뜰에서 캐내어졌다.

3) 아프리카에서 어느 날 몇몇 고구마 채굴자들이 우연히 대단히 큰 다이아몬드를 캐냈다.

4) 그들은 눈보라 후에 눈을 치우는 힘든 일을 했다.

162. Do the honors (*v.*) – 주인 역할을 하다.

1) 내 상사는 회사의 연례 연회에서 내게 우리 지사를 대표하여 주인 역할을 하도록 부탁했다.

163. Do over (*v.*) – 다시하다.

1) 너의 숙제에는 잘못 된 것이 너무 많다. 다시 하도록 해라.

2) 나는 내 아파트의 실내 장식이 맘에 안 든다. 그래서 다시 하고 싶다.

164. Double-check (*v.*) – 재확인하다.

1) 나는 문을 잠근 것으로 생각한다. 하지만, 재확인 해야겠다.

2) 너는 여행을 떠나기 전에 여행일정을 재확인 해야만 한다.

3) 너는 오븐이 꺼져 있는지 재확인 했니?

4) 그녀는 그녀의 글을 재확인 했고, 몇 개의 사소한 오류들을 발견했다.

5) 나는 내일 일정을 재확인해야겠다.

165. Double-cross (*v.*) – 동의해 놓고 다른 일을 함으로써 배신하다.

1) 그 중앙정보부 요원은 국가의 1급 비밀을 적에게 주어버림으로써 정부를 배신했다.

2) 나를 배신하려 들지 마라.

** Double-dealing (*adj., n*) – 배반하는, 배반

1) 매춘업주들로부터 돈을 받은 불성실한 경찰관들이 심각한 곤경에 처해있다.

** Double standard (*n.*) – 위선적인 이중 잣대.

1) 아이를 가진 남자가 재혼하는 것은 괜찮고, 여자가 그렇게 하는 것은 안 된다면, 그것은 위선적인 이중의 기준을 적용한 것이다.

** Double talk (*n.*) – 말과 생각과 행동이 다른 것

1) 그녀는 표리부동하다. 그녀는 네 앞에서는 항상 좋은 말만하지만, 네 등 뒤에서는 다르게 말한다.

2) 전화를 통해서 그녀는 나를 만나면 반가울 것이라고 말했고 나는 그것을 믿었는데, 후에 그것은 그녀가 생각과 말을 다르게 한 것임이 드러났다.

166. Doubt (*n., v.*) – 의심하다. 믿지 않다. 확실치 않다. 의심

1) "너는 경제가 곧 회복 될 것이라고 생각하니? 나는 그렇게 생각하지 않는다."

** Beyond doubt (*adv.*) – 분명히

1) 2-3년 안에 경기가 나아질 것이라는 것은 분명하다.

167. Give the benefit of the doubt (*v.*) - 유죄로 판명되기 전에는 무죄라고 믿는 것

1) 명백한 증거 없이는 죄인이라고 판명되기 전까지는 무죄라고 믿어야만 한다. 유죄라고 판명되기 전까지 모든 사람은 무죄이다.
2) 그녀는 학생들이 부정행위를 했다고 생각했지만, 유죄로 판명되기 전에는 무죄로 인정해야 하기 때문에 그들을 시험에서 통과 시켰다.

168. Double up (*v.*) - (1인용 방 등을) 함께 쓰다.

1) 우리는 새 직원들에게 자리를 마련해 주기위해 방을 함께 써야만 했다.
2) 방이 하나밖에 없다. 그래서 우리는 밤에 방을 함께 써야만 할 것이다.

169. Down-to-earth (*adj.*) - 현실적, 실질적, 센스 있는

1) 그 계획은 실현 가능성이 있어 보인다. 하지만 정말로 잘 될까?
2) 그는 그의 현실적인 경영 기법으로 인해 많은 사랑을 받는다.

170. Drag on (*v.*) - 천천히 오랫동안 계속하다.

1) 그 모임은 저녁까지 오랫동안 계속되었다.
2) 뜨거운 날씨가 오랫동안 계속되고 있다. 결코 끝나지 않을 것인가?

** Drag out (*v.*) - 오래 끌다.

1) 나는 이 모임이 오래가지 않기를 바란다. 그 모임은 너무 길게 가는 경향이 있다.

171. Draw a (the) line (*v.*) - 분명히 하다. 한계를 정하다.

1) 때때로, 도덕적, 비도덕적이라는 것의 명백한 한계를 정하는 것이 쉽지 않다.
2) 나는 매달 유흥에 쓰는 돈의 한계를 명백히 정해야 한다.

172. Dream of (*v.*) - 상상하다. 생각하다.

1) 나는 항상 내 사업을 하고 싶은 상상을 한다. 나는 아마도 공상가일지도 모른다.
2) 눈 내리는 성탄절을 꿈꾸는 것은 달콤하다.

173. Dress up (*v.*) - 정식적으로 또는 우아하게 잘 차려입다.

1) 금요일 밤의 파티에는 우리 정장을 입는 것이 어때?
2) 너는 정장을 차려 입으면 매우 멋있어 보인다.

174. Drop off (*v.*) - 맡기다.

1) 나는 세탁소에 옷 몇 가지를 맡겨야 한다.
2) 나 좀 가까운 역에 내려주겠니?

175. Drop out (*v.*) – 중도에 그만두다. 자퇴하다.

1) 몇몇 학생들은 1학년 때 대학을 그만둔다.

2) 그는 경제적 어려움으로 인해서 학교를 그만두었다.

** Dropout (*n.*) – 졸업 전에 학교를 그만두는 사람.

1) 그는 고등학교 중퇴자이다. 그래서 그는 좋은 직업을 구하는데 어려움을 겪을 것이다.

2) 중퇴자들이 대개 필요한 기술들이 결여되어 있어 우리 회사는 그들을 고용하지 않는다.

176. Due to (*prep.*) – ~에 의해 야기된, ~ 때문에

1) 많은 산불들이 부주의하게 꺼진 불들로 인해 발생한다.

2) 그 경기는 비 때문에 취소되었다.

** Due (*adj.*) – 지불 기일이 된, 지불해야할, 빚진

1) 내 전화비는 오늘이 지불 기일이다.

2) 지불해야 할 돈은 42달러 95센트 이다.

3) 나의 과제는 다음 주가 기한이다.

** Dues (*n.*) – 부과금, 회비

1) 수영 클럽의 연간 회비는 120달러이다.

2) 회비는 매월 5일에 납부해야 된다.

177. Dwell on (*v.*) – (~의 생각 등에서) 쉽게 벗어나지를 못하다.

1) 너의 실수에 집착하지 말라.

2) 그녀는 항상 과거 일에 집착해서 산다.

E

178. Easy come, easy go (clich) – 쉽게 얻은 것은 쉽게 잃는다. (속담)

1) 짐은 많은 돈을 상속 받자마자. 쉽게 들어온 돈이었기 때문에 그는 사치스럽게 돈을 쓰기 시작했다. 쉽게 얻는 것은 쉽게 잃는다.
2) 짐이 얻은 돈은 빨리 써졌다. 그의 친구가 쉽게 얻는 것은 쉽게 잃는다고 그에게 말했다.

179. Eat one's words (*v.*) –한 말을 취소하다. 하고 싶은 말을 삼키다.

1) 나는 나의 상사에게 불평을 하고 싶었으나 참았다.
2) 그는 그의 화난 상사 앞에서 할 말을 삼켜야만 했다.
3) 그녀는 그 게임에서이길 것이라고 모든 사람들에게 말했으나 졌다. 이제 그녀는 그녀가 한 말을 취소해야 한다.

180. Edge out (*v.*) – 근소한 차이로 이기다. 몰아내다.

1) 뉴욕은 토론토를 아슬아슬한 경기로 이겼다.
2) 그녀는 더 나은 자격을 가진 사람에 의해 그 자리를 얻지 못했다.

**** to be on edge (*v.*) – 염려와 긴장이 되고 초조하다**

1) 그는 오늘 마음이 초조하고 긴장되어있다.
2) 나는 인터뷰 결과를 기다리며 마음이 초조하다.

181. Eke out (*v.*) – 근근히 꾸려나가다.

1) 대부분의 농부들은 간신히 생활을 꾸려나간다.
2) 많은 가족들이 경제위기로 인해 겨우 생활을 꾸려나가고 있다.

182. End up (*v.*) – 끝내다. 결국 ~로 끝나다.

1) 그 축구 경기는 한국이 일본을 2:0으로 이기며 끝났다.
2) 만약 그가 계속해서 버는 돈보다 더 쓴다면, 그는 결국에는 파산 법정에 서게 될 것이다.
3) 그들은 결국 이혼으로 끝났다.

183. Enjoy oneself (*v.*) – 즐거운 시간을 갖다.

1) 즐거운 시간을 가지세요.
2) 지난 밤 파티에서 즐거운 시간을 가졌습니까?

184. Enough is enough – 이제 그만 충분함

1) 당신의 잔소리에 너무 질렸어. 이제 그만 좀 해요.
2) 그녀가 이미 빌려간 돈에 추가해서 그녀가 돈을 더 빌려달라고 부탁했을 때, 그 녀의 성난 아버지는 "이제 그만 좀 해"라고 말했다.

185. Every now and then / Every ones in a while (*adv.*) – 이따금

1) 우리는 이따금 외식하기를 좋아한다.
2) 나는 이따금 영화 보러 가기를 좋아한다.
3) 우리는 함께 많은 시간을 보내곤 했었다. 그러나 이제는 이따금씩만 만난다.

** Every so often (*adv.*) – 이따금

1) 우리는 그곳에 많이 가곤 했다. 그러나 지금은 이따금만 간다.

186. Every single (*adj.*) – 매, 각, 하나 하나 (대개 강조하여)

1) 나는 지난해 이래로 매일 매일을 열심히 일해오고 있다.
2) 나는 네가 나를 위해 한 모든 일에 대해 감사한다.

** Every other (*adj.*) –하나 걸러

1) 우유배달원은 격일로 온다.
2) 우리는 한 주 걸러 토요일마다 대단히 많은 식료품을 산다.

F

187. Face to face (*adv.*) – 직접 서로 맞서서, 서로의 면전에서

1) 그 두 권투선수들은 서로 마주보고 서서 한판승부를 위해 싸울 준비가 되었다.
2) 나는 그를 직접 만나지는 못했지만 그에 관해 좋은 평을 들어 왔다.
3) 직접 대면해서 말하자.

188. Face up to (*v.*) – 사실로 받아들이다. 용감하게 맞서다.

1) 만약 그가 그의 술 마시는 문제를 사실로 받아들이지 않는다면 그는 그것을 극복할 수 없을 것이다.

189. Face value – 액면가격, 표면상의 가치, 액면그대로

1) 이 희귀한 은 동전은 액면가가 500달러이다.
2) 나는 그가 거짓말을 하리라고는 전혀 생각지 않고 그의 말을 액면그대로 받아들였다.

190. Fair and square (*adv.*) – 정직하게, 공정하게

1) 우리는 정직하게 그 게임에서 이겼다.
2) 우리의 이익을 공정하게 나누자.

** Fair play (*n.*) – 정직하고 정당한 행동

1) 스포츠 행사들은 공정한 경기를 위해 심판들을 고용한다.
2) 양쪽의 변호사들은 공정한 작전이나 매너에는 관심이 없었다.

191. Fair-weather friend (*n.*) – 친구가 오직 형편이 좋을 때 만 친구가 되어주는 사람

1) 그는 내가 도움이 필요할 때는 전혀 도움을 청할 수 없는 그런 류의 친구이다.
2) 나는 내가 형편이 좋을 때 만 찾아주는 친구들을 갖느니 차라리 친구들이 없는 것이 낫다.

192. Flunk out (*v.*) – 실패하다. 성적이 나빠서 학교에서 또는 과목에서 탈락하다.

1) 열심히 공부해라. 그렇지 않으면 학교에서 탈락할 것이다.
2) 그들은 그들의 딸이 학교에서 탈락했을 때 충격을 받았다.

193. Fall all over (*v.*) – 지나친 애정표시를 하다.

1) 그녀는 그에게 대중 앞에서 지나치게 애정표시를 하지만 그것이 그를 전혀 무안하게 만들지 않는다.

194. Fall back on (*v.*) – 도움을 받기 위해 또는 필요한때 의지하다.

1) 모든 사람들은 도움이 필요할 때 의지할 수 있는 훌륭한 교육을 받아야한다.
2) 그는 의지할 사람도 없는 고아이다.
3) 너는 항상 나에게 기댈 수 있다.
4) 예금 이율이 너무 낮아서 예금에 의지해야만 하는 것이 힘들다.

** Fall back (*v.*) – 후퇴하다.

1) 군대는 안전 상 적선 뒤로 후퇴해야만 했다.
2) 적군은 반격으로 후퇴했다.

195. Fall behind / Fall behind in (*v.*) – 뒤쳐지다. 남들보다 느리다

1) 그녀는 신용카드 대금을 제때 갚지 못해서 빨리 갚아야 한다.
2) 나는 학과 공부들에서 뒤지고 싶지 않기 때문에 공부해야 한다.

196. Fall for (*v.*) – ~에게 반하거나 사랑의 느낌을 받다. 속임수를 당하다.

1) 그녀를 처음 보았을 때 그는 사랑의 감정을 느꼈다.
2) 그는 그가 만나는 모든 여자들에게 반한다.
3) 그녀는 그에게 거짓말을 했고 그는 속임수를 당했다.

** Fall in love (*v.*) – 사랑의 감정을 갖다.

1) 우리는 처음 만났을 때 서로 사랑의 감정을 느꼈다.
2) 나는 첫눈에 그와 사랑에 빠졌다.

197. Fall off (*v.*) – 감소하다.

1) 회사의 영업실적이 감소해왔기 왔기 때문에 아마 임시 해고가 있을 거야.
2) 이번 학기에 학생 등록이 현저히 줄었다.

198. Fall out (*v.*) – 말다툼하다. 사이가 벌어지다.

1) 그들은 조그만 일로 말다툼한 뒤 사이가 멀어졌다.
2) 그녀는 말다툼 후로 그녀의 옆집 사람들과 교제를 해오고 있지 않다.

199. Fall through (*v.*) – 실패하다. 망쳐지다.

1) 나의 휴가 계획이 시간을 낼 수가 없게 되어 망쳐졌다.
2) 해외로 갈 그녀의 계획들이 무산되었다.

200. Far cry (*n.*) – 매우 다른 것

1) 당신의 말은 진실과 매우 다르다.
2) 이 시계는 가짜 롤렉스로서 내가 기대했던 것과 아주 다르다.
3) 이 영화는 대부분의 한국영화와는 아주 다르다.

201. Far-off (*adj.*) - 먼

1) 그는 먼 섬으로 가고 싶어 한다.
2) 대학교의 신입생에게는 졸업은 멀고 결코 실현될 것 같지 않을 것처럼 보인다.

202. Fed up / Fed up with (*adj.*) - 진저리나다. 싫증나다.

1) 그는 그의 아내의 잔소리에 진저리가 났다.
2) 내가 일을 하는 식들에 대한 너의 끊임없는 불평에 나는 진저리가 난다.

203. Feel like verb + ing (*v.*) - 무엇인가 하고 싶은 감정이다.

1) 무엇인가 먹을 것을 좀 사고 싶은 기분이다.
2) 오늘은 공부하고 싶은 기분이 아니다.

204. Feel like a million dollars / Look like a million dollars (cliché) - 최상의 컨디션이다.

1) 그는 나를 사랑한다. 그리고 그 것이 나를 최고로 기분 좋게 만든다.
2) 너는 그 새 옷을 입으니 대단히 아름답게 보인다.

205. Fifty-fifty (*adj.*) - 반반의

1) 재산을 반은 너에게 반은 나에게로 나누자.
2) 기상예보가 오늘은 비올 확률이 반반이라고 했다.

206. Fight off (*v.*) - 싸워 물리치다.

1) 나는 많은 비타민 C를 복용함으로서 감기를 떨쳐버리려고 노력하고 있다.
2) 우리의 군인들이 용감하게 적을 물리치고 있다.

**** Fight it out (*v.*) - 한쪽이 이길 때까지 싸우다. 몸부림치다.**

1) 그 권투선수들은 그들 중의 한 명만 남아 서 있을 때까지 싸웠다.
2) 계속되는 소비자 유치 전쟁에서 큰 회사들은 몸부림치고 있다.

207. Figure on (*v.*) - 계획하다. 기대하다.

1) 우리는 하여튼 우리의 결혼식에 많은 사람들을 기대하지 않았다.
2) 나는 급여의 인상을 기대하고 있었으나 이루어지지 않았다.

208. Figure out (*v.*) - 해답을 찾다. 풀다. 이해하다.

1) 이 컴퓨터 프로그램을 풀기 위해 도움을 청해도 될까요?
2) 왜 나의 컴퓨터가 종종 다운되는지 이해를 못하겠어요.

209. Fill in (*v.*) - 빈칸에 글을 써넣다. 대체하다.

1) 신청서를 기재하여 저 바구니에 넣으세요.

2) 요리사가 아파서 곧 누군가로 대체해야 될 필요가 있다.

**** Fill out (*v.*) – 양식을 작성 / 완성하다.**

1) 나는 아직 나의 세금신고를 하지 않았다. 곧 세금 신고서를 작성해야 한다.
2) 나는 등록 양식 서를 기재하여 지난주에 보냈다.

210. Fill up (*v.*) – 가득 채우다.

1) 연료탱크가 거의 비어서 채워야겠다.
2) (주유소에서) 가득 채워 주세요.
3) 세탁기 물이 가득 찬 후에 세제를 넣는 것이 가장 좋다.

211. Find out (*v.*) – ~에 대한 정보를 얻다. 알아내다.

1) 그 영화가 몇 시에 시작하는지 알아보았니?
2) 나는 그 장학프로그램에 대한 정보를 알아냈다.

212. Fine feathers do not make fine birds (proverb) – 멋있게 보이고 멋있게 말하고 멋있는 옷을 입는 사람이 꼭 멋있는 사람은 아니다.

1) 그/녀는 좋은 옷을 입고 좋은 차를 몰고 그리고 미소를 많이 짓는다. 그러나 물건들이 꼭 좋은 사람을 만드는 것은 아니다.

213. Finish up (*v.*) – 완전히 끝내다. 마무리 짓다.

1) 나는 나의 일을 빨리 끝내고 집에 가고 싶다.
2) 그는 그의 숙제를 마무리 짓고 있다. 그러고 나서 영화를 보러 갈 예정이다.

**** Finished with (*v.*) – 관계, 임무 등을 끝내다.**

1) 그는 그의 말을 전혀 지키지 않기 때문에 나는 그와의 관계를 끝냈다.
2) 내가 너에게 빌려준 책 다 보았니?

**** Finished (*adj.*) – 망쳐진, 끝난, 숙련된, 완성된, 완벽한, 완전히 가공된**

1) 그는 정치인으로서는 끝났다.
2) 그 회사는 파산했다. 이제 끝났다.
3) 그 가구에 완벽한 모습을 주기 위해서는 약간의 마지막 손질이 필요하다.
4) 이것은 완성된 제품이다.

214. First-class (*adj., adv.*) – 최상의 서비스의, 뛰어난, 일등급의

1) 일등실의 승객들은 자연적으로 삼등실의 승객들보다 더 나은 서비스를 받는다.
2) 우리는 일류호텔에 머물렀다.
3) 우리는 당신이 주문한 선물 세트를 일등급으로 보냈다.

215. First come, first served - 먼저 오는 사람이 먼저 서비스를 받음

1) 예약은 필요 없다. 방들은 먼저 오는 사람 순으로 빌려준다.
2) 그 100대의 컴퓨터들은 먼저 오는 사람에게 제공이 된다.

216. Fit in / Fit in with (*v.*) - 적합하다. 적응하다.

1) 이 커튼들이 저것들보다 색상 면에서 더 적합하다고 본다.
2) 그녀는 사진클럽의 다른 멤버들과 잘 어울린다.

217. Fix up / Fix up with (*v.*) - 수선 / 수리하다. 꾸미다. 장식하다. 고치다. 제공하다. 주선하다. 소개하다.

1) 우리는 방 하나를 공부방으로 사용하기 위해 수리했다(꾸몄다).
2) 나는 배가 고프다. 무엇인가 만들어야 되겠다.
3) 나는 그에게 직업을 주선했다.
4) 우리는 그에게 멋진 소녀를 소개했다.

218. Follow through (*v.*) - 시작한 일을 끝내다. 시작된 일을 완성하다.

1) 또 다른 프로젝트를 시작하기 전에 이미 시작된 일을 완성하라.
2) 나는 내가 시작한 일을 끝내기를 좋아한다.

**** Follow up (*v.*) - 추가적인 것을 통하여 이전의 행동을 좀 더 효과적으로 만들다. 수행하다. ~에 대한 정보를 추구하거나 주다.**

1) 당신의 이력서를 그들에게 보내시오. 그리고 일주일정도 후에 전화를 걸어 좀 더 효과적으로 추진하시오.
2) 유능한 서비스 맨은 제품을 판 후 전화를 걸어 제품에 대해 묻고 더 많은 정보를 가르쳐준다.
3) 좋은 도표가 있는 안내서를 참고하시오.
4) 우리는 내일 학습의 복습과 함께 그 이야기에 대해 더 배울 것이다.

219. Fool around (*v.*) - 게으름 피다. 쓸데없는 짓을 하며 시간을 낭비하다.

1) 게으름 피울 시간이 없어요. 나는 할 일이 많아요.
2) 쓸데없이 돌아다니며 시간을 낭비하지 마라. 그렇지 않으면 나중에 후회 할 것이다.
3) 나쁜 무리들과 어울려 다니지 마라. 그렇지 않으면 문제가 생길 거야.

220. Foot in the door (*v.*) - 무엇인가를 얻기 위한 첫 번째 단계

1) 그것은 시간제 직위였다. 그러나 나는 그 회사에 발을 들여놓기 위한 첫 번째 단계로 그것을 받아들였다.
2) 이것은 단지 임시직이다. 그러나 누가 알아? 그것이 첫 번째 단계일지.
3) 이것은 일단 발을 들여 놓기 위한 entry level position 이다.

221. For all – ~에도 불구하고

1) 군인들이 우리의 국가를 위해 공헌해온 것에도 불구하고 그들은 제대로 대접받지 못하고 있다.
2) 그는 많은 돈과 멋진 가족이 있다. 그러나 그럼에도 불구하고 그는 행복하지 않다.

222. For all the world (*adv.*) – 결코, 절대로

1) 나는 너에 대해 결코 어떤 것도 바꾸지 않겠다.

**** Forever and ever (*adv.*) – 영원히, 항상**

1) 이 날의 기억은 영원히 나와 함께 있을 것이다.
2) 일들은 오직 동화에서만 영원하다.

**** For good (*adv.*) – 영원히, 영구적으로**

1) 그녀는 영원히 갔다. 그리고 돌아오지 않을 것이다.
2) 그는 결국 영구적으로 술과 노름을 끊었다.

223. For sure (*adv.*) – 의심할 여지없이, 확실하게

1) 나는 이것이 정말이라는 것을 안다.
2) 당신은 그녀가 확실히 돌아올 것이라는 것을 압니까?

224. For the best (*adj., adv.*) – 좋은, 최상의, 운 좋게, 잘

1) 그에게는 안됐어요. 하지만 나머지 사람들에게는 잘된 일이예요.
2) 가끔 나쁜 상황들이 오히려 아주 잘된 일로 판명된다.

**** For the better (*adj., adv.*) – 호전된, 더 나은 것을 위한**

1) 그의 음주량을 줄이는 것은 호전된 것이다.

**** For the worse (*adj., adv.*) – 더 나빠지는**

1) 그는 새 직위를 받았는데 그것이 더 나쁘게 되었다.
2) 그 환자의 상태가 더 나쁘게 변했다.
3) 그들이 결혼했을 때 그들은 좋을 때나 나쁠 때나 서로를 사랑할 것을 맹세했다.

225. Freeze over / Freeze up (*v.*) – 얼음으로 덮이다. (긴장감 등으로) 기능을 못하다.

1) 호수가 얼을 때 우리는 스케이팅을 하러 간다.
2) 지난밤에 너무나 추워서 물관이 얼었다.
3) 그는 학급 앞에서 얼어붙어 그의 연설을 전혀 할 수가 없었다.

**** Freeze out (*v.*) – 제외하다. 불친절한 대우로 몰아내다.**

1) 그는 그 고급클럽에 가입하고 싶었으나 회원자격은 그를 제외시켰다.

226. From hand to hand (*adv.*) **- 이 사람에서 저 사람으로, 여러 손을 거쳐**

1) 그들의 부모가 죽은 후 그 아이들은 그들의 아저씨와 아주머니에게 영구적인 법적 양육권이 주어졌을 때까지 여러 손을 거쳐야 했다.
2) 우리 가족은 모두 나누어 쓴다. 옷조차도 돌려가며 입는다.
3) 그 유명한 그림은 내가 소유할 때까지 많은 손을 거쳤다.

227. From the bottom of one's heart / With all one's heart (*adv.*) **- 진심으로**

1) 그는 그녀를 진심으로 사랑했다.
2) 나를 위해 당신이 한 모든 일에 대해 진심으로 감사한다.

228. From time to time (*adv.*) **- 가끔**

1) 그는 가끔 나를 방문한다.
2) 그는 가끔 와인 한잔을 마시기를 좋아한다.

229. From way back (*adj., adv.*) **- 오래 전부터**

1) 우리는 오래 전인 고등학교 시절부터 아는 사이이다.
2) 우리는 방금 만났다. 그러나 오래 전부터 알아 온 듯한 느낌이다.

G

230. Get across (*v.*) – 뜻을 분명하게 전달하다.

1) 나는 그 일을 그들에게 설명했다. 그러나 내 생각에 그들에게 명확하게 뜻을 전달한 것 같지는 않다.
2) 그 교수는 어려운 물리학 이론을 쉽고 명확하게 학생들에게 전달 할 수가 없었다.
3) 나는 당신에게 어떻게 나의 생각을 이해시킬지 모르겠다.
4) 나는 그가 떠나기 전에 간신히 그에게 나의 뜻을 이해시켰다.

**** Get it (*v.*) – 이해하다. 잡다.**

1) 나는 그것을 내가 할 수 있는 한 명확하게 설명했다. 이해가 되었는가?
2) 나는 감기가 심하게 걸렸다. 당신은 걸리지 않기 바란다.
3) 개들은 가서 물어오는 것을 좋아한다. 당신이 작대기를 던지면 그들은 가서 잡을 것이다.

231. Get along / Get along with (*v.*) – 진전을 보다. 친구가 되다.

1) 당신의 학습이 어떻게 되어가고 있는가?
2) 나는 최근에 나의 상사와 잘 지내지 못하고 있다.
3) 가장 좋은 친구도 항상 잘 지내지는 않는다.
4) 당신은 그와 잘 지내는가?

232. Get around (*v.*) – 여기저기 다니다. 피하다. 널리 알려지다.

1) 그녀의 자동차가 정비소에 들어가 있기 때문에 여기저기 다니는 것이 힘들었다.
2) 학생들은 숙제를 피하는데 있어서는 기발하다.
3) 그녀는 규칙을 잘 피할 줄 안다.
4) 나쁜 뉴스가 좋은 소식보다 종종 더 빨리 퍼진다.

233. Get at (*v.*) – 이해하다. 방법을 찾다. 의미하다.

1) 그 이야기의 주요 주제는 이해하기가 힘들었다.
2) 진실은 종종 발견하기가 어렵다.
3) 그 고양이는 새를 잡을 수 있는 모든 것을 시도했다.
4) 내가 의미하고 있는 것은 이것이다, 우리는 더 종종 대화가 필요하다.

234. Get away (*v.*) – 탈출하다. 자유롭게 되다.

1) 세 명의 죄수들이 지난 밤 교도소에서의 폭동 중에 탈출했다.

2) 내 몸과 마음을 재충전하기 위해 한 이삼일 다 접고 떠나고 싶다.
3) 그 십대 소년이 가출을 했다.

** Get away with (v.) – 벌을 받거나 잡히지 않고 하다.

1) 범죄인들은 잠시 동안은 그들의 범죄에 대가를 치르지 않고 놓여 날수도 있지만 조만간 그들은 대가를 치른다.
2) 그 좀도둑들은 많은 액수의 현찰과 보석을 훔쳐 달아났다.
3) 당신은 이일을 저지르고 그냥 빠져나갈 수 없다.

235. Get back at (v.) – 보복하다.

1) 많은 사람들이 그들을 모욕하는 사람들에게 보복을 할 필요성을 느낀다.
2) 그는 성공함으로써 그를 비방했던 사람들에게 보복했다.
3) 그는 그녀를 모욕했다. 그래서 그녀는 그와 싸움으로서 보복을 했다.

** Get even (v.) – 손실도 없고 이득도 없다. 빚이 없다. 보복하다.

1) 나는 두 가지 주식에 돈을 약간 투자했다. 한 달 뒤에 하나는 10%가 내렸고 다른 것은 10%가 올랐다. 그래서 손실도 이득도 없다.
2) 그들이 그 모임에서 나를 모욕한 후에 나는 우리의 사업거래를 중단함으로서 보복을 했다.
3) 나는 언젠가 그녀에게 받은 것을 되돌려 주겠다.

** Break even (v.) – 이기지도 지지도 않다.

1) 우리는 마침내 그 거래에서 비겼다. 그리고 처음에 투자했던 금액을 되찾았다.

236. Get by / Get by with (v.) – 겨우 생존하다. 운영하다. 지나가다.

1) 그녀는 연금으로 살아간다.
2) 경제가 많은 가족들을 감소된 수입으로 겨우 살아가게 만들었다.
3) 그 트럭은 길게 늘어선 자동차들이 지나가도록 가장자리로 비켰다.

237. Get down to (v.) – 집중하다. 주의를 집중하다. 시작하다.

1) 일에 집중하자.
2) 중간고사가 다음 주이다. 집중적으로 공부를 해야 할 때다.

238. Get a hold of (v.) – 사람을 만나거나 연락하다.

1) 그에게 중요한 소식을 전해야하기 때문에 그와 연락이 되어야한다.

** Get hold of (v.) – 얻다.

1) 임박한 이혼이 그녀를 그녀가 할 수 있는 한 재산을 빨리 손에 넣도록 만들었다.

239. Get in / Get in with (v.) – 도착하다. 들어가다. (승용차에) 타다. 환심을 얻다.

1) 당신의 전화를 못 받아서 미안하지만 나는 하루 종일 밖에 있다가 이제 막 들어왔다.

2) 그 기차는 약 5시 20분에 도착한다.

3) 우리가 다른 차들을 막고 있으니 빨리 차에 타라.

4) 그녀는 정말 그녀의 감독의 환심을 사고 싶어 한다.

**** Get on /Get on with (*v.*) – 차에 타다 (버스, 기차, 비행기 등). 계단을 올라가서 앉다. 진보하다. 친하게 되다. 계속하다(중단 후)**

1) 승객 여러분! 지금 타십시오. 비행기가 30분 후에 떠납니다.

2) 그는 정말 그의 회사에서 진전하고 있다.

3) 그녀는 그녀의 새 남자 친구와 잘 지내고 있는가?

4) 계속 일을 해야 한다 그렇지 않으면 따라 잡기가 힘들다.

240. Get off (*v.*) – 내리다. 제거하다

1) 우리는 다음 정거장에서 내려야 한다.

2) 그녀는 소파에서 일어나 저녁식사를 준비하기 시작했다.

3) 그것을 내 가슴에서 털어 내니 기분이 한결 좋다.

**** Get off easy / Get off with (*v.*) – 많은 벌을 받지 않고 빠져나가다. 무거운 벌을 피하다.**

1) 그 도둑은 잡혔는데 어떻게 해서 쉽게 풀려났다.

2) 말을 듣지 않는 그 아이는 자신이 벌을 많이 받지 않고 쉽게 빠져나갔다는 것을 알았다.

3) 그 범죄인은 매우 가벼운 형으로 중벌을 면했다.

**** Get off one's back (*v.*) – 비난을 멈추다.**

1) 당신은 항상 나를 비난한다. 이제는 그만하고 나를 혼자 있게 놔두시오.

241. Get out / Get out of (*v.*) – 떠나다. 내리다. 피하다. 풀려나다. 이익을 얻다. 얻다 배우다.

1) 나는 이곳이 좋지 않다. 여기서 나가자.

2) 그녀는 몇 시에 수업이 끝나는가?

3) 그는 자동차에서 내려 작은 상점으로 들어갔다.

4) 어떻게 해서 한 새가 새장에서 나와 자유를 찾아 날아갔다.

5) 나는 이 수업을 즐기지 않지만 내가 할 수 있는 한 최대한으로 배우고 있다.

6) 나는 이 세미나에서 새로운 무엇인가를 얻었다.

7) 나는 이 거래에서 아무 것도 얻은 것이 없다.

242. Get over / Get over with (*v.*) – 회복하다. 극복하다. 끝내다.

1) 그는 마침내 전쟁의 아픈 기억을 극복했다.

2) 그녀는 승진되지 못한 아픈 기억이 있었다. 그러나 극복하고 있고 인생을 잘 살 고 있다.

3) 나는 이것을 빨리 끝내고 싶고 내 인생을 살아가고 싶다.

243. Get the brush-off (*v.*) - 불친절하게 취급받다. 무시당하다.

1) 나는 그녀를 만나기 위해 그녀의 집에 잠시 들렀으나 나는 그녀로부터 냉대를 받았다.
2) 그는 그의 혁신적인 아이디어가 모임에서 무시당했다고 느꼈다.

244. Get the feel of (*v.*) - 만지거나 취급해 봄으로서 배우다.

1) 컴퓨터는 재미있는 기계이다. 조만간 만져보기를 바란다.
2) 2-3주가 걸렸으나 그는 곧 그의 새 임무에 대해 배웠다.
3) 이 실크를 만져봐. 대단히 부드러워.

245. Get to (*v.*) - 시작하다. 우연히 시작하다. 도착하다. 불쾌하게 하다. 결정을 내리다.

1) 쇼핑을 가고 싶다. 그러나 돈을 쓸 여유가 있는지 생각해 보아야겠다.
2) 우리는 최근의 친목회에서 서로를 알게 되었다.
3) 우리는 기대했던 것보다 더 일찍 호텔에 도착했다.
4) 그의 무안하게 하는 장난이 그를 불쾌하게 했고 그는 매우 화가 났다.
5) 우리는 모든 가능성을 고려한 것 같다. 이제는 요점으로 들어갑시다.

** Get to the bottom of (*v.*) - 진짜 원인을 찾아내다.

1) 당신의 불행한 감정에 대해 얘기합시다. 그래서 우리가 정말 그 문제의 핵심으로 들어가 원인을 찾아낼 수 있는지 봅시다.

** Get at the heart of (*v.*) - 가장 중요한 사실을 찾다. 가장 중요한 의미를 이해하다.

1) 내가 공부할 때 나는 그 자료의 가장 중요한 사실을 알아내려 한다.
2) 나는 당신의 이야기에서 핵심을 이해했는지 잘 모르겠다.

246. Get together (*v.*) - 함께 만나다. 모이다.

1) 언제 점심이나 저녁을 먹으러 함께 만날까요?
2) 만나서 점심을 먹으며 당신의 제안에 대해 토의해 보자.

247. Get up (*v.*) - 잠자리에서 나오다. 일어서다.

1) 7시다. 일어나야 될 시간이다.
2) 그는 그 노인이 자리에 앉도록 좌석에서 일어났다.

248. Give a hard time (*v.*) - 곤경이나 문제를 주다. 불평하다.

1) 나의 상사가 오늘 나를 힘들게 했다.
2) 나의 최선을 다 했으나 그는 여전히 나를 힘들게 괴롭혔다.
3) 나를 더 이상 힘들게 하지 마라. 그만 하면 됐어.

**** Give a pain (*v.*) – 괴롭히다. 고통을 주다.**

1) 나는 너의 행위가 너무 혐오스러워. 그리고 그 것이 나를 괴롭힌다는 사실을 알기바래.
2) 옆집에서 들리는 그 시끄러운 음악이 정말 고통이야.

249. Give back (*v.*) – 돌려주다.

1) 그는 잠시 들려서 그가 빌린 돈을 돌려주고 싶어한다.
2) 너는 언제 그것을 돌려 줄 것이니?

250. Give in / Give in to (*v.*) – 양보하다. 항복하다.

1) 당신은 말다툼 할 때마다 이길 수 없다. 가끔은 양보해야만 한다.
2) 중동지역의 위기는 오직 한쪽이 항복해야 풀릴 것 같은 생각이다.

251. Give off (*v.*) – 방출하다. 보내다.

1) 어떤 화학 반응들은 독가스를 방출한다.
2) 마이크로 오븐은 방사선을 방출한다.
3) 많은 차량들이 독가스들을 방출하고 그것들은 공기를 심각히 오염시킨다.

252. Give out (*v.*) – 알려지게 하다. 나누어주다. 다 쓰여지다.

1) 그 회사는 다음 월요일에 언론에 알리기로 결정했다.
2) 우리는 모든 초콜릿 칩 과 코코넛 과자들을 나누어주었다.
3) 내 차의 엔진이 마침내 다 소모되었다.

**** Give away (*v.*) – 선물로 만들다. 비밀을 노출하다.**

1) 내가 서울을 떠날 때 나는 내 소지품들을 사람들에게 선사했다.
2) 그의 직원 중 한사람이 그의 회사의 비밀을 유출 한 혐의로 잡혔다.

253. Give up / Give up on (*v.*) – 중단하다. 포기하다. 기대를 접다.

1) 현대의 연구원들은 담배를 끊기보다 마약을 끊는 것이 더 쉽다고 믿는다.
2) 그녀가 주말을 포기하고 일하는 것을 좋아하지 않는다는 것을 알기 때문에 그녀의 상사는 그녀에게 오버타임으로 일할 것을 부탁하지 않았다.
3) 그들은 새집을 사고 싶어하는 그들의 꿈을 접었다.
4) 그 여자는 그녀의 아들이 마약복용으로 체포된 후에 그에 대한 희망을 버렸다.

254. Give voice / Give voice to (*v.*) – 말하다.

1) 대통령은 최근의 파업들과 부진한 경제에 대한 그의 염려를 표했다.
2) 오늘 날 시민들은 다양한 주제들에 목소리를 높이기 위해 단체에 참가한다.

255. Go about (*v.*) – 돌다.

1) 많은 학교들이 재정적인 어려움을 겪고 있다는 소문이 돌고 있다.

** Go around (*v.*) – 돌다. 한 장소에서 다른 장소로 또는 한 사람에서 다른 사람으로 가다.

1) 문제가 있는 그들 관계에 대한 소문이 한동안 돌았다.
2) 그는 설교를 하면서 시골로 돌아다닌다.
3) 당신은 남의 소문(잡담)이나 말하면서 돌아다녀서는 안 된다.

256. Go ahead (*v.*) – 시작하거나 진행하다. 바로 망설임 없이 진행하다.

1) 질문을 해도 될까요? 그럼요. 하세요.
2) 우리는 바로 우리의 프로젝트를 진행할 수 있다.
3) 먼저 가세요. 저는 약 2-3분 후에 따라잡겠습니다.

** Go on / Go on with (*v.*) – 계속하다. 진행하다. 발생하다.

1) 당신의 대화를 중단해서 미안해요. 계속하세요.
2) 꽤 재미있군요. 계속해서 나머지 이야기를 말 해주세요.
3) 여기 무슨 일 있나요?

257. Go along (*v.*) – 진전하다. 진행하다.

1) 컴퓨터를 배우는 것이 내가 진전할수록 더 쉬워진다.
2) 그녀의 일상적 운동은 진행될수록 더 쉬워졌다.

** Go along with (*v.*) – 동의하다. 동행하다.

1) 우리는 당신의 의견이 마음에 든다. 그러나 회사는 지금 당장 그것을 따를 여유가 없다.
2) 다음 토요일에 서울에 가는데 나하고 동행하시겠습니까?

258. Go off (*v.*) – 떠나다. 울리기 시작하다. 터지다. 갑자기 꺼지다.

1) 그는 명성과 부를 찾아 떠났다.
2) 자명 시계는 매일 아침 7시에 울린다.
3) 그는 그 총이 장전되어 있었다는 것을 몰랐고 그것은 뜻밖에 발포되었다.
4) 내가 TV를 보고 있던 중에 갑자기 전기가 나갔다.

** Go off with (*v.*) – (허락 없이 무엇인가 또는 누군가와) 떠나다.

1) 내 여동생이 허락도 없이 나의 새 구두를 가져갔다.

259. Goof off (*v.*) – 쓸데없이 돌아다니다. 빈둥거리며 시간을 낭비하다.

1) 만약 그가 계속해서 빈둥거리면 아마도 해고당할 것이다.
2) 우리는 너무나 열심히 일을 해왔다. 잠시 그냥 좀 돌아다니자.
3) 아이들은 대개 그들의 부모가 없을 때 빈둥거리며 시간을 낭비한다.

260. Go out (*v.*) **- 밖으로 나가다. 유흥가에 가다. 일을 중단하다. 동정이나 연민으로 마음이 움직이다.**

1) 그는 방금 나갔는데 약 2-3분 후에 돌아 올 것이다.
2) 우리친구들 중 몇몇과 이번 주 말에 나갈까 (유흥을 위해)?
3) 그 공장이 재정적 어려움으로 인해 2주전에 작업을 중단했다.
4) 그 노동자들은 새 계약에 동조할 수 없어서 파업에 들어갔다.
5) 그녀는 먹여야 할 어린아이들이 딸린 불쌍한 과부이다. 그래서 나는 그녀를 동 정한다.

261. Go over (*v.*) **- 조심스럽게 또는 자세히 조사하거나 연구하다. 방문하다. 내려가다.**

1) 이 보고서를 다시 자세히 봅시다. 그리고 알아낼 수 있는 것이 있는지 봅시다.
2) 그들은 그들의 여름휴가 때 런던을 방문했다.
3) 저녁 먹으러 저 새 식당에 가자.
4) 그는 언덕을 내려갔고 우리는 그의 소식을 전혀 듣지 못했다.

262. Go steady (*v.*) **- 같은 사람하고만 데이트하다**

1) 그들은 그들끼리만 데이트하기로 결정했다.
2) 그들은 한동안 그들끼리만 데이트를 했으나 곧 별로 공통점이 없다는 것을 깨달았다.

263. Go through (*v.*) **- 승인을 받다. 자세히 연구하거나 감정하다. 경험하다. 장소를 지나다.**

1) 그녀의 지원서가 재검토 위원회의 승인을 얻었다.
2) 나는 나의 책을 모두 뒤졌으나 당신이 빌려 준 책은 찾지 못했다.
3) 그들은 지난 2-3개월 동안 많은 어려움을 겪었다.
4) 저 문을 지나가시오 그러면 오른쪽에 있는 그녀의 방을 찾을 수 있을 것이다.

**** Go through with** (*v.*) **- 완성하다. 완성하기 위해 추구하다. 어려운 것을 끝내다.**

1) 나는 박사과정에 입학이 되었으나 그럴만한 가치가 없다고 생각했기 때문에 끝까지 추구하고 싶지 않았다.
2) 우리는 우리의 처음 계획을 추구하기로 결정했다.

264. Go under (*v.*) **- 실패하다. 파산하다. 가라앉다.**

1) 비틀거리는 경제와 형편없는 판매로 인해 그의 사업은 실패했다.
2) 많은 배들이 최근의 태풍으로 인해 가라앉았다.

**** Go down** (*v.*) **- 작동을 중단하다. 가라앉다.**

1) 오늘 사무실의 컴퓨터가 다운되었다.

2) 부동산 가격이 내려가고 있다.

**** Go up (*v.*) – 증가하다. 오르다.**

1) 1월 1일 이래로 이익이 100% 증가했다.
2) 쌀값이 3개 월 만에 두 배로 올랐다.
3) 기온이 오르고 있다. 오늘은 정말 뜨거운 날이 될 꺼야.

265. Go with (*v.*) – 조화가 되다. 동행해서 나가다.

1) 저 연두색 재킷이 저 푸른색 치마와 잘 어울린다.
2) 그의 셔츠는 그의 타이와 조화가 안 된다.
3) 우리는 몇몇 직원들과 종종 저녁 먹으러 간다.

266. The grass is always greener on the other side of the fence (cliché) – 잔디는 항상 담 너머에 있는 것이 더 푸르다.(속담) 사람들은 종종 자기가 가지고 있는 것이 남의 것만 못하다고 생각한다.

1) 그는 그의 친구의 직업을 원했다. 그러나 그것은 남의 잔디가 더 푸르게 보이는 또 하나의 경우였다.
2) 그녀는 보통 다른 사람들이 그녀보다 더 행복하다고 생각한다. 항상 남의 것이 더 좋아 보인다.

267. Great oaks grow from little acorns (*Proverb*) – 인내심이 필요하다. 위대한 사람들이나 훌륭한 물건들은 대단히 큰 참나무가 작은 도토리 열매에서 시작하는 것처럼 보기에 하찮은 것으로부터 시작되었다.

1) 토마스 에디슨의 인생은 참나무가 도토리에서 자라는 좋은 예이다.

268. Grow on / upon (*v.*) – 더 강렬해지다. 습관이 되다. 좋아지다.

1) 그는 그녀를 처음에는 좋아하지 않았다. 그러나 시간이 흐르면서 그는 그녀를 좋아하게 되었다.
2) 처음에 그녀는 그 아이디어를 좋아하지 않았으나 나중에 좋아하게 되었다.
3) 당신이 우리의 서울 사무실로 전근 가고 싶어하기를 바란다.

269. Grow up (*v.*) – 성숙해 지다.

1) 그들의 아이들 모두가 다 자라서 집에서 떠났다.
2) 선생님은 그녀의 철없는 학생들이 성숙해 지기를 바랬다.
3) 아이들은 곧 자라서 어른이 될 것이다.

H

270. Hand down (*v.*) – 죽은 후 무엇인가를 후손들에게 남기다. 주다.

1) 그녀의 집은 그녀의 부모로부터 물려진 것이다.
2) 신화들과 전설들은 세대에서 세대로 이어 내려온다.
3) 법원은 무죄판결을 내렸다.

**** Hands down (*v.*) – 쉽게**

1) 우리는 그 경기를 11대 0으로 쉽게 이겼다.
2) 그는 그 시험이 어려웠다고 생각했지만 쉽게 합격했다.

271. Hand in hand (*adv.*) – 긴밀히 연결되거나 연관된. 손을 잡고

1) 그 두 사무소들은 긴밀하게 관련이 되어 그 일을 했다.
2) 어떤 커플들은 공원에서 손을 잡고 걷고 있었다.

272. Hand in (*v.*) – 제출하다.

1) 우리는 언제 우리의 기말 보고서를 제출하나요?
2) 소득세신고서는 다음 금요일까지 제출되어야한다.

**** Hand out (*v.*) – 배포하다.**

1) 교수들은 대개 수업 첫날 수업일정표를 나누어준다.
2) 그 판매원은 새 제품의 샘플을 나누어주었다.

**** Handout (*n.*) – 공짜로 주어진 것(거지에게). 기부. 인쇄물**

1) 그 거지는 공짜를 바라면서 지하도 근처에 앉았다.
2) 그는 모든 제공을 거지에게 주는 동냥으로 보아 일체 받지 않았다.
3) 그 교수님은 우리에게 우리의 여름과제와 관련된 인쇄물을 나누어 주었다.

273. Hand over (*v.*) – 지휘권을 양도하다. 주다. 포기하다.

1) 그 퇴임하는 대법관은 그의 책임들을 그의 계승자에게 넘겼다.
2) 그가 퇴직할 때 그는 사업의 지휘권을 그의 아들에게 양도 할 것이다.
3) 시험 때는 메모쪽지의 사용이 불허된다. 그것들을 나에게 달라.

274. Hang around (*v.*) – (게으르게, 어슬렁거리며, 무익하게) 시간을 보내다.

1) 그는 대개 그에게 나쁜 평판을 주는 나쁜 무리들과 시간을 보낸다.

2) 그녀의 퇴임이후 그녀는 집 주변에서 더 많은 시간을 보내오고 있다.

3) 우리가 점심을 함께 하기위해 내가 외출 준비를 할 때까지 여기서 좀 기다려 줄 수 있나요?

**** Hangout (*n.*) – 사람들이 모여서 마시고 먹고 격식 없이 잡담하는 곳.**

1) 2가에 있는 그 작은 식당은 학생들이 모이는 인기 장소이다.

**** Hangover (*n.*) – 과음 한 후의 불쾌한 증상**

1) 지난 밤 과음으로 인해 그는 여전히 몸이 좋지 않다.

275. Hang in / Hang in there (*v.*) – 포기하지 않다. 꾸준하다.

1) 나는 당신이 어려운 시기를 보내고 있다는 것을 안다. 그러나 포기하지 말라.

2) 그 직업은 어렵다. 그러나 조금 더 꾸준하면 할 수 있다.

**** Hang on (*v.*) – 어딘가에 꽉 매달리다. 전화를 잡고 기다리다.**

1) 그는 일 년 전에 임시로 해고당했다. 그러나 그는 그의 회사가 곧 그를 재고용 하리라는 희망 속에 기다리고 있다.

2) 119구조 팀이 올 때까지 로프를 잡고 있어라.

3) 더 나은 직업을 찾을 때까지 현재의 직업을 잡고 있는 것이 더 현명하다.

4) 잠시만 기다려요. 그녀가 통화를 끝내는 대로 연결하여 드리겠어요.

**** Hang up (*v.*) – 전화통화를 끊다. 고리에 걸다.**

1) 누군가 문을 노크하고 있어서 이만 전화를 끊어야 하겠다.

2) 당신이 전화를 끊었을 때 나의 말이 끝나지 않았었다. 지금 전화를 끊지 마라. 나는 말이 아직 다 끝나지 않았다.

3) 당신은 그림이 어디에 걸리기를 원하는가? /이곳에 거시오.

**** Hang-up (*n.*) – 무엇인가에 대한 (비정상적인) 두려움.**

1) 그녀의 차사고 이래로 그녀는 운전에 대한 두려움이 있다.

2) 비행기가 종종 추락하므로, 어떤 승객들은 비행기 타는 것에 대한 두려움이 있다.

3) 많은 군인들이 전쟁에 대해 두려움을 느낀다.

276. Happy hour (*n.*) – 술집이나 레스토랑 등에서 칵테일이나 음식이 디스카운트 된 가격으로 나오는 시간

1) 오우크 트리 라운지에서의 해피아워는 저녁 6시부터 8시까지다.

2) 그들은 항상 닭 날개를 공짜로 주기 때문에 나는 그들의 해피아워를 좋아한다.

277. Haul away (*v.*) – 실어가다.

1) 그 쓰레기차는 월요일마다 부엌쓰레기를 실어가고 재활용되는 것들은 목요일마다 가져간다.

2) 그 난폭한 데모꾼 들이 경찰에 의해 연행되어 갔다.

278. Have a ball (*v.*) – 즐거운 시간을 갖다.

1) 그 파티는 사실 꽤 지루했다. 그러나 하여튼 나는 즐거운 시간을 가졌다.
2) 그는 아이들을 서커스로 데리고 가서 재미있는 시간을 보냈다.

279. Have an eye for (*v.*) – 훌륭한 감각을 가지다.

1) 그녀는 색깔 조화와 실내장식에 뛰어난 감각을 가지고 있다.
2) 당신은 음악을 들을 줄 아는 귀와 예술작품을 볼 줄 아는 안목을 기르는 것이 필요하다.

**** Have an eye on (*v.*) – (원하는 것을 강도를 가지고) 주시하다. 몹시 관심을 가지다.**

1) 내가 식품을 사고 있는 동안 아이들을 잘 보세요.
2) 그는 한동안 그녀에게 몹시 관심을 가졌다.

280. Have been around (*v.*) – 자신을 돌볼 수 있는 경험과 능력을 갖다. 많은 곳을 다녔고 많은 일을 했다.

1) 당신하고 나는 오랫동안 많은 경험을 쌓아서 우리자신을 돌볼 수가 있다. 그러나 그녀는 아직 충분히 그렇지 못하고 순진하다.
2) 그는 경험도 많고 지식도 풍부해서 나는 그를 좋아한다.

281. Have done with (*v.*) – 끝내다.

1) 내가 빌려준 책 다 보았니?
2) 내가 처음 생각했던 것보다 더 복잡한 것이라서 아직 끝내지 않았다.
3) 이 일을 끝내고 다음 일을 착수하자.

282. Have it out (*v.*) – 의견의 불일치나 문제를 공개토의나 싸움 등을 통해 해결하다. 수술로 제거하다.

1) 우리는 둘 다 서로에게 감정이 좋지 않으므로 털어놓고 얘기하는 것이 좋겠다.
2) 지금 당장 털어놓고 얘기하자. 그래서 끝내자.
3) 3개월 전에 그는 그의 신장제거 수술을 받았다.

283. Have no use for (*v.*) – 참을 수가 없다. 싫어하다. 필요 없다.

1) 나는 동물들을 학대하고 함부로 취급하는 사람들을 참을 수가 없다.
2) 그는 믿을만한 사람이 아니기 때문에 그를 싫어한다.
3) 나는 이 의자가 필요 없으니 가져가시오.

**** Of use – 유용한**

1) 내 일을 하는데 컴퓨터가 유용하게 쓰인다.

284. Have on (*v.*) – 입고 있다. 계획하다.

1) 그녀는 낡은 청바지와 빨간 티셔츠를 입고 있다.
2) 당신은 걱정이 있는 것처럼 보인다. 무슨 생각을 하고 있는지 말해줘요.

285. Have one's hands full (*v.*) – 많은 일로 바쁘다. 압도당하다.

1) 우리는 지금 너무나 할 일이 많고 바빠서 더 이상 주문을 받을 수가 없다.
2) 그녀는 일하면서 아이들 셋을 키우느라 쩔쩔 맬 정도로 바쁘다.

286. Have over (*v.*) – 집으로 초대하다.

1) 언제 저녁식사 같이 하게 그들을 초대하자.
2) 나는 당신의 가족과 당신을 주말에 초대하고 싶다.
3) 당신을 오늘 저녁 집으로 오게 해서 함께 축구경기를 보고 싶다.

287. Have the courage of one's convictions (*v.*) – 자신의 신념대로 행동하는 용기가 있다.

1) 성공하는 사람들은 그들의 신념대로 행동하는 용기가 있다.
2) 만약 그의 신념대로 밀고 나가는 용기가 없었다면 그는 아마 오래 전에 포기했을 것이다.

288. Have two strikes against one (*v.*) – 계속해서 두 번이나 어려움을 겪다. 자신에게 불이익이 되는 일이 있다.

1) 그는 벌써 두 번이나 연거푸 찍혔다. 한번은 회의에 늦었고 그 다음에는 상사 앞에서 문을 쾅 닫았다.
2) 그는 벌써 두 번이나 불이익을 가져올 수 있는 일을 했기 때문에 조심하는 편이 났다.

289. Head above water (*n.*) – 재정적 어려움에서 벗어나 있다.

1) 사업이 형편없고 간신히 재정적 어려움에서 벗어나 있다.
2) 나는 일을 두 곳이나 하면서도 재정적 어려움에서 벗어나는 것 같지 않다.

290. Heart goes out to – 동정심을 가지다.

1) 당신은 많은 어려움을 겪었기 때문에 동정심이 간다.
2) 우리는 술 취한 운전사에게 치인 가엾은 동물에게 동정심을 느꼈다.

** Have a heart (*v.*) – 동정심을 가지다. 배려하다.

1) 당신은 동정심을 가지고 저 불쌍한 남자를 도와야 한다.

291. Heart-to-heart (*adj.*) – 개인 적이고 진실한, 솔직한

1) 나는 그와 솔직한 대화를 하고 싶다.
2) 우리는 마음을 터놓고 진실하게 대화를 오래 했다. 그리고 그것이 우리 사이를 더 좋게 만들었다.

292. Help oneself / Help oneself to (*v.*) – (부탁하지 않고) 스스로 대접하다.

1) 그것은 뷔페 식 점심이라 모든 사람들이 각자 스스로 음식을 갖다 먹는다.

2) 나는 샐러드와 스프를 한 접시 더 먹을 거야.

3) 호텔들의 손님들은 가끔 여분의 타월을 물어보지 않고 갖다 쓴다.

293. Help out (*v.*) – 누군가가 도움이 필요할 때 도움을 주다. 돕다.

1) 당신이 파티준비로 너무 바쁘면 내가 도와 줄 수 있다.

2) 그녀가 새 차를 샀을 때 그녀의 부모가 도와주었다.

3) 그는 집 주변에서 집안일을 도와주는 것으로 매주 용돈을 받는다.

294. Hinge on / Hinge upon (*v.*) – 의지하다. ~에 의해 결정이 되다.

1) 많은 경제학자들이 한국 경제의 변화는 정부의 빅딜 정책에 달렸다고 말한다.

2) 우리의 휴가는 우리의 재정 상태에 달렸다.

295. Hit it off (*v.*) – 잘 지내다.

1) 그들은 잘 지내더니 곧 베스트 프렌드가 되었다.

2) 우리는 그냥 사이가 좋다.

296. Hit the ceiling (*v.*) – 대단히 화를 내다.

1) 나의 게으른 동료가 감독관직으로 승진했다는 것을 알았을 때 나는 대단히 화를 내었다.

2) 그 보수비용이 얼마가 들것인가를 알았을 때 그는 대단히 화를 내었다.

297. Hit the jackpot (*v.*) – 대박을 터뜨리다. 대단한 성공을 얻다.

1) 어떤 행운의 사람이 지난 밤 복권 추첨에서 2천만 불의 대박을 안았다.

2) 그 여자는 대박을 터뜨렸을 때 기뻐서 비명을 질렀다.

298. Hit the road (*v.*) – (특히 차로) 떠나다.

1) 휴일의 교통체증이 시작되기 전에 우리는 떠나야겠다.

2) 아. 벌써 7시군. 떠나는 것이 좋겠어요. 대화 재미있었어요. 다음에 다시 들리겠어요.

299. Hold back (*v.*) – 자제하다. 못하게 하다. 나타내지 않다.

1) 경찰은 군중들을 자제시키기 위해 범죄 장소에 비상선을 쳤다.

2) 너의 좋지 못한 태도가 너의 인생을 살아가는데 걸림돌이 되게 하지 말라.

3) 그는 그의 구좌를 잃지 않기 위해 방지책으로서 어떤 정보는 노출하지 않았다.

300. Hold down (*v.*) – 억압하다.

1) 독재 정부들은 다양한 수단을 통해 국민들을 억압한다.

2) 경찰이 투입되어 시끄러운 공연 군중을 자제시켰다.

301. Hold it (*v.*) **- 누군가 무엇을 하는 것을 막다. 멈추다**

1) 경찰이 좀도둑을 잡았다 그리고 그에게 바로 거기에 멈추라고 명령했다.
2) 거기 잠깐만. 그것은 사실이 아니 예요.

**** Hold on** (*v.*) **- 기다리다. 멈추다. 꾸준히 견디다.**

1) 잠깐만 기다릴 수 있나요? 나는 지금 바쁩니다.
2) 잠깐 만 기다리세요. 그녀가 통화를 끝내는 대로 전화를 연결 해 드리겠어요.
3) 그가 산을 내려갈 때 그는 구명줄에 끈질기게 매달렸다.

302. Hold in (*v.*) **- 속에 간직하다.**

1) 자신의 감정을 속에 담아두는 것은 건강에 좋지 않다.
2) 당신의 감정을 속에 담아 두지 말고 건강하게 해소할 수 있는 길을 찾아라.

303. Hold off / Hold off on (*v.*) **- 연기하다.**

1) 한 2-3 주 당신의 휴가계획을 미룰 수 있습니까?
2) 돌아다니며 알아볼 때까지 컴퓨터 사는 것을 연기해라.
3) 우리가 좀 더 알게 될 때까지 결혼을 미루어야 하겠어요.

**** On hold - 연기된, 대기 중 (전화에서)**

1) 그 건축 계획은 경제가 좋아질 때까지 연기 중이다.
2) 그 전화선이 통화 중인데요. 대기 중으로 돌리겠어요.

**** Hold over** (*v.*) **- 연기하다. 계획했던 것보다 더 오래 계속하다.**

1) 지금 모든 정보가 없으므로 다음 주로 우리의 회의를 연기할 수 있을 까요?
2) 대중의 요구로 그 공연은 일주일 더 계속될 예정이다.

304. Hold one's head up (*v.*) **- 창피스러워 하지 않고 자신을 가지다.**

1) 당신은 좋은 남자다. 자신을 가지고 그 소문에 걱정하지 마라.

**** Keep your chin up** (*v.*) **- 용기를 가지고 문제를 직면하다.**

1) 시기가 어렵다는 것을 안다. 그러나 용기를 가지고 헤쳐 나가라.
2) 당신이 직업을 잃었다는 소식에 유감이다. 그러나 용기를 가지고 일을 해 나가라. 나는 당신이 곧 다른 직업을 찾으리라 확신한다.

305. Horns of a dilemma (*n.*) **- 두 가지 선택이 있으나 어떤 것도 만족스럽지 못하고 하고 싶지도 않음.**

1) 그녀는 그녀가 진퇴양난에 빠진 것을 알았다. 그녀가 아이를 가지면 그녀의 직업을 계속할 수 없고, 그녀의 직업을 계속하면 아이를 잘 기를 수가 없다.

306. Hot air (*n.*) - 과장된, 감정이 섞인 말도 안 되는 말

1) 그녀는 그만두겠다고 항상 협박하지만 모두 감정에서 나온 말이다.

2) 그가 하는 말은 거의 과장된 것들이다.

307. Hot potato (*n.*) - 대부분 열띤 논쟁을 일으키고 해결을 보기 힘든 질문이나 문제점

1) 정치나 종교는 항상 열띤 논쟁을 일으키고 해답을 얻기 힘들다.

2) 천주교에서 피임의 문제는 확실히 열띤 논쟁을 일으키고 해답을 얻기가 쉽지 않은 주제이다.

** Hot water (*n.*) - 곤경

1) 그녀는 대중 앞에서 종교에 관한 말을 함으로서 곤경에 빠졌다.

2) 그는 너무 많은 숙제를 하지 않았으므로 곤경에 빠져있다.

** Hot seat (*n.*) - 문제를 일으킬 소지가 많은 자리

1) 큰 도시의 시장은 문제가 되는 자리이다. 이것은 도시의 현상적인 세금 인상 문제 때문이다.

I

308. If anything (*adv.*) – 대신, 오히려

1) 일요일은 따스하지가 않을 것이다. 대신 서늘할 것이다.
2) 고양이들은 나쁜 애완용 동물이 아니다. 오히려 그들은 꽤 좋은 벗이다.

309. If worse comes to worst – 만약 최악의 사태가 되면

1) 만약 최악의 사태가 벌어지면 우리는 그 항거가 잠잠해질 때까지 대학교를 폐쇄할 것이다.
2) 최악의 사태 시에는 공장을 닫지 않기 위해 약간의 노동자들을 임시로 해고해야 할 것이다.

310. Ill at ease (*adj.*) – 불안 초조하고 불편한

1) 많은 승객들은 그들이 처음 비행기를 탈 때 불안 초조하고 불편하다.
2) 그가 그렇게 그녀를 쳐다보는 것이 그녀를 불편하게 했다.

311. I tell you what / Tell you what – 내가 생각했던 아이디어가 있어요.

1) 당신은 오늘 하이킹하고 싶어 하는 것을 안다. 그러나 비가 오고 있어요. 내 생각에는 팝콘이나 만들고 영화나 보자.
2) 그 중국 음식점은 오늘 영업하지 않는다. 내 생각에는 오늘은 이탈리언 음식을 먹으러 가고 다음에 중국 음식을 먹자.

312. Impose on / upon (*v.*) – 강요하다, 불편하게 하다, 이익을 취하다, 부담을 주다, 영향을 미치다.

1) 강요하고 싶지는 않지만 당신 스테레오의 볼륨을 줄여 주겠습니까? 나는 공부를 하려고 합니다.
2) 그는 예고도 없이 찾아오기 때문에 항상 우리를 불편하게 한다.
3) 너무 오래 있음으로 당신에게 부담을 주고 싶지 않다.
4) 정부는 국민들에게 높은 세율을 부과한다.
5) 오랫동안 일하는 것이 나에게 과로하게 만든다.

313. In addition (*adv.*) – 여분으로, 게다가

1) 그는 나에게 공연티켓을 사는 것 외에도 저녁식사까지 대접했다.
2) 내가 이미 주문했던 것 말고 두 개의 책꽂이를 더 주문하고 싶다.
3) 훼밀리 사이즈 외에 펄스널 사이즈 피자를 한 개 더 가져오시오.

314. In advance (*adv.*) – 미리. 앞서서. 전에

1) 나는 한 주 계획을 미리 세우는 것을 좋아한다.
2) 정찰 군들은 정규군보다 먼저 전쟁터에 간다.
3) 그녀의 아이디어들은 대개 다른 직원들에 의해 제공된 생각들보다 앞섰고 더 나은 것들이었다.

315. In and out (*adv.*) – 들어오고 나가고

1) 그녀는 온종일 들락거렸다. 그리고 언제 돌아올지 모른다.
2) 나는 온종일 들락거릴 거야. 나에게 할 말이 있으면 오늘 저녁 7시 이후에 전화해.

316. In any case / In any event / At all events (*adv.*) – 확실히, 하여튼, 어떤 일이 있더라도

1) 지금 당장은 직원이 너무 많아 채용을 하지 않는다. 그러나 어떻게 해서라도 조직내에 당신을 위한 자리를 마련 할 수 있는 것만은 확실하다.
2) 언제 돌아올지 확실하지는 않으나 하여튼 12월까지는 돌아 올 것이다.

317. In arrears / In arrears on (*adv.*) – 의무적으로 납입해야 하는 일에 연체된

1) 그들은 3개월이나 집세를 내지 못해서 쫓겨났다.
2) 그녀는 그녀의 신용카드를 포함해서 매달 내는 고지서 모두가 연체된 상태에 있다.

318. In a sense (*adv.*) – 어떤 면에서는

1) 승진이 되면 더 많은 일을 해야 하기 때문에 어떤 면에서는 나는 급여를 더 받고 싶지 않다.
2) 이런 저런 이유들로 헤어지는 것이 어떤 면에서는 그들에게는 더 나은 일이었다.

319. Inasmuch as (*conj.*) – ~라는 사실 때문에, 때문에

1) 날씨가 우리가 기대했던 것만큼 좋지 않기 때문에 하와이 여행을 연기할 것이다. 사실은 매일 비가 오고 있다.
2) 정치인들이 간청을 하여 그는 마음을 바꾸어 재선에 출마하고 있다.

320. In behalf of / In one's behalf (*prep.*) – ~의 이익을 위하여

1) 그 기념비는 한국의 독립을 위하여 생명을 바친 모든 사람들을 위해 세워졌다.
2) 평화봉사단원들은 권리를 박탈당한 사람들을 위해 세계 여러 곳에서 일을 한다.

****On behalf of / On one's behalf – 위하여, 대신하여**

1) 어린이 옹호자들은 모든 곳의 어린이들을 위해서 일을 한다.
2) 나의 할머니를 대신해서 여러분 모두에게 여러분들의 관대함과 친절에 감사한다.
3) Tokyo 경제 정상회담에 참석하고 있는 대통령을 대신하여 국무총리가 그 장례식에 참석했다.

321. In case (*conj.*) – 만약

1) 만약 내가 늦게까지 일해야 되면 당신이 어디 있을지 알려줘요.
2) 비가 올 것을 대비해 우산을 가져갈 것이다.

** In case / Just in case (*adv.*) – 필요하다면, 조심으로서

1) 긴급 할 때를 대비하여 여분의 돈을 가져가는 것이 났다.
2) 나는 대개 수표나 신용카드로 지불한다. 그러나 신용카드나 수표를 받지 않을 경우를 대비해 약간의 현금을 가져갈 것이다.
3) 길을 잃거나 지연이 되는 경우를 대비해 나의 전화번호를 가져가가시오.

** In case of (*prep.*) – ~의 경우에

1) 만약 졸음이 올 경우에는 그 약을 중단하라고 의사가 말했다.
2) 불이 난 경우에는 건물을 탈출하기위해 계단을 사용하시오.

322. In charge (of) (*adv., adj., prep.*) – 권한이 있는, 책임지는, 담당하는

1) 대통령은 그가 떠나 있을 때는 부통령에게 권한을 남긴다.
2) 닥터 리는 고참 외과의이고 또한 응급실을 책임진다.
3) 누가 복사기를 담당하는가?

** On the charge of (*prep.*) – 혐의로

1) 세 명의 남자가 밀수 혐의로 오늘 일찍 체포되었다.
2) 그 여자는 사기와 횡령혐의로 유죄를 입증받았다.

323. In circulation / Into circulation (*adj.*) – 평소와 같이 일하는, 회전이 되는

1) 그 경제학자는 2년 전에 실직한 이래로 직업을 잡지 못했다.
2) 회사 내의 정보에 의하면 새 앨범이 명절시기에 맞춰 다음 주 초에 상점들로 배송이 될 것이라고 했다.

324. In common (*adv.*) – 함께 나누는, 공동으로

1) 행복한 커플들은 대개 공통되는 흥미가 많다.
2) 그들은 같은 동네에서 자랐고 같은 학교를 다녔고 비슷한 직업을 선택했기 때문에 많은 공통점이 있다.

325. In consequence (*adv.*) – 결과로서, 결국에, 그러므로

1) 그는 그의 매니저와 말다툼을 했고 그 결과로서 해고당했다.
2) 강우량은 기대치보다 훨씬 더 많았고 그래서 대단한 홍수가 발생했다.

**** In consequence of (*prep.*) – 때문에, 결과로서**

1) 그의 부인의 학대하는 성격 때문에 그는 그의 부인으로부터 이혼하는 것이 허락되었고 아이들의 양육권도 주어졌다.
2) 그 학생은 계속되는 자신의 결석 때문에 질책을 받았고 경고를 받았다.

326. In consideration of (*prep.*) – ~를 고려하여, 때문에

1) 그 상은 그녀가 지역사회에 공헌 한 것을 고려하여 주어졌다..
2) 당신이 가외로 많은 일들을 한 것을 고려해서 나는 기꺼이 원래 계약했던 것보다 더 많이 지불하고 싶다.

327. In defiance of (*prep.*) – ~에 불복종하여

1) 그녀는 부모님의 통행금지에 불복종하여 늦게 집에 왔다.
2) 직원들은 그 회사의 노 스트라이크 정책에 불복종하여 파업에 들어갔다.

328. In dispute (*adj.*) – 논쟁 중

1) 그 강도 행각에서 그가 담당한 역할이 논쟁중이다.
2) 최근의 사기와 부패 혐의를 들며 조합지도자들이 회사의 연금계획을 논쟁 중에 있다.

329. In earnest (*adj., adv.*) – 진지하게, 진지한 의도로, 사실은, 정말

1) 그녀는 작가가 되고 싶은 그녀의 목표를 위해 진지하게 일했다.
2) 몇몇 소방관들이 천정이 무너져 내렸을 때 열심히 일하고 있었다.
3) 나는 농담하고 있지 않다. 내가 말한 것은 진심이다. 당신의 일의 질을 높이던가 아니면 해고이다.

330. In effect (*adj., adv.*) – 사실은, 사실, 효력발생의, 운용되는

1) 그들이 사실 무슨 말을 하고 있나?
2) 사실 그들이 말하는 것은, 한주일 더 컴퓨터 시스템이 작동치 않을 것이라는 거다.
3) 사실 열심히 공부하는 것은 당신의 미래를 위해 보험을 들어두는 것이다.
4) 오늘 부터 효력이 발생되는 그 새 법률은 어떤 이유로든지 경찰이 아무나 세워서 조사할 수 있게 하는 것이다.

**** In fact (*adv.*) – 사실은**

1) 사람들은 어떤 일들은 정말 하기 쉽다고 하지만 사실은 그것들이 항상 하기 쉬운 것은 아니다.
2) 그것이 진품 같지만 사실은 교묘하게 만든 모조품이다.

**** In force (*adj.*) – 실제의, 작용중인, 유효한**

1) 새 마약법이 현재 작용 중이고 재범들은 엄하게 다루어 질 것이다.

2) 직원들이 경쟁사로부터 시간제 일을 맡는 것이 금지되어 있는 그 회사의 정책이 아직 유효하다.

331. In evidence (*adj.*) - 쉽게 눈에 띄는, 현저한

1) 겨우 이른 3월인데 봄이 완연하다.
2) 거리 곳곳마다 빈곤과 공항이 현저하다.

332. In favor of (*prep.*) - ~의 편에서, ~를 지지하여

1) 대부분의 노동자들은 회사의 최근의 계약조건을 선호한다.
2) 나는 주 5일 근무를 지지한다.

333. In full swing (*adj.*) - 풀가동 중인, 최상의 활동 중에

1) 그 공연은 내가 도착했을 때 이미 한창이었다.
2) 서서히 시작하더니 지금은 명절 쇼핑시즌이 무르익었다.

334. In general (*adv.*) - 일반적으로, 대부분이, 전체적으로

1) 비록 그들의 광고지에서 좋다고 주장하는 것만큼은 아니지만 일반적으로, 그것은 좋은 프로그램이다.
2) 미국의 서남부는 대부분이 덥고 건조하다.
3) 나의 학급에 있는 학생들은 전체적으로 행실이 바르다.

335. In half (*adv.*) - 반으로

1) 그는 사과를 반으로 잘랐다.
2) 내가 할일을 반 밖에 하지 않았기 때문에 내 용돈이 반으로 줄었다.

336. In honor of (*prep.*) - 경의를 표하여, 축하하여

1) 퇴직하는 김교수에게 경의를 표하기 위해 환송파티가 열릴 것이다.
2) 어린이날은 아이들을 축하하기위해 제정되었다.

337. In kind (*adv.*) - 상품이나 서비스나 음식등 돈이 아닌 것으로 지불하다.

1) 그는 그의 여자 친구를 속였고 그녀는 나중에 다른 것으로 복수했다.
2) 리츠칼튼 호텔이나 하이야트리전시 호텔은 정도는 서비스의 차원에서 정도는 다르지만 다른 것에서는 같다.

** Kind of - 오히려

1) 전구가 두어개 나가서 이 안이 좀 어두운 편이다.
2) 당신이 한 일에 대해서는 동의하지만 당신이 사용한 방법에 대해서는 동의할 수 있을지 모르겠다.

338. In (the) light of (*adj.*) – 고려하는, 참작하여

1) 우리는 당신이 최근에 우리에게 보고한 그 정보를 고려하여 그 일을 다시 조사하기로 결정했다.
2) 거리의 사람들의 어려움을 돕기 위한 그녀의 헌신을 참작하여 새 병원의 한 병동을 그녀의 이름을 따서 하기로 결정했다.

339. In line (*adv.*) – 줄서서

1) 우리는 표를 샀고 그들이 우리를 입장시킬 때까지 줄서서 있어야 했다.

** In line (for) (*adj.*) – 다음 순번, 적당한 제한안에

1) Mr. Kim 의 상사는 그가 승진에 있어 다음 순번이라고 말했다.
2) 정부는 물가를 적당한 선에 안정시키기 위해 무엇인가를 할 필요가 있다.

** In line with (*prep.*) – ~와 조화되어, 동의하는

1) 그 새로운 제안은 회사의 전체적인 정책과 조화된다.
2) 행정실장은 그 학생의 행위가 대학교의 정책들에 위반되어 경고장을 발행했다.
3) 그 회사의 고용제도는 새 연방법에 준한다.

** On the line – 위험한, 위험한 처지에, 전화선에

1) 당신은 그 프로젝트에 성공해야 한다. 그렇지 않으면 당신직업이 위태롭다.
2) Mr. Lee 가 전화했는데 당신하고 통화하고 싶어 한다.

340. In part (*adv.*) – 부분적으로, 어떤 면에서

1) 나는 나의 직업을 그만두었다. 그 한 이유가 더 이상 직업이 즐겁지가 않았고 또한 보수도 작아서였다.
2) 그들은 어떤 면에서 그 집의 매매가치를 높이기 위해 개축을 했다.

341. In particular (*adv.*) – 구체적으로, 특히

1) 나는 영문학에서도 구체적으로 말한다면 낭만주의를 전공했다.
2) 나는 휴가 중에서도 특히 해변에서 느긋하게 즐기는 휴가를 좋아한다.
3) 그는 먹는 것을 좋아하는데 특히 과일과 야채를 좋아한다.

342. In person (*adv.*) – 직접

1) 교장선생님이 직접 고등학교 댄스파티에 나타났다.
2) 나의 지난 번 급여에서 뗀 금액에 대해서 직접 얘기할 수 있을까요?

343. In place (*adv.*) – 제자리에, 원래자리에

1) 그녀의 딸의 방은 엉망이었다. 하나도 제자리에 없었다.
2) 너의 물건들을 원래자리에 놓아라.

3) 그는 정리를 잘한다. 모든 것이 항상 제자리에 있다.

**** In place of / Instead of (*prep.*) – 대신에**

1) 그들은 내가 주문한 중간 사이즈의 야채 피자대신에 큰 페페로니 피자를 보냈다.
2) 모든 사람들이 놀랍게도 그는 오랫동안 사귄 그의 약혼녀 대신에 방금 만난 여자와 결혼을 했다.

**** Out of place (*adj., adv.*) – 부적절한, 어울리지 않는**

1) 나만이 양복을 입고 있어서 부적절한 느낌이 들었다.
2) 대단히 큰 그 소파는 그 작은 거실에 어울리지 않았다.

344. In print (*adj.*) – 인쇄되거나 출판된, 여전히 발행자에 의해 판매되는

1) 그녀는 발행된 그녀의 책을 보는 날을 갈망한다.
2) 미안하지만 그 책은 더 이상 발행이 안 된다.
3) 6백만 부 이상이 인쇄되어 있다.

**** Out of print – 더 이상 인쇄가 안 되는, 더 이상 발행이 안되는**

1) 그 책은 인쇄중단이다.
2) 당신이 주문한 그 책은 발행이 안 된다.

345. In private (*adv.*) – 개인적으로, 비밀로

1) 개인적으로 말 좀 할 수 있을까요?
2) 그 전화가 개인적인 것이라 그녀는 아무도 없는데서 혼자서 받았다.

**** In public (*adv.*) – 공개적으로, 다른 사람들이 있는 곳에서**

1) 사람들은 혼자 있을 때보다 공개 장소에 있을 때 다르게 행동한다.
2) 그 사고 후 그들이 함께 공개석상에 나타난 것은 처음이다.

346. In question (*adj.*) – 거론중인, 의심이 되는

1) 거론이 되고 있는 그 사람들은 더 이상 회사에 근무하지 않는다.
2) 의심이 되는 그날 그는 그 지역에 없어서 그는 그 범죄를 저지를 수가 없었다.

347. In reference to / With reference to / In regard to (*prep.*) – 관련되어, 관하여

1) 나는 가장 최근의 전기요금과 관련하여 전화를 하고 있는데요.
2) 그는 H사와의 거래는 무산되었지만 S사와의 거래에 관련해서는 좋아 보인다고 했다.
3) 우리는 팀의 최근 패배에 관하여 회의를 했다.

**** In relation to / With relation to (*prep.*) – 관련하여, 비교하여, 관하여**

1) 대화는 회사에서의 나의 미래에 관한 것이었다..
2) 그녀는 그녀의 미래에 도움이 될 것과 관련하여 전공을 선택했다.

** In respect to / With respect to (*prep.*) – 관련하여, 관하여

1) 그 새로운 법이 어떻게 사람들에게 영향을 줄지에 관해 이야기합시다.

2) 경영진은 그의 작업활동에 관해 그에게 말했다..

348. In return (*adv.*) – 보답으로

1) 나는 그녀에게 선물을 주었는데 그녀는 보답으로 저녁을 샀다.

2) 딕은 내가 내 차를 수리하는 것을 도왔다. 그 보답으로 나는 그를 저녁식사에 초대했다.

349. Ins and outs (*n.*) – 어떤 활동이나 과정의 자세한 것

1) 그는 그 지역의 모든 정치적 상황을 자세하게 안다.

2) 그 서비스 맨은 내 컴퓨터 시스템에 대해 자세히 알았다.

350. In short order (*adv.*) – 지체 없이

1) 당신이 무엇을 원하는지 말해 그러면 지체 없이 끝내어 놓을 테니.

2) 우리는 모든 일을 그가 원하는 대로 지체 없이 했다.

351. In short supply (*adj.*) – 충분하지 않은

1) 오늘날, 정직한 사람이 많지 않은 것 같다.

2) 몇몇 후진국들에서는 의료용품과 음식이 부족하다.

352. Inside / Inside of (*prep.*) – 안에

1) 그의 어머니는 그에게 그의 방에 들어가서 청소를 하라고 했다.

2) 등산객들은 동굴 속에 머무름으로서 그 폭풍에서 살아남았다.

** Inside out (*adj.*) – 안쪽 면이 뒤집혀진

1) 그녀는 그녀의 재킷을 뒤집어 입었다.

2) 우리는 빨래를 널기 전에 속을 뒤집었다.

3) 그는 너무 피곤한 바람에 그의 셔츠를 뒤집어 입었다.

353. Insofar as (*adj.*) – ~하는 한

1) 내가 할 수 있는 한, 나이에 불구하고 일을 계속 할 것이다.

2) 그가 할 수 있는 한, 시간이 조금씩 날 때마다 그의 프로젝트를 했다.

354. In spite of (*prep.*) – ~에도 불구하고

1) 짙은 안개에도 불구하고 그 비행기는 무사히 착륙했다.

2) 봄날의 폭우에도 불구하고 그들은 캠핑을 갔다.

** Notwithstanding (*adj., adv.*) – ~에도 불구하고

1) 나는 어떤 반대에도 불구하고 나의 계획을 진행할 것이다.

2) 세계 환경지도자들이 습지개발 제안을 반대했지만 그럼에도 불구하고 그 제안은 국회에서 통과되었다.

355. In stock (*adj.*) – 팔 물건이 있는, 현재 보유하고 있는, 무엇인가를 팔 준비가 되어 있는

1) 품목들이 너무 빨리 팔리면, 물건을 계속해서 들이기가 어렵다.
2) 당신이 주문한 신발들이 지금 들어와 있다.

** Out of stock (*adj.*) – 팔 물건이 없는

1) 그 광고된 컴퓨터는 지금 팔 물건이 없다. 그래서 그들은 그녀에게 뢰인 첵(나중에 물건이 들어오면 연락해 주겠다는 약속의 카드)을 주었다.
2) 그 품목들은 지금 품절이다.

356. In substance (*adv.*) – 주요 부분이나 기본적 부분에서, 본질적으로

1) 이 두 전축들은 가격만 제외하고 기본적으로 같다.
2) 그의 주장은 꽤 신빙성 있게 들리지만 일반적으로 본질적인 것이 결여되어 있다.

357. In terms of (*prep.*) – 특히 ~에 관해, ~에 관해서는

1) 경기 능력에 있어서 금년의 팀은 작년 팀에 비교가 안 된다.
2) 인정받음에 있어서 교사들은 대개 많이 받지 못한다.

358. In that (*conj.*) – 때문에, ~의 이유로

1) 가을은 신선한 과일과 야채들이 풍부한 시기이기 때문에 나는 가을을 좋아한다.

359. In the air (*adv.*) – 모든 사람들의 생각 속에, 일반적인 느낌

1) 청중이 새 영화의 세계적인 특별 개봉을 기다렸을 때 기대감과 흥분감이 모든 사람들의 생각 속에 가득했다.
2) 이제 4월이다. 봄이 완연해.
3) 벌써 크리스마스 분위기이다.

** Up in the air – 해결되지 않은, 결정되지 않은

1) 최근 선거의 승리자가 여전히 결정되고 있지 않다.
2) 그녀가 제때에 졸업을 할 수 있을지는 결정되지 않고 있다.
3) 그 문제들은 여전히 해결되지 않고 있다.

360. In the first place (*adv.*) – 시작시, 처음에

1) 나는 처음부터 그에게 약혼했다고 말했다.

361. In the least (*adv.*) – 조금도

1) 나는 조금도 야구를 이해하지 못한다.

2) 그녀는 조금도 그에게 관심이 없다.

362. In the main (*adv.*) – 일반적으로, 대부분, 대체적으로

1) 일반적으로 대부분의 사람들이 돈을 벌기위해 열심히 일한다.
2) 대체적으로 그 영화는 흥행에 성공했다.

363. In the nick of time (*adv.*) – 아주 중요한 시점에 / 순간에

1) 그녀는 막 떠나려던 참이었는데 아슬아슬하게 그가 그녀를 만났다. / 잡았다.
2) 나는 겨우 시간에 맞춰 숙제를 끝냈다.

364. In the running (*adj., adv.*) – 경쟁 / 도전 중, 이길 기회가 있는

1) 그는 확실히 새 매니지먼트 자리에 도전하고 있다.
2) 4명의 학생들이 학급의 반장자리를 향해 경쟁하고 있다.

365. In the saddle (*adj., adv.*) – 명령 / 지휘를 하는 위치에

1) 사장 대행이 지휘를 하고 있고 일들은 순조롭게 가고 있다.

366. In the same boat (*adj., adv.*) – 같은 상황에

1) 우리 모두는 같은 상황에 있기 때문에 서로 도와야 한다..
2) 판매가 감소됨에 따라 급여삭감의 예상이 곧 현실화 될 것이다. 더 나쁜 일은 회사가 수백 명의 노동자들을 임시로 해고 했다. 우리는 모두 같은 처지에 있다.

367. In the wake of (*prep.*) – 따르는, 바로 후, 결과로서

1) 지난 주 폭우가 오고 나서 작은 댐들 중의 약간이 파괴되었다.
2) 경제불황으로 인해 많은 사람들이 한시적으로 해고당했다.

368. In time (*adj., adv.*) – 너무 늦지 않게, 때에 맞춰

1) 비행기를 탈 수 있는 시간에 맞춰 공항에 도착했다.
2) 교통체증이 심했으나 나는 환영파티시간에 맞추어 갔다.

369. In touch (*adj.*) – 소식을 교환하는, 말하거나 쓰는, 연락하는

1) 그녀는 그녀가 떠나있는 동안 우리와 계속해서 소식을 주고받을 것이라고 약속했다.
2) 나는 대학교 친구들 중 많은 사람들과 계속 연락을 한다.

370. In trust (*adj., adv.*) – 신탁하는, 맡기는

1) 그 돈은 그가 21세가 될 때까지 신탁에 맡겨졌다.
2) 그 자선가는 장학기금으로 $10,000,000을 신탁에 맡겼다.

371. In view of (*adv.*) - 고려하여

1) 그의 최근의 활동을 고려하여, 그 경영진은 그의 재계약을 하지 않기로 결정했다.

2) 그 공장은 침체되고 있는 경제와 인상되고 있는 인건비를 고려해서 가동을 중단했다.

372. Invite over (*v.*) - 방문 할 것을 부탁하다.

1) 나는 스미스씨 가족을 보았고 그들을 저녁식사에 초대했다.

2) 그는 나를 크리스마스에 초대를 했지만 내가 갈 수 있는지 확실하지 않다.

J

373. Jack up (*v.*) – 잭으로 들어 올리다. 가격을 올리다.

1) 자동차 수리공은 기계로 자동차를 들어 올려 펑크 난 타이어를 갈았다..
2) 농부들은 인플레이션에 맞서 그들의 곡식 가격을 올렸다.

374. Jazz up (*v.*) – 더 생기 있고 열광하게 만들다.

1) 새 소파와 커피 테이블이 그들의 거실을 더 생기 있게 만들었다..
2) 실내수리가 확실히 그 호텔을 더 산뜻하게 만들었다.
3) 그 밴드는 굉장한 라이트 쇼로 공연을 한층 더 열광스럽게 했다.

375. Join hands or forces (*v.*) – 합치다. 공통된 원인이나 활동 등으로 서로 모이다.

1) 경영진과 노동자들이 그 프로젝트를 제때에 끝내기 위해 힘을 합쳤다.
2) 다수의 의료진들이 에이즈와 사스를 퇴치하기위해 서로 모였다.

376. Join (*v.*) – 조직의 일원이 되다. 등록하다.

1) 스키클럽에 멤버가 되고 싶니?
2) 싫어. 나는 헬스클럽에 등록하고 싶어.

**** Join in (*v.*) – 참석하다. 참가하다. 다른 사람들과 함께 ~을 하다.**

1) 토론에 참석할 것인가?
2) 그 가수가 노래의 후렴을 불렀을 때 청중들이 함께 불렀다. 그들 중의 많은 사람들이 그 가사를 외어서 알고 있었다는 것이 명백했다.
3) 그녀는 세계야생조수 재단의 연례모금행사에 참가하는 것이 대단히 행복했다.

**** Join up (*v.*) – 군대에 가다. 입대하다.**

1) 우리나라가 전쟁으로 가면, 자격있는 모든 남자들이 군대에 가야 할 것이다.
2) 그 대학생은 봄 학기가 끝난 후 입대하기로 결심했다.

K

377. Keel over (*v.*) – 뒤집어엎다. 내려앉다.

1) 대단한 강풍이 그 작은 어선을 뒤집어엎었다.
2) 그 지휘자가 주저앉아 죽었을 때 그는 오케스트라를 지휘하고 있었다.

378. Keep after (*v.*) – 꾸준히 무엇인가에 대해 다시 말하고 또 다시 말하다.

1) 그는 내가 재촉하지 않으면 나에게서 빌려간 돈을 갚지 않을 것이다.
2) 그녀는 그녀의 딸에게 공부를 하라고 말하고 또 말하고 해야 한다.

379. Keep an eye on (*v.*) – 조심해서 살피다. 한시도 한눈을 팔지 않다.

1) 내 가방을 잠시만 좀 봐 주시겠습니까?
2) 나는 심부름을 가야하는데 나를 위해 내 아이들을 좀 봐 주시겠습니까?

380. Keep at (*v.*) – 계속하다. 꾸준히 매달리다.

1) 나는 숙제를 끝낼 때까지 계속해야 한다.
2) 나는 그것이 끝나고 또 정확하게 되었을 때까지 꾸준히 했다.

381. Keep down (*v.*) – 억압하다. 제한하다. 진보하는 것을 막다.

1) 당신은 당신의 성질을 다스리는 것을 배워야한다.
2) 우리는 비용을 줄이려 노력한다. 그러나 현재의 경제 상황으로 보아 어렵다.
3) 좋은 학생들은 진보를 막기가 어렵다.

382. Keep from (*v.*) – 자신이 ~하는 것을 막다.

1) 그녀는 수업 중에 말을 참지 못하는 것 같다.
2) 그는 술을 삼가하지 못하는 것 같다.

** Keep on (*v.*) – 계속하다. (대개 현재 분사)

1) 우리는 거의 떠날 준비가 되었다. 그러나 그 연사는 계속해서 말을 했다.
2) 그녀의 의사는 그녀에게 식사 사이에 먹는 것을 삼가하라고 했으나 그녀는 계속해서 그렇게 했다.
3) 그녀에게 접촉하는 것을 금지하는 법원의 명령에도 불구하고 그는 계속해서 그녀를 괴롭힌다.
4) 선생님이 그만하라고 요구한 후에도 학생들은 계속해서 잡담들을 했다.

** Keep on with (*v.*) – ~을 계속하다.

1) 그는 기금이 중단된 후 에도 계속해서 그의 연구를 했다.

** Keep up (with) (*v.*) – ~을 계속하다. 좋은 상태를 유지하다. 간격을 유지하다.

1) 운동프로그램을 계속하는 것은 시간과 노력이 걸린다.
2) 당신은 당신의 주택 부금을 계속 잘 내어야한다. 그렇지 않으면 은행이 압류할 것이다.
3) 최근의 비와 그로 인해 계속되는 곡식의 부족이 계속 가격을 올렸다.
4) 당신은 너무 빨리 걸어서 내가 보조를 맞추기가 힘들다.

383. Keep one's chin up (*v.*) – 용기를 가지고 곤경에 대처하다.

1) 시기가 어려운줄 나는 안다. 하지만 용기를 가지고 대처하라.
2) 당신이 직업을 잃었다는 것이 유감이다. 그러나 용기를 가지고 대처하라. 나는 당신이 곧 새 직업을 찾으리라는 것을 확신한다.

384. Keep one's distance (*v.*) – 가까이 또는 친밀하게 되는 것을 피하다. 거리를 두다.

1) 나는 그들을 신용하지 않기 때문에 거리를 둔다..
2) 그 불은 너무나 뜨거워서 소방수들은 거리를 두어야했다.

385. Keep track of (*v.*) – ~에 대해 계속 정보를 받거나 문서를 간직하다.

1) 나는 고등학교 시절의 친구들과 연락이 되도록 노력한다.
2) 그들은 자주 이사해서 계속 추적하기가 힘들다.

** Lose track of (*v.*) – ~을 계속하거나 계속해서 연락하는 것에 실패하다.

1) 그의 연설은 너무나 빙빙 돌아 나는 그의 논점을 잃었다.
2) 내가 학생이었을 때 알았던 친구들 중 다수와 연락이 두절되었다.

386. Kick around (*v.*) 거칠게 대우하다. 한가하게 얘기를 주고받다. 무관심 속에 돌아다니다.

1) 너의 남동생에게 거칠게 구는 행동을 중지해라.
2) 우리는 스페인으로 2주간 가는 것에 대해 한가하게 얘기를 주고받았다.
3) 무가치의 채권 증서 발행 가능성이 오랫동안 돌았다. 그것은 결코 새로 나온 말이 아니다.

387. Kick off (*v.*) – 축구에서 게임을 시작하는 킥을 하다. 시작하다.

1) 그 이끄는 멤버가 다른 팀으로 게임을 시작하는 공을 찼다.
2) 그 캠페인은 인터뷰와 공공장소에 모습을 보임으로서 시작되었다.

** Kickoff (*n.*) – 시구하기. 무엇인가의 시작

1) 그것은 멋있는 시구였다.
2) 새 축구 시즌의 시구는 흥분되는 축하 의식이다.

388. Kick oneself (*v.*) - 후회하다. 유감으로 여기다.

1) 주식시장에서 현명치 못한 선택을 한 것에 대해 후회하고 있다..
2) 나는 그것을 하기 위한 용기가 없어서 유감이었다.

389. Kick out (*v.*) - 내보내다 (강요하여). 쫓아내다. 내 던지다.

1) 그 소년은 그의 반 친구를 몹시 때렸기 때문에 학교에서 쫓겨났다.
2) 그 집주인은 그의 세들은 사람들이 3개월이나 집세를 내지 않아 쫓아냈다.

390. Kick up (*v.*) - 문제를 크게 하다. 악화되다.

1) 내 상사는 아주 작은 실수들이라도 크게 문제를 삼는다.
2) 그 여자 노인의 신경통이 악화되고 있다. 그녀는 아프다.

391. Kill off (*v.*) - 완전히 또는 대량으로 파괴하다.

1) 인근 지역의 공장에서 나오는 오염된 폐수가 근처에 있는 바다의 해양생물들을 완전히 죽였다.
2) 한 종류의 생물이라 할지라도 다 죽이는 것은 자연의 균형을 깨트릴 수 있다.

392. Knock out (*v.*) - 지치게 하다. 의식을 잃게 하다.

1) 태양과 힘든 일이 나를 지치게 했다.
2) 그 챔피언은 첫 번째 라운드에서 도전자를 의식을 잃게 만들었다.

393. Knock it off (*v.*) - 그만두다. 끝내다.

1) 그들은 한 시간이나 논쟁을 하고 있다. 그래서 나는 그들에게 그만하라고 말했다.
2) 나는 한 시간 안에 일을 끝낼 수 있다고 확신한다.

394. Know-it-all (*adj., n.*) - 모든 일에 대해서 다 아는 것처럼 생각하거나 행동하는 사람

1) 나는 그의 무엇이든지 다 아는 것 같은 태도와 거만한 행동을 싫어한다.
2) 그녀는 정말 무엇이든지 다 아는 것 같이 행동하는 사람이고 그것이 나를 미치게 마든다.

395. Know one's way around (*v.*) - 세상일이 어떻게 돌아가는지 이해하다. 어떤 일에 경험과 기술이 있다.

1) 세상 물정에 밝은 사람은 곤경에 처함이 없이 타운을 잘 돌아다닌다.
2) 그녀는 기업 구조를 잘 알기 때문에 새 직무를 잘 해 낼 것이다.

L

396. Lay away (*v.*) **– 미래에 사용하기위해 저축하거나 따로 떼어놓다. 상품을 지불될 때까지 보관하다.**

1) 우리의 매년하는 여행을 위해 우리는 약간의 돈을 저축한다.
2) 이 상품을 내가 돈을 다 지불할 때까지 보관해 두시오.

**** Layaway** (*adj., n.*) **– 대금을 지불하는 제도, 다 지불될 때까지 무엇인가를 잡다(보관하다).**

1) 내가 이 스테레오를 사기위해 레이어웨이 제도를 이용할 수 있을까요?
2) 나를 위해 그것을 레이어웨이로로 해주세요.

397. Lay in (*v.*) **– (식량 등을) 구해서 저장하다.**

1) 그 농부는 6톤의 짚을 구해서 저장했다. 그래서 그는 추운 겨울 동안에 그의 가축들을 먹일 수 있을 것이다.
2) 우리는 비상시를 위한 식량을 저장하기 위해 여분의 냉동고를 가지고 있다.

398. Lay off (*v.*) **– 노동자들을 내보내다. 직장에서 내보내다.**

1) 그녀는 지난 해 잠정적으로 해고 되었고 아직 새 직장을 찾지 못했다.
2) 만약 경제가 향상되지 못하면 많은 노동자들이 잠정적으로 해고 될 것이다.

**** Layoff** (*v.*) **– 대개 직장에서 임시로 내보내는 것**

1) 경제 침체기에는 종종 대량 임시 해고가 있다.
2) 재정적인 어려움이 임시 해고로 연결되었다. 그러나 회사는 해고된 노동자들 중 많은 사람들을 7월 말 전에 재고용 할 것을 희망하고 있다.

399. Lay out (*v.*) **– 펼쳐놓다. 계획에 따라 조정 배열 등을 하다. 돈을 쓰다.**

1) 그 요술사는 테이블위에 6장의 카드를 펼쳐놓았다.
2) 어떤 사람들은 그들의 미래가 이미 그들을 위해 배열되어 있다고 믿는다.
3) 나는 나의 결혼식을 위해 만달러를 쓸 예정이다.

400. Lead off (*v.*) **– 시작하다. 먼저 가다.**

1) 그 밴드는 그것의 옛날 노래 들 중의 하나로 시작했다. 그러고 나서 그들의 더 최근의 히트곡과 섞어 본격적으로 연주에 들어갔다.

2) 그 연사는 우스운 이야기로 시작했다.

401. Lead on (*v.*) – 바람직하지 못한 무엇으로 누군가를 유혹하다.

1) 그녀는 그를 유혹했다. 그러나 그녀는 부정한다.
2) 그는 나를 유혹했고 나는 그를 정직하다고 믿었다. 그러나 그것이 나에게 많은 돈을 손해 보게 했다.

402. Lead up to (*v.*) – 서서히 준비하거나 접근하다.

1) 그 회사는 더 젊은 사람들을 서서히 고용하고 그것의 판매를 더 활성화시키기 위한 노력으로 더 나이든 직원들의 해고를 서서히 준비하고 있다.
2) 나는 그녀가 아픈 줄 알았다. 그러나 그녀의 죽음으로 서서히 다가가는 징조는 보지 못했다.

403. Leave off (*v.*) – 무엇인가 하는 것을 멈추다. 어디로 가는 길에 무엇인가를 남기다 / 맡기다.

1) 나는 나의 프로젝트를 완성하기 전에는 멈추지 않을 것이다.
2) 나는 항상 내가 읽은 책 안에 서표를 끼워둔다. 그래서 내가 어디에서 멈추었는지 안다.
3) 그는 일하러 가기 전에 그의 아들을 탁아소에 맡긴다.

404. Leave out (*v.*) – 생략하다. 포함하지 않다.

1) 나는 그녀에게 나의 작업(원고)을 교정하고 중요하지 않은 모든 정보는 생략하라고 부탁했다.
2) 내가 가르칠 때 덜 중요한 약간의 부분은 생략하기를 좋아한다.
3) 아무도 그녀를 기억하지 못했기 때문에 그녀는 파티에서 외톨이가 되었다.

405. Lend a hand / give a hand (*v.*) – 돕다. 보조해주다.

1) 내가 이 아파트로 이사했을 때 나의 친구들이 도와주러 왔었다.
2) 그녀는 종종 교회의 사교모임들에 보조를 한다.
3) 당신이 그 무거운 상자를 옮기는데(드는데) 내가 도와주겠다.

406. Lend oneself to (*v.*) – 적합하다.

1) 어떤 법률들은 다양한 해석을 하는데 적합하다.

407. Lend out (*v.*) – 빌려주다.

1) 그 은행은 적당한 이율로 돈을 빌려준다.
2) 그는 그의 좋아하는 비디오테이프를 빌려주고 다시는 그것을 보지 못했다.

408. Less than (*adv.*) – 아닌, 조금도 아닌

1) 그들의 시험점수 결과로 그들은 기쁘지 않았다..
2) 그들은 그들의 딸의 허락없이 한 비밀결혼 소식에 조금도 신나지 않았다.

** Less than no time (*n.*) – 매우 빠르게

1) 그 파티가 매우 빨리 끝난 것 같았다.
2) 나는 아주 신속하게 당신이 필요한 카피를 마련 할 수 있다.

409. Let down (*v.*) – 실망시키다. 속도를 늦추다.

1) 나를 실망시키지 마시오.
2) 나는 그녀를 신용했다. 그러나 그녀는 나를 실망시켰다.
3) 우리는 거의 다 끝났다. 그러니 아직 일의 속도를 늦추지 말라.

** Letdown (*n.*) – 실망, 낙심

1) 그가 정말 원했던 직업을 제공받지 못했기 때문에 대단한 실망이었다.

410. Let go (*v.*) – 무엇인가를 그대로 지나가게 하다. 무엇인가를 잡고 있는 것을 중지하다. 단념하다.

1) 그 소년들은 창문을 깬 것으로 그녀가 그들에게 소리를 지를까봐 무서웠다. 그러나 그녀는 그것을 문제 삼지 않았다.
2) 그는 이렇게 그 자신을 내버려두어서는 안된다. 그렇지 않으면 그는 곧 타락하게 될 것이다.
3) 당신은 용서하고 잊어버리는 것이 필요하다. 그냥 단념하지 그래? 더 나은 인생이 당신을 기다리고 있다.

411. Let off (*v.*) – 일이나 의무에서 벗어나다. 벌을 조금 받거나 또는 전혀 없이 내보내다. 폭발하다.

1) 그 학생들은 학교에서 담배를 피우다가 잡힌 뒤에 쉽게 풀려났다.
2) 그 판사는 그 교통위반자를 단지 경고만 하고 풀어주었다.
3) 그 화난 남자는 화를 터트린 후에 기분이 나아졌다.

** Let off steam / Blow off steam (*v.*) – 넘치는 신체적 에너지나 강한 부정적인 기분 들을 내보내다.

1) 만약 건전한 방법으로라면 화를 분출하는 것은 괜찮다.
2) 그 여자는 넘치는 신체적 에너지를 내보내기위해 조깅을 했다.

412. Let out (*v.*) – 떠나게 하다. 오도록 (가도록) 허락하다.

1) 우리의 영어 선생님은 벨이 울리자마자 우리를 나가게 했다.
2) 반대로 우리의 수학 선생님은 절대로 정시에 우리를 내보내지 않는다..
3) 그는 그의 개가 운동하도록 밤마다 내보낸다.

** Let the cat out of the bag (*v.*) – 비밀을 말하거나 드러내다.

1) 그들은 일주일 전에 갈라섰고 조용히 감추었다. 그러나 그들 친구들 중에 한 사람이 지난밤에 그 비밀을 말했다.

413. Let up (*v.*) – 속도를 늦추거나 덜 집중적인

1) 비가 이제 덜 온다.
2) 눈발이 조금 약해졌지만 앞으로 더 온다.

414. Lick and a promise (*n.*) – 성급하고 부주의하고 불만족스러운 일

1) 오늘 날 많은 노동자들이 성급하고 부주의하고 만족스럽지 못하게 작업을 하기 때문에 건물들이 오래가도록 지어지지 않는다.
2) 나는 서두르고 있었다. 그래서 바닥을 형편없이 닦았다.

415. Lick one's boots (*v.*) – 아첨하다.

1) 속담-현명한 왕은 친구들이나 충고자들이 그에게 아첨하는 것을 원하지 않는다.
2) 그는 그의 직원들이 그에게 아첨해 주기를 기대하는 사람이다.

416. Lie down (*v.*) – 수평의 자세로 쉬다.

1) 그녀는 그녀의 두통이 사라질 때까지 침대에 누웠다.
2) 나는 잠시의 낮잠을 위해 누웠다. 그리곤 거의 5시간이나 잤다.

417. Lightning never strikes twice (in the same place). (a cliché) – 행운은 반복해서 (같은 장소에)오지 않는다.

1) 그는 5년 전에 일백만 불에 당첨되었다. 그리고 어리석게 그 모두를 탕진했다. 그는 여전히 복권을 산다. 그러나 행운은 반복해서 오지 않기 때문에 나는 그 가 다시 당첨되리라고는 생각지 않는다.

418. Light up (*v.*) – 갑자기 밝아지다. 담뱃불을 켜다.

1) 그의 신부가 통로를 걸어오자 그의 얼굴은 갑자기 밝아졌다.
2) 피로연 후에 신랑의 들러리는 시가에 불을 붙였다.

419. Line up (*v.*) – 줄을 형성하거나 줄에서다. 마련 / 준비 / 주선하다. 차례로 놓다

1) 사람들은 표를 사기위해 줄을 섰다.
2) 그들은 자선공연을 위해서 몇몇의 좋은 악단들을 주선했다.
3) 그녀는 침실 선반에 그녀의 가족사진들을 차례로 놓았다.

420. Give lip service / Pay lip service (*v.*) – 증명이나 뒷받침 없는 헛된 말

1) 어떤 정치인들은 지역의 프로그램에 헛된 공약을 많이 하고 그들이 당선된 뒤에는 그 지역을 위해서 거의 아무 것도 하지 않는다.
2) 그는 그의 여자 친구에게 그냥 헛된 말을 한다.
3) 그녀가 말하는 것을 믿지 말라. 그것은 그냥 헛된 말이다.

421. Live off (*v.*) – ~에서 제공된 것으로 살다.

1) 그는 그의 연금으로 산다.
2) 그들은 그들의 저축으로 산다.
3) 그는 꾸준히 나가는 직업이나 저축도 없기 때문에 그의 친구들에 의지해서 산다.

** Live off the fat of the land (*v.*) – 일할 필요없이 편히 살다.

1) 나는 일찍 퇴직하기위해 충분한 돈을 모으고 싶고 일하지 않고 편히 살고 싶다.
2) 일하지 않고 편히 살 수 있다면 좋지 않을까요?

422. Live on (*v.*) – 계속해서 살다. 자신을 지원하다.

1) 당신의 친절한 행동이 영원히 내 가슴 속에 살아있을 것이다.
2) 많은 나이들은 사람들이 적은 수입으로 산다.

423. Live up to (*v.*) – ~에 따라서 살다. 채우다. 만족시키다. 실망시키지 않다.

1) 나는 나의 이상에 따라서 살려고 노력한다.
2) 나는 당신의 기대에 맞추어 살려고 태어나지 않았고 당신 역시 나의 기대에 맞추어 살려고 태어나지 않았다. 그러나 우리가 서로의 다름을 받아들일 수 있다면 그것은 아름다울 것이다.

424. Long face (*n.*) – 슬픈 표정

1) 왜 그녀는 오늘 아침 슬픈 표정을 짓고 있나요? 그녀에게 무슨 일이 있나요 ?
2) 그가 그의 여동생을 때린 것에 대해 그의 아버지가 벌을 주었을 때, 그 소년은 슬픈 표정을 짓고 울기 시작했다.

425. Look after (*v.*) – 돌보다.

1) 나는 기꺼이 집 없는 동물들을 돌볼 것이다.
2) 나는 집 없는 동물들을 돌보는 것이 나의 의무이고 즐거움이라고 생각한다.
3) 나의 부모님들은 그들이 슈퍼마켓에 간 동안 나의 남동생을 잘 돌보라고 나에게 부탁했다.
4) 너의 할머니를 돌봐드려라.

426. Look at (*v.*) – 처리하다. 고려하다. 검토 / 조사하다. 초점을 맞추다. 집중하다.

1) 당신은 그 문제를 객관적으로 처리해야 한다.
2) 우리는 나이 들어감에 일들을 다른 시각으로 본다.

3) 그 의사는 환자의 병력을 검토했다.
4) 떡갈나무 위에 있는 저 아름다운 입내새*를 보아라

427. Look at the world through rose-colored glasses (*v.*) - 모든 것을 좋고 아름답게만 보다. 낙천적이다.

1) 나는 종종 세상을 좋고 아름답게만 본다.
2) 많은 십대들이 세상을 멋있고 아름답게만 보는 경향이 있다.

428. Look back (on) (*v.*) - 자신의 과거를 생각하거나 기억하다.

1) 나는 가끔 나의 어린아이 시절을 생각한다.
2) 나는 과거를 돌아보지 않으려 애쓴다. 오히려 현재와 미래에 집중하려 한다.

429. Look down on or upon (*v.*) - 경멸하다. 다른 사람들은 열등하다고 여기다. 존경심의 결여를 보이다.

1) 그는 그보다 덜 행운인 사람들은 누구든지 경멸한다.
2) 나를 낮추어 보지 말라.
3) 어떤 부자들은 가난한 사람들을 열등하게 보아 존경심을 보이지 않는다.

430. Look for (*v.*) - ~을 찾다. 수색하다.

1) 나는 열쇠를 찾기 위해 온 집안을 다 뒤져오고 있는 중이다.
2) 이제 국회에서의 그녀의 임기가 끝나서 개인적인 분야에서 직업을 구하고 싶어 한다.
3) 나는 새 직업을 구하고 있다.

431. Look forward to (*v.*) - 기대하다. (대개 즐거움을 가지고)

1) 우리는 곧 당신을 만나기를 기대 할 것이다.
2) "당신은 다가오는 당신의 결혼식으로 행복함에 틀림없다." "네, 나는 그것을 정말 기대하고 있습니다."
3) 나는 이번 여름에 유럽으로의 여행을 기대하고 있다.

432. Look in on (*v.*) - 점검 / 조사 등을 위해 잠깐 들르다.

1) 나의 친구는 가끔 나의 어머니가 어떠신가 보기위해 잠깐 들린다.
2) 그 걱정하는 어머니는 자고 있는 아기가 어떤가 보기위해 잠깐 들렸다.
3) 그 간호사는 가끔 환자를 점검하기위해 들린다.

433. Look into (*v.*) - 조사하다.

1) 없어진 문건의 일을 즉시 조사하시오.

---

* 입내새 : 북 아메리카에 살고 있는 노래하는 새이며 회새과 갈색의 깃털을 가지고 다른 새들의 노래를 흉내 냄.

2) 나는 그 일을 조사했고 그 문건에 대해서 무슨 일이 일어났는지 알아냈다.
3) 경찰은 그 범죄를 조사했고 그것을 해결했다.

434. Look out (for) (*v.*) – 조심하다, 정신을 바짝 차리다.

1) 보초는 적 군대의 움직임을 날카롭게 주시하도록 명령받았다.
2) 조심해, 차가 이리로 오고 있어!

435. Look over (*v.*) – 대강 훑어보다.

1) 소득 보고서를 훑어 볼 기회가 있었나요?
2) 예, 대강 훑어 보고나서, 내 소견을 조금 적었어요.

436. Look up (*v.*) – 찾다. 찾아내다. 방문하다.

1) 김박사님 전화번호를 찾아주세요.
2) 나는 종종 내 사전에서 단어들을 찾아본다.
3) 반창회에 가서 옛 동창들을 찾아보는 것은 재미있다.

** Look up to (*v.*) – 우러러 보다. 존경하다.

1) 그 남자는 보통 사람에 지나지 않지만, 그의 아들은 그가 마치 세상에서 가장 위대한 사람인양 존경한다.
2) 많은 사람들이 그의 업적 때문에 전 대통령인 빌 클린턴을 존경한다.

437. Lose one's heart (to) (*v.*) – 사랑에 빠지다. 좋아하게 되다.

1) 그녀의 첫 데이트 전에, 그녀의 어머니는 너무 빨리 사랑에 빠지게 되지 않도록 주의를 주었다.
2) 그는 그녀를 처음 본 순간 사랑에 빠졌다.

438. Lose one's temper (*v.*) – 화내다.

1) 코치는 그 선수에게 화를 자제하고 성질을 부리지 말라고 말했다.
2) 그래요, 저 지금 화났어요, 하지만 그가 먼저 계속 저의 성질을 건드렸어요.

439. Lose out (*v.*) – 지다, 패배하다.

1) 우리는 그 게임에 이기기를 원했지만, 다른 팀에게 졌다.

** Lose out on (*v.*) – 놓치다.

1) 그는 그의 만성적 게으름 때문에 승진 기회를 놓쳤다.

440. Lose track of (*v.*) – 소식이 끊어지다. (중간에) 잊어버리다.

1) 우리는 그와 소식이 끊겨서, 그가 무엇이 되었는지 알지 못한다.
2) 그녀는 고등학교의 친구들과 소식이 끊기지 않도록 노력했으나, 해가 지나감에 따라서

연락을 하고 지내는 것이 더욱더 어려워졌다.

3) 늦어서 죄송합니다. 골프를 하는 동안에 시간 가는 줄을 몰랐어요.

441. Luck out (*v.*) – 행운이다.

1) 난 참 운이 좋아, 시험이 연기되었어.

2) 그는 그가 그녀를 만난 것을 대단한 행운으로 여겼다.

** In luck (*adj.*) – 행운의

1) 공항에 가는 동안에 교통 정체가 정말 심하였다. 그러나 내가 탈 비행기가 한 시간 연기되어 행운이었다.

2) "우리는 오늘 행운이다. 상대편의 유명한 선발 투수가 감기가 걸려서 오늘 출전하지 않는다."라고 감독이 발표했다.

** Out of luck (*adj.*) – 불운의

1) 그는 그들의 관계를 지키기 위해 그녀에게 다시 한 번 기회를 줄 것을 원했지만 뜻대로 되질 않았다. 그녀는 그와 이야기 하는 것 초차 거절했다.

M

442. Mad as a hornet (*adj.*) – 매우 화가 난

1) 그는 누군가가 그의 차에 침입해서 그의 카세트와 테이프들을 훔쳐 간 것을 발견하고는 매우 화가 났다.

2) 그녀는 그가 두 시간 이상이나 늦은데다가 전화조차 하지 않아서 그녀의 사장이 매우 화가 났을 것이라는 것을 알고 있었다.

443. Make a difference (*v.*) – ~의 본질을 변화시키다. 관계가 있다.

1) 당신이 부자이건 가난하건 상관이 없다.

2) 네가 만약에 집을 팔기로 마음을 먹는다면, 칠을 새로 하는 것이 파는 조건에 큰 차이를 만들 것이다.

444. Make a fool of (*v.*) – 속이다. 바보로 만들다.

1) 그는 회사의 성탄 파티에서 술에 취한 채 싸우려 드는 행동을 함으로써 스스로를 바보처럼 만들었다.

2) 그 여자는 그녀부부가 다른 사람들과 있을 때면 그녀의 남편을 바보로 만들려고 시도 한다.

445. Make a hit (*v.*) – 성공하다, 히트하다. 유행하다.

1) 그 음반 회사는 그들이 새로 계약한 밴드가 그들의 데뷔 앨범에서 성공을 하기를 바랬다.

2) 그녀의 새로운 종류의 일상복은 파리 패션쇼에서 크게 성공했다.

446. Make a mountain out of a molehill / Make a federal case out of nothing / Make a big issue out of nothing (a cliché) – 아무것도 아닌 것을 큰 문제로 삼다.

1) 아무것도 아닌 것을 큰 문제로 삼지마라. 그것은 단지 작은 일일 뿐이다.

2) 당신은 왜 항상 아무것도 아닌 것을 크게 문제 삼는가? 나는 겨우 10분 늦게 집에 왔을 뿐인데.

447. Make a practice of (*v.*) – 규칙적으로 연습하다.

1) 너는 좀 더 규칙적으로 공부를 해야만 한다.

2) 그는 규칙적으로 일찍 일어나는 습관을 들여 직장에 늦은 적이 없다.

448. Make a virtue of necessity (*v.*) – 어려움을 쾌히 극복하다.

1) 그들은 주식 시장이 붕괴되었을 때, 그들의 돈을 모두 잃었지만, 그들은 어려움을 쾌히 극복해 내였고, 그들의 손실을 잘 회복하고 있다.

** Make the best of it (*v.*) – 좋지 않은 상황에서 최선을 다하다(불평 없이).

1) 나는 내가 원하던 학교에 입학하지 못했지만, 지금 내가 다니고 있는 곳도 또한 좋은 대학이고, 나는 최선을 다하고 있다.
2) 그는 보수가 좋지 않은 직장에서 일하는 것을 싫어했지만, 그는 최선을 다했고, 학교에 다니면서 그의 진로를 모색했고, 그는 지금 변호사가 되었다.

449. Make ends meet (*v.*) – 겨우 꾸려나가다. (최저)생활비를 마련하다.

1) 대부분의 사람들은 봉급으로부터 겨우 생활을 꾸려 나갈 수 있기 위해 힘들게 일한다.
2) 경제적 상황과 함께 그것은 최저 생활비를 마련하기위한 몸부림이다.

450. Make fun of (*v.*) – 조롱하다, 우습게 만들다.

1) 그들은 그가 옷을 우스꽝스럽게 입는다고 생각하기 때문에 그를 조롱한다.
2) 그녀는 그가 그녀의 친구들 앞에서 그녀를 우습게 만들었기 때문에 그를 꾸짖었다.

451. Make hay while the sun shines (a cliché) – (어떤 특정한 일을 하기 위한) 좋은 기회를 놓치지 않다. 기회를 잡다.

1) 우리는 단지 적은 저축액을 가지고 있지만, 때를 놓치지 않기 위해서 네가 학비로 썼으면 좋겠다.
2) 땅값이 지금 높다. 그래서 기회를 놓치지 않기 위해 우리가 쥐고 있는 땅의 약간을 팔 것이다.

** Make the most of it (*v.*) – 최대한 이용하다.

1) 내게 제안된 일자리는 내가 원하던 곳은 아니었지만, 나는 그들의 제안을 받아들일 것이고 최대한 이용할 것이다.
2) 너무나 적은 수의 학생들이 학교도서관을 충분히 사용한다.

452. Make light of (*v.*) – 대단치 않게 취급하다. 소홀히 여기다.

1) 너의 업적을 너무 자랑하지 마라, 하지만 너무 소홀히 취급하지도 말아라.
2) 그는 좋은 경영인 이지만, 그의 노동자들이 너무 종종 직면하는 문제를 소홀히 여긴다.

** Make much of (*v.*) – 실제보다 더 가치가 있는 양 보이게 하다.

1) 신문들은 그들의 발행부수를 늘리기 위해 별것 아닌 이야기를 종종 실제보다 과장한다.

453. Make love (*v.*) – 성관계를 맺다.

1) 그 영화는 검열관에게 우리 젊은이들에게 사랑 없는 성관계를 조장한다는 느낌을 주었기 때문에 상영금지 되었다.

454. Make off with / Make away with (*v.*) – 훔치다.

1) 그 도둑은 밝혀지지 않은 액수의 현금과 보석을 훔쳐갔다.

2) 다람쥐가 도토리를 훔쳤다.

455. Make oneself at home (*v.*) – (마치 집에 있는 것처럼) 편안히 하다.

1) 그녀는 친구에게 들어와서 편히 있으라고 말했다.
2) 몇 분 있으면 준비되니까 편히 계세요.

456. Make one's mark (*v.*) – 명성을 얻다. 흔적을 남기다.

1) 그녀는 발레리나로서 명성을 얻기를 원했다.
2) 어네스트 헤밍웨이는 기자로 그의 경력을 시작하였지만, 소설가와 단편작가로 명성을 얻었다.

457. Make one's way (*v.*) – 길을 찾다. 살기위해 열심히 일하다.

1) 대단히 많은 군중들 속에서 길을 찾는다는 것은 쉬운 일이 아니었다.
2) 그는 고아였고 그를 도와줄 사람이 아무도 없었기 때문에 살기 위해 열심히 일 해야만 했다.

458. Make out (*v.*) – 보고 구별하다. 이해하다. 작성하다. 써넣다. 잘하다. 화합하다. 키스하고 껴안다.

1) 안개가 너무 짙었기 때문에 그 운전자는 신호등을 잘 구별할 수가 없었다.
2) 나는 두 번째 문단의 세 번째 문장을 잘 이해할 수가 없다
3) 장보러 가기 전에 그녀는 대개 살 목록을 작성한다.
4) 그는 지원서를 작성했지만, 그들은 그에게 자리를 제안하지 않았다.
5) 너는 물리학 수업을 잘 하고 있니?
6) 나는 그녀가 그와 잘 어울린다고 생각하지는 않았지만, 그들이 잘 화합하고 있다고 추측한다.
7) 그녀는 대부분의 아이들이 저녁 시간을 키스를 하며 보냈기 때문에 그 파티가 지루하다고 생각했다.

459. Make over (*v.*) – 권리를 양도하다. 다시하다. 다시 고치다.

1) 그 노인의 재산은 그의 아들에게 양도되었다.
2) 우리는 실내장식이 완전히 마음에 들지 않기 때문에 그것을 다시하고 싶다.
3) 그 집은 완전히 새로 고쳐야 될 필요가 있다. 그래서 우리는 새 페인트 작업으로 시작할 것이다.

460. Make sure (*v.*) – 확실히 하다. 확인하다.

1) 나는 그녀가 내일 아침 7시에 도착하리라고 생각한다. 하지만, 우리는 항공사에 전화를 걸어 확인하는 것이 더 좋다
2) 잠자리에 들기 전에 전등을 끄고 문을 잠그는 것을 확인해라

461. Make up (of, for, to) (*v.*) – (이야기를) 꾸미다. 구성하다. 보충, 벌충, 보상하다. (불평 등)만족시키다. 화해하다. 반복하다. 결정하다. 화장하다.

1) 말도 안 되는 얘기를 늘어놓지 말고 내게 진실을 얘기해라.

2) 뉴욕시는 5개의 독립구로 되어있고, 각각의 독립구는 몇 개씩의 군으로 구성되어 있다.
3) 그는 지난주에 학교에 결석을 했기 때문에 그가 빠뜨린 부분을 보충해야만 한다.
4) 나는 내가 그동안 너에게 관대하지 못했음을 안다. 하지만 나는 그것을 네게 보상하고 싶다.
5) 나는 지난 번 우리가 싸운 것이 내 잘못이었기 때문에 네게 사과를 한다. 우리 화해하고 지난 일은 잊어버리고 지난날처럼 친구가 될 수 있으면 좋겠다.
6) 저는 지금 시험을 치루기에 너무 아픕니다. 다음에 보면 안 되겠습니까?
7) 나는 이번 여름휴가를 프랑스로 가기로 결정했다.
8) 그녀는 매일 아침 화장을 한다.

** Make-up / Makeup (*n.*) – 화장, 보충(벌충) 시험

1) 그녀는 너무 창백해 보이기 때문에 약간의 화장을 하는 것이 좋겠다.
2) 기말시험을 치루지 않은 모든 학생들에게 보충 시험을 치루는 것이 허락되었다.

462. Make waves / Causing waves (*v.*) – 문제를 일으키다.

1) 직장에서 문제를 일으키는 것은 좋은 생각이 아니다.
2) 만약 그가 계속 문제를 일으킨다면, 그는 쫓겨날 것이다.

463. Man of his word (*n.*) – 약속을 지키는 사람

1) 나의 아버지는 그가 의미하지 않은 어떤 것을 말하는 적이 없으시다. 그분은 신용이 있는 분이시다.
2) 우리가 아직 계약에 서명을 하지는 않았지만, 그는 신용있는 사람이기 때문에 나는 이 계약을 마무리 하는 것에 대해서 별로 걱정하지 않는다.

464. Many hands make light work (proverb) (격언) – 함께 일을 하면 힘든 일도 쉬워 진다. 백짓장도 맞들면 낫다.

1) 그 일은 쉽지 않겠지만, 우리가 함께 힘을 모으면 제시간에 끝낼 수 있을 거야. "백짓장도 맞들면 낫다"는 속담을 기억해.

465. Matter of course (*n.*) – 당연한 일

1) 도움이 필요한 사람을 돕는 것은 그녀가 자비스러운 천성을 가졌기 때문에 그녀에게 자연스러운 일이다.
2) 계속 열심히 공부하고 학점에 대해서는 염려하지 마라. 나는 네가 잘해 내리라고 확신한다. 그것은 당연한 일이다.

466. Matter of fact (*n.*) – 사실

1) 그는 여기에서 오랜 기간 동안 일해 왔다. 사실 그는 우리가 창업했을 당시부터 이곳에서 일해 왔다.
2) 그들 아직도 연애하니? 그래. 실은 그들은 약혼했어.

467. Measure up to (*v.*) - (어떤 상황, 표준, 기대 등에) 잘 맞추다.

1) 그는 한 번도 그의 아버지의 기대에 부응하지 못했다.
2) 사람들은 종종 스스로 자신에게 가장 엄격한 비평가가 되어서, 그들이 정한 표준에 좀처럼 맞추지 못한다.

468. Meet with (*v.*) - 우연히 또는 계획해서 만나다. 경험하다. 겪다.

1) 그들은 신혼여행 중이었는데, 우리를 만나기 위해 시간을 내었다.
2) 1997년 12월 많은 아시아의 국가들은 경제적 공황을 겪었다.
3) 낚시 배는 황해의 폭풍 속에서 재난을 겪었다.

** Meet up with (*v.*) - 우연히 만나다. 약속해서 만나다. 겪다.

1) 나는 그 식당에서 저녁 7시에 너를 만날 것이다.
2) 복도에서 우연히 그를 만났다.
3) 서울 가는 길에 대단한 교통정체를 겪었다.

** Meet (*v.*) - 우연히 또는 계획해서 만나다. 목표에 도달하다. 만족시키다.

1) 우리는 좁은 다리에 도달했을 때 대단한 교통정체를 겪었다.
2) 나는 수년간 만나지 못했던 옛 친구를 쇼핑몰에서 우연히 만났다.
3) 나는 그곳에서 오후 7시에 당신을 만나겠다.
4) 두 강들이 이곳에서 만나 근처의 바다로 들어간다.
5) 정부는 그들의 국민들이 필요로 하는 것을 만족시키기 위해 노력해야 한다.
6) 그 회사는 그 해의 영업목표를 달성했다.

469. Melt in one's mouth (*v.*) - 맛이 있다.

1) 이것은 매우 부드럽고 맛있어서, 입안에서 살살 녹는다.

470. Mental telepathy (*n.*) - 과학적으로 설명될 수 없는 초감각적 지각에 의한 대화

1) 최근의 연구는 일란성 쌍둥이의 정신적 텔레파시 같은 몇 가지 재미있는 사실에 대해서 상세히 보도했다.
2) 나는 근래에 몇 년 동안 보지 못한 옛 친구에 대해서 생각하고 있었는데, 오늘 아침 그로부터 편지를 받았다. 그것이 내가 정신적 텔레파시의 가능성에 대해서 고려해 보도록 만들었다.

471. Miss out (on) (*v.*) - (즐거움이나 이익을 얻을) 기회를 놓치다.

1) 그는 야영을 갈 기회를 놓치고 싶지 않았지만, 기말 시험이 더 중요했다.
2) 너는 야영을 가지 않음으로써 많은 즐거운 일들을 겪을 기회를 놓쳤다.

472. Mix up (*v.*) - 혼동하다. 섞다. 실수하다. 연관(교제)하다.

1) 학생들은 종종 kitchen과 chicken을 혼동한다.

2) 저를 위해서 샐러드를 섞어 주시겠습니까?

3) 나는 그가 말하는 것을 들었지만, 우리가 지난번에 이야기 한 때보다 지금 그가 그의 입장에서 말한 것이 더 혼동되었다.

4) 그는 단지 나쁜 패거리들과 어울렸을 뿐 나쁜 사람은 아니다.

473) Monkey business (*n.*) – 비윤리적이고, 불법이고, 속임수를 쓰는 활동, 쓸데없는 일

1) 경찰은 그 작은 가게가 불법 도박의 은신처였다고 확신하지만 거기서 그런 불법 활동이 있었다는 것을 증명할 수는 없었다.

2) 그의 어머니는 그에게 쓸데없는 일을 집어치우고 숙제를 하라고 말했다.

N

474. Nail down (*v.*) - 결정을 보다. 매듭을 짓다. 검거하다.

1) 회사가 파산으로 가는 것을 막길 원한다면 우리는 이 계약을 매듭지어야만 한다.
2) 그 팀은 시즌 마지막 경기에서 결승리그로 가는 것이 결정 되었다.
3) 경찰이 마약 판매상을 검거했다.

475. Name of the game (*n.*) - 표면과는 달리 내용이 다른 일

1) 우승을 하는 것이 단순하게 보일 수 있지만, 그렇지 않다. 가끔 우승이라는 것은 보이는 것과는 다른 일이다.
2) 그 사건은 단순한 뇌물 사건인 것처럼 보이지만, 많은 사람들은 정부의 부패가 이유라고 생각한다.

476. Natural-born (*adj.*) - 그 나라에서 출생한 시민, 타고난 소질이 있는

1) 그의 부모님은 귀화한 시민들이나, 그는 시민권을 가지고 태어났다.
2) 모차르트는 타고난 음악 천재인 것처럼 보인다.

477. Never mind (*v.*) - 상관하지 않다.

1) 전화 좀 받아주겠니? 아, 그만 둬. 그냥 내가 받을께.

478. Next door (*adv.*) - 바로 옆(집, 아파트, 빌딩, 사무실 등)에

1) 그들은 제과점 바로 옆에 있는 피자집 위에 살았다.
2) 이분은 림 여사입니다. 바로 옆집으로 이사 왔어요.
3) 새 비디오 대여점이 미용실 바로 옆에서 개업을 했다.

** Next-door (*adj.*) - 바로 옆의

1) 그녀는 나의 바로 옆집의 이웃이다.

479. Nightlife (*n.*) - 밤의 유흥

1) 어느 도시에나 밤의 유흥이 많다. 도시들은 환락으로 무성하다.
2) 우리가 휴가를 갈 때면, 우리는 문화적 매력과 밤의 유흥을 즐긴다.

480. Nip and tuck (*adj., adv.*) - 매우 아슬아슬하게

1) 그 축구경기는 매우 막상막하였지만, 홈팀이 끝나기 몇 분 전에 겨우 승리했다.

2) 금년의 인디 500 경기는 매우 아슬아슬했다.

481. Nip in the bud (*v.*) – 초기에 방지하다.

1) 교장은 십대들에게 있어서 싸움은 흔한 일이라는 것을 알았지만, 그는 문제를 조기에 방지하기 위해서 그들을 정학시켰다.
2) 흡연과 그리고 그 외의 중독성 행동은 초기에 방지된다면 효과적으로 극복할 수 있다.

482. Nobody's fool (*n.*) – 영민하고 자신이 무엇을 하는지 잘 아는 사람.

1) 그들은 그들이 임시교사를 잘 이용할 수 있을 거라 생각했지만, 그는 그가 함부로 착취할 수 없는 영민한 사람이라는 것을 그들에게 보여주었다.

483. No doubt (*adv.*) – 의심할 여지없이

1) 그는 부자이고 유명하다. 그는 인간이 원할 만한 모든 것을 가지고 있다. 그가 행복하다는 것은 의심의 여지가 없다.
2) 그녀가 상을 받을 만한 자격이 된다는 것을 의심하는 사람은 아무도 없었다.

** To be sure (*adv.*) – 의심할 여지없이, 확실히

1) 그 대회는 그의 경력에서 가장 큰 것이다. 하지만 그가 우승하리라는 것은 확실하다.
2) 그녀는 천천히 일하지만, 조직적이고 차근차근하게 일을 매우 잘 한다.

484. No good (*adj.*) – 소용없는, 좋지 않은

1) 나는 내 고물차가 쓸모없기 때문에 없앨 예정이다.
2) 그는 사람을 다루는 기술이 없기 때문에 매니저로서는 좋지 않다.
3) 나는 좀 더 높은 급여를 받기위해 협상을 시도했지만, 소용이 없었다.
4) 그는 항상 그 자신이 옳다고 생각하기 때문에 그와 논쟁하는 것은 소용이 없다.

** Of no avail / To no avail (*adj.*) – 소용없는, 성공적이지 못한

1) 나는 아직도 머리가 아프기 때문에 약을 먹은 것이 소용이 없었다.
2) 그 계획은 쓸모없어졌다. 그래서 그들의 힘든 노력이 소용없어졌다.
3) 새 컴퓨터 프로그램을 배우려는 그녀의 노력은 소용이 없었다.

485. No longer (*adv.*) – 더 이상 ~ 않다.

1) 당신이 찾는 사람은 더 이상 여기 살지 않는다.
2) 당신이 건 전화번호는 더 이상 사용되지 않는다.
3) 나는 옛날에는 단 것을 즐기곤 했는데, 지금은 더 이상 먹지 않는다.
4) 나는 오랜 시간 그를 좋아해 왔지만, 이제는 더 이상 관심이 없다.

486. No matter what / No matter how (*adv.*) – ~할지라도, ~에도 불구하고

1) 그가 뭐라고 말하든, 그는 아직도 너를 사랑한다.

2) 그는 열심히 공부했음에도 여전히 시험에서 불합격 하였다.

487. No sweat (*adv.*) – 쉽게(힘들이지 않고)

1) 나는 내가 힘들이지 않고 그 일을 정시에 끝낼 것이라고 확신한다.
2) 그것은 별로 어렵지 않다. 나는 네 컴퓨터를 고칠 수 있다.

488. Not bad (*adj.*) – 나쁘지 않은, 괜찮은

1) 나는 내가 이 생선의 맛을 좋아하게 되리라고는 생각해 본 적이 없는데 나쁘지는 않다.
2) 나는 그 영화가 형편없을 것이라고 생각했지만, 그리 나쁘지는 않았다.

489. Not for the world (*adv.*) – 결코 ~하지 않을

1) 나는 결코 네 감정을 상하게 하지는 않을 거야.
2) 결코 나는 너를 버리지 않을 것이다.

490. Nothing succeeds like success (proverb) (금언) – 하나의 일에 성공을 하면 다른 일에도 성공하기 쉽다. 성공은 계속 성공을 부른다.

1) 동물사료 사업에서 성공한 후 그는 다른 벤처 사업에도 투자하였고, 그것 역시 성공이었다. 성공은 계속 성공을 부르기 마련이다.

491. Not know which way to turn (*v.*) – 어려운 처지에서 어찌할 바를 모른다.

1) 그녀가 실직하고 집세를 치룰 돈도 없었을 때, 그녀는 어찌해야 할 바를 몰랐다.
2) 조기 퇴직과 빈약한 연금을 받아들이도록 강요받았을 때, 그는 정말로 어찌 해야 할 바를 몰랐다.

492. Not the only fish in the sea (*n.*) – 세상에 오직 그 사람만 있는 것은 아님, 여러 명 중의 한명

1) 나는 그가 멋있는 사람인 줄 알고 있어. 하지만 세상에 남자가 그 하나 뿐은 아니잖니? 나는 네가 다른 사람을 찾을 수 있을 것이라고 확신한다.

**** Not the only pebble on the beach (*n.*) – 쓸 수 있는 유일한 사람, 여러 명 중의 한 명**

1) 세상에 그녀만 있는 것이 아니야. 너는 곧 다른 사람을 찾을 거야.

493. No use crying over spilled milk (*proverb*) (금언) – 이미 발생한 일에 대해 후회하거나 불평해도 소용없다. 지난 일은 후회해도 소용없다.

1) 그들은 결승전에서 패했다. 하지만 후회해도 소용없다.
2) 나는 그들이 내게 일자리를 제안 할 것이라고 확신했었다. 하지만 그들은 그러지 않았다. 아, 이제 울어도 소용없다.

**** No use (*n.*) - 소용없음, 무익**

1) 옛 부귀영화에 대해서 이야기 해봐야 아무런 소용이 없다. 과거는 지나간 것이고 이미 끝난 것이다.
2) 그는 아무도 도와주지 않기 때문에 그에게 도와 달라고 말해봐야 소용이 없다.
3) 그녀는 이미 결심을 했기 때문에 그녀에게 편지를 보내도 아무 소용없다.

494. No wonder (*adj.*) - 놀랄 필요 없는, 당연한

1) 그녀는 지성 있고, 매력있고, 철저히 전문적이다. 그들이 그녀에게 감명을 받은 것은 전혀 놀랄 일이 아니다.
2) 네가 이 식당을 좋아하는 것이 놀랄 일이 아니다. 그들의 서비스는 훌륭하고, 음식은 매우 맛있다.

O

495. Oddball (*n.*) – 약간 이상한 사람

1) 내 이웃인 조지는 약간 이상한 사람이다. 그는 외톨이로 시간을 보내고 누구와도 어울리지 않는다.

**** Off-center (*adj.*) – 이상한**

1) 그는 이상한 사람이다. 그래서 우리는 그를 결코 파티에 초대하지 않는다.
2) 이 그림은 약간 이상하다.

**** Off center (*adv.*) – 정확하게 한 가운데가 아닌**

1) 이 그림은 가운데에서 약간 어긋났다, 그래서 우리는 그것을 조정해야한다.

496. Of age (*adj.*) – (성인의 권리와 책임을 수행할 수 있도록 법에 의해 허락된) 연령의

1) 그녀는 이제 운전을 할 수 있는 나이다. 그래서 그녀는 운전면허를 따기 원한다.
2) 투표를 하기 위해 적어도 21살이 되어야 한다.
3) 만약 20살 이라면 아직 선거할 수 있는 나이가 아니다.

497. Of course (*adv.*) – 당연히, 물론

1) 그가 그녀를 사랑하니? 물론 그는 그녀를 사랑한다.
2) 나를 기억하니? 물론이지. 나는 너를 기억해.

498. Off again, on again (*adj.*) – 불확실한, 이어졌다 끊어졌다.

1) 그들은 이어졌다. 끊겼다 하는 불확실한 관계를 가지고 있다.
2) 비가 하루 종일 내리지 않았지만 오락가락 했기 때문에 그 테니스 경기는 취소되었다.

**** Off and on / On and off (*adv.*) – 이따금, 불규칙적으로**

1) 그날동안 전기가 불규칙적이었다.
2) 우리는 저녁이나 사교적 모임에서 그들을 이따금 본다.

499. Off balance (*adj.*) – 불균형의

1) 세탁기가 균형이 맞지 않아, 큰 소음을 낸다.
2) 내 차의 타이어들이 균형이 맞지 않아, 승차감이 별로 좋지 않았다.

500. Off duty (*adj.*) – 비번의, 쉬는 날의(종종 관료에게 사용)

1) 비번인 경관이 범인을 체포했다.
2) 그 의사는 오늘 쉬는 날이어서, 아마 골프를 치고 있을 것이다.

**** On one's day off (*adv.*) – 쉬는 날에, 비번 날에(종종 일반인들에게 적용)**

1) 너 쉬는 날 대개 뭐하니?
2) 난 쉬는 날이면 대개 정원 손질을 하며 시간을 보내곤 한다.
3) 나는 쉬는 날에는 대개 쇼핑을 가곤 한다.

**** On duty (*adj.*) – 근무 (중) (자신의 책임부서에서)**

1) 닥터 샤키스는 오늘 근무이다.
2) 그는 한국 해군에 현역으로 복무중이다.
3) 직원들은 위급한 상황이 아니면 근무 중에 개인적인 전화를 받는 것이 허락되지 않는다.

501. Off one's chest (*adj.*) – 자신의 고민거리를 누군가에게 말하다. 마음에서 털어놓다.

1) 나는 내 상사에게 그가 나를 공평하게 대우하지 않았음을 이야기 하였다. 그 이후 그가 나를 대하는 것이 달라지지는 않았지만, 나는 내 마음속을 털어 놓은 뒤 훨씬 기분이 나아졌다.
2) 그는 그녀의 이야기를 들었고, 그녀의 마음속을 털어놓도록 했다.

502. Off the cuff (*adv.*) – 즉석에서

1) 그는 즉석에서 연설하는 것을 더 좋아한다.
2) 그는 제시된 계획에 대해서 즉석에서 설명을 했다.

**** Off-the-cuff (*adj.*) – 즉석의, 준비 없이**

1) 그는 즉석에서 연설하는 것에 놀라운 재능을 가지고 있다.
2) 그는 굉장한 즉석연설을 했다.

503. Off the top of one's head (*adj., adv.*) – (깊이 생각하지 않고) 그냥 생각나는 대로

1) 그녀는 깊이 생각할 시간을 갖지 않았다. 그녀는 질문에 그냥 생각나는 대로 답했다.
2) 그는 그가 쓴 것에 대해서 생각을 짜내지 않았다. 그는 그냥 생각나는 대로 썼다.

**** Offhand (*adj., adv.*) / offhanded (*adj.*) – 계획 없이, 깊이 생각하지 않고 바로**

1) 나는 좀 생각을 하지 않고는 바로 그것을 회상해 낼 수가 없다.
2) 그 정치가는 몇 가지 민감한 현안문제들에 대해서 깊은 생각 없이 논평했다.

504. Of late (*adv.*) – 최근에

1) 최근에 그는 평소의 낙천적 모습이 아니었다.
2) 최근에 그 신문은 중요한 문제 보다는 하찮은 문제들에 초점을 맞춰왔다.

505. Of one's own free will / Of one's own accord (*adv.*) **– 자발적으로, 외부의 영향 없이**

1) 너 그 계약에 외부의 영향 없이 자발적으로 서명하려고 하니?
2) 그래, 나는 그것에 내 의향대로 서명하려고 해.
3) 1년간의 휴무는 내 의지에서 나온 결정이다.

506. On account of (*prep.*) **– ~를 위하여, ~의 이유로써, ~ 때문에**

1) 그는 그의 건강상의 이유로 좀 더 따뜻한 남부지역으로 이사를 하고 싶어 한다.
2) 그들은 그들 나라의 팽팽한 정치상황 때문에 이민을 갔다.
3) 그녀는 교통 체증 때문에 늦게 도착했다.

507. On the average (*adv.*) **– 평균해서, 대개**

1) 평균적으로, 나는 3000마일에 한 번씩 자동차 오일을 교환한다.
2) 평균적으로, 나는 한 달에 100달러를 용돈으로 사용한다.

508. On approval (*adv.*) **– (대부, 신용장)등을 받기 전에 요구되는 기준**

1) 그녀는 물품이 당장 배달되길 원했지만, 그들은 신용장 승인이 나야만 배달하므로 기다려야만 했다.
2) 우리는 당신의 신용 신청허가에 의해서 신용카드를 발급 할 수 있다.
3) 우리는 당신이 점검 매매의 조건으로 이 물품을 산다면 당신에게 환불을 보장할 수 있다.

509. On call / At call (*adj.*) **– (의사나 간호원 등) 호출 대기 중의, (사전 통보 없이) 돈을 갚으라고 요구하는**

1) 스미스 의사가 오늘 당직 외과의사다.
2) 그 자리는 호출 대기를 해야만 하는 자리이지만, 어쨌든 나는 그 제안을 받아들였다.
3) 그 남자는 긴급하게 그 지역의 은행에서 온콜조건으로 많은 액수의 돈을 빌렸다. 지금 그 채권자는 돈을 갚을 것을 요구하지만 그는 갚을 준비가 되어있지 않다.

510. Once and for all (*adv., n*) **– 단 한번, 확실하게**

1) 확실하게 그 대답은 "아니다."이다.
2) 그 일을 한 번에 확실하게 끝마치도록 하자.

511. Once in a while (*adv.*) **– 이따금, 가끔**

1) 우리는 종종 그들과 저녁식사를 하러 나간다.
2) 나는 종종 내 동료들과 커피를 마시러 나간다.
3) 낯선 사람이 되지 말고 종종 들려서 우리를 좀 만나라.

512. On the condition that (*conj.*) – 만약, ~라는 조건으로

1) 나는 네가 진심이라는 조건으로 너의 사과를 받아들이겠다.
2) 나는 2년 상환에 10%의 이자로 은행에서 약간의 돈을 빌렸다.
3) 나는 네가 설거지를 한다는 조건으로 기꺼이 저녁을 준비하겠다.

513. On edge (*adj.*) – 긴장한, 불안한, 신경이 곤두선,

1) 그 불쾌한 사건은 사무실에 있는 모든 사람의 신경을 곤두서게 했다.
2) 그의 불쾌한 어조는 그가 아직 신경이 곤두서있다는 것의 결정적인 증거였다.

514. On end (*adv.*) – 곧추 선, 중단 없이, 계속해서

1) 그는 그녀의 말에 너무나 화가 나서 그의 머리털이 곤두섰다.
2) 그녀는 부과된 숙제를 몇 시간째 중단 없이 했지만 그것은 미완으로 남았다.
3) 나는 이 기사를 쓰기위해 계속해서 몇 시간째 노력하고 있지만, 끊임없는 방해거리들이 내가 그것을 끝마치지 못하게 하고 있다.
4) 몇 시간째 계속 비가 내리고 있다.

515. One of these days (*adv.*) – 조만간

1) 그는 아내에게 조만간에 차고를 청소하겠다고 약속했다.
2) 우리 조만간 커피나 술 한잔하러 만납시다.

516. On faith (*adv.*) – 신뢰로써, 의심 없이

1) 네가 만약 그와의 관계를 지키고 싶다면 너는 그가 말하는 것을 신뢰로써 받아들여야 한다.
2) 그녀는 신뢰로써 그녀의 차를 팔았지만, 그는 그녀에게 결코 돈을 지불하지 않았다.

517. On guard (*adj.*) – 조심하는

1) 대도시에 가면 소매치기가 많기 때문에 조심해야 한다.

** Off guard (*adj.*) – 방심한

1) 포도주를 몇 잔 마신 후에, 그는 방심을 해서 그 비밀을 그녀에게 말했다.
2) 주자는 투수가 방심을 하고 있는 것이 보였기 때문에 홈으로 도루를 했다.

518. On hand (*adv.*) – 사용할 수 있게, 가까이

1) 그 비서는 응급사태를 대비해서 여분의 의약품을 보관하고 있다.
2) 나는 공부할 때, 항상 내 사전을 가까이 둔다.

519. On one's hands (*adj., adv.*) – ~의 책임인, 돌보는, 수중에 있는

1) 처리해야 할 일이 많기 때문에, 그녀는 7월 말까지 휴가를 연기해야만 했다.
2) 그 일들은 지금 그의 책임 하에 있다.

** Off one's hands – 돌보지 않아도 되는, 수중에서 떠난, 책임에서 벗어 난

1) 그녀의 아들은 21세가 넘었고, 그녀의 품을 떠났다. 그래서 그녀는 그 아들의 빚에 대해 책임이 없다. 그래서 그는 그의 빚을 갚기 위해서 직업을 찾아야만 한다.
2) 그 임무가 끝나고 마침내 내 책임에서 떠나 기쁘다.

520. On one's honor (*adj.*) – ~의 명예를 걸고

1) 그 학생들은 그들의 명예를 걸고 시험을 보았고, 아무도 부정행위를 하지 않았다.

521. On one's mind (*adj.*) – ~의 생각 속에

1) 그녀는 집에서 먼 곳에 있지만, 그녀의 가족은 여전히 그녀의 마음속에 있었다.
2) 나는 내 친구와 한 달 전에 말다툼을 했지만 아직도 앙금이 가시지 않았다.
3) 너 지금 무슨 생각하니? 너 지금 무슨 생각하고 있음에 틀림없어.

522. On one's own (*adj.*) – 완전히 독립한

1) 부모님이 돌아가신 후 그는 스스로 완전히 독립해서 살았다.
2) 나는 네 숙제를 도와 줄 시간이 없다. 너는 스스로 해야만 한다.
3) 그녀가 완전히 혼자라는 생각은 그녀를 불안하게 만들었다.

523. On the part of / On one's part (*adj.*) – ~편의, ~에게 있는, ~의 탓인

1) 그 사고는 운전자 측의 부주의 탓으로 돌려졌다.
2) 그가 돈을 훔쳤지만, 그녀는 그를 신고하지 않았다.

524. On one's shoulders (*adj., adv.*) – 책임이 있는

1) 가족을 돌봐야 하는 책임이 그녀의 어깨를 무겁게 눌렀다.
2) 그 회사의 성공이 대부분 그에게 달려있다.

525. On one's toes (*adj.*) – 활동할 준비가 되어있는, 정신을 바짝 차린

1) 훌륭한 변호사는 항상 정신을 바짝 차리고 있어서, 거의 실수를 하지 않는다.
2) 근무 중인 경찰은 정신을 바짝 차리고 있어야 한다.

526. On paper (*adj., adv.*) – 서류상, 이론상

1) 우리는 서류상 합의점을 찾을 수 있었고, 그 계약은 성사 되었다.
2) 많은 취업 희망자들이 서류상 훌륭해 보인다. 하지만, 그들은 종종 기대에 부응해서 일을 잘하지 못한다.

527. On purpose (*adv.*) – 일부러, 고의로

1) 경찰은 그 불이 방화에 의해 시작되었다고 생각한다.
2) 그 공공연한 못된 반칙은 우연이 아니다. 그것은 일부러 그런 것이다.

528. On record (*adj.*) – 공개적으로 알려진, 기록된

1) 학생들의 비행은 학교 기록부에 기록된다.
2) 그 정치인은 다가오는 선거에 대한 그의 입장을 기록하여 밝혔다.
3) 많은 옛 기록들이 소실되어서 더 이상 기록이 남아있지 않다.

529. On sale (*adj.*) – 특정한 기간 동안에 할인된 가격으로 판매하는

1) 그 대학의 봄 기금 모금 행사에서 많은 물품들이 할인된 가격으로 제공되었다.
2) 통상적으로 1200달러에 팔리는 한 디자이너의 옷이 500달러로 할인되었다.

530. On schedule (*adv.*) – 예정대로

1) KE 460 항공편이 예정대로 착륙했다.
2) 악천후 때문에 제주도로 가는 배가 예정대로 떠나지 못했다.

531. On the air (*adj., adv.*) – 방송중의, 방영될

1) 그 골프 경기가 오후에 방송될 예정이다.
2) 그 기록영화는 다음 주 토요일 9번 채널에서 방영될 예정이다.

532. On the contrary (*adv.*) – 반대로, 오히려

1) 그는 그가 그 경기에서 이길 것이라고 생각했지만, 오히려 패했다.
2) 사람들은 그녀가 동물을 좋아하지 않을 것이라고 생각했지만, 반대로 그녀는 동물권리 옹호자의 한 사람이다.

533. On the face of it (*adv.*) – 표면상으로, 외견상으로

1) 그의 이야기는 표면상으로는 이치에 맞는 것 같았지만, 면밀히 따져보면 이치에 전혀 맞지 않았다.
2) 외견상으로, 그러한 상황에서 그녀의 행동은 예기치 못한 것으로 보였다.

534. On the go (*adj.*) – 활동적이고 바쁜

1) 그녀는 내가 아는 한 가장 원기왕성한 사람이다. 그녀는 항상 활동적이고 바쁘다.
2) 그의 새로운 일자리는 많은 출장을 포함한다. 그리고 그를 항상 활동적이고 바쁘게 한다.

535. On the house (*adj.*) – (레스토랑이나 바 등에서 손님에게 무료로 주는 것)공짜의

1) 그들은 우리가 한 시간이나 음식을 기다렸기 때문에 우리에게 음료를 공짜로 제공했다.
2) 많은 식당들이 손님을 끌기 위해서 청량음료를 무료로 제공한다.

536. On the line (*adj.*) – 즉시 사용할 수 있는, 준비된, 위태로운

1) 지금 당신의 전화가 와 있습니다.
2) 그녀는 그녀의 평판이 위태롭다는 것을 깨달았고, 그것이 그녀가 최선을 다하도록 동기를 부여했다.

** Lay it on the line / Put it on the line (*v.*) – 숨김없이 분명하게 공개적으로 말하다. 쓰다.

1) 나는 내가 직선적으로 말하는 것을 네가 기분 나빠 하지 않았으면 좋겠다. 네가 하는 일이 만족스럽지 못하다.
2) 나는 네가 마음속에 많은 것을 감추고 있는 것을 안다. 숨김없이 말해주지 않을래?
3) 그 회사는 1백만 달러를 사원 건강계획을 위해서 사용했다.

** On line / Online (*adj.*) – 컴퓨터 시스템에 연결이 되어있는, 즉시 이용할 수 있는, 작동이 잘 되는

1) 요즈음 모든 은행은 온라인 체계를 갖추고 있다.
2) 내 컴퓨터가 얼마 전에 작동 불능이 되었지만, 지금은 작동이 정상적이다.

** Off-line (*adj.*) – 컴퓨터 시스템에 연결이 되어있지 않은, 작동이 안 되는

1) 인터넷이 하루 종일 작동이 안 되었다.
2) 컴퓨터가 작동이 안 되었기 때문에 나는 은행에서 돈을 인출할 수가 없었다.

537. On the lookout for (*adj.*) – 자세히 살피다 (기대감을 가지고).

1) 그 에이전시는 항상 새로운 인재를 찾기 위해 자세히 살핀다.
2) 그녀는 항상 싼 물건을 잘 찾는 사람으로 평판이 나있다.
3) 경찰은 최근 화재들의 방화범을 샅샅이 수색하고 있다.

538. On the run (*adj., adv.*) – 바쁜, 서두르는, 황급히

1) 나도 너를 도와주고 싶지만, 회의가 있어서 급히 가는 중이라 그럴 수 없다.
2) 우리는 그녀를 저녁 식사에 초대하고 싶지만, 그녀는 항상 바쁘다.

539. On the point of (*prep.*) – 막 ~하려고 하는, 막 ~하려는 시점에서

1) 그들이 마침내 그에게 승진을 제안했을 때 그는 막 사표를 제출하려고하는 시점에 있었다.
2) 그의 연설은 매우 통렬해서, 그녀는 막 울려고 했다.

540. On the spot (*adj., adv.*) – 그 당장, 즉석에서, 어려운 처지에

1) 그녀의 반항은 그가 그녀를 즉석에서 해고하는 이유가 되었다.
2) 세 명의 증인과 결정적인 증거가 그 강도를 궁지로 몰고 갔다.
3) 그는 임대료가 없기 때문에 어려운 처지에 놓여 있다.

541. On the spur of the moment (*adv.*) – 충동적으로

1) 그녀는 충동적으로 짐을 싸서 하와이로 일주일간 떠났다.
2) 그는 충동적으로 그 약속을 했고, 그것을 후회하면서 살았다.

542. On the strength of (*prep.*) - ~를 근거로

1) 그 계약은 그 회사의 평판을 근거로 성사되었다.
2) 그는 예술가로서의 그의 경험을 바탕으로 화랑을 열었다.

543. On the way / on one's way (*adj., adv.*) - 오는 중, 가는 중, 여행 중

1) 나는 집에 가는 중이고, 20분 이내에 도착할 것이다.
2) 나무위의 새싹들은 봄이 오고 있다는 좋은 신호이다.
3) 나는 클리블랜드로 가는 중이었으나, 대신 워싱턴 D.C로 갔다.

544. On time (*adj., adv.*) - 예정된 시간에

1) 평소와 같이 6시 기차가 정시에 도착하지 않았다.
2) 그녀의 저녁 데이트 상대는 정시에 왔지만, 그녀는 아직 준비되지 않았다.
3) 학생들은 그 수업이 결코 정시에 시작되지 않았다고 불평했다.

545. On top of (*prep.*) - ~에 대해 잘 아는, 게다가, ~위로, 지배(관리)하는

1) 현대의 멀티미디어는 우리가 세계의 최신뉴스와 사건에 대해 잘 알도록 해준다.
2) 그는 암으로 진단받았고, 게다가 실직까지 했다.
3) 사과 하나가 나무에서 떨어져서 그의 머리 위를 때렸다.
4) 그는 일을 관리하기 위해서 여분의 시간을 투자한다.

** On top of the world (cliché) - 성공적으로 느끼는, 매우 기쁜

1) 그녀가 영어과목에서 A+를 받았을 때, 그녀는 매우 기뻤다.

546. Open doors (*v.*) - 기회를 주다. 문을 열다. 시작하다.

1) 그 장학기금은 도움을 필요로 하는 많은 청소년들을 위해 시작되었다.
2) 비스트로 식당은 20년 전 오늘 개업했다.

547. Open one's eyes (*v.*) - 눈을 뜨다. 사실을 보다.

1) 시골에서의 성장은 내게 자연의 아름다움에 대한 눈을 띄어주었다.
2) 눈을 떠서 사실을 보아라.

548. Open one's heart (*v.*) - (마음을 열어) 사랑이나 동정을 주다. 신뢰하다. 마음을 터놓다.

1) 작은 고양이 한 마리가 나의 마음을 열게 했다.
2) 적십자사가 시민들에게 마음을 열어 헌혈을 할 것을 요청하고 있다.
3) 고아들을 보았을 때, 그녀는 동정을 느꼈고, 보다 나은 삶을 영위시키기 위해 그녀의 남은 일생을 헌신하도록 만들었다.
4) 그녀는 너무 늦기 전에 그의 마음을 열라고 간청했다.

549. Out of breath (*adj., adv.*) - 숨이 가쁜

1) 6Km의 경주 후에 달리기 주자들은 숨이 가빴다.

2) 흡연이 심폐기능에 영향을 주기 때문에, 흡연자들이 달리기를 하면, 더 빨리 숨이 가쁘게 된다.

550. Out of one's character (*adj., adv.*) - ~의 일반적인 성격이나 행동과는 다른

1) 그는 열심히 공부했고 부정행위와는 거리가 멀어보였지만, 그럼에도 불구하고, 기말시험에서 부정행위를 하다가 적발되었다.

**** in character - ~의 일반적 성격이나 행동에 일치하는**

1) 그녀의 시간과 능력을 필요로 하는 사람을 위해 자원 봉사하는 것은 그녀의 성격과 잘 일치하는 좋은 면이다.

551. Out of hand (*adv.*) - 조정 할 수 없는, 조절 할 수 없는, 통제 할 수 없는

1) 그의 부모님은 그의 행동을 통제할 수 없어서, 부모님은 그에게 2주간 외출을 금지 한다는 벌칙을 결정하셨다.

2) 몇몇의 이웃들이 도를 넘어선 남학생들의 사교파티를 신고하기 위해서 경찰에 전화했다.

552. Out of line (*adj.*) - 부적절한, 줄이 바르지 않은

1) 그의 논평은 부적절했고, 의장이 그를 비난했다.

2) 너의 최근 행동은 학교 정책에서 어긋난 것이었다. 그래서 우리는 이번 학기의 나머지 기간 동안 정학시키는 수밖에 달리 방도가 없다.

3) 유치원의 선생님이 계속해서 주의를 주었지만, 그 아이들은 계속 줄에서 벗어났다.

553. Out of luck (*adj.*) - 운수가 나쁜

1) 나는 은행이 문을 닫기 전에 은행에 도착하려고 했지만, 운이 나빴다.

2) 그 팀은 준결승까지 진출했지만, 결승전에서는 운이 나빴다.

554. Out of nowhere (*adv.*) - 갑자기, 뜻밖에

1) 나는 고속도로 순찰대를 못 보았기 때문에, 제한 속도보다 더 빨리 운전 했는데, 그때 갑자기 순찰대원이 나타나 나를 쫓기 시작했다. 그래서 나는 결국 법정에 섰고 120달러의 벌금을 선고 받았다.

555. Out of order (*adj., adv.*) - 규칙에 위배되는, 순서가 바뀐, 고장 난

1) 그 학생의 행동은 규칙에 위배되는 것이었기 때문에, 그는 질책을 받았다.

2) 어린 아이들은 종종 알파벳의 순서를 바꾸어 말한다.

3) 나는 커피 자판기가 고장 난 것을 알리기 위해 그 회사에 전화를 걸었다.

556. Out of print (*adj.*) - 더 이상 인쇄되지 않는

1) 그는 많은 작품을 썼고, 그의 시대에는 많이 읽혔으나, 근래에 그의 작품은 더 이상 출판

되지 않는다.

** In print – 인쇄된, 출판된

1) 그 작가의 애호가들은 그들이 오랫동안 기다리던 속편이 출판되었다는 것을 듣고 기뻤다.
2) 새 천문학 교과서가 곧 출판될 것이다.

557. Out of season (*adv.*) – 제철이 아닌, 이용하거나 구할 수 없는

1) 토마토는 지금 제철이 아니기 때문에, 우리가 먹는 모든 것은 온실 토마토이다.
2) 그녀의 복장은 계절과 맞지 않는다. 한 여름에도 계속 스웨터를 입는 것은 이상하다.

558. Out of the question (*adj.*) – 생각할 수조차 없는, 고려될 수 없는

1) 너의 추가 대출 요구는 고려될 수조차 없다.
2) 그녀에 있어서 실패라는 것은 생각할 수조차 없었다. 그녀는 그녀가 모든 일에서 성공해야만 한다고 느낀다.

** In question – 고려(거론) 되고 있는

1) 나는 거론 되고 있는 사람들의 명단을 만들었지만, 승진할 만한 모든 사람들을 포함시켰는지 확실하지 않다.

559. Out of the running (*adv.*) – 승리할 기회가 없는, 승산이 없는

1) 그녀는 그 자리에 승산이 없다고 생각했지만, 그럼에도 불구하고 그녀는 그 자리를 얻었다.
2) 내가 돈을 건 말들은 출발문부터 대개 승산이 없다.

560. Over one's head (*adj., adv.*) – ~을 이해하거나 상대하는데 있어서 능력이 미치지 않는

1) 컴퓨터를 완전히 이해하는 것은 내 능력 밖이다.
2) 이것은 어려운 논문이고 몇몇 부분이 내 능력 밖이라는 것을 인정한다.
3) 죄송하지만, 저는 그 질문에 대답을 할 수가 없습니다. 그 결정은 저의 권한 밖으로서 회사의 누군가에 의해 내려진 것입니다.

P

561. Pack off (*v.*) – (짐 싸서 또는 챙겨서) 보내다.

1) 그들이 마침내 아이의 짐을 싸서 여름 캠프로 보냈고, 안도의 한숨을 내 쉬었다.
2) 그 소년은 여름 휴가동안에 집에 있기를 원했지만, 그의 부모님들은 짐을 싸서 그를 유럽으로 보냈다.

562. Pain in the neck (*n.*) – 불유쾌한 것. 귀찮거나 성가신 존재(것)

1) 내 동료들 중의 하나는 매우 불쾌하고 귀찮은 존재이다.
2) 많은 학생들이 작문을 귀찮게 생각한다.

563. Pair off / Pair up (*v.*) – 그룹을 짓거나 쌍으로 나누어지다. 짝짓다. 관련이 되다.

1) 쌍쌍이 다음 춤을 위해서 짝을 지었다.
2) 주최자는 초대 손님들을 나이와 관심사항에 따라 그룹을 지었다.
3) 나는 테니스의 복식 경기에서 그와 짝이 되었다.
4) 이씨는 일을 하기 위해 김씨와 함께 팀이 되었다.

564. Pawn off (*v.*) – 속여서 처분하다.

1) 그 보석상은 그 반지를 원래의 가치보다 훨씬 더 높게 속여서 팔았다.
2) 그녀의 동료들은 그녀에게 대개 많은 양의 일을 속여서 떠맡긴다.

565. Partake (in, of) (*v.*) – 참여(참가)하다. ~의 몫을 받다. ~을 함께 사용하다(나누다.)

1) 많은 사람들이 그 회사의 연례 춘계 모임에 참석한다.
2) 초대 손님들은 그 행사에 열심히 참가하였다.
3) 파티를 즐기는 사람들이 뿔모양 장식에 담겨있는 음식과 마실 것을 나누어 먹었다.

566. Part and parcel (*n.*) – 떼어 놓을 수 없는 부분. 불가분의 관계

1) 초과근무는 그 계약과 떼어 놓을 수 없는 부분인 것 같았다.
2) 부상은 운동선수가 되는 것과 불가분의 관계이다.

567. Part with (*v.*) – 포기하다. 헤어지다.

1) 그녀는 사귀어 온 친구들과 헤어지는 것이 슬펐지만, 그녀는 떠나서 새로운 일을 하기를 간절히 원했다.

2) 그녀의 가족과 떨어지는 것이 그녀에게 매우 아픈 경험인 것처럼 보인다.

568. Pass away (*v.*) - 죽다. 지나가다. 중단하다.

1) 나의 할아버지는 고령의 나이인 98세에 돌아가셨다.
2) 시간은 우리가 실감하는 것보다 훨씬 더 빨리 지나간다.
3) 그 약의 효과가 그치는 데는 두어 시간이 걸린다.

569. Pass on (*v.*) - 전하다. 넘겨주다.

1) 유전적 성질은 한세대에서 다음세대로 전해진다.
2) 대학의 학생들은 종종 그들의 교과서들을 다른 학생들에게 물려준다.

570. Pass out (*v.*) - 배포하다. 기절하다.

1) 그녀는 그 회사의 광고 전단을 배포하기 위해서 고용되었다.
2) 너의 시험지만 가지고 나머지 시험지는 다른 학생들에게 돌려라.
3) 그녀는 그녀의 자매의 사고 소식을 들었을 때 기절했다.

571. Pass over (*v.*) - 그냥 지나치다. 생략하다.

1) 이 문제는 당분간 거론하지 않고 지금 현재의 안건만 다룹시다.
2) 그 영화에 대한 너의 비평에서 내가 가장 중요한 부분이라고 본 부분을 생략한 것 같다.

572. Pass up (*v.*) - 거절하다.

1) "쵸콜릿 좀 드시겠어요?" "아니요, 괜찮습니다. 다이어트 중이라 거절하겠습니다."
2) 그들의 일자리 제안은 매력적이었지만, 그녀는 좀 더 나은 자리를 찾기 위해서 거절했다.

573. Patch up (*v.*) - 화해하다. 구멍 난 곳을 때우다. 수리하다.

1) 그들은 그들의 관계를 호전시키기 위해 화해했다.
2) 우리는 장마철이 시작되기 전에 지붕을 수리해야만 한다.

574. Pave the way (*v.*) - 개발이나 진행 등을 더 쉽게 만들다.

1) 교육이 경제적 성공을 더 쉽게 만든다는 것은 사실이 아니다.
2) 그녀의 가족 혈통은 그녀가 미국의 명문대학에 입학하는 것을 더 쉽게 만들었다.

575. Pay back (*v.*) - 갚다, 보복하다.

1) 그는 그들에게 그들의 모욕을 보복할 방법을 찾을 것이라고 그들에게 다짐했다.
2) 그 팀 전원은 작년 결승전에서의 치욕적인 패배를 갚기 위해서 혈안이 되어 있었다.

576. Pay for (*v.*) - ~의 결과로 고통을 겪다.

1) 젊은 시절은 우리가 실수를 하고 그것에 대해 잊을 수 있는 때다. 성인기는 우리가 저지른 잘못의 결과로 고통을 겪는 시간이다.

2) 만약 네가 지금 담배를 끊지 않는다면, 당신은 나중에 그로 인해 고통을 겪을 것이다.

577. Pay up (*v.*) – 전액을 지불하다.

1) 우리는 그 일이 완료된 후 3주후가 아니라, 완료된 후 즉시 임금을 지불 받을 것이라고 예상했다.
2) 장기 휴가를 떠나기 전에 너의 신용카드의 빚 전액이 지불 되어있나 확인하는 것이 현명하다.

**** Pay off (*v.*) – 전액을 지불하다. 임금을 지불하고 해고하다. 이익을 남기다. 보람이 되는.**

1) 내 집에 대한 장기주택 담보대출자금을 상환하였다. 그래서 나는 더 이상 은행에 빚이 없다.
2) 마침내 그녀는 그녀의 오랫동안 밀린 전화요금을 다 갚을 수가 있었다.
3) 직물 공장에 대한 그의 투자는 큰 이익이 남지는 않았지만, 그는 안락한 생활은 할 수 있었다.
4) 내 영어 능력을 향상 시키는 것은 어려웠다. 하지만, 높은 영어 능숙도를 요구하는 좋은 직업을 얻었을 때, 그것이 참 보람이 되었다.

578. Penny wise and (but) pound foolish (*proverb.*) (격언)– 호미로 막을 것을 가래로 막는다. 기와 한 장 아끼려다 대들보를 썩힌다.

1) 그는 작은 녹슨 부분을 고치는 시간을 할애하지 않아, 지금은 그곳에 큰 구멍이 생겼다. 그는 호미로 막을 것을 가래로 막았다.
2) 그녀는 중고 세탁기를 사는 것이 이익을 얻는 것이라고 생각했지만, 그것은 몇 주가 지나지 않아서 고장이 났고, 몇 푼 아끼려다 더 큰 손해를 보게되었다.

579. Pep up (*v.*) – 격려하다.

1) 코치의 중간 쉬는 시간의 연설은 낙심한 축구팀을 격려했다.
2) 좋은 선생님들은 어떤 반에 들어가든지 항상 학생들을 격려해준다.

**** Pep talk – 격려의 말**

1) 코치가 격려의 말을 한 다음에, 그 팀은 경기장으로 들어갔고 그들은 그 시즌 최고의 경기를 펼쳤다.
2) 내가 기분이 우울해질 때, 내 친구는 대개 내 기분이 좋아지게 하는 격려의 말을 통해서 나를 도와준다.

580. Perk up (*v.*) – 기분이나 기운을 되찾거나 또는 되찾게 하다.

1) 공부하기 싫어하는 학생들은 그들의 교수님이 휴강을 발표하자 기뻐했다.
2) 뜨거운 커피 한잔은 내가 기운을 되찾게 한다.
3) 내 고양이는 내가 고양이 박하를 줄때면 언제나 활기를 되찾는다.

581. Pick and choose (*v.*) – 아주 꼼꼼히 마음대로 선택하다.

1) 그의 아버지는 그에게 이제는 꼼꼼히 직업을 선택해야 할 시기라고 말했다.
2) 일찍 오는 손님들은 판매 품목 중에 가장 좋은 것을 마음대로 선택한다. 늦게 오는 손님들은 남은 것들 가운데서 고르게 된다.
3) 우리는 바쁘다. 자세히 고를 시간이 없다. 그냥 하나 가지고 가자.

582. Pick at (*v.*) – 식욕이 없는 듯 조금씩 먹다. 아주 조그만 일들로 트집을 잡거나 비평을 하거나 괴롭히다.

1) 그는 까다로운 식성을 가지고 있어서 모든 음식을 식욕이 없는 듯 조금씩 먹다.
2) 그녀는 그녀의 상급자가 그녀가 하는 작은 실수까지도 트집을 잡고 괴롭혀서 직장을 그만 두려고 한다.

** Pick on – 골리다, 계속해서 귀찮게 하다.

1) 그 학생은 다른 학생들이 자기를 계속 귀찮게 군다고 그의 선생님에게 말했다.
2) 그는 학습지진아이기 때문에 많은 학급 친구들로부터 골림을 받았다.

583. Pick out (*v.*) – 선택하다. 고르다.

1) 그녀는 그녀의 남자친구가 그녀의 생일 선물로 아름다운 드레스를 골랐기 때문에 매우 기뻐했다.
2) 그는 세이 백화점에서 옷을 골라서 샀다.

584. Pick up (*v.*) – 집어 올리다. 태우다. (지나는 길에) ~을 찾다. 받다(전파 등을 타다), 쉽게 배우다. 향상하다.

1) 그는 그 무거운 상자를 집어 올렸다.
2) 학교 버스는 학생들을 태우기 위해 멈추었다.
3) 나는 집에 가는 길에 세탁소에서 내 정장을 찾을 것이다.
4) 관제탑은 713 비행기로부터 조난 신호를 수신했다.
5) 어린이가 외국어를 배우는 것이 더 쉽다.
6) 그는 뒤 쳐져 있지만, 그의 교육과정을 빨리 향상 시킬 수 있을 것이라고 확신한다.

585. Pin down (*v.*) – 명확하게 지적하거나 설명하다. 결론짓다. 확답하게 하다.

1) 현대적 기술을 사용하여 그 고고학자는 그 화석의 나이를 명확하게 설명 했다.
2) 그녀는 자신의 직업을 좋아하지는 않지만, 그 이유를 명확하게 설명할 수는 없다.
3) 나는 급여의 인상을 원하지만, 이 건을 거론하여 나의 상사가 확답하게 하기에는 너무 이르다.

** On pins and needles (*n.*) – 안절부절한 상태

1) 그녀는 그 일자리를 지원한 이래로 안절부절 못해왔다.
2) 그 학생들은 그 시험 결과를 기다리는 동안 안절부절 하지 못했다.

586. Pit-a-pat (*adv.*) – 가슴이 두근거리는

1) 봄이 가까이 다가올 때면 나의 가슴은 두근거린다.

2) 그가 그녀에게 청혼 했을 때, 그녀의 가슴은 설랬다.

587. Play down (*v.*) – 중요치 않게 취급하다. 강조하지 않다.

1) 자동차 판매원은 그 차의 단점을 극소화하고 장점만 강조했다.

2) 그는 현명한 사람이다. 그리고 항상 자신의 능력과 지식수준을 겸허히 낮춘다.

**** Play up (*v.*) – 강조하거나 과장되게 알리다.**

1) 그 신문은 그 작가의 예술적 재질을 너무 과장되게 논평했다.

2) 그는 그가 소녀들에게 인기있다는 사실을 과장되게 떠벌리기를 좋아한다.

**** Play up to (*v.*) – 아첨으로 ~의 환심을 사려하다.**

1) 그녀는 승진하기 위해 그의 사장에게 아첨으로 환심을 사려고 해왔다.

2) 그는 여성들의 허영심을 자극하고 환심을 사서 그것으로 이익을 취했다.

588. Play havoc with / Raise havoc with (*v.*) – 대단한 혼란을 일으키다. 파괴하다. 비판을 일으키다.

1) 폭우는 그 지역의 전기에 대단한 혼란을 일으켰다.

2) 그 연구원의 비윤리적 동물취급은 동물생존권을 주장하는 단체들 사이에 대단한 비판을 일으켰다.

589. Play hooky (*v.*) – 허락 없이 학교를 빠지다. 농땡이 치다.

1) 교장은 그 세 학생들에게 학교에 무단결석하는 짓에 대하여 경고했다.

2) 만약 그들이 무단결석을 계속한다면, 그들은 졸업을 할 수 없을 것이다.

590. Play on / upon (*v.*) – 자신의 목적을 위하여 다른 사람의 기분이나 바램 등을 이용하다. 영향을 미치다.

1) 어떤 사람들은 다른 사람들의 공포심을 이용하고 싶어 한다.

2) 그 연설은 그 젊은이의 정치적 욕망에 영향을 미쳤다.

591. Play politics (*v.*) – 자신의 이익을 위해서 영리하게 또는 교묘히 사람을 조종하다. 책략을 쓰다.

1) 그녀는 그녀가 원하는 것을 얻기 위해 교묘히 책략을 쓴다.

2) 대통령 후보자들은 총선에 몇 년 전부터, 중요한 지역에서 교묘히 책략을 쓴다.

592. Play it safe (*v.*) – 안전을 위하여 위험이나 손실을 피하다. 안전을 추구하다.

1) 그는 필요 없는 모험을 하여 모든 것을 잃지 않기 위해 주식시장에서 위험을 피할 것이다.

2) 나는 위험을 피하고 싶다. 그래서 달걀을 한 바구니에 담은 적이 없다.(한 종목에 집중 투자하지 않는다.)

593. Plow back (*v.*) – (사업에) 소득을 재투자 하다.

1) 그는 종업원들을 위해 회사 이익의 50%를 재투자하고, 스톡옵션을 제공하겠다고 약속했다.

594. Plow into (*v.*) – 강력하게 돌진하다. 열정적으로 ~을 하다.

1) 모터사이클 한대가 덤불 속으로 강하게 쳐 박혔다.
2) 그는 열정적으로 그의 일을 했고, 자정까지 끝마쳤다.

** Plug away (*v.*) – 고집하다. 주장하다. 일을 꾸준히 하다.

1) 그 소년은 그가 정답을 쓰고 성취감을 느낄때까지 그 어려운 수학 문제를 물고 늘어졌다.
2) 그 건설 인부들은 일을 꾸준히 열심히 했고 예상보다 일찍 그 건물을 완성했다.

595. Plug in / into (*v.*) – 전기를 꼽다.

1) 만약 다리미가 가열되기 원한다면, 전원을 연결해야 한다.
2) 내가 코드를 소켓에 꽂았는데도, 그것은 작동하지 않았다.

596. Plunge into (*v.*) – 갑자기 어떤 상황에 처하게 하다. 돌입하다. 뛰어들다.

1) 그녀는 이번이 마치 그 책을 마무리 할 수 있는 마지막 기회인양 일에 몰두했다.
2) 다이빙 선수가 완벽하게 입수를 했을 때, 관중들은 박수갈채를 보냈다.
3) 실직한 그 사람이 다리에서 얼음처럼 차가운 물로 뛰어내려서 자살했다.
4) 국왕 살해가 그 두 국가를 전쟁 상황으로 몰고 갔다.

597. Point out (*v.*) – 지적하다. 알리다.

1) 아주 소수의 사람만 그들의 결점을 지적받을 때 감사해한다.
2) 여행 안내인이 역사 유적지와 그리고 다른 재미있는 곳들을 알려주었다.

598. Poles apart (*adj.*) – 극과 극의, 아주 다른

1) 새로 결혼한 많은 커플들은 그들이 많은 점에서 서로 아주 많이 다르다는 것을 발견한다.
2) 그들의 성격과 삶에 대한 견해는 극과 극이다.

599. Polish off (*v.*) – 재빨리 해치우다. 재빨리 먹어 치우다.

1) 소년은 저녁을 재빨리 먹어치웠기 때문에 친구들과 나가서 놀 수 있었다.
2) 나는 숙제를 재빨리 해치우고는 영화를 보러 나갔다.

600. Possessed of (*adj.*) – 소유한

1) 그는 놀라운 기지가 있었고, 훌륭한 마음을 가졌다.
2) 내 남동생은 대단한 잠재력을 가지고 있다.

3) 우리는 이사를 했고, 2001년 5월 31일부터 그 집을 소유했다.

601. Pot calling the kettle black (cliché) – ~묻은 개가 ~묻은 개를 나무란다.

1) 그들의 논쟁은 시장이 경찰서장을 무능력하다고 비난하고, 경찰서장이 뭐 묻은 개가 뭐 묻은 개 나무란다고 응답했을 때 시작되었다.

602. Press one's luck / Push one's luck (v.) – 성공률이 희박함에도 불구하고 일을 강행하다.

1) 신중한 사람들은 성공률이 희박한 경우에 일을 강행하지 않는다.
2) 그 선생님은 버릇없는 학생들에게 자만하지 말라고 했다.

603. Prevail on / upon (v.) – 성공적으로 설득하다.

1) 그가 성실한 만큼이나 부자이고 권력이 있다는 것을 내가 믿도록 나를 설득했다.
2) 그 변호사의 변론은 배심원들에게 그의 의뢰인이 무죄라는 것을 성공적으로 설득했다.

604. Prey on / upon (v.) – 먹이를 낚아채서 먹다. 수탈하다. 해로운 결과를 초래하다.

1) 부엉이는 쥐를 잡아 낚아채서 먹는다.
2) 우리 사회의 젊은이들과 의지할 곳 없는 사람들은 가장 수탈을 당하기가 쉽다.

605. Pride (oneself) on (v.) – 자랑스럽게 여기다.

1) 우리는 우리의 성취로 인해 종종 자부심을 갖는다.
2) 너는 네 재능을 자랑스럽게 생각해야 한다.

** Take pride in – 자랑스럽게 여기다.

1) 나는 나의 글 쓰는 능력을 자랑스럽게 여긴다.
2) 부모님들은 종종 그들 자식의 재능을 자랑스럽게 여긴다.

606. Promise the moon (v.) – 불가능 한 것 또는 지킬 수 없는 것을 약속하다.

1) 그는 그녀에게 지킬 수 없는 약속들을 했고, 그녀는 매우 깊이 실망했다.
2) 지킬 수 없는 약속을 할 수는 없지만, 최선을 다해서 너를 돕겠다.

607. Pull in / pull into (v.) – 도착하다. 차가 들어오다.

1) 그 기차는 예정보다 5분 늦게 도착했다.
2) 그는 우리가 말한 대로 차도에 차를 대고 있다.

608. Pull off (v.) – 어려움에도 불구하고 해내다. 성취하다.

1) 그 첼로 연주자는 그가 서울 교향악단과 계약을 성사시켰을 때, 매우 기뻐서 어쩔 줄을 몰랐다.
2) 세 명의 강도가 대담하게도 지역은행에서 낮에 강도행각을 벌였다.

609. Pull (oneself) together (*v.*) – 침착성이나 자제성을 되찾다.

1) 침착성을 되찾도록 노력해라.
2) 그는 실직을 했고, 은행에서 그의 집을 압류했다. 하지만, 상황은 나아지고 있고, 그는 천천히 확실하게 침착함을 되찾고 있다.

**** Pull through (*v.*) – (병이나 불행 등으로부터) 회복 하다.**

1) 가족 친구로부터 빌린 빚은 우리가 경제적 어려움으로부터 회복하게 했다.
2) 수술은 완전한 성공이었고 환자는 곧 회복될 것이다.
3) 그 회사는 이 어려운 시기로부터 회복해서 장래를 바라보아야만 한다.

**** Pull together (*v.*) – 협력하다.**

1) 그 계획을 성공하기 위해서 우리는 협력 해야만 한다.
2) 이 일을 하기 위해서 우리 모두는 협력 해야만 한다.

610. Pull over (*v.*) – 길 가장자리에 차를 멈추다.

1) 고속도로 순찰대원이 그녀가 과속했다고 가장 자리에 차를 정지시켰다.
2) 운전자는 차를 가장자리에 정지시키고 그의 차의 후드를 열었다.

**** Pull up (*v.*) – 와서 정지하다. 와서 멈추다.**

1) 존은 새 스포츠카를 타고 와서 건물 앞에 멈췄다.
2) 운전사는 속도를 늦추고는 도로 연석 옆에 정지했다.
3) 그가 내 옆에 와서 차를 멈춰 섰을 때 나는 주차장에 앉아있었다.

611. Puppy love (*n.*) – 청소년들의 미숙한 사람.

1) 풋사랑은 멋있다. 하지만 그것은 시작처럼 빨리 사그러진다.

612. Pure and simple (*adj.*) – 간단히 말하자면

1) 간단히 말하면, 네 청구서를 지불하는 것은 네 문제이다.
2) 간단히 말하면, 내 삶의 목표는 환경보호가가 되는 것이다.

613. Push around (*v.*) – (우월권을 가지고) 불공평한 대우를 하거나 괴롭히다.

1) 아무도 그가 왜 자기 아내가 자기를 괴롭히도록 내버려 두었는지 이해할 수 없었다.
2) 그의 어머니는 그에게 그의 남동생을 괴롭히지 말라고 말했다.
3) 나를 강압적으로 괴롭히지 마라.

614. Put all one's eggs in one basket (*v.*) – 노력, 희망, 투자 등을 모두 한 곳에 쏟아 붓다.

1) 나는 내 모든 돈을 한 회사에 투자 하지는 않을 것이다. 왜냐하면 그것은 내 모든 달걀을 한 바구니에 넣는 것과 똑같을 것이기 때문이다.

2) 너의 모든 달걀을 한 바구니에 넣는 것은 위험하고, 네가 이익을 얻을 수 있는 기회를 제한한다.

615. Put an end to (*v.*) – 중단하다. 끝내다.

1) 그녀는 학교제도에서 체벌을 끝내자고 주장한다.
2) 경찰은 폭력 범죄를 근절시키기 위해 경계 태세를 강화해오고 있다.

616. Put away (*v.*) – 적당한 장소 또는 제자리에 두다. 갇히다.

1) 책과 학용품을 사용하고 나면 제자리에 잘 놓아라.
2) 그의 변호사는 그에게 그가 2년 형을 살게 될 것이라고 이야기 했다.

** Put away / Put aside (*v.*) – 저축하다. 떼어 놓다.

1) 예외 없이, 매달 나는 내 미래를 위해 약간의 돈을 저축한다.
2) 너는 돈을 받을 때마다 약간의 돈을 저축해야만 한다.

617. Put down (*v.*) – 내려놓다. 진압하다.

1) 가방을 내려놓으시죠.
2) 학생들의 폭동을 막기 위해 국가 경비대를 불러야만 했다.
3) 그 싸움은 그 소년들 중의 한명이 다른 소년을 깎아 내렸을 때 시작되었다.

618. Put off (*v.*) – 역겹게 하다. 흥미를 잃게 하다. 연기하다.

1) 그녀의 뚱한 성질은 사람들을 역겹게 하지만, 그녀는 정말 나쁜 사람은 아니다.
2) 영어를 공부하는 것이 어렵다고 흥미를 잃지 말라. 공부하기를 계속하라. 그러면 잘 할 수 있을 것이다.
3) 그녀의 약혼자는 그들의 결혼 날짜를 계속 미루지만, 그녀는 그가 언젠가 그녀와 결혼할 것이라는 것을 확신한다.
4) 그녀는 너무 늦을 때까지 공부하는 것을 계속 미뤘다.

619. Put on (*v.*) – 입다. (스토브에) 올려놓다. 작동하다. 가장하다.

1) 기온이 꽤 낮다. 만약 따뜻한 코트를 입지 않는다면 너는 추울 것이다.
2) 차 끓일 물을 올려놓아라.
3) 그는 브레이크를 밟았지만, 그 차는 계속 언덕을 내려갔다.
4) 그녀는 항상 잘난 척을 한다.

620. Put out (*v.*) – 끄다, 짜증나게 하다.

1) 소방관들이 그 화재를 진화하는데, 몇 시간이 걸렸다.
2) 잠자리에 들기 전에 전등을 끄도록 해라.
3) 진료실에서 두 시간이나 기다려야 했을 때 나는 정말 짜증이 났다.

621. Put two and two together (*v.*) **- 알려진 사실을 토대로 추론하다. 판단을 내리다.**

1) 그녀는 추론을 해서 그녀의 아기가 기저귀를 갈아주기를 원했다는 것을 알아내었다.
2) 그는 결국 추론을 통해, 그가 공부하지 않으면, 그 과정을 통과하지 못할 것이라는 것을 깨달았다.

622. Put through (*v.*) **- 성공적으로 완성하다. (전화에서) ~와 연결되다.**

1) 그 제안은 성공적으로 완성하기에 어렵지 않을 것이야. 우리가 우리의 머리를 맞댄다면 그것을 할 수 있다.
2) 그 가족은 그들의 두 아들이 성공적으로 대학을 마치게 하기 위한 충분한 저축액을 가지고 있다.
3) 이 전화를 입학관리실로 연결해 주실 수 있습니까?

623. Put up (*v.*) **- 짓다, 들어 올리다. 숙소를 제공하다. 팔려고 내어놓다.**

1) 우리는 새 차고를 지을 계획을 짜고 있다.
2) 그 강도들은 스키 마스크를 하고는 우리에게 손을 들라고 말했다.
3) 당신은 호텔에 갈 필요가 없다. 우리는 여분의 침실을 당신에게 제공할 수 있다.
4) 그들의 사업이 파산했을 때, 그들은 그들의 집을 팔기 위해 내어놓았다.

**** Put up with** (*v.*) **- 견디다. 참다.**

1) 그는 그의 아들의 퇴폐적인 생활방식을 견디기를 거절했다.
2) 우리가 환경오염을 묵과하며 살아가는 한, 야생동물들은 계속해서 죽어갈 것이다.
3) 그는 아내의 끊임없는 잔소리를 더 이상 견딜 수 없었기에 이혼했다.

624. Put words into one's mouth (*v.*) **- (허락, 권리 등이 없이) 대신 말을 하다.**

1) 그녀 대신 말하지 마라, 그녀는 스스로 이야기 할 수 있다.
2) 그는 그 판매원이 허락 없이 말을 계속했기 때문에 짜증이 났다.

Q

625. Quite a (*adj.*) – 뛰어난, 대단한

1) 대단히 많은 군중들이 연례 꽃 축제를 보기위해 모였다.
2) 이것은 새롭게 발굴된 한 예술가의 뛰어난 전시회다.
3) 그녀의 학생들은 그녀가 대단히 좋은 선생님이라고 생각한다.

626. Quite a few (*adj., n.*) – 꽤 많은

1) 그 폭풍은 많은 집들을 파괴했고, 꽤 많은 사람들을 고립된 채 남겨두었다.
2) 우리가 서울에 도착하려면 아직도 꽤 많은 거리가 남아있다.
3) 꽤 많은 사람들이 지난밤 파티에 왔었다.

627. Quite a bit (a little, a few) (*adj., n.*) – 꽤 많은

1) 나는 집에 가기 전에 해야 할 일들이 아직도 많다.
2) 지난밤에 꽤 많은 눈이 내렸다.
3) 여전히 팔아야 될 꽤 많은 물건들이 남아있다.

R

628. Rain check (*n.*) **- 다음 기회를 의미하는 뜻 (개인 간이나 상점에서 물건을 살 때, 그 물건이 없을 경우 카드를 써주면 상점에서 나중에 그 물건이 들어오면 연락을 해줌.)**

1) 나 감기가 걸려서 네 저녁초대에 응하지 못할 것 같은데, 다음에 갈 수 있을까?
2) 그 상점 주인은 실망해 하는 손님에게 rain check을 제안했고, 그 물건이 새로 공급되면 그들에게 연락해 주겠다고 약속했다.

629. Rain out (*v.*) **- 비 때문에 옥외 행사를 부득이 중단 또는 연기하다.**

1) 그 회사의 연례 야유회는 비 때문에 연기되었다.
2) 어제의 야구 경기는 비 때문에 연기되었다.

630. Rainy day (*n.*) **- 앞으로 필요한 때, 궁 한때**

1) 나는 앞으로 필요할 때를 대비해서 저축을 해오고 있다.
2) 그녀는 장래를 위해 돈을 저축한다.
3) 다람쥐는 궁한 때를 대비해서 도토리를 비축한다.

631. Reach out (*v.*) **- 다른 사람들과 유대관계를 갖거나 이해하려고 노력하다.**

1) 너는 친구가 될 사람을 찾기를 원한다면 다른 사람들과의 유대관계를 가져야 한다.

632. Reckon with (*v.*) **- ~을 고려해 넣다. ~인가가 상황을 바꿀 수 있는 것들 중의 하나라고 여기다.**

1) 농부는 날씨를 고려해야하고 다양한 곡식들을 심어야한다.

**** be reckoned with - 무시해서는 안될, 중요한**

1) 그는 중요한 사람으로 보이지는 않는다. 그러나 그는 무시해서는 안 되는 큰 사업가이다.
2) 오늘날 십대들은 무시되어서는 안되는 그룹이다.

633. Refine (*v.*) **- 향상시키다. 다듬다.**

1) 그는 고급단계 시험을 시도하기 전에 그의 영어 문법과 어휘에 대한 지식을 향상시켜야만 한다.
2) 그 교수는 그녀에게 개요를 제출하기 전에 다듬을 것을 요구했다.

634. Relative to (*prep.*) – ~에 관하여, ~에 관계가 있는, ~에 비례하는

1) 그 쟁점은 도덕성과 관련이 있다.
2) 공급은 수요에 비례한다.
3) 비싸거나 싸다는 의미는 개인의 수입과 관계가 있다.

635. Rent out (*v.*) – 세를 주다.

1) 나는 방이 세 개나 있는데, 그중에 하나를 세를 주고 싶다.
2) 그들이 세를 얻기를 원했던 그 집은 이미 세가 나갔다.

636. Ride on (*v.*) – ~에 달려있다.

1) 그 선거결과는 유권자들에 대한 그녀의 인기에 달려있다.

637. Ride for a fall (*v.*) – (자신을 과신하여) 무모한 짓을 하다.

1) 그 사업가는 너무나 사치스러운 집을 지었다 그리고 그가 버는 것 보다 더 빨리 써버리고 있다. 그는 무모한 짓을 하고 있다.
2) 그는 집을 위해 은행으로부터 너무 많은 돈을 빌렸다. 그는 무모한 짓을 하고 있다.

638. Ride out (*v.*) – 성공적으로 살아남다. 이겨내다.

1) 그 작은 돛배는 폭풍우를 이겨내었고, 별다른 큰 손상 없이 계류장으로 돌아왔다.
2) 기민한 정치가들은 군중의 마음이 얼마나 변덕스러운지를 알고 기꺼이 대부분의 추문들을 견뎌낸다.

639. Get rid of (*v.*) – 제거하다. 면하다.

1) 나는 이 낡은 의자를 버리고 새것을 사고 싶다.
2) 우리는 마침내 우리 집을 다시 꾸미었고, 거실의 볼품없는 가구들을 버렸다.

**** to be rid of (*v.*) – 놓이다. 자유롭게 되다.**

1) 그녀는 그녀가 수학교수로부터 벗어났다고 생각했으나, 그녀의 여름 시간표에서 그의 이름을 다시 보았을 때, 그녀는 대단히 놀랬다.

640. Right along (*adv.*) – 문제없이, 지체 없이

1) 기상이변에도 불구하고, 그 비행기는 지체됨 없이 날아서 예정대로 착륙했다.

**** Right away (*adv.*) – 즉시, 지체 없이**

1) 만약 우리가 해질녘 전에 정상에 도착하길 원한다면, 우리는 지금 즉시 출발하는 편이 좋다.
2) 만약 우리가 지금 즉시 출발한다면 약 30분 후면 우리는 그곳에 가 있을 것이다.
3) 홍수의 피해를 받은 사람들은 지금 당장 도움을 필요로 한다.

641. Ring up (*v.*) – (금전 등록기로) 계산하다.

1) 이 손님의 계산을 끝내는 대로 당신의 물품을 계산해 드리겠습니다.
2) 그는 내 구매품을 금전등록기로 계산하고는 내가 25,950원을 내야 한다고 말했다.

642. Rip into (*v.*) – 맹렬히 공격하다. 아주 심하게 몰아세우다. 비난하다.

1) 사자 한 마리가 관중들이 바라보는 가운데, 동물 사육사를 맹렬히 공격했다.
2) 그녀의 상사는 그녀가 일주일에 세 번 지각한 것에 대해 그녀를 아주 심하게 몰아세웠다.

**** Rip off (*v.*) – 훔치거나 정당한 가격을 지불하지 않고 가져가다. 바가지 씌우다.**

1) 그는 그가 마침내 현행범으로 잡히기 전까지 그 상점에서 수개월간 도둑질을 했었다.
2) 한국을 방문한 몇몇 방문객들은 파렴치한 바가지 행위를 당한 것에 대해서 불평했다.

**** Rip-off (*n.*) – (도둑행위 같은) 바가지 행위**

1) 그 가격은 너무 높아서, 바가지나 다름없다.

643. Rip up (*v.*) – 조각조각 찢다.

1) 그의 편지는 그녀를 매우 화나게 만들어서 그녀는 그것을 조각조각 찢어버렸다.
2) 그 숙제는 너무나 형편없었기 때문에, 선생님은 그것을 찢어서 쓰레기통에 던져버렸다.

644. Rise up (*v.*) – 항거하다. 들고 일어나다.

1) 자유가 인정되지 않을 때, 결국은 사람들이 들고 일어날 것이다.
2) 그 노동자들은 노동조합을 가질 그들의 권리를 지키기 위해 항거할 것을 권유 받았다.

**** Give rise to (*v.*) – ~을 일으키는 원인이 되다. 일으키다.**

1) 컴퓨터 칩의 개발이 정보세대를 일으키는 원인이 되었다.
2) 조선술은 많은 다른 산업들을 일으키는 원인이 되었다.

645. Rob the cradle (*v.*) – 상당한 나이 차이가 나는 사람과 결혼하거나 성관계를 갖다.

1) 오늘날 어떤 남자들은 십대들과 성 관계를 맺음으로써 성적인 착취를 한다.
2) 그가 그녀를 그의 아내로 선택했을 때 그는 정말 그녀를 유린하는 것이었다.

646. Roll in (*v.*) – 엄청나게 들어오다.

1) 표들이 할인 판매되었고, 최신집계에 따르면 돈이 엄청나게 굴러들어 오고 있다.
2) 그들은 그들이 할 수 있는 모든 일을 했고, 이제는 손을 떼고 앉아서 선거결과가 엄청나게 들어오는 것을 주시했다.

647. Roll back (*v.*) – 이전 상태로 가격을 낮추다.

1) 경영진은 그들이 현재 임금을 유지하는 동안 이전 상태로 가격을 낮추기를 희망한다.
2) 새 사업을 위한 시도로, 그 여행 회사는 1980년대에 제시된 가격과 경쟁하기 위해서 그

들의 가격을 이전 상태로 낮추었다.

648. Roll up (*v.*) – 둘둘 말다. 축적하다.

1) 파티가 끝난 후 우리는 양탄자를 둘둘 말아서 그것을 세탁소에 가져다주어야만 했다.
2) 그 회사는 노동자들에게 팔을 걷어 부치고 그들의 작업을 다 끝내도록 요청했다.
3) 그는 우표를 수집해서 판돈으로 대단히 많은 재산을 축적했다.

649. Rough up (*v.*) – (위협, 협박 등으로) 때리다. 망가뜨리다.

1) 하교해서 집에 가는 동안에 이군은 근처 고등학교에 다니는 두어명의 불량배들에게 잡혀 구타를 당했다.
2) 그 권투선수는 처음 세 회 동안 매번 그의 상대를 때려 눕혔고, 4회에는 T.K.O 승을 거두었다.

**** a diamond in the rough – 천연 그대로, 정련되지 않은**

1) 그녀는 다듬어지지 않은 다이아몬드와 같다. 그녀는 굉장한 가능성을 가지고 있다.
2) 지금 초창기 컴퓨터들은 정련되지 않은 다이아몬드처럼 보여진다.

650. Round off / round out (*v.*) – (소수점을 떼거나 반올림해서) 가장 가까운 자연수로 만들다. 멋있게 끝내다. 둥글게 만들다.

1) 그 시험의 평균점수는 87)69였고, 반올림해서 88점이었다.
2) 우리는 맛있는 딸기 쇼트케이크로 저녁을 훌륭히 마쳤다.
3) 나는 식당 방에 있는 식탁의 날카로운 가장자리를 둥글게 만들어줄 사람이 필요하다.

**** Round up (*v.*) – (짐승의) 무리를 모으다. 찾아 나서서 데려오다. 반올림하다. (그 다음으로 가장 높은 숫자로 올리다.)**

1) 날이 어두워지고 있다. 우리는 해지기 전에 장구들을 모아서 텐트를 쳐야한다.
2) 모든 사람들을 다 찾아 데리고 와서 집에 갈 준비를 하자.
3) 87)69를 반올림 하면 88이다.

651. Rub down (*v.*) – 문지르다. 마사지 하다.

1) 어떤 사람들은 안마를 받기위해 여자 마사지사나 남자 마사지사를 찾아간다.
2) 그 치료사는 근육을 이완시키기 위해 내 등을 문질렀다.

652. Rule on (*v.*) – (법적인)판결을 내리다.

1) 배심원은 판사에게 논쟁 중에 있는 그 문제에 대해서 판결을 내릴 것을 요청했다. 그래서 그 판사는 피고에게 무죄를 선고했다.
2) 대법원은 최근에 거대한 담배 소송에 대한 판결을 통과시켰다.

** Rule out (*v.*) – 제외하다. 배제하다.

1) 배심원들은 평결에 이르기 전에 증명되지 않은 증거는 배제해야만 한다.
2) 결정이 내려 질 때는 직원들의 제안들이 배제되어서는 안 된다.

653. Run across / Run into (*v.*) – 우연히 부딪치다. 우연히 만나다.

1) 나는 쇼핑센터에서 메리와 우연히 마주쳤는데 그녀가 마을에 돌아 온줄 몰랐었기 때문에 놀랬다.
2) 김씨와 나는 같은 건물에서 일하기 때문에 항상 우연히 만나게 된다.

654. Run after (*v.*) – ~의 뒤를 쫓다.

1) 그는 여자들의 뒤를 쫓아다니기를 좋아하는 사냥개이다.
2) 그 소년은 그가 할 수 있는 한 최대한 빨리 그 공을 쫓아갔다.

655. Run a risk / Take a risk (*v.*) – 모험을 하다. 위험에 처하다.

1) 나는 위험에 처하는 것을 원하지 않는다. 그래서 나는 수영을 하지 못하기 때문에 배에 탈 때면 항상 구명조끼를 입는다.
2) 너의 눈이 다칠지도 모르는 모험을 하지 말고, 보안경을 써라.
3) 나는 모험을 하고 싶지 않기 때문에, 나의 재산을 한 곳에 모두 걸지 않도록 노력한다.

656. Run around (*v.*) – (친구와) 놀러 이리저리 돌아다니다.

1) 나는 할 일이 많아서 그녀의 심부름을 해주면서 여기저기 돌아다닐 시간이 없다.
2) 지금 현재 그는 그의 친구들과 이리저리 놀러 돌아다니는 것을 좋아하지만, 그가 결혼한 후에는 정착할 것이다.

657. Run a temperature (*v.*) – 열이 있다.

1) 의사를 빨리 불러라, 아기한테 높은 열이 있다.

658. Run away from (*v.*) – 도망가다.

1) 집에서 세 번 가출한 후에 그 소년은 가출소년 보호소로 보내졌다.
2) 그 소녀들은 물풍선을 가지고 쫓아오는 소년들로부터 비명을 지르며 도망쳤다.

** Run away with (*v.*) – 훔쳐서 도망가다. (부모의 허락 없이) 남녀가 도망가다. 쉽게 받다.

1) 그녀는 금고에서 돈과 서류들을 꺼내서는 그것들을 가지고 도망갔다.
2) 그들은 누군가가 그들을 말리기 전에 도망가서 결혼했다.
3) 다크호스로 지목된 사람이 일등상을 쉽게 받았다.

659. Run down (*v.*) **– (시계 등이)서다. (배터리 등이)죽다. 비평하다. 형편없는 상태가 되다. 지칠 때까지 추격하다. (자동차가) 치다.**

1) 자명종 시계의 배터리가 다 닳았다.
2) 그는 그의 주차등을 켜 놓은 채로 놓아두었고, 그의 차의 배터리가 다 방전 되어 버렸다.
3) 만약에 네가 사람들로 하여금 일을 잘하게 하고 싶다면, 그들을 비평하기 보다는 칭찬하는 것이 좋다.
4) 그 작은 농가는 완전히 형편없는 상태이다.
5) 개가 토끼를 추적했다.
6) 오토바이 운전자가 행인을 거의 칠 뻔 했다.

**** Run-down** (*adj.*) **– 낡고 헐은, 수리가 요구되는**

1) 그 도시는 하층민들의 낡은 공동주택들을 개선하기 위해 재원을 마련해야 한다.
2) 마라톤을 뛴 것이 존을 기진맥진하고 피곤하게 만들었다.
3) 우리 동네 길에 있는 오래되고 낡은 집이 마침내 수리 중에 있다.
4) 이곳은 서울의 재건축이 요구되는 낡은 지역이다. 그래서 정부는 이 지역에 새로운 타운을 지을 계획이다.

660. Run for (*v.*) **– 출마하다.**

1) 그 상원위원은 재선을 위해 뛰겠다고 발표했다.
2) 그녀는 주 의회에 들어가기 위해 출마중이다.

661. Run off (*v.*) **– 복사하다. 급히 떠나다. ~을 떠나게 하다. 배수하다.**

1) 우리는 그 광고전단을 3천장을 복사해서 배부했다.
2) 싸우고 있던 소년들이 경찰을 보자마자 황급히 떠났다.
3) 그 저수지는 산에서 흐르는 물에 의존하고 있다.

662. Run out (of) (*v.*) **– 몽땅 다 써버리다. (운, 돈 등이) 다 떨어지다.**

1) 휴지를 좀 더 사오세요. 다 써버렸습니다.
2) 그는 대개 봉급날 전에 돈을 다 써버린다.
3) 우리는 다음 주유소에서 멈추는 것이 좋겠다. 연료가 다 떨어져가고 있다.
4) 우리는 고속도로에서 연료가 다 떨어져서 도로 서비스에 연락해야만 했다.

**** Run through** (*v.*) **– (얼마 안가서)다 써버리다.**

1) 그 미망인은 그녀가 받은 유산을 2-3 년 만에 다 써버렸다.
2) 학생들은 그들의 과제를 아주 빨리 해치웠다. 그것은 너무 쉬웠다.

663. Run over (*v.*) **– 차로 치다. 재빨리 훑어보다. (물 등이) 넘치다.**

1) 자동차로 다람쥐를 친 것은 끔찍한 경험이었다.

2) 그 음주운전자는 행인을 치고 나서 속도를 줄였다.
3) 학생들은 그 들의 기말고사를 치루기 전에 복도에서 노트를 빠르게 훑어보며 서 있다.
4) 그녀는 물을 잠그는 것을 잊어버려서, 물이 싱크대에서 넘쳐서 바닥에 흘렀다.

664. Run short (*v.*) – 부족하다.

1) 그녀는 돈이 부족해서, 봉급날이 될 때까지 돈을 조금 빌려 달라고 나에게 요청했다.
2) 우리는 우리에게 돈이 부족해지고 있다는 것을 깨달을 때까지 굉장히 즐거운 시간을 보냈다.

665. Run out on (*v.*) – 저버리다.

1) 그녀는 그녀의 아기를 저버렸다.
2) 그는 그의 가족을 저버렸다.

666. Run up (*v.*) – (빚이)늘다. 오르다. (기 등을)게양하다.

1) 그녀는 그녀의 신용카드 빚이 많아져서 그녀의 가난한 남편이 대금을 지불하도록 청구서를 남겨 놓았다.
2) 그들은 전화 요금을 많이 썼고 마침내 그들의 전화가 끊겼다.
3) 석유수출국 기구는 원유의 가격을 인상하고 있다.
4) 국경일에 국기를 게양하는 것이 애국적으로 보인다.

S

667. Safe and sound (*adv.*) – 무사히, 안전하게

1) 깨지기 쉬운 소포가 무사히 배달되었다.
2) 그녀의 부모님들은 그녀가 집에 무사히 도착 할 때까지 걱정하였다.
3) 데이비드는 해외여행을 갔다가 무사히 돌아왔다.

668. Save face (*v.*) – 체면을 살리다.

1) 나는 사람들에게 체면을 살릴 기회를 주는 것을 좋아한다.
2) 누군가에게 체면을 살릴 기회를 준다는 것은 그들로부터 존경을 얻을 수 있는 좋은 방법이다.

669. Save one's breath (*v.*) – (말해도 소용없기 때문에)말을 아끼다. 말하지 말라.

1) 그는 고집이 세기 때문에 그의 마음을 바꾸지 않을 것이다. 그러므로 그에게는 말을 하지 말라.

670. Save up (*v.*) – 저축하다. 모으다.

1) 그들은 지금 집을 장만하기 위해 저축을 하고 있는 중이기 때문에 휴일에도 거의 놀러 나가지 않는다..
2) 그녀는 그녀가 사무실 주변에서 찾은 고무밴드와 종이 클립을 모은다.

671. Savings account (*n.*) – 예금계좌

1) 그는 최근에 그 지역 은행에 예금계좌를 하나 개설했다.

** Checking account (*n.*) – 수표 계좌

1) 나는 나의 예금계좌를 해약하고 거기에 있는 예금을 나의 수표구좌에 넣고 싶다.

672. Scare away / Scare off (*v.*) – 무서워서 도망가게 하다.

1) 그 짓는 개가 배달부를 무서워 도망가게 했다.
2) 그들의 관계 초기에 그는 그녀를 좋아했지만, 그녀의 타인에 대한 배려없이 자기식대로만 하는 행동에 그는 점점 멀어졌다.

673. Scratch one's back (*v.*) – (상대방도 나를 도울 것이라는 전제 하에) 도움을 주다.

1) 만약에 내 숙제를 도와주면, 나는 영화를 보여 줄께, 우리 서로 돕고 살자.

** From scratch (*adv.*) - 거의 빈손으로, 거의 아무것도 없이

1) 그녀는 이것저것 남은 재료로 음식 만드는 것을 좋아한다.
2) 그는 맨주먹으로 그의 사업을 시작했다.

674. Screen out (*v.*) - 정화 과정에 의해 제거하다. 면접, 테스트 등으로 가려내다.

1) 천연 자원국에서 물속의 불순물을 걸러내기 때문에, 그 물은 마시기에 안전하다.
2) 그 회사는 짧은 명부와 면접을 통해서 지원자들을 가려내고 있다.

675. Search one's heart / Search one's soul (*v.*) - ~의 행위 또는 욕망의 이유나 진실을 알아내려 노력하다. 마음을 헤아리며 곰곰이 생각하다.

1) 그는 그의 부모님의 기대와 그의 욕망을 모두 충족시킬 타협점을 찾아내기 위해 곰곰이 생각했다.
2) 나는 내 삶에서 정말로 원하는 것이 무엇인지 알기 위해 곰곰이 고민을 해왔다.

676. Second thought (*n.*) - 생각의 변화 (좀 더 깊이 생각한 후)

1) 그녀는 여름 계절학기를 듣기를 원했었다. 그런데 생각의 변화를 통해, 여름에는 수업을 듣지 않고 쉬기로 결정했다.
2) 나는 하와이에 가기로 결정했다. 그러나 다시 생각을 하고 있고, 발리가 더 이국적으로 보인다.

677. See about (*v.*) - 생각해 보다. 고려해 보다. 검토해 보다.

1) 그녀는 승진에서 누락된 것에 대해서 화가 났으나, 그녀의 상사는 그녀가 계속 열심히 일하면, 고려해 보겠다고 말했다.
2) 우리는 깨진 물관들을 조사해보기 위해 배관공을 불렀다.
3) 인사과장은 수일 이내에 본사로의 나의 전근을 검토해 보겠다고 약속했다.

678. See daylight (*v.*) - (좋은) 결과를 보다.

1) 우리는 이 프로젝트를 2~3년간 작업해오고 있고, 마침내 좋은 결과를 보기 시작하고 있다.
2) 나는 1998년이래로 이 책을 써오고 있다. 그리고 2003년 후반에는 좋은 결과를 볼 것이라고 확신한다.

679. See off (*v.*) - 배웅하다.

1) 우리가 너를 배웅하러 공항으로 갈께.
2) 그는 그녀를 역으로 태워다 주고는 그녀가 떠나는 것을 보기위해 기다렸다.

680. See through (v.) – 간파하다. ~가 어려움을 극복하도록 도와주거나 끝까지 지켜 보다. 과제나 임무 등을 끝내다.

1) 시험을 치루지 않은 것에 대한 그의 핑계는 너무 빈약해서, 어린아이라고 할지라도 그것을 간파할 수 있었을 것이다.
2) 그녀의 가족과 친구들은 그녀가 어려움을 극복하도록 끝까지 지켜 주었기 때문에, 그녀는 그들의 친절에 보답을 하고 싶어 한다.
3) 그 계획은 내가 예상했었던 것 보다 훨씬 크지만, 나는 그것을 끝마치고 싶다.

681. Sell off (v.) – (헐값으로) 팔아 치우다.

1) 나는 한국으로 돌아가기 위해 가전 기구들을 헐값으로 팔아치웠다.
2) 그는 그의 우량주식들을 다 팔고 있다. 그리고 부동산에 재투자하고 있다.

**** Sell out (v.) – 전부 팔다. 이익을 위해 배반하다.**

1) 봄 세일기간에 남성복이 기대했던 것 보다 빨리 매진되었다.
2) 그 가게의 크리스마스 관련 상품들은 품절이다.
3) 그 노동조합은 타협의 마지막 시점에서 회원들을 배반했다.

682. Send back (v.) – 반환하다. 반품하다.

1) 그것은 그녀가 주문한 상품이 아니었기 때문에 그녀는 그것을 반품했다.
2) 나는 금목걸이를 한 개 홈쇼핑 TV 채널에서 샀다. 그러나 그것은 내가 원하는 것이 아니기 때문에 반품할 것이다.

683. Send for (v.) – ~을 주문하다. ~을 부르러 보내다.

1) 나는 카탈로그에서 나이키 신발 한 켤레를 주문했다.
2) 나는 약 10분전에 택시를 부르러 보냈다.
3) 그는 그의 아내가 매우 아팠기 때문에 의사를 부르러 보냈다.

684. Send out (v.) – (우편으로)발송하다.

1) 이 소포들은 오늘의 우편물들과 함께 발송되어야 한다.
2) 우리 대학의 언어학교는 대단히 많은 광고지를 발송한다.
3) 어떤 고객들은 그들의 신용카드를 직접 받아가기를 더 좋아하지만 대부분은 우편으로 발송되어진다.

**** Send over (v.) – (보통 가까운 거리에) ~을 시켜서 보내다. 파견하다.**

1) 우리는 배달 서비스에 전화를 걸어서 이 패키지들을 운반하게 가능한 빨리 누군가를 보내달라고 했다.
2) 그는 우리의 저녁 데이트를 지킬 수 없어서 우리 집으로 꽃을 보냈다.

3) 국제연합군이 평화유지 활동을 하기 위해 사라예보로 파견되었다.

685. Send up (*v.*) – 감옥(교도소)에 보내다. 올리다.

1) 그 피고는 유죄로 판결되어서 5년에서 7년 동안 감옥에 보내졌다.
2) 난파선으로부터 살아남은 사람들은 작은 섬에 다다라서 불꽃을 올렸다.

686. Serve up (*v.*) – 차려내다.

1) 주 요리 전에 스프와 샐러드가 차려나온다.
2) 그 요리사는 매우 맛있는 음식을 준비해서 차려내었다.

687. Set about (*v.*) – 시작하다.

1) 그는 사용법을 이해할 수 없었기 때문에 그 기계의 조립을 시작할 수 없었다.
2) 그녀는 컴퓨터를 5년 전에 배우기 시작해서 괄목할 만한 진보를 이뤄냈다.

** Set in (*v.*) – (~하기) 시작하다.

1) 그들이 정상에 도달하기 전에 폭풍우가 시작되었다.
2) 그 조그만 낚싯배가 항구에 도착하기 전에 강풍이 불기 시작했다.
3) 여름보다 겨울에 밤이 일찍 시작된다.
4) 갑자기 시작된 그의 병이 그의 가족에게 충격을 주었다.

688. Set against (*v.*) – 강하게 반대하다.

1) 그녀는 그녀의 딸의 약혼자가 술꾼이기 때문에 딸의 결혼을 강하게 반대한다.
2) 그 모임은 너무나 논쟁적일 것이기 때문에 나는 그 모임에 가는 것에 단연코 반대한다.

** Set (*adj.*) – 결심한, 준비된

1) 나는 공부를 더 하기 위해 대원원에 갈 것을 결정했다.

689. Set aside (*v.*) – (특별한 목적으로)따로 떼어 비축하다. (잠시) 접어두다. 관심을 두지 않다.

1) 아버지는 나의 대학 교육을 위해서 매달 약간의 돈을 따로 비축하신다.
2) 그 새로운 사업은 부주의하게 방치되기에는 너무나 중요하므로 원래의 계획은 일시적으로 접어놓았다.

690. Set back (*v.*) – ~의 진행을 더디게 하다. 비용이 들다.

1) 폭우가 예정되었던 건물의 개축 계획을 지연시켰다.
2) 그의 실무 경험의 부족은 진전을 더디게 하였지만, 그의 열망과 그의 능력은 그가 모든 장애물들을 극복하는데 도움을 주었다.
3) 그들이 집을 개축하는데 175,000달러 이상이 들었다.

691. Set down (v.) – 적어두다. 내려놓다. ~의 탓으로 돌리다.

1) 그들은 그들이 합의한 모든 것을 기록하기로 하고, 나중에 다시 모이기로 결정했다.
2) 그는 책상위에 그 책을 내려놓았다.
3) 나는 내가 원했던 자리를 얻지 못했는데, 그것을 나의 경험부족으로 돌렸다.

692. Set fire to (v.) – 불을 내다. 불이 옮겨 붙다.

1) 방화범이 지난 한달 사이에 세 곳의 비디오 대여점에 불을 질렀다.
2) 불꽃은 타는 건물에서 옮겨 나와 이웃 건물들에 옮겨 붙었다.

693. Set forth (v.) – 명확하게 설명, 또는 발표하다, 출발하다.

1) 두 달에 한 번씩 열리는 정기 회의에서 그 회사의 새로운 회계정책이 발표되었다.
2) 대통령은 부패를 방지하기위한 새로운 운동을 제안하라고 그의 보좌관들에게 명령했다.
3) 그들은 멕시코로의 여행을 출발했다.

694. Set off (v.) – 폭발시키다. 강조하다.

1) 매년 8월 15일이면, 많은 사람들이 우리나라의 독립을 기념하기 위해 폭죽을 터뜨린다.
2) 지난주 더블린에서 터진 폭탄에 대해서 누구도 책임지려 하지 않았다.
3) 그녀가 입은 블라우스는 그녀의 눈 색깔과 대조가 되어 선명하게 보였다.
4) 회색빛 벽이 화려한 녹색 카펫이 더해지면서 강조되었다.
5) 적포도주 빛 커튼이 상아색 벽과 하얀 장식을 정말로 눈에 띄게 한다.

695. Set on / upon (v.) – 공격하게 하다. 공격하다.

1) 그 집의 주인은 그의 개에게 침입자를 공격하게 하였다.
2) 이스라엘 군대는 지난밤 일찍 가자지구에서 성난 팔레스타인 사람들로부터 공격을 받았다.

696. Set one's heart on (v.) – 몹시 원하다.

1) 그녀는 유럽에 몹시 가고 싶어 했지만, 그녀의 나쁜 성적이 그녀의 여행을 취소할 수밖에 없도록 만들었다.
2) 그는 아직 모르고 있지만, 그녀의 여자친구는 큰 사파이어와 다이아몬드로 된 결혼반지를 몹시 원하고 있다.

697. Set out (v.) – 아는 장소에 놓다. 심다. 설명하다.

1) 나는 집 없는 고양이들을 위해 항상 한 접시의 음식을 내어놓는다.
2) 그녀는 매년 여름에 토마토 묘목을 심는다.
3) 그의 직원들은 그가 결정을 내리기 전에 모든 진상에 대해서 다 설명을 해야만 했다.

698. Set up (v.) – 차리다. 만들다. 설립하다. 권위를 세우다. 필요한 것으로 지원하다.

1) 그녀가 밤마다 하는 허드렛일은 저녁식탁을 꾸미고 접시를 내어놓는 것이다.

2) 그 학교는 경영학을 전공한 학생들이 졸업 후에 직업을 찾는 것을 도와주는 특별프로그램을 만들었다.
3) 나는 출판 회사를 설립하기를 원한다.
4) 그는 개인 사업을 설립해서 대단히 많은 돈을 벌었다.
5) 그의 가족은 그가 식당을 개업하는데 도움을 주었다.

699. Settle down (*v.*) – 안착하다. 안정된 생활을 하다. 조용히 하다.

1) 그들은 조용한 가족 지향의 지역에서 안착하기를 희망한다.
2) 대부분의 사람들은 그들이 결혼한 다음에는 안정된 생활을 하는 경향이 있다.
3) 학생들은 선생님께서 교실로 들어오자마자 조용히 했다.

700. Settle for (*v.*) – (만족하지는 않지만 할 수 없이) 받아들이다.

1) 그는 그의 자전거를 100달러에 팔고 싶었지만 할 수 없이 65달러에 만족할 수밖에 없었다.
2) 그녀는 수백만 달러를 가진 부자와 결혼하고 싶어 했으나 1백만 달러를 가진 사람과 결혼하는 것에 만족해야했다.
3) 나는 좀 더 나은 직장을 찾기 원했지만 그냥 현재의 직장을 받아들였다.

701. Settle on / upon (*v.*) – 결정을 보다.

1) First Merit회사는 최근에 대단히 많은 회사 정책을 바꿨으나, 결국에 그들을 다음 10년으로 인도해줄 것으로 기대되는 새 정책으로 결정을 보았다.
2) 두 은행의 자산을 어떻게 합병하는가 하는 문제가 지난 주 회의에서 결정이 되었다.

702. Settle up (*v.*) – 결말을 짓다. 분쟁을 해결하다.

1) 빨리 돈을 지불하고 이곳에서 떠나도록 하자, 그렇지 않으면 우리는 음악회에 늦을 거야.
2) 소송의 화해는 변칙적인 기금모음에 대해 그들의 계속되는 분쟁을 그들이 해결할 것을 요구한다.

** Settle with (*v.*) – 합의를 보다.

1) 그는 표 판매 이익에 대한 정당한 자기 몫을 돌려받기 위한 그 회사와의 분쟁에서 합의를 보았다.
2) 그녀는 그녀의 은행 계좌를 즉시 결재해야 한다. 그렇지 않으면 그 서비스는 종료될 것이다.

703. Shake down (*v.*) – (돈을)강탈하다. 빼앗다.

1) 그 지역의 사업 소유주들로부터 돈을 갈취하려던 경찰관들이 붙잡혔다.
2) 마피아는 작은 사업주들을 협박하여 돈을 갈취하거나 그들의 사업들을 망하게 하는 것으로 종종 비난받는다.

704. Shake off (*v.*) – 제거하다.

1) 그 스파이는 누군가 자기를 미행하고 있음을 알고, 떨쳐버리려고 했으나 소용이 없었다.
2) 그녀는 스토커를 떨쳐버리고 싶으나 어떻게 그를 떨쳐버릴 수 있을지 방법을 모른다.

705. Shake up (*v.*) – (긴장, 걱정, 혼란 등으로) 몹시 불안하게 하다.

1) 그 소름 끼치는 범행은 온 동네를 몹시 불안하게 만들었다.
2) 강제해고와 조기 퇴직에 대한 뉴스는 모든 직원들을 몹시 불안하게 했다.

706. Shape up (*v.*) – (행위, 몸매, 태도 등을)다듬다. 개발하기 위하여 기대되는 일을 하다. 행동이나 일을 향상하다.

1) 중간고사가 끝난 후 그녀의 선생님은 만약에 그녀가 새로 마음먹고 공부하지 않으면 그 과목에서 낙제할 것이라고 말했다.
2) 그의 아버지는 그가 행동을 바르게 하기 시작하지 않으면 따로 나가 살 집을 구해야 할 것이라고 말했다.
3) 나의 몸매가 정말 좋지 않다. 나는 정말 내 몸매를 다듬어야할 필요가 있다.

707. Ship out (*v.*) – 다른 장소로 수송하다.

1) 우리는 모든 상품을 곧 다른 장소로 수송할 예정이다.
2) 만약 모든 화물들이 오늘 안에 선적된다면, 3일 후에는 도착할 것이다.

708. Shoot for (*v.*) – 목적을 달성하기 위해 시도 또는 노력하다.

1) 그는 6월 개장을 위해 시도했으나, 해낼 수 없었다.
2) 그들은 댄스 경연대회에서 1등상을 위해 노력하고 있다.

709. Shoot off (*v.*) – 발포하다. 쏘아 올려서 터뜨리다.

1) 육군은 2002년 8월 전에 새 미사일을 발사하기로 결정했다.
2) 들뜬 군중들이 독립일을 기념하여 폭죽을 쏘아 올렸다.

710. Show into / out (*v.*) – 안으로(밖으로) 안내하다.

1) 제가 집안으로 안내하겠습니다.
2) 제가 밖으로 안내하겠습니다.

711. Show off (*v.*) – 자랑하다. 전시하다.

1) 그는 공부를 하고 있어야 하는데, 그의 친구들에게 그의 새 차를 자랑하느라고 바쁘다.
2) 그녀는 과시하는 것을 좋아하고, 그녀의 부를 자랑할 수 있는 모든 기회에 흔쾌히 달려든다.

712. Show up (*v.*) – 도착하다, 오다, 나타나다, 드러나다.

1) 딱 한번 모든 사람들이 정시에 도착했다.

2) 그 악단은 그들의 연주회에 정시보다 한 시간 이상이나 늦게 도착했다.
3) 그녀가 저녁식사에 나타나지 않았을 때 그녀의 가족들은 걱정하기 시작했다.
4) 정기 감사 때 많은 부기 오류들이 드러났다.

713. Shrug off (*v.*) - 떨쳐버리다. 경시하다.

1) 그녀는 승진되지 못한 것에 대한 실망을 떨쳐버리고, 계속 일을 하였다. 그녀가 다음에 승진할 것이라는 것은 확실하다.
2) 그의 가족과 친구들이 그에게 여러 제안을 했으나, 그는 그것들을 경시했다.

714. Shut down (*v.*) - 휴업하다. 중지하다.

1) 그 회사는 노동 분쟁이 해결될 때까지 공장의 문을 닫았다.
2) 그 회사는 매년 여름 두 주간 휴업을 한다.

715. Shut off (*v.*) - 끄다. 차단하다.

1) 잠자러 가기 전에 TV 전원을 껐는지 확인하시오.
2) 물 부족은 아마 수자원공사가 격 주말로 물의 공급을 차단할 것이라는 것을 의미한다.

716. Shut out (*v.*) - 따돌리다. 제외하다. 들어오는 것을 막다.

1) 그녀는 그녀의 동업자가 주례 회의에서 그녀를 철저히 따돌리는 것을 느꼈다.
2) 우리는 소음이 밖에서 들어오는 것을 막기 위해 모든 창문을 닫았다.

717. Shy away from (*v.*) - 두려움이나 혐오스러움으로 피하거나 가버리다.

1) 학생들은 새로 온 선생님의 질문에 두려운 듯 피했다.
2) 새끼 고양이는 일반적으로 낯선 사람들을 피한다.

718. Sick and tired of (*adj.*) - (반복되거나 아주 오래 끄는 불쾌한 일로) 몹시 성가신, 지겨운

1) 나는 하루 종일 전화 받는 것이 정말 귀찮다.
2) 나는 그녀의 불평을 듣는 것이 지겹다.

719. Side by side (*adv.*) - 가까이 함께, 나란히

1) 그들의 집은 1번가에 나란히 위치해 있다.
2) 그들은 교실에서 항상 나란히 앉는다.
3) 옷들이 진열창에 나란히 전시되어 있었다.
4) 그들은 오후 내내 같이 놀았다.

720. Side with (*v.*) - 편들다.

1) 그녀는 그가 옳던 그르던 그의 편을 든다.

2) 그는 그의 결근 요청에 응해준 사장에게 감사했다.

**** Side against (*v.*) – ~의 편을 들지 않다.**

1) 그녀가 친구라고 생각했던 많은 사람들이 그녀의 편을 들어주지 않았다.
2) 노동자들이 노조의 편을 들지 않고 경영자들의 편을 들어주는 것을 보는 것이 흔치 않은 일이다.

721. Sign in (*v.*) – 입장할 때 등록표나 명부 등에 성명을 기재하다.

1) 시험을 치르는 학생들은 시험장에 들어갈 때 성명을 기재해야 한다.
2) 월요일 아침, 직원들은 출근할 때, 성명을 기재해야 한다.

**** Sign out (*v.*) – 떠날 때 기재하다.**

1) 종업원들은 출근할 때나, 교대를 끝내고 퇴근할 때, 자신들의 이름을 기재해야만 한다.

722. Sign off (*v.*) – 방송에서 종료 신호와 함께 (그날의) 방송을 끝내다.

1) 그 방송사는 매일 밤 같은 시각에 정규방송을 끝낸다.
2) 그 뉴스의 진행자는 항상 "안녕히 주무세요"라는 말로 방송을 끝맺는다.

723. Sign on (*v.*) – 고용계약서에 서명하다. 자원해서 하다.

1) 여름 일자리에 관심이 있다면, 지금 고용계약서에 싸인을 해야 합니다.
2) 많은 연예계 인사들이 홍수 피해자들을 돕기로 서명했다.

**** Sign up (*v.*) – 동의서에 서명하다. 등록(참가)하다. 서명하다.**

1) 그는 지난주에 해군에 지원했다.
2) 그 대학은 그들의 여름집중과정에 더 많은 학생들이 등록하기를 바라고 있다.

724. Sign over (*v.*) – 서명하여 합법적으로 양도하다.

1) 그는 그의 집의 증서를 양도했다.
2) 그녀는 그녀의 양자가 나이가 웬만히 들면 그녀의 재산을 그에게 양도할 것이다.

725. Sit back (*v.*) – 느긋하게 쉬다. 떨어져 있다.

1) 나는 은퇴 한 후에, 느긋하게 쉬면서 인생을 즐길 것이다.
2) 나는 그녀가 그녀의 아이들이 하고 싶은 내로 내버려 두었다는 것을 믿을 수가 없다.

726. Sit in (on) (*v.*) – 참가하다. 참관하다.

1) 그는 법인의 자금 모금 전문가이기 때문에 재무회의에 참가하도록 요청받았다.
2) 신임 교사는 교장의 수업 중 한 시간을 참관할 수 있는지 물었다.

**** Sit on (*v.*) (참석하여) – ~의 임무를 수행하다. ~의 멤버이다. 지연하다.**

1) 그 재판에 참석한 12명의 사람들은 그 피고가 유죄라는 것을 알아냈다.

2) 그는 은퇴했지만, 여전히 이사회의 일원이다.

727. Size up (*v.*) - 어림잡다. 평가(측정)하다. 표준이나 요구사항에 미치다.

1) 그 카운슬러는 그 다툼에 연루된 모든 사람들과 면담한 후에 그 문제를 평가했다.
2) 그는 그 상황을 파악하기 위해 약간의 시간을 더 필요로 했다.
3) 그 면접자가 그녀를 평가하고 있다는 생각이 그녀를 불편하게 했다.

728. Skeleton in the closet (*n.*) - 숨겨진 창피한 비밀

1) 거의 모든 사람들은 적어도 한가지씩의 창피한 비밀을 가지고 있다.(털어서 먼지 안 나는 사람 없다.)

729. Sketch out (*v.*) - 윤곽을 그리다.

1) 그의 상사는 그들이 다른 팀들을 만나기 전에, 그에게 그의 제안의 대략적인 윤곽을 그려보도록 요청했다.
2) 그 건축가는 제안된 건물 건축 계획의 윤곽을 그렸다.

730. Skin and bones (*n.*) - 매우 마르고 영양실조에 걸린, 피골상접

1) 흉작이 휩쓴 나라의 사진들은 피골이 상접한 어린아이들의 끔찍한 장면을 보여주었다.
2) 그 고양이는 지금은 건강하지만, 내가 그것을 발견했을 때는 아사직전이었고, 단지 뼈와 가죽밖에 남지 않았었다.

731. Skin-deep (*adj.*) - 매우 얕은, 깊은 의미가 없는, 피상적인

1) 그는 그가 세계사를 공부해왔다고 주장하지만, 그의 지식은 매우 얕다.
2) 그녀는 나의 친구인 척 하지만, 그녀의 우정은 깊이가 없다.
3) 그녀의 아름다움은 피상적이다.

732. Skip out (on) - 허락 없이 (수업 등을) 빠지다.

1) 그 소녀는 그녀의 친구를 만나기를 원했기 때문에 학교를 무단결석했다.

** Skip over (*v.*) - 생략하다.

1) 선생님은 재미없게 보인다고 제3장을 생략했다.

733. Slap down (*v.*) - 무례하게 거절하다. 자기보다 지위가 낮은 사람이 말을 못하도록 막다.

1) 그녀는 그녀의 상관에게 불평을 전했지만, 그는 아주 냉정하게 그녀가 말도하지 못하게 했다.
2) 경영진은 직원들의 임금인상 요구를 단번에 거절했다.

** Slap in the face (*n., v.*) - 모욕(하다). 실망이나 당황 하게하다.

1) 그녀가 나의 전화에 대답하지 않은 것은 나에 대한 모욕이었다.

2) 그는 그의 좌천은 그에 대한 모욕이라고 느꼈다.

3) 너의 공개적인 무례는 모욕적이었다.

734. Sleep a wink (*v.*) – 잠깐 눈을 붙이다.

1) 그는 그의 계획에 대해 너무 많이 걱정해서 잠시도 눈을 붙일 수 없었다.

735. Sleep on it (*v.*) – 결정하기 전에 하루 밤 생각해 보다.

1) 나는 그 모임에 가입하고 싶지만, 내가 시간여유가 있는지 잘 모르겠다. 내게 하루 밤 생각해 볼 여유를 주면 내일 대답을 해 주겠다.

2) 저를 초청해 주셔서 감사합니다만, 제게 하루 밤 생각할 수 있도록 시간을 주시면, 내일 당신께 답을 드리겠습니다.

736. Slip away (*v.*) – (알지 못하는 사이에) 눈에 띄지 않게 지나가다.

1) 내가 바쁠 때 시간은 알지 못하는 사이에 지나가 버리는 것 같다.

2) 그들이 깨닫기도 전에 휴가 한 달이 벌써 지나가 버렸다.

**** Slip out (*v.*) – 눈치 채지 않게 조용히 떠나다 (빠져나가다.)**

1) 우리는 피곤했기 때문에 파티에서 일찍 조용히 떠났다.

2) 그녀는 저녁식사 후에 친구들을 만나기 위해 조용히 집에서 빠져나갔다.

737. Slip of the tongue (*n.*) – 전혀 생각하지 않은 실수로 한 말.

1) 그는 비밀을 누설하려고 했던 것은 아니다. 그것은 실수로 한말이다.

2) 연설도중에 말실수를 하지 않도록 노력해라.

**** Slip up (*v.*) – 실수 하다.**

1) 은행 창구직원의 서랍에서 200달러 이상 돈이 모자라는 것을 보면, 그 행원은 돈을 세면서 실수한 것이 틀림없다.

2) 나는 시험을 잘 풀었는데, 마지막 문제에서 실수를 했다.

738. Slow down (*v.*) – 속도를 늦추다, 천천히 하다. 천천히 가게하다.

1) 속도 좀 늦춰, 서두를 이유 없잖아.

2) 그는 평상시처럼 바쁘다. 하지만, 조만간 시간의 여유를 가질 것이다.

3) 그 공장은 제품의 수요가 줄어들었기 때문에 그들의 생산 속도를 늦추었다.

739. Smash up (*v.*) – 완전히 박살내다.

1) 교통사고로 그의 차는 완전히 박살났다.

2) 술에 취한 운전자가 벽을 향해 돌진해서 그의 차가 박살났다.

740. Smooth over (*v.*) - 사태를 수습하다. 진정시키다.

1) 정부는 그 추문을 무마 시키려고 노력하고 있다.
2) 그는 노사관계 상호의 불만을 잘 절충하는데 능숙하다.

741. Snap out of it (*v.*) - 나쁜 감정, 느낌, 버릇, 또는 병 등으로부터 빨리 회복되다.

1) 그녀는 결혼하자마자, 그녀의 우울한 감정에서 벗어났다.
2) 그가 시험결과를 처음 들었을 때 매우 실망했지만, 그는 곧 마음을 추스르고 다시 공부에 전념했다.

742. Snap up (*v.*) - 몹시 원하여 재빨리 사버리다(가져가다).

1) 고객들은 우리가 특가 판매한 크리스마스 상품들을 재빠르게 다 사갔다.
2) 아이들은 그녀가 식탁에 쿠키판을 놓기도 전에 쿠키를 다 집어 먹었다.

743. Sneak up on (*v.*) - 몰래 접근하다.

1) 그는 그녀에게 몰래 가까이 갔는데, 그 행동이 그녀를 깜짝 놀라게 해서 그녀는 비명을 질렀다.

** Sneak into / onto (*v.*) - 몰래 눈치 채지 않게 들어가다.

1) 두세 명의 학생들이 지각을 해서 뒷문을 통해서 조용히 눈치 채지 않게 들어왔다.
2) 배에 무임승차 하려던 두 젊은이들이 잡혔다.

744. Snowed in (*v.*) - 폭설 속에 갇히다.

1) 그들은 폭설 때문에 눈 속에 삼일 간 갇혀있었다.

745. So far, so good - 아직까지는 좋다.

1) 우리는 그녀가 사업인으로 성공할 수 있을지 걱정했지만, 지금까지는 잘해오고 있다.
2) 모든 징조들이 경제호전을 가르치고 있으며 지금까지는 좋다.

746. Only so many (*adj.*) - 한정된 숫자의

1) 내가 하루에 할 수 있는 일들은 한정되어 있다.
2) 그들은 메이저리그 야구 사무국과의 협정에 의해 각각의 카드에 대해서 한정된 수량만큼만 발행 할 수 있다.
3) 내가 하루에 할 수 있는 일들은 한정되어 있다.

** Only so much (*adj.*) - 한정된 양의

1) 나는 할 일은 많은데 시간은 한정되어 있다.
2) 나는 집수리에 쓸 수 있는 돈이 한정되어 있다. 나머지 돈은 다른 일을 하는데 필요하다.

747. Something (else) (*adj.*) - 보통이 아닌(똑똑한, 매우 아름다운, 멋있는 등등)

1) 그녀의 새 머리 모양은 정말로 멋있다.
2) 그래, 그녀는 정말로 특별한 사람이야.
3) 새 콜벧 스포츠 자동차는 정말 멋있다.

** Something else again - 다른 것, 별개의 것

1) 책을 빌리는 것과 허락 없이 그것을 갖는 것은 다르다.

748. So-so (*adj.*) - 아주 좋지도 나쁘지도 않은, 그저 그런

1) 그 영화는 그저 그랬다.
2) 음식은 참 맛있었는데, 서비스는 별로였다.

749. So that (*conj.*) - ~하기 위해, 그래서, ~의 결과로써

1) 나는 집을 구하기 위해 두세 곳의 부동산 중개사에게 전화를 걸 예정이다.
2) 회의가 소집되었다. 그래서 우리는 그 문제를 토의할 수 있었다.
3) 파티를 할 컨디션이 나아지도록 나는 거의 하루 종일 누워 있었다.

** So as to (*prep.*) - ~하기 위해서

1) 소포들이 제때에 도착하게 하기 위해서 일찍 발송해라.
2) 나는 해외여행을 하기 위해, 최대한 많은 돈을 저축하기 원한다.

** So ~ that - (형용사나 부사와 함께 쓰여서)몹시 ~해서 ~하다.

1) 그녀는 몹시 아름다워서 모든 사람이 그를 주목한다.
2) 지하철이 몹시 붐벼서 겨우 끼어들 수 가 있었다.
3) 그는 시험을 매우 잘 봐서 딘즈 리스트에 올라갔다.

750. Sort out (*v.*) - 분류하다.

1) 그의 직업은 우편물을 분류하는 것이다.
2) 이 편지들을 알파벳순으로 분류해라.

751. Sought after (*adj.*) - 구해지는, 추구되어지는, 찾으려 애써지는

1) 그의 첫 영화는 매우 성공적이어서 많은 사람들이 그녀를 찾는다.
2) 수집가들은 오래된 동전들의 희소성과 가치 때문에 그것들을 찾으려 애쓴다.
3) 고가구들은 항상 인기가 있다.

752. Sound off (*v.*) - 크게 또는 불평조로 말하다.

1) 그 학생들은 그들의 형편없는 성적들을 받았을 때 크게 불평조로 떠들어댔다.

753. Sound out (*v.*) **- 다른 사람의 생각 또는 느낌을 조심스럽게 타진하다.**

1) 그녀는 사장에게 1주일간의 휴무를 조심스럽게 타진했다. 그러나 요청을 하지 않기로 결정했다.
2) 그 회의는 회비인상에 대한 회원들의 생각을 타진하기 위한 것이다.

754. Space out (*v.*) **- 간격을 두다.**

1) 그녀는 좋은 학생이다. 하지만, 가끔씩 멍해진다.
2) 나는 모든 것을 한꺼번에 시도하는 것보다는 간격을 두는 것을 좋아한다.

755. Speak for (*v.*) **- ~을 대변하다. 요구(청구)하다.**

1) 나는 지금 동물들을 포함한 모든 생물들의 권리를 대변하기 위해 여기에 있다.
2) 당신은 나를 대변할 필요가 없다. 나는 내 자신을 위해 말할 수 있다.
3) 한 남자가 그녀에게 같이 춤출 것을 제안했으나, 그녀는 이미 춤 요청을 받아 같이 출 사람이 있다고 했다.

756. Speak of the devil and he appears (*proverb*) **- 호랑이도 제말하면 온다.**

1) 호랑이도 제말하면 온다더니, 우리가 짐에 대해 이야기 하고 있었는데, 저기 짐이 온다.

757. Speak out (*v.*) **- 저항하다. 자유로이 자신의 의견을 말하다.**

1) 압박을 받는 자들은 그들의 주장을 낼 때까지 결코 그들의 운명을 개선할 수 없다.
2) 요즘 노동자들은 종종 경영진에게 자유로이 의견을 제시한다.

**** Speak up** (*v.*) **- 큰 목소리로 말하다.**

1) 모든 사람들이 들을 수 있게 큰 소리로 말씀해 주세요.

**** Speak well for** (*v.*) **- 좋은 증거이다.**

1) 그가 쓴 논문은 그의 모교를 나타내는 좋은 증거이다.
2) 그의 최근의 편지들은 화해가능성에 대한 좋은 증거이다.

758. Speed up (*v.*) **- 속력을 내다 (내게 하다)**

1) 우리가 일하는데 좀 더 속력을 내야한다. 그렇지 않으면 우리는 이일을 끝마치기 위해 주말에도 일해야 한다.
2) 그 회사는 생산속도를 증가시키기로 결정했다.

759. Spell out (*v.*) **- 분명하고 이해할 수 있게 하다. 천천히 한자씩 읽다. 약자를 쓰지 않고, 전체를 다 쓰다.**

1) 선생님은 학생들이 그 문제를 이해할 수 있도록 설명했다.
2) 그녀는 그녀의 이름을 크게 한자씩 읽었다. "N-a-n-c-y."
3) 당신의 이름 전체를 써주시기 바랍니다.

760. Split off (*v.*) - 쪼개다. 분리하다.

1) 우리는 썩은 나뭇가지들을 쪼개서 불쏘시개로 썼다.

2) 본사로부터 영업부를 분리하려는 경영진의 결정은 잘 받아들여지지 않았다.

**** Split up (*v.*) - 쪼개다. 헤어지다.**

1) 그들은 그 일을 분업해서 더 빠르게 끝냈다.

2) 그들은 원만하게 잘 지내지 못하기 때문에 헤어질 예정이다.

761. Spread out (*v.*) - 널리 펴놓다. (시간적, 공간적으로) 넓게 간격을 두다. 널리 퍼지다.

1) 그녀는 천을 넓게 펴놓고 그 위에 고추들을 올려놓았다.

2) 우리는 할 일들을 모든 사람들에게 공평하게 분배해 주었다.

3) 휴대폰의 사용은 전국에 걸쳐 널리 퍼져있다.

762. Spring up (*v.*) - 나타나다, 일어나다.

1) IT 기업들이 갑자기 생겨나는 것 같았다.

2) 인권단체들이 전국에 걸쳐서 생겨났다.

763. Spruce up (*v.*) - 말쑥하게 단장하다.

1) 그녀는 많은 종류의 의상을 가지고 있고 언제나 말쑥하게 차려입는다.

2) 친구들이 올 예정이면 우리는 언제나 집안을 깔끔하게 단장한다.

764. Square off (*v.*) - 싸울 자세로 들어가다.

1) 선생님이 도착했을 때 두 소년들은 막 싸우려는 찰나에 있었다.

765. Square with (*v.*) - 동의하다. 맞다.

1) 그녀의 이야기는 사실과 다르다.

766. A square peg in a round hole. - 어느 특정한 장소나 임무 등에 잘 맞지 않는 사람.

1) 그녀는 그녀의 직장이 그녀와 잘 맞지 않는다고 느꼈기 때문에 그만 두었다.

767. Square up (*v.*) - 빚을 청산하다.

1) 내 모든 빚을 청산하고 나서, 나는 긴 휴가를 가질 예정이다.

2) 지난번에 당신이 점심값을 냈으니 이번에는 내가 내겠다. 나는 공평한 것을 좋아한다.

768. Stack up (*v.*) - 포개다. 쌓아놓다.

1) 그의 상사는 그에게 늦게 까지 남아서 내일 트럭에 선적될 상자들을 쌓는 것을 도와 달라고 요청했다.

2) 나는 납부금을 연체했고, 그래서 청구서들이 쌓여있다.

769. Stamp out (*v.*) - 근절하다. 억압하다. 밟아서 끄다. 틀로 찍어내다.

1) 관세당국은 멸종위기 동물들의 수입과 판매를 근절하기 위해 노력하고 있다.
2) 히틀러나 스탈린 같은 독재자들은 민주주의를 근절시키려는 시도에서 실패했다.
3) 우리는 모닥불을 밟아서 끈 후에 그 위에 물을 부었다.
4) 조폐국은 대중의 수요를 충족시키기 위해 노벨평화상 기념주화를 더 많이 주조해 내고 있다.

770. Stand a chance (*v.*) - 가능성이나 희망을 갖다.

1) 그녀는 그녀가 국회의원으로 선출될 가능성을 가지리라고 생각하지 않았다.
2) 네가 진지하게 달라붙어서 공부하기를 시작하지 않는다면, 너는 그 과정을 통과할 가능성이 없다.

771. Stand by (*v.*) - 옹호하다. 지키다. 돕다. 대기하다.

1) 그녀는 그녀가 매우 곤란한 시절에 그녀를 도와준 친구에게 경의를 표하기 위해 파티를 열었다.
2) 승객들은 게이트에 대기해서 그들의 자리를 확인해야 한다.

**** Stand up for (*v.*) - 편들다, 옹호하다. 지키다.**

1) 그녀는 항상 자신의 남동생 편을 든다.
2) 사람들이 그를 비난할 때면, 그녀는 항상 그를 옹호해 주었다.
3) 우리는 자신들의 절대권리를 지키도록 사람들에게 용기를 주어야한다.

772. Stand for (*v.*) - 견디다.(축약된 모양이나 형상으로) 상징하다. 의미하다.

1) 나는 학생들이 교실에서 싸우는 것을 참지 않을 것이다.
2) $표시는 달러를 상징한다.

773. Stand off (*v.*) - 잘 견디다. 저항하다. 격퇴하다.

1) 동맹국들은 격렬한 적군의 공격을 잘 견디어 내었다.
2) 적이 우리나라를 공격했지만 우리의 군대가 격퇴했다.

**** Standoffish (*adj.*) - 냉담한, 불친절한.**

1) 그녀는 멋있지만, 약간 쌀쌀맞다.

774. Stand on (*v.*) - 주장하다. (의견 등) 자신의 입장을 취하다.

1) 그는 변호사를 선임할 수 있는 그의 헌법상의 권리를 주장했다.
2) 투표자들은 낙태문제에 대해서 그 대통령 후보자가 어떤 주장을 하는지 알고 싶어 했다.

**** Stand one's ground (*v.*) - 자신의 믿음을 주장하고 변호하다. 자기 입장을 지키다. 도망대신 맞서 싸우며 자신의 입장을 지키다.**

1) 그는 모든 사람들이 그를 비난할 때, 당당히 자신의 믿음을 변호했다.

2) 우리의 군인들은 적들이 공격할 때 도망가지 않고 맞서 싸웠다.

**** Stand on one's own feet (*v.*) – 독립하다. 스스로에게 의지하다.**

1) 그녀의 부모님들은 그녀가 이제 독립해서 살 때가 되었기 때문에 그녀에게 더 이상 그녀가 내야하는 청구서등을 갚아주지 않겠다고 말했다.

2) 그녀가 18살이 되었을 때, 그녀는 직업을 가졌고, 독립해서 자주적으로 살기 시작했다.

775. Stand out (*v.*) – 눈에 띄다. 계속해서 반대하다. 탁월하다.

1) 시장에서 동종의 제품과 비교할 때, 우리의 제품은 탁월하게 눈에 띈다.

2) 합의가 이루어진 후에도 불만있는 약간의 노동자들은 계속해서 반대했다.

3) 그 팀은 경기를 잘하지만, 그중에서도 그들의 센터는 눈에 띈다.

776. Stand up to (*v.*) – 용기를 내서 맞서다.

1) 그의 친구들은 자기네들이 그를 지지할 테니 그 불량배에게 용감히 맞서 싸우라고 말했다.

2) 그녀는 모든 생물들은 존중되어야만 한다는 그녀의 신념을 위해서 용기를 내서 맞섰다.

777. Start out (*v.*) – (직업, 경력, 인생 등을)시작하다. 가기 시작하다.

1) 그는 신문배달 소년으로 시작해서 지금은 신문사의 주인이 되었다.

2) 나는 그들이 휴가를 가기 전에 그들을 만나길 원했으나, 내가 그들의 집에 도착했을 때, 그들은 이미 떠난 뒤였다.

**** Start up (*v.*) – 작동하다. 시작하다.**

1) 추운 날씨에도 불구하고, 엔진이 한 번에 시동이 걸렸다.

2) 학교는 여름동안에 방학하고 9월에 개학할 것이다.

778. Stay away (*v.*) – 가까이 하지 않다. ~에서 멀리 떨어지다.

1) 마당에서 놀되 정원에 들어가지는 말아라.

2) 몸무게를 줄이기를 원하면, 간식을 멀리해야 한다.

3) 그는 그 젊은이에게 그의 딸에게 가까이 하지 말라고 했다.

779. Stay over (*v.*) – 한 장소에서 추가로 더 머무르다.

1) 우리는 그들을 방문했을 때, 그의 집에서 이틀 더 머물렀다.

2) 그들은 그들의 여행이 너무 좋았기 때문에 한주를 더 머무르기로 결정했다.

780. Stay put (*v.*) – 떠나거나 옮기지 않고 그대로 머무르다.

1) 그가 그의 어머니에게 전화를 걸어 지금 막 걸어서 집으로 가려고 한다고 하자, 그의 어머니는 아들을 차로 태우러 오겠다고 그냥 거기 움직이지 말고 있으라고 말했다.

2) 폭우나 폭설시는 고속도로에서 운전하는 것보다 그냥 움직이지 않는 것이 항상 현명하다.

3) 새 직업을 구하는 것은 어렵다. 현재 있는 곳에 그대로 있어라.

781. Stay up (*v.*) - 밤을 새우다. 잠자지 않다.

1) 그녀는 올빼미처럼 밤늦게까지 자지 않고 있는 것을 좋아 한다.
2) 우리는 지난밤에 텔레비전을 보기는 했지만, 밤늦게까지 앉아 있지는 않았다.

782. Steamed up (*adj.*) - (보통 부정적인 의미로) 몹시 흥분하거나 화내는

1) 그는 좋은 사람이기는 하지만, 종종 작은 일에 몹시 흥분하곤 한다.
2) 그는 컴퓨터가 작동하지 않는 것을 알게 되자 흥분하며 화를 냈다.

** Worked up (*adj.*) - 흥분한, 화난, 걱정하는

1) 너무 걱정 하지 마라, 모든 일이 잘 될거야.
2) 그는 그가 하지도 않은 일로 비난을 받았기 때문에 흥분해 있다.

** Fired up (*adj.*) - (보통 긍정적이고 경쟁적인 느낌) 몹시 흥분한, ~을 몹시 하고 싶어 하는

1) 전반전이 끝난 후 감독의 용기를 주는 스피치는 팀원들에게 힘을 내어서 경기를 이기도록 용기를 북돋아 주었다.

** Run out of steam - 기운이 빠지다.

1) 그는 너무 많은 시간 일을 해왔기 때문에, 이제 진이 빠지기 시작했다.
2) 권투선수들은 서로 상대방이 먼저 기운이 빠지기를 바라며 서로 주먹질을 했다.

783. Step aside (*v.*) - 옆으로 비키다. 양보하다.

1) 그 안내인은 이미 표를 가진 사람들이 극장 안으로 들어갈 수 있도록 줄을 서 서 기다리는 사람들이 옆으로 비켜서도록 요청했다.
2) 그는 다른 후보자가 선거에서 이길 확률이 더 높다고 생각해서 자진해서 양보했다.

784. Step down (*v.*) - 높은 지위에서 물러나다. 높은 곳에서 낮은 곳으로 내려오다.

1) 그 사장은 계약기간이 만료되기 전에 퇴진하도록 압력을 받았다.
2) 그의 사퇴이유는 건강과 관련이 있다.

** Step up (*v.*) - 승진하다. 증가하다. (낮은 곳에서 위로) 올라가다.

1) 그녀의 진급은 확실히 한 단계 올라간 것이고, 회사의 부사장이 되려는 그녀의 목표에 더 근접하였다.
2) 우리는 수요에 미리 맞추어 생산량을 늘렸다.
3) 부엌에 들어가기 위해서는 위로 올라가야 한다.

785. Step in (*v.*) - 끼어들다. 간섭하다. 잠시 들어가다.

1) 누가 다치기 전에 그는 싸움을 말리기 위해 끼어들었다.
2) 제 사무실로 잠깐 들어오시겠습니까? 당신과 이야기 하고 싶습니다.

**** Step out (*v.*) – 잠시 밖으로 나가다.**

1) 그의 비서는 그가 잠깐 자리를 비웠다고 이야기 했다.
2) 그는 커피를 마시기 위해 잠깐 나갔다.

**** Step into (*v.*) – 아무 어려움 없이 차지하거나 얻다. ~로 들어가다.**

1) 그녀가 그렇게 좋은 자리를 그렇게 빨리 차지하다니 그녀는 참 운이 좋았다.
2) 그는 대학을 졸업하자마자, 그의 아버지 회사의 좋은 자리를 차지해 들어갔다.
3) 내 상관은 내게 잠시 그의 사무실로 들어와 달라고 요청했다.

786. Stick around (*v.*) – 한 장소에 머무르다. 근처에 머무르다.

1) 잠시 후면 일 끝나니까, 근처에서 잠깐만 있어줄래?
2) 그녀는 별 달리 할 일이 없었기 때문에, 그녀의 친구들이 쇼핑을 마칠 때까지, 근처에서 기다리면서 머물렀다.

787. Stick by (*v.*) – 충실하게 남다.

1) 사람들은 결혼 할 때 상대방에게 좋을 때나 나쁠 때나 충실할 것을 맹세한다.
2) 좋은 친구란 네가 어려울 때, 네 옆에 충실히 남는 사람들이다.

788. Stick one's neck out (*v.*) – 모험을 하다.

1) 그녀의 신용은 아주 나쁜데, 그는 모험을 감수하고 그녀에게 1만 달러를 빌려주었다.
2) 대립되는 정책에서 대통령을 지지했을 때 그는 정말 모험을 했다. 그러나 끝에 가서 보상을 잘 받았다.

789. Stick out (*v.*) – 눈에 띄다. 분명하다. 튀다.

1) 그는 굉장히 키가 큰데다가, 그의 곱슬머리를 파랗게 물들여서, 어떤 사람들 속에서도 쉽게 눈에 띈다.
2) 그 초록색 차는 어떤 주차장에서도 눈에 띈다.

790. Stick to (*v.*) – 고집하다. 고수하다. 주장하다.

1) 그녀는 일단 한번 일을 시작하면, 그것이 끝날 때까지 놓지 않는다.
2) 사람들은 더 이상 오래된 전통을 고수 하지 않는 것 같다.

**** Stick with (*v.*) – 계속해서 하다(어려운 일들을). 계속 ~하다.**

1) 대학을 졸업하는 것은 어렵다. 하지만, 계속해서 열심히 공부해라. 보상이 크다.
2) 그의 친구들 중 여럿이 그녀를 싫어함에도, 그는 여전히 그녀를 좋아했다.
3) 그는 아내와 이혼했고, 그의 아이들이 18세가 될 때까지 계속 그들의 양육비를 대어야 한다.

791. Stir up (*v.*) – (기분, 감정 등을) 휘젓다. 움직이다.

1) 그는 항상 문제를 일으키려고 시도했기 때문에 해고되었다.

2) 그는 그녀가 다른 사람을 만나는 것을 몰랐기 때문에 그녀의 애정 도피는 그의 마음을 휘저어 놓았다.

792. Stock up on (*v.*) **– ~을 비축해 두다.**

1) 시골에 사는 사람들은 대개 겨울을 대비해서 식량을 비축해 놓는다.

**** Store up** (*v.*) **– 저장하다.**

1) 다람쥐들은 겨울동안에 먹기 위해서 도토리와 호두를 비축한다.
2) 우리는 우리의 주요 식품과 그밖에 식품들을 보관하기 위해 부엌 옆의 창고를 사용한다.

793. Stop off / over (*v.*) **– (~로 가는 도중에) 잠깐 들르다. 잠깐 머무르다.**

1) 한국의 집으로 돌아가는 도중에 우리는 하와이에 잠시 들렀다.
2) 그는 일을 마치고, 맥주를 마시기 위해 친구들과 잠시 들렸다.
3) 그녀는 시부모님께 저녁 식사 후 커피와 후식을 드시러 오시라고 전화 했다.

794. Stow away (*v.*) **– 적당한 곳에 보관하다. (공짜로 배, 비행기, 기차 등에) 몰래 타다.**

1) 우리는 우리의 성탄절 장식을 내년까지 적당한 곳에 치워놓았다.
2) 그 난민은 잡히지 않을 것을 바라면서 그 배에 무임승차 했다.

**** A stowaway** (*n.*) **– 무임승차를 위해 기차나 배 등에 숨는 사람**

1) 로마에서 시카고로 비행하고 있던 중, 승무원들이 무임승차한 사람을 발견했다. 그들은 비행기가 O' Hare 공항에 도착했을 때 그를 세관에 넘겼다.

795. Straight away (*adj.*) **– 즉시, 망설임 없이**

1) 그의 아버지는 그에게 즉시 집으로 오라고 말했다.
2) 그는 좀처럼 돌려서 말하지 않는다, 그래서 즉시 요점을 말했다.

796. Straighten out (*v.*) **– 해결하다. (행동, 생각 등을) 바로 잡다. 바르게 고치다.**

1) 우리 사이에 뭔가 바로 잡아야 할 일이 있어.
2) 그들은 그들의 망나니 아들을 바로잡는데 사관학교가 도움이 될 거라고 생각했다.

**** Straighten up** (*v.*) **– (행동 등을) 바로 잡다. 깔끔하게 정리하다.**

1) 너는 이 새해부터 행동을 잘 해야 한다.
2) 이 벽장은 지저분해서 정리를 해야 한다.

797. Stretch the point (*v.*) **– 예외를 만들다. 진실을 말하지 않는다.**

1) 그는 그에게 이익이 될 것이라고 생각하면, 언제든지 예외를 만든다.
2) "숨기려고 하지 말고 진실만을 말해."

798. Stretch out (*v.*) - 쭉 뻗다. 늘이다.

1) 하루의 격무를 마치고나서 기지개를 펴고, 저녁 식사 전에 잠깐 눈을 붙이는 것은 기분이 좋다.
2) 학생들은 대개 그들의 10분 휴식 시간을 늘리려고 시도를 하고, 대개 15분의 휴식을 취하게 된다.

799. Strike it rich (*v.*) - 뜻밖의 대 횡재를 하다.

1) 그는 유정을 찾음으로써 뜻밖의 대 횡재를 하였다.
2) 그녀의 꿈은 복권에 당첨되어 갑작스럽게 횡재를 하는 것이다.

800. Strike out (at) (*v.*) - 무차별로 때리다.

1) 그는 화가 났을 때, 그 주변에 있는 것들을 물불가리지 않고 때린다.

** Strike out (*v.*) - 삭제하다. 선을 그어 지우다.

1) 그녀의 편집장은 그녀에게 몇 개의 어색한 표현을 지우도록 요구했다.
2) 그래서 그녀는 그것들을 지웠다.

801. Strike up (*v.*) - 음악을 힘차게 연주하다. 시작하다.

1) 그 악단은 행사가 시작되자 국가를 힘차게 연주했다.
2) 우리는 대학에서 만나 즉시 평생을 같이할 우정을 시작했다.

802. String along (*v.*) - (속임수로) 매달리게 하다. 따르다. 협조하다.

1) 그녀는 그를 사랑했는데, 그는 그녀와 결혼 할 의사가 없으면서도 그녀가 그에게 매달리게 했다.
2) 내 결정은 이래요. 저와 새 계약을 체결하든지, 아니면 놓아주세요, 저를 속임수로 잡아두지 마세요.
3) 그들은 그의 계획에 동의하지 않았으면서도, 그의 계획을 따르기로 결정하고, 무슨 일이 일어나나 관망하기로 했다.

** Pull strings (*v.*) - 이득을 위해 ~의 영향력이나 권력을 이용 또는 사용하다.

1) 신씨는 그녀가 만약에 그 자리를 원한다면 그가 그녀를 위해 힘을 써 줄 수 있다고 말했다.
2) 그는 너를 위해 힘을 써 줄 수 있다.

803. Strip (*v.*) - 벗다, 약탈하다. 벗겨서 제거하다.

1) 나체 무희가 무대를 가로질러서 춤을 추었다.
2) 내란은 그 나라의 가장 귀중한 재산인 사람들을 빼앗아 갔다.
3) 목수는 오래된 칠을 벗겨낸 다음, 그 진열장을 사포로 문지른 다음에 다시 니스를 칠하였다.

804. Subject to (*adj.*) - ~의 지배 하에 있는, ~하기 쉬운, 영향을 받는

1) 1995년 6월 1일 이후에 이 회사에 채용된 근로자들은 새로운 은퇴정책의 적용을 받는다.

2) 모든 수수료와 서비스 비용은 알리지 않고 바뀔 수 있다.
3) 동남아시아는 몬순시즌에는 태풍의 영향에 놓인다.

805. Sum up (*v.*) – 요약하다.

1) 그 강의는 두셋의 간단한 문장으로 요약될 수 있다.
2) 나의 사장은 우리 회의의 주요 안건을 요약해서 편지를 쓸 것을 요구했다.

806. Summon up (*v.*) – (용기, 기운, 열정 등을)모으다. 불러일으키다.

1) 그녀가 마침내 노래할 용기를 내었을 때는 이미 많은 사람들이 집으로 떠난 뒤였다.
2) 타고난 연설가들은 대개, 청중들의 열정을 불러일으키는 것이 쉽다고 생각한다.

807. Sure enough (*adv.*) – 기대했던 대로

1) 그는 그녀와 결혼하기로 약속했다. 기대했던 대로, 그가 청혼했다.
2) 일기예보는 주말에 폭풍을 예보했고, 기대했던 대로, 주말에는 강풍을 동반한 폭우가 내렸다.

808. Survival of the fittest (*n.*) – 적자생존(주어진 환경에 가장 적절히 순응하는 생명체는 살아남고, 그렇지 않으면 소멸된다는 의미)

1) 자연세계는 적자생존의 극명한 예를 보여주는 좋은 장소이다.
2) 점점 경쟁이 심해지는 세상에서 사는 우리의 삶 또한 적자생존의 한 예이다.

809. Swallow one's pride (*v.*) – (자존심을 죽이고) 받아들이다. 견디다.

1) 그가 강등되었을 때, 그는 자존심을 죽이고, 그 회사를 위해 계속 일하기로 결심했다.

**** Swallow ones' words (*v.*) – 자신의 말을 철회하다.**

1) 그들은 그가 결코 공군에서 소령이 되지 못할 것이라고 말했지만, 그는 소령이 되었고, 그들이 한 말을 취소하도록 강요받았다.
2) 그녀를 가장 신랄하게 비판했던 비평가들은 그녀가 그래미상을 받자 그들이 한 말을 철회할 수밖에 없었다.

**** Swallow one's feelings (*v.*) – 감정을 억누르다.**

1) 그가 처음 그 대학의 거절 편지를 받았을 때, 그는 망연자실 했으나, 몇 주가 지난 후 그의 감정을 억누르고 다시 삶을 살아갈 수 있었다.

810. Swallow up (*v.*) – 삼키다. 파괴하다.

1) 한 거대 복합 기업이 그 작은 기업을 삼켰다.
2) 그녀는 자신이 마치 삼켜질 것 같이 느껴지기 때문에 많은 군중들을 싫어한다고 말했다.

811. Swear by (*v.*) – (진실이나 정직의 표시로서) 맹세나 서약을 하다. ~에 대단한 자신감을 갖다.

1) 그는 그가 가진 모른 거룩한 것에 대고 충실하겠다는 서약을 했다.
2) 새 대통령이 서약을 할 때, 그는 취임선서라고 불리는 것을 한다.
3) 그녀는 그 상표를 대단히 좋아해서 그 것에 대단한 자신감을 가지고 있다.

**** Swear in (*v.*) – 법적인 선서를 하고 취임하게 하다. 선서하고 임무를 수행하게 하다.**

1) 대통령은 대법원의 대법관을 선서시키고 취임하도록 했다.
2) 배심원들이 선서를 한 바로 후에, 그들 중의 한 사람은 병 때문에 배심임무로부터 제외되었다.

812. Swear off (*v.*) – ~을 끊겠다고 맹세하다.

1) 그녀는 임신한 후에 금연하겠다고 맹세했다.
2) 그는 금주하겠다고 몇 번이나 맹세했지만, 그럼에도 불구하고 여전히 술을 마신다.

813. Sweep off one's feet (*v.*) – 강한 충동으로 들뜨게 하다.

1) 그녀는 그의 매력적인 모습에 그녀의 마음이 들떴다.
2) 그녀는 멋있는 남자를 보면 쉽게 마음이 들뜬다.

814. Swim with the stream – 대세에 편승하다.

1) 그는 그 제안된 계획에 반대했지만, 만약 자신이 그 회사에 머물기를 원한다면, 대세를 따르는 것이 가장 좋은 선택일 수 있다고 결정했다.

**** Swim against the stream or current – 대세에 역류하다. 거스르다.**

1) 사람들은 대개 대중의 의견에 거스르려 시도하기 보다는 시류를 따른다.

T

815. Tag along (*v.*) **– 바짝 따라 다니다. (대부분 원하여지지 않는)**

1) 나 별로 할 일이 없는데, 너 쇼핑할 때 따라다녀도 괜찮겠니?
2) 나의 개는 내 뒤를 항상 바짝 따라 다니기 때문에 내가 산책하는 동안 집에 있지 않으려 한다.

816. Take a chance (*v.*) **– 모험을 하다.**

1) 그녀는 집을 떠나 도시에서 직장을 구하는 모험을 하기로 했다.
2) 그녀는 대개는 낯 선 사람을 잘 도와주지 않는데, 이번에는 모험을 했다.

817. Take advantage of (*v.*) **– 자신의 이익을 위해 부당하게 이용하다. 적절히 잘 이용하다.**

1) 그는 너그러운데, 어떤 사람들은 그의 너그러움을 부당하게 이용한다.
2) 학생들은 새 도서관을 적절히 잘 이용했다.

818. Take after (*v.*) **– 닮다. 뒤쫓다.**

1) 그는 그의 아버지의 외모와 버릇을 빼 닮았다.
2) 그 개는 다람쥐를 뒤쫓았다.

819. Take apart (*v.*) **– 분해하다. 심하게 비평하다.**

1) 내 동생은 라디오와 시계를 분해하는 것을 좋아한다.
2) 그 학생의 주된 논증은 교수에 의해서 심하게 비평 받았다.

820. Take at one's word (*v.*) **– ~의 말을 그대로 믿다.**

1) 그녀는 그가 다시는 그녀에게 거짓말 하지 않겠다고 말했을 때, 그 말을 그대로 믿었다.

821. Take back (*v.*) **– 반환하다. 철회하다.**

1) 나는 바지 한 벌을 반환하고 돈을 되돌려 받았다.
2) 그 싸움은 그 소년들 중의 한명이 다른 소년에 대해 말한 것을 철회하지 않음으로 일어났다.

822. Take care of (*v.*) **– 돌보다, 처리하다.**

1) 그는 그의 아내가 장보러 간 사이 그의 아기를 돌보았다.
2) 그녀는 일을 하고 그리고 그녀의 어머니도 돌보기 때문에 그녀와 연락이 닿는 것은 쉽지 않다.
3) 우리는 휴가가기 전에 이 청구서들을 처리해야 한다.

4) 몸조심 해.

** Take care (*v.*) - 조심하다.

1) 그는 직장에 자주 지각을 해서 그의 상사는 그에게 조심하지 않으면 직장을 잃을 것이라고 말했다.

823. Take charge (*v.*) - 이끌다. 책임을 맡다.

1) 그는 승진이 되었고, 2004년 1월 1일부터는 그 부서를 이끌게 것이다.
2) 그녀의 어머니께서 안 계시는 동안, 그녀가 집안을 책임졌다.

824. Take down (*v.*) - (글로)적다. 메모하다. 떼어내리다. 분해하다.

1) 그는 나의 전화번호를 적었다.
2) 우리는 한 주간 더 성탄트리를 분해하지 않기로 결정했다.
3) 그 오래된 트뤼하우스를 뜯어 내리고 그 자리에 새 것을 지읍시다.

825. Take effect (*v.*) - 효력을 발생하다. 합법적으로 운용되기 시작하다.

1) 의사는 그 약이 바로 효과가 발생할 것이라고 그에게 말했다.
2) 새 정책은 다음 달의 첫 근무일부터 효력을 발생할 것이다.

826. Take exception (*v.*) - 불쾌하게 받아들이다. 문제 삼다.

1) 그녀는 논쟁적이서 누가 무슨 말을 하든 문제를 삼는다.
2) 그는 내 논평을 문제 삼을 타당한 이유가 없었다.

827. Take for (*v.*) - 잘못 알다(보다). 잘못 간주하다.

1) 경찰관은 콧수염이 있는 그 남자를 마약 판매상으로 오인하였다.
2) 나는 저 키 큰 여성을 선생님으로 잘 못 봤다.

828. Take for granted (*v.*) - ~의 가치를 느끼지 못하고 당연한 것으로 받아들이다.

1) 사람들이 그의 관대함을 당연하게 느낀 것이 그를 기분 상하게 했다.
2) 많은 사람들이 너무 늦을 때까지 그들의 부모의 존재를 당연하게 여긴다.
3) 우리 인간들은 자연을 당연한 것으로 여긴다.

829. Take heart (*v.*) - 용기를 내다.

1) 용기를 내어라! 네가 정말 열심히 일을 하면 그것을 할 수 있다.
2) 60세의 나이에 그녀가 학교로 돌아가서 컴퓨터 과학을 공부하는 것은 용기를 낸 것이다.

830. Take in (*v.*) - 포함하다. 입장하다. 받아들이다. 짧게 줄이다. 속이다. 거처를 제공하다.

1) 대영제국은 영국, 스코틀랜드, 웨일즈, 아일랜드를 포함한다.

2) 지난여름 롯데 월드에는 1억 명이상이 입장했다.
3) 그녀는 길 잃은 동물들을 받아 들여서 먹인다.
4) 그 보험회사는 그들의 상품을 팔기위해 속임수로 사람들을 끌어들였다.

831. Take in stride (*v.*) - 좋은 일이건, 나쁜 일이건 모든 일을 그대로 받아들이고 앞으로 나아가다. 모든 일을 쉽게 잘 해결해 나가다.

1) 그의 상사와 수년 동안 논쟁한 끝에 그는 일들을 있는 그대로 받아들이고 지나가는 것을 배웠다.
2) 그는 일들을 그대로 수용하는 방법을 배웠기 때문에, 그가 실패 하더라도 별로 당황하지 않는다.
3) 당신은 일들을 있는 그대로 받아들이고 나가야한다. 그렇지 않으면 당신은 늘 마음이 우울하고 화가 날 것이다.

832. Take into account (*v.*) - 고려하다. (어떤 일을 결정함에)

1) 우리는 교통상황을 고려하지 않았기 때문에 오페라에 늦었다.
2) 모든 것을 고려해서 계산하면 그 여행은 약 6000달러가 들을 것이다.

** Take into consideration (*v.*) - 고려하다.

1) 우리는 사람들의 실수를 고려하지 않았기 때문에 새 집을 건축하는 것이 좀 더 일찍 끝날 것이라고 생각했었다.
2) 우리는 빙판길을 고려해서 공항에 도착하는데 더 많은 시간을 할애해야한다.

** Take under consideration (*v.*) - 신중히 생각하다.

1) 한 회사가 나에게 더 좋은 자리를 제안했고, 나는 신중히 생각해야만 한다.

833. Take it (*v.*) - 참다. 견디다. ~로 받아들이다.

1) 다른 아이들이 그를 괴롭히고 있고, 그는 더 이상 그것을 참을 수 없다.
2) 그것은 농담으로 한 말이었는데, 그녀는 그것을 개인적으로 받아들였다.

** Take it out on (*v.*) - ~에게 자신의 화풀이를 하다.

1) 그녀는 화가 나면, 아이에게 화풀이를 한다.

** Take it or leave it (*v.*) - 그대로 받아들이든가 또는 그만 두든가 하다.

1) 그 팀은 이것이 그들의 마지막 제안인데 그것을 받아들이든지, 그만두든지 하라고 그에게 말했다.

834. Take it easy (*v.*) - 심한 일을 피하다. 천천히 여유 있게 지내다. 진정하다.

1) 그녀는 너무 열심히 일해 왔다. 그래서 그녀의 상사가 그녀에게 좀 천천히 쉬어가면서 하라고 말했다.

2) 만약에 몸이 좋지 않으면 조금 쉬는 것이 좋겠다.

3) 대개 그의 남편은 아이들에게 너무 엄했다. 그래서 그녀는 그에게 아이들을 너무 심하게 하지 말라고 요구했다.

835. Take liberties with (*v.*) – 지나치게 친근하게 굴어 불쾌하게 만들다. 마음대로 많이 고치다. 허락도 없이 마음대로 쓰다.

1) 그 남자는 그 젊은 여비서에게 지나치게 친근하게 굴어 불쾌하게 만든 것을 후회했다.

2) 그 편집자는 그 작가의 글을 마음대로 많이 고쳤다고 고발당했다.

3) 그 소녀는 그녀의 룸메이트의 개인소지품을 마음대로 사용했다.

836. Take notice of (*v.*) – 주의를 집중하다. 관심을 가지다.

1) 빈약한 입안과 장려 때문에, 대중들은 그 행사에 별 관심을 가지지 않았다.

2) 그녀는 놀랄 정도로 아름다워서, 사람들이 즉시 그녀에게 주의를 집중한다.

837. Take off (*v.*) – ~을 벗다. 증가하다. 떠나다. 이륙하다. ~로 부터 시간을 내다.

1) 사원에 들어갈 때는 신발을 벗어야만 한다.

2) 집중적인 광고 캠페인이 있은 후 매출이 많이 증가했다.

3) 비행기는 4:05분에 이륙할 예정이었으나, 폭우로 인해서 출발이 연기되었다.

4) 그는 시간을 내서 하와이로 놀러갔다.

838. Take on (*v.*) – 고용하다. 떠맡다.

1) 경제 부흥은 그 회사로 하여금 1000명의 새 직원을 고용하도록 하였다.

2) 그녀는 이미 해야 할 일이 너무 많았기 때문에 그 계획을 맡을 수가 없었다.

839. Take one's time (*v.*) – 서두르지 않고 천천히 하다.

1) 그의 어머니는 그에게 급하게 서두르지 말고 천천히 시간을 가지고 숙제를 하라고 했다.

2) 대개 서두르지 않고 천천히 하는 사람은 거의 실수를 하지 않는다.

840. Take out (*v.*) – 꺼내다. 짜내다. (사교로) 데리고 나가다.

1) 그는 출근 전에 냉동고에서 고기를 꺼내 놓았다. 그래서 그것은 녹을 시간이 충분할 것이다.

2) 과자들이 오븐에서 꺼내질 준비가 되었다.

3) 그의 어머니가 그에게 저녁식사 후에 쓰레기를 내어 놓으라고 말했다.

4) 그는 가끔 그녀를 데리고 나간다. 하지만 그들은 단지 친구일 뿐이다.

841. Take over (*v.*) – (지배권이나 경영권 등을) 계승하다. 점령하다.

1) 새 경영진이 경영권을 계승했다. 그래서 직원들은 많은 변화가 있을 것을 예상한다.

2) 그가 은퇴하면서, 그의 아들이 사업을 계승했다.

842. Take place (*v.*) – **발생하다, 일어나다.**

1) 그 행사는 Palace 극장에서 개최될 것이다.
2) 그 사고는 사거리 교차로에서 일어났다.

843. Take steps (*v.*) – **조처를 취하다, 계획이나 조정등을 하다.**

1) 그 회사는 자사 제품을 향상시키기 위해 필요한 조처를 취하고 있다.
2) 그는 그의 업무 수행을 향상시키기 위해 조처를 취할 것을 약속했다.

844. Take to (*v.*) – **좋아하게 되다. 마치 습관적으로 해 왔던 것처럼 하다.**

1) 그는 곧바로 그녀를 좋아하게 되었다.
2) 그녀는 자신이 수영하는 것을 좋아하게 되리라고 생각하지 않았었으나 물고기인양 수영을 좋아하게 되었다.

845. Take the law into one's own hands (*v.*) – **범법자나 악행자를 법적인 절차를 거치지 않고 직접 벌을 주다**

1) 경찰들은 폭도들이 자기들 임의대로 행동하기 전에 도착했다.
2) 자경단원이란 자신들 임의대로 죄를 주거나 보복을 하는 사람들이다.

846. Take to heart (*v.*) – **깊이 영향(상처)을 받다.**

1) 그녀는 그녀의 친구의 죽음에 상처를 받았다.
2) 그는 종종 화가 나서 한 말에 마음의 상처를 받는다.

847. Take turns (*v.*) – **차례로 하다, 교대로 하다.**

1) 우리는 고속도로에서 교대로 운전했다.
2) 우리는 교대로 저녁식사 접시들을 씻는다.

848. Take up (*v.*) – **흥미를 개발하다. 시작하다. 줄이다. (공간 등을) 차지하다.**

1) 그녀는 작년에 조깅을 시작해서 조깅애호가가 되었다.
2) 우리는 다음 직원회의에서 병가에 관한 문제를 다루기 시작할 것이다.
3) 이 바지는 1인치 정도 줄여져야 한다.
4) 저 소파는 너무 많은 공간을 차지한다.

**** Take up with** (*v.*) – **~와 교제를 시작하다. ~와 돌아다니기 시작하다.**

1) 그녀와 교제를 시작했기 때문에, 그는 그의 다른 친구들을 무시한다.
2) 그가 그 패거리들과 같이 다니기 시작하면서 그의 행동은 변했다.

849. Talk back (*v.*) – **무례하게 대답하다. 말대꾸 하다.**

1) 그녀의 부모님은 그녀가 선생님께 말대꾸 한 것에 대해서 벌을 주었다.

2) 그는 상사에게 말대꾸했기 때문에 해고되었다.

850. Talk down (to) (*v.*) – 경시하다. 얕보다. 짐짓 우월감을 가지고 상대를 낮춰보는 듯이 말하다.

1) 그녀는 나를 얕보고, 그리고 내 일을 경멸한다.
2) 그는 모든 사람에게 거만하게 말하기 때문에 별로 사랑 받지 못한다.

851. Talk into (*v.*) – ~을 설득해서 ‥하게 하다

1) 나는 춤추러 가고 싶지 않았으나 그의 설득에 넘어가서 갔다.
2) 너는 그녀가 수업에 빠지도록 꾀었다.

** Talk out of (*v.*) – ~을 설득해서 ‥하지 못하게 하다

1) 나는 그가 도박을 하지 말도록 설득했다.
2) 우리는 그가 그의 친구들과 싸우지 못하도록 설득했다.
3) 그들은 그녀가 공부를 끝마칠 때까지 결혼하지 말도록 설득하고 싶어 한다.

852. Talk out (*v.*) – 충분히 토론해서 해결하다.

1) 우리는 많은 문제들을 가지고 있지만, 충분한 토론을 통해 해결하려고 노력하고 있다.
2) 나하고 무슨 문제가 있다면, 대화를 통해 풀어보자.

** Level with (*informal., v.*) – 솔직하다. 솔직하게 다 말하다.

1) 협상자들은 그 문제를 해결하기위해 회의에서 서로에게 솔직했다.
2) 그 소년의 아버지는 그의 아들이 축구선수가 되기를 바라지만 그의 아들은 스포츠인이 되는 것을 싫어한다. 그 소년은 그의 아버지와 솔직하게 털어놓고 얘기해야한다.
3) 그는 결국 그의 아내에게 주식에서 많은 돈을 잃었고 예금이 한 푼도 남아있지 않다고 솔직하게 다 말했다.

853. Talk over (*v.*) – 자세히 의논하다. 자세히 얘기하다.

1) 나는 내 결정들을 실행에 옮기기 전에 자세히 의논하고 싶다.
2) 그녀는 지금 바쁘지만, 나중에 너와 자세히 이야기 할 수 있을 것이다.

854. Tear down (*v.*) – 부수다. 헐다, 몹시 비난하다.

1) 그들은 오래된 건물을 헐고 현재 그 자리에 새 건물을 지을 예정이다.
2) 그는 그들의 총아였으나, 그의 새 영화가 인기순위에서 밀리자 그 영화사는 그를 몹시 비난했다.

** Tear up (*v.*) – 갈기갈기 찢다.

1) 그녀는 그 편지를 읽고 나서는 갈기갈기 찢었다.
2) 그것의 내용이 그녀의 마음을 상하게 했기 때문에 그녀는 그것을 갈기갈기 찢어 버렸다.

855. Tell off (*v.*) - 몹시 야단치다.

1) 사장은 화를 참지 못하고 그녀를 몹시 야단쳤다.

2) 그녀는 우리에게 형편없는 서비스를 했기 때문에 몹시 야단을 맞아도 당연하다.

856. Think about (*v.*) - 생각하다, 고려하다. 회상하다, 기억하다

1) 내 형은 해외로 나가는 것에 대해 생각 중이다.

2) 내 여자 친구는 자기에게 내 카메라를 빌려줄 것을 생각해 보라고 부탁했다.

3) 그는 그의 딸에게 방으로 가서 자기 자신의 행동에 대해서 생각해 보라고 말했다.

**** Think of (*v.*) - 고려하다. 생각하다, 기억하다, 상상하다, 제안하다**

1) 우리 가족은 작은 도시로 이사 가는 것을 고려하고 있다.

2) 나는 그녀의 이름을 기억해 낼 수가 없다.

3) 위대한 미술, 음악 또는 문학이 없는 삶이 어떨지 나는 상상할 수가 없다.

4) 저녁을 먹기에 좋은 장소를 하나 제안해 주시겠습니까?

857. Think better of (*v.*) - 재 고려하여 더 나은 결정을 하다. 마음을 바꾸다.

1) 그는 직장을 그만둘 예정이었으나 마음을 바꾸었다.

2) 그녀는 그 돈을 훔치려고 생각했었으나 마음을 고쳐먹었다.

858. Think nothing of (*v.*) - 일상으로 생각하다. 대수롭지 않게 생각하다.

1) 그녀의 룸메이트는 늦은 밤에 시끄러운 음악을 연주하는 것을 대수롭지 않게 생각한다.

2) 그는 물건을 빌리고는 되돌려주지 않는 것을 대수롭지 않게 생각한다.

859. Think over (*v.*) - 심사숙고하다. (결론에 도달하기 전에) 깊이 생각하다.

1) 결론을 답하기 전에 시간을 가지고 깊이 생각해라.

2) 나는 이미 충분히 숙고했고, 그 자리를 받아들이기로 결심했다.

**** Think twice (*v.*) - 재고하다.**

1) 그들은 그들의 아들에게 학교를 자퇴하기 전에 다시 한 번 생각해보라고 부탁했다.

2) 고리대금업자에게 돈을 빌리기 전에 다시 한 번 생각해봐라.

860. Throw away (*v.*) - 버리다, 낭비하다.

1) 아직 읽지 않았으니 이 잡지들을 버리지 말라.

2) 그는 그의 돈을 경마장에서 낭비했다.

3) 그는 주색에 그의 돈을 낭비했다.

**** Throw out (*v.*) - 버리다, 거부하다, 떠나게 하다.**

1) 그녀는 낡은 구두를 버리고 새것을 샀다.

2) 상사는 회의 전에 그 아이디어를 거부했다.

3) 그는 화재경보기를 작동시켰기 때문에 학교에서 퇴학당했다.

861. Throw up (*v.*) – 토하다.

1) 그 학생은 술을 많이 먹은 후 토했다.

862. Tide over (*v.*) – 곤란한 시기에 도움이 되다.

1) 만약 네가 25 달러를 빌려줄 수 있다면, 월급날이 될 때까지 내게 큰 도움이 될 텐데.

863. Tie down (*v.*) – 묶다, 제한 / 속박하다.

1) 그 소년들은 그들의 야영용품을 밴 지붕에 싣고는 묶었다.
2) 그녀는 공부에 얽매여서 거의 나가지 않는다.

**** Tie up (*v.*) – 정지 · 정체시키다. 방해받다. 돈을 한곳에 모두 투자해서 쓸 수 없게 하다.**

1) 그 사고로 교통이 두 시간 이상 정체되었다.
2) 그녀는 아침 내내 회의에 참석해야 하지만, 점심 후에는 시간이 있다.
3) 그의 모든 돈은 그가 25살이 될 때까지 신탁자금에 묶여있다.

864. Tie in (with) (*v.*) – ~과 관련이 있다.

1) 그들은 그 책과 관련된 영화를 발표 할 것이다.
2) 그 용의자의 자백은 증거와 관련이 있다.

865. Tighten up (*v.*) – 더 꼭 조이다.

1) 우리는 책장들을 붙여 놓은 다음에, 나사로 꼭 조일 것이다.
2) 그 바퀴들은 더 꽉 조여져야만 할 것 같다.

866. Time and again / Time after time (*adv.*) – 반복해서

1) 나는 그녀에게 나갈 때 문을 세게 닫지 말라고 몇 번이나 요청했지만, 그녀는 아 직도 그렇게 한다.
2) 나이 많은 환자들은 잘 잊어버리는 경향이 있기 때문에 약을 먹도록 몇 번이고 주지시켜야 한다.

867. The time is ripe. – 시간이 적당하다. 시기가 무르익다.

1) 그녀는 적당한 시기가 되면 결혼하겠다고 말한다.
2) 국회의원들은 이 법을 입법할 시기가 무르익었다고 믿는다.

868. Tip off (*v.*) – 사전, 혹은 내부 정보를 제공하다.

1) 경찰들은 사전정보를 입수해서 은행 강도들이 침입할 때 기다리고 있었다.
2) 한 친구가 그녀의 사무실에서 곧 일자리 하나가 나올 것이라는 것을 내게 미리 가르쳐 주었다.

869. To-be / To be (*adj.*) – ~이 될

1) 그녀는 그녀의 미래의 시어머니를 껴안았다.
2) 그는 항상 될 것은 된다고 믿어왔다.

870. To be sure (*adv.*) – 의심할 여지없이, 확실히

1) 확실히, 우리는 그 경기대회에서 이길 거야.
2) 그 새로운 시스템이 작은 결함도 없이 컴퓨터 네트워크에 연결되었지만, 틀림없이 앞으로 문제들이 발생할 것이다.

871. To blame (*adj.*) – 책임 있는, 비난 받아야할

1) 그들은 그 램프를 깬 것이 누구의 잘못인지 알기를 원했다.
2) 밝혀졌듯이, 그들의 막내인 존이 잘못했다.

872. To date (*adj., adv.*) – 현재까지

1) 지금까지 10명이 채 안 되는 학생이 이 과목에 수강신청을 했다.
2) 지금까지 대학당국은 등록에 관한 서류를 보내지 않았다.
3) 현재까지, 우리의 실험 자료는 결론이 나지 않았다.

** Up to date – 최신지식, 정보, 방법 또는 스타일에 편승한

1) 그 조사는 가장 최근의 자료에 기초하고 있다.
2) 경찰은 진행 중인 수사에서 어떠한 진전이라도 보이면 그 가족들에게 알려 주겠다고 약속했다.

** Out of date – 구식의, 시대에 뒤진, 유행이 지난

1) 그녀가 더 이상 사용되지 않는 옛날 자료를 사용했기 때문에 그녀의 보고서에는 결함이 있었다.
2) 찢어진 청바지와 발목까지 덮는 긴 치마는 구식이다.

873. Tone down (*v.*) – 완곡히 하다. 부드럽게 하다.

1) 그녀는 좀 더 적절하고 전문적으로 행동할 것을 요구받았다.
2) 그는 격앙된 말을 좀 더 부드럽게 고친 후 편지를 보냈다.
3) 그녀는 그녀의 아파트를 부드러운 색으로 칠했다.

** Tone up (*v.*) – 더 강하게, 더 건강하게, 더 밝게, 또는 더 생동감 있게 하다.

1) 그는 더욱 강해지기 위해 일주일에 두 번씩 역기를 든다.
2) 좋은 실내 장식가는 가장 우중충한 아파트라도 생동감 있게 만들 수 있다.

874. Too bad (*adj.*) – 참으로 안된, 유감스러운

1) 참으로 불행하게도 그 회사의 인재였던 Tom이 임시 해고를 당하였다.
2) 유감스럽게도 그 회사가 좋은 직원들을 많이 잃고 있다.

875. Top off (*v.*) - **마지막 마무리를 해서 완성하다.**

1) 우리는 저녁에 샐러드를 먹었고, 아이스크림 선데로 마무리를 했다.
2) 그들은 휴가로 호주에 갔고, 돌아오는 길에 싱가포르에서 3일을 보내면서 그들 의 휴가를 마쳤다.

876. Toss off (*v.*) - **빠르고, 쉽게 일을 처리하다. 힘들게 생각함이 없이 쉽게 말하다.**

1) 그녀는 그녀의 직업분야에 대단히 숙련되어, 일어나는 어떤 문제든지 쉽게 해결할 수 있다.
2) 우리는 두 잔의 margarita 칵테일을 단번에 들이키고는 저녁을 먹으러 갔다.
3) 그의 강연자로서의 명성은 청중들이 점점 지루해 한다고 보일 때마다 즉흥적으로 재미있고 우스운 말들을 쉽게 하는 그의 능력에 기반한다.

877. To the best of one's knowledge - ~가 아는 한, ~의 아는 범위에서는

1) 내가 아는 한 그녀는 독신이다.
2) 내가 아는 한 그는 정직하고 성실한 사람이다.

878. To the fore (*adj., adv.*) - **지도적 입장에서, 앞으로, 눈에 띄는**

1) 회의 동안, 몇 가지 주요한 사항들이 중요하게 거론되었다.
2) 훌륭한 전략가로서의 그의 능력이 전쟁기간동안 눈에 띄었다.

879. To the good (*adv.*) - **아주 잘 된, 이익이 된.**

1) 우리는 서울에 갈 수가 없었지만, 오히려 이번 일은 모두 잘 되었다. 우리는 집에 일찍 도착했고, 일하러 돌아가기 전에 이삼 일을 쉴 수 있었다.
2) 그녀는 꽃을 팔아서 80 달러의 이익을 보았다.

880. To the letter (*adv.*) - **그대로, 세심하게 주의를 기울이며**

1) 그는 그녀의 지시를 그대로 따랐다.
2) 그 판사는 법에 적힌 그대로 그녀의 의무를 수행할 것을 맹세했다.

881. To the wall (*adv.*) - **피할 수 없는 상황에**

1) 그의 사업실패는 그를 피할 수 없는 상황으로 몰고 갔다.
2) 그녀는 심각한 상황에 처해있었다. 하지만 그녀는 그런 처지에 전에도 있어 보았으며, 그녀가 처한 상황에서 다시 성공할 수 있는 길을 찾을 것은 확실했다.
3) 재정적 어려움 때문에 집을 잃는 것이 그녀를 극한상황으로 몰아갔다.

882. Touch off (*v.*) - **폭발시키다, ~의 발단이 되다.**

1) 침대에서 담배를 피운 것이 화재의 원인이 되었다.
2) 단장과의 불화가 그 코치의 사직결심을 야기했다.

883. Touch on (*v.*) **– 간단히 언급하다.**

1) 그는 임금인상에 대해서 간단히 언급한 후 다른 문제로 넘어갔다.
2) 임신중절반대슬로건 표제에도 불구하고, 그 기사는 임신중절에 관해서 겨우 간단히 언급했다.

884. Touch up (*v.*) **– 약간 수정하거나 더하여 더 향상시키다, 조그만 흠이나 긁힌 곳 등에 페인트로 살짝 칠하다.**

1) 그 아파트는 그리 나쁜 상태가 아니어서, 단지 조금만 손보면 된다.
2) 너는 네 차의 녹이난 지점이 더 나빠지기 전에 페인트로 살짝 칠해야 한다.

885. Track down (*v.*) **– 추적하여 찾아내다.**

1) 경찰은 강간범이 다시 범죄를 저지르기 전에 그를 추적하여 찾아내길 바란다.
2) 그녀는 그녀의 연구논문에 필요한 정보를 찾아내기 전에 도서관에서 거의 하루 전체를 보냈다.

886. Trade in (*v.*) **– 새로운 제품 구입 시 사용하던 것을 주고 약간 싸게 구입함 (특히 자동차 구입시)**

1) 그는 그의 낡은 컴퓨터를 새것으로 보상 구입할 것이다.
2) 그 차 판매인은 내가 새 차를 사는 것에 대해 관심을 보이자, 내가 보상 구입 하게 하려고 노력했다.

887. Trade on (*v.*) **– 가능한 최대한도로 이용하다. 남용하다.**

1) 그 정치가는 선거에서 이기기 위해 그의 할아버지의 평판을 최대한 이용했다.
2) 그 교수는 그가 10년 이상 아무런 책도 출간한 적이 없기 때문에 그의 명성을 최대한 이용하고 있다.

888. Trial and error (*n.*) **– 시행착오, 최상의 해결책을 찾을 때까지 여러 가지 방법들을 시도하는 일**

1) 대부분의 과학자들은 시행착오를 통해서 그들의 문제를 해결한다.
2) John은 그의 대수 문제를 시행착오 방법을 이용해서 풀었다.
3) 부모들은 시행착오를 통해서 자녀를 양육하는 방법을 배운다.

889. Trick or treat (*n.*) **– 미국의 관습으로 할로우윈 데이에 아이들이 집집마다 돌아다니며 사탕이나 과자 등을 달라고 할 때 쓰는 말로써 주지 않으면 해코지로 장난을 치는 경우가 있다.**

1) 할로우윈 데이에 아이들은 과자를 얻으러 밖으로 나갔다.
2) 그들은 "Trick or treat."을 외치며 사람들의 집 문들을 두드린다.

890. Trip up (*v.*) – 넘어지거나 실수하게 하다.

1) 소매치기를 하려던 범인이 근처에서 조깅을 하던 비번인 경찰관에 의해 넘어졌다.
2) 꽤 많은 학생들이 시험 볼 때 함정문제들에서 실수를 했다.

891. Try on (*v.*) – (어떤가 보기 위해) 입거나, 신거나, 써보다

1) 그녀는 몇 개의 코트를 입어보았으나 그녀가 원하는 것을 찾지 못했다.
2) 저는 제게 어울리나 보기 위해 이 치마를 입어보고 싶습니다.

892. Try out (for) (*v.*) – 경험, 시험 등을 하다.

1) 회사들은 시장에 내놓을 것을 결정하기 위해 수백 가지의 디자인을 실험해본다.
2) 그는 도자기 만들기를 시도해보았으나 좋아하지는 않았다.
3) 그는 수영팀에 들기 위해 테스트를 받아보았으나 뽑히지 않았다.

893. Tune in (*v.*) – 특정 방송을 청취(시청)하기 위해 채널을 조정하다.

1) 드라마왕건을 보기 위해 9번을 틀어라.
2) 나는 내 라디오의 안테나를 조정했고, 그래서 지금은 98)6의 쿨 FM을 들을 수 있다.

894. Tune up (*v.*) – 악기를 조율하다. 기계, 엔진 등을 조정하다. (특정 활동을 위해) 준비하다.

1) 우리가 클럽에 도착했을 때 그 밴드는 악기만 조율하고 있었다.
2) 그녀는 엔진을 튜닝하기 위해 차를 안으로 몰고 들어갔다.
3) 당신은 마지막 시험 전에 당신의 기술을 다듬어야 할 필요가 있다.

895. Turn away (*v.*) – 보내 버리다, 거절하다.

1) 그녀는 자기 딸을 보내 버릴 수가 없었다.
2) 그 고객은 이미 너무 많이 술을 마셨기 때문에 한 술집에서 거절 되었다.

896. Turn down (*v.*) – 거절하다. 소리나 밝기, 온도 등을 낮추다.

1) 경영진은 내 임금인상 요구를 거절했다.
2) 우리는 우리 이웃에게 전화를 걸어 그가 너무 크게 틀어 놓은 전축의 소리를 줄 여줄 것을 요구했다.
3) 온도를 낮추어라, 너무 덥다.

**** Turn up (v.) – 우연히 발견되거나 나타나다. 볼륨, 온도 등을 높이다.**

1) 나는 상자들을 뒤적이고 있었는데, 거기에서 내가 잃어버린 줄 알았던 신용카드가 우연히 발견되었다.
2) 우리의 연구는 새 정보를 우연히 발견했다.
3) 볼륨을 높여주시겠습니까? 그들이 뭐라고 말하는지 들리지가 않습니다.

897. Turn in (*v.*) **– 제출하다, 돌려주다, (경찰에)인도하다, 밀고하다, 잠자리에 들다.**

1) 너는 모든 과제를 학기의 마지막 주까지는 제출해야만 한다.
2) 조에게 토요일까지는 비디오테이프를 반납해야 한다고 말해라.
3) 한 밀고자는 현상금 때문에 그를 고발했다.
4) 나는 피곤해서 오늘은 일찍 잠자리에 들려고 한다.

898. Turn off (*v.*) **– 물, 전기, 엔진 등을 끄다, 방향을 바꾸다, 싫증, 혐오하게 하다.**

1) 너 전열기구 끄는 것을 잊었더구나, 그래서 내가 껐다.
2) 우리는 다음 출구에서 방향을 바꾸어야 한다.
3) 결코 실수하지 않는다고 주장하는 사람들은 나를 역겹게 한다.

**** Turn on** (*n.*) **– 전기, 수도, 엔진 등을 켜다. 관심, 성적인 흥미 등이 생기게 하다.**

1) 복도의 등은 자동으로 켜지고 꺼진다.
2) 에어컨 좀 켜주세요.
3) 채널 30번 좀 틀어주세요.
4) 그는 매우 매력적이어서 그녀가 그를 볼 때면 성적인 호기심이 발동한다.
5) 천문학 과목이 정말 재미있어서 나는 내 전공을 바꿀까 생각했다.

899. Turn of the century (*n.*) **– 한 세기의 말과 다음 세기 초의중간시기**

1) 세기말은 대개 갈등과 소동의 시기이다.
2) 자동차는 19세기 말에 도입되었다.

900. Turn one's back on (*v.*) **– (도움이 필요할 때) 외면하다.**

1) 나는 그가 내 친구라고 생각했는데, 그는 내가 도움이 필요할 때 외면했다.
2) 나는 네가 내 도움이 필요할 때 외면하지 않겠다.

901. Turn one's stomach (*v.*) **– (속을) 메스껍게 하다**

1) 그 방에서 나는 강한 냄새가 그의 속을 뒤집어 놓았다.
2) 그 사고는 너무 끔찍해서 그녀의 속을 메스껍게 하였다.

902. Turn out (*v.*) **– 끄다, 생산하다, 조립하다, 결과가 되다, 참석하다, 판명되다, 쫓아내다, 안팎을 뒤집다**

1) 잠자리에 들기 전에 전등을 꺼주시기 바랍니다.
2) 새 프린터는 1분에 60장을 인쇄한다.
3) 지금은 자동차를 조립하는데 로봇들이 사용되고 있기 때문에 많은 노동자들이 일자리를 잃었다.
4) 나는 그 연구계획이 어떤 결과가 나올지 모르지만, 최선을 다할 것이다.
5) 수천 명의 사람이 그 락 콘서트에 참석했다.

6) 그녀가 이혼했다는 그 소문은 거짓으로 판명 났다.

7) 이전 세입자들은 집세를 내지 않았기 때문에 쫓겨났다.

8) 그는 잃어버린 차 열쇠를 찾기 위해 그의 주머니를 뒤집었다.

903. Turn over (*v.*) – (책장 등을) 넘기다. 뒤집어엎다, 시동이 걸리다. 곰곰이 생각하다.(경찰에) 넘기다.

1) 배터리가 다 방전되었기 때문에 엔진의 시동이 걸리지 않는다.

2) 결론을 내리기 전에 이삼일 마음의 여유를 가지고 곰곰이 생각해 봐라.

3) 피고는 유죄판결 후에 주 교정관들에게 인계되었다.

**** Turnover (*n.*) – turn over의 명사형, 이직 또는 그 자리를 메꾸기 위해 고용되는 사람들의 수, 페이스트리 종류 (대개 사과)**

1) 이 지역에서 교사들의 이직률은 상당히 높다.

2) 이 사과 페이스트리들은 매우 맛있다.

904. Turn to (*v.*) – 도움을 받기 위해 ~에 의지하다. 일을 시작하다. 참조하다.

1) 그 난민들은 중국 정부에 도움을 요청했으나, 그들은 신변보호 대신 북한으로 송환되었다.

2) 교과서의 24쪽을 참고하기 바랍니다.

U

905. Underage (*adj.*) – 미성년의

1) 그는 미성년자이기 때문에 술을 사도록 허가되지 않는다.
2) 그는 미성년이기 때문에 운전면허를 딸 수 없다.

906. Under arrest (*adj.*) – 체포된

1) 그 여성은 가게에서 물건을 훔친 죄로 체포되었다.

907. Under fire (*adj.*) – 공격을 받는, 비난, 비평을 몹시 받는

1) 그 군대는 심한 공격을 받아서 후퇴할 수밖에 없었다.
2) 일본은 그들의 교과서를 수정하라는 요구를 거절함으로써 몹시 비난을 받아왔다.
3) 새 법은 그 것이 제정되기도 전에 몹시 비난을 받았다.

908. Under the table (*adv.*) – 비밀리에

1) 그는 적은 급료를 받았지만, 비밀리에 뇌물을 받았기 때문에 부자가 되었다.
2) 그녀는 비밀리에 그에게 약간의 돈을 주었다.

909. Up against (*adj.*) – (많은 어려움 등에) 당면하고 있는

1) 그 두 회사를 합병하려는 계획은 많은 문제에 당면해 있다.
2) 존은 직장을 잃을 것이기 때문에, 피할 수 없는 어려움에 당면하고 있다.

910. Up front (*adj.*) – 매우 솔직한, 공개적인

1) 그 서비스 회사는 그들의 유지비용에 대해서 매우 투명하다.
2) 그 시장은 그의 정치적인 신념과 정책에 대해서 매우 솔직했다.

911. Ups and downs (*n.*) – 오르내림, 좋을 때와 나쁠 때 (기복)

1) 모든 사람에게는 좋을 때와 나쁠 때가 있다.
2) 성공적인 삶이란 나쁜 때보다 좋은 때가 더 많다.

912. Up to (*prep.*) – ~에 달린, ~하고 있는, 준비(각오)등이 되어있는

1) 네가 원하기만 하면 그 자리는 네 것이다. 그것은 완전히 네게 달려있다.
2) 쿵하는 큰 소리를 들었기 때문에, 엄마는 그들이 무엇을 하고 있는지 궁금해 했다.
3) 아무런 증거도 없지만, 그녀는 그녀의 이웃이 좋지 않을 것이라고 확신했다.

4) 그는 퇴원을 했고, 한두 주후에는 직장으로 돌아갈 준비가 될 것이다.

913. Use up (*v.*) – 다 써버리다.

1) 그녀는 케이크를 만드는데 모든 버터를 다 써버리고는 내일 아침식사를 위해 더 준비하는 것을 잊어버렸다.
2) 그는 배구를 하는데 모든 힘을 다 써버려서 지금은 춤추러 가고 싶지 않다.
3) 우리는 샴푸를 다 써버려서 새로 더 사야 된다.

V

914. Vote (*v.*) **- 투표하다.**

1) 민주당은 모든 등록된 선거권 자에게 다가오는 선거에 투표하라고 요청하고 있다.

**** Vote for** (*v.*) **- ~에 우호적으로 (찬성하여) 투표하다.**

1) 유권자들은 2대1로 세금인상에 찬성투표를 했다.

**** Vote against** (*v.*) **- 반대하여 투표하다.**

1) 학교 위원회는 더 많은 교사를 채용하자는 제안에 반대투표를 했다.

915. Vote down (*v.*) **- 부결하다.**

1) 제안된 수정안은 7대 3으로 부결되었다.
2) 입법 위원회는 수입 증가 제안을 부결시켰다.

916. Vote in (*v.*) **- (투표로) 선출하다.**

1) 그는 근소한 표차로 당선되었다. 그리고 아직 우리는 그가 일 처리 하는 방식을 좋아한다.
2) 김씨는 연례 주주회의에서 선출되었다.

W

917. Wait on (*v.*) – (식당, 가게, 병원 등 공공시설에서) 웨이터나 웨이트리스 등으로서 시중들다.

1) 그들은 그들보다 늦게 온 다른 고객들이 이미 안내되었음에도 불구하고, 아직 그들이 안내되지 못한 이유를 알고 싶어 했다.
2) 그는 테이블에서 시중드는 시간제 직을 가지고 있다.

918. Wake up (*v.*) – (잠 또는 정신적인 면에서) 깨다. 깨우치다.

1) 나는 보통은 6시 경에 잠에서 깬다.
2) 그는 늦잠을 잤기 때문에 1교시 수업에 빠졌다.
3) 그 연사는 매우 영감적이어서 많은 청중들에게 난민들의 어려운 처지를 알게 해 주었다.

919. Walk away from (*v.*) – 떠나거나 저버리다, (사고 등에서) 거의 다치지 않고 살아나다.

1) 나는 어린 아이들의 양육을 저버리는 어떤 사람도 존경할 수 없다.
2) 그녀는 운 좋게도 긁힘 하나 없이 그 사고로부터 무사했다.

**** Walk away with / walk off with (*v.*) – 훔쳐서 달아나다. 자신의 실력으로 따가다.**

1) 그 도둑은 내가 다른 고객을 도와주고 있는 동안 시계를 훔쳐서 달아난 것이 틀림없다.
2) 러시아 팀이 금메달을 땄다.

920. Walk of life (*n.*) – 사회계층, 생활, 직업 등등

1) 모든 사회계층에서 온 사람들이 그 회의에 참석했다.
2) 그들은 그들의 딸과 딸이 결혼하고 싶어 하는 남자가 사회계층이 다르기 때문에 결혼을 반대했다.

921. Walk out (*v.*) – 파업하다. 갑자기 나가다. 버리고 떠나다.

1) 교사들은 그들의 임금 인상과 다른 이익들에 대한 요구를 당국이 듣게 하기 위한 운동으로 파업을 했다.
2) 승진이 거부되자, 그는 말 한마디 없이 사무실을 나가버렸다.
3) 그녀는 그녀의 세 아이를 버리고 떠나고는 다시는 돌아오지 않았다.

922. Walk over / Walk all over (*v.*) – (누군가를)존중이나 배려 없이 마음대로 하다.

1) 왜 그녀는 그가 자기를 함부로 대하도록 놓아두는지 나는 모르겠다.
2) 그는 매우 무기력한 사람이라 그녀의 아내가 그를 아무렇게나 대하도록 놓아둔다.

923. Warm up (*v.*) – 더워지다. 덥히다. 준비운동하다.

1) 이번 주말로 가면서 날씨가 따뜻해 질 것이다.
2) 나는 저녁을 위해 스프를 조금 데웠다.
3) 운동선수들은 경기 전에 준비운동을 한다.

924. Wash out (*v.*) – 물로 씻어 제거하다, 씻어 내다.

1) 이 셔츠에 커피 얼룩이 있어서 나는 그것을 씻어내야만 한다.
2) 블루베리 열매의 얼룩은 지워지지 않는다.
3) 폭우가 옥수수 밭을 쓸어버렸다.

925. Waste away (*v.*) – 점점 약해지고 야위어지다.

1) 그녀의 아내가 죽은 후, 그는 슬픔으로 약해져 가는 것 같다.

926. Waste one's breath (*v.*) – 말해도 소용없다.

1) 그녀에게 말하는 것은 소용없다. 그녀는 충고를 받아들이지 않는다.
2) 말해도 소용없어. 그녀는 마음을 바꾸지 않을 거야.

927. Watch out (*v.*) – (자동차 등을 운전할 때) 조심하다.

1) 그 도로에서 밤에 운전할 때는 사슴에 주의해라.
2) 도로를 건널 때는 차의 왕래를 조심해라.

928. Water down (*v.*) – (적당히 조절하여) 강도를 약하게 (물을 타서)

1) 편집자가 신문사의 사주를 유화하기 위해 그 기사를 약하게 조절하기 전까지, 그는 그 기사가 지금까지 자기가 쓴 기사 중에 최고의 기사라고 생각했다.
2) 이 음료들은 마치 물을 탄 것 같다.

929. Ways and means (*n.*) – 의회의 예산 위원회, ~을 위한 방법이나 재원.

1) 그는 의회 예산위원회로 선출되었다.
2) 그는 여행할 돈도 없고 돈을 마련할 방법도 없다.

930. Wear down (*v.*) – (사용이나 마찰의 결과로) 썩다, 부식하다, 지치게 하다.

1) 침식은 수년에 걸쳐서 산을 깎았다.
2) 아이들을 가르치는 것은 보람이 있지만, 그것은 정말 사람을 지치게 한다.

** Wear out (*v.*) - 너무 많이 써서 못쓰게 되다(하다). 피곤하게 하다.

1) 그녀는 그녀의 청바지가 닳아서 못쓰게 될 때까지 입었다.
2) 그는 세 달꼴로 두 켤레의 운동화를 닳게 한다.
3) 오늘은 너무나 힘든 날이어서, 나는 지금 대단히 피곤하다.
4) 오랜 시간동안의 하이킹이 나를 지치게 했다.
5) 교실의 학생들이 너무 활동적이어서 그들은 그녀를 지치게 하고 있다.

931. Wear off (*v.*) - 점차 사라지다. 점차 마모되다.

1) 그들은 결혼 한지 고작 6개월이 지났을 뿐인데, 그들의 사랑은 벌써 시들기 시 작하고 있다.
2) 묘석에 새겨진 이름은 오래전에 닳아 없어졌다.

932. Weed out (*v.*) - (잡초 등을) 제거하다.

1) 이번 주말에 나는 나의 헌 옷들을 버릴 것이다.
2) 우리는 아이들을 보호하기 위해 유해한 인터넷 사이트를 제거해야만 한다.

933. Weigh down (*v.*) - 짓누르다. 압박하다.

1) 밤새내린 눈이 상록수들을 짓눌렀다.
2) 올림픽 방송이 상업 광고들로 짓눌렸다.
3) 그 트럭은 무거운 타일 짐들로 눌려있다.
4) 직원들은 회사의 파산 계류 때문에 압박감을 느끼고 있다.

934. What have you / What not (*n.*) - 그 밖의 여러 가지

1) 나는 내 자신을 소개했고 그들에게 나의 이름, 내가 어디서 왔는가, 왜 여기 있는가, 등등을 말했다.
2) 우리는 우유, 빵, 버터 그리고 그밖에 여러 가지를 사야한다.

935. What if - 만약 ~하면 어찌할 것인가? 가정해서

1) 네가 1백만 달러를 찾게 된다면 어떻게 할 것인가?
2) 그는 그가 졸업 후에 직업을 얻지 못하면 어떻게 하나 생각했다.
3) 만약 내가 이번 출장을 가지 않으면 어떻게 될까?

936. A while ago (*adv.*) - 조금 전에

1) 나는 좀 전에 그를 보았다.
2) 나는 조금 전에 내 사전을 여기에 놓아두었는데, 없어져 버렸다.

** A while back (*adv.*) - 수 주 또는 수개월 전에

1) 그녀는 여기에서 좀 오래전에 일했었는데, 우리는 그녀가 떠난 뒤로 그녀의 소식을 듣지 못했다.

2) 우리는 거기에 얼마 전에 낚시 하러 갔었는데, 오염이 많이 되어있어 실망했다.

937. Wide of the mark (*adj., adv.*) – 과녁에서 빗나간, 왜곡된, 사실이 아닌

1) 그녀의 처음 두발은 과녁에서 빗나갔다.
2) 그의 예산 위기에 대한 발언은 많이 빗나갔다.

**** Wide-awake (*adj.*) – 완전히 잠이 깬.**

1) 누군가 내게 새벽 3시에 전화를 했다. 전화를 끊은 후, 다시 잠을 청했으나 나는 완전히 잠이 깨었다.

938. Win out (over) – ~에게 이기다, ~보다 낫다.

1) 대개 성실하게 일하고 부지런한 것이 아첨보다 낫다.

**** Win one's way (*v.*) – 힘든 일을 통하여 또는 힘들게 인생에서 성공하다.**

1) 그는 대단한 유머 감각과 친절한 천성을 가졌기 때문에 그녀의 마음을 얻었다.

939. Win over (*v.*) – ~을 설득해서 ~편으로 만들다.

1) 그는 단지 그 자신이 됨으로써 그녀를 자기편으로 만들었다.
2) 그의 명료한 발표와 강한 논리는 마침내 그들을 설득해서 자기편으로 만들었다.

940. Wind up (*v.*) – ~로 끝나다, 마무리하다, (태엽 등을) 감다.

1) 그 영화는 전형적인 해피엔딩으로 끝났다.
2) 지금 하던 일을 마무리하고 30분정도 후에 그 식당에서 당신들과 합류 하겠습니다.
3) 그는 자명종 시계의 태엽을 감아 놓는 것을 잊었기 때문에 늦게 일어났다.

941. Wipe off (*v.*) – 표면을 닦다.

1) 이 탁자는 닦아야 한다.
2) 텔레비전 화면을 닦아라.

**** Wipe out (*v.*) – 닦아내다. 제거하다. 파괴하다.**

1) 그녀는 녹제거제를 뿌리고는 녹을 닦아 냈다.
2) 그 토네이도는 지역 휴양지에 있는 수십 채의 집들을 휩쓸었다.
3) 오늘의 교전은 전쟁의 신속한 종결을 위한 모든 가능성을 다 없애버렸다.

942. Within reason (*adj., adv.*) – 적당하게(한), 적절하게(한)

1) 그 회사는 파업 중인 노동자들의 요구를 적절히 수용할 것이다.
2) 그녀의 아버지는 적절한 선에서 그녀가 원하는 어떤 차던지 사주기로 약속했다.

943. With good grace (*adv.*) – 품위 있게, 친절하게, 상냥하게, 공손히

1) 그들은 일들이 자신들이 원하는 방향으로 가지 않을 때라도, 항상 품위있게 행동한다.

2) 작고하신 내 할머니는 사람들을 아주 친절히 대하곤 하셨다.

** With bad grace (*adv.*) – 불손하게, 악의로

1) 그 팀은 가장 최근의 패배를 불손하게 받아들이며 그들의 코치를 당황하게 만들었다.

944. With no strings attached (*adv.*) – 조건 없이

1) 그는 아무런 조건 없이 그녀가 차를 고치는 것을 도와주고 싶다고 말했다.

2) 나는 네가 그 계획을 끝내도록 아무런 조건없이 도와주겠다.

945. With open arms (*adv.*) – 반갑게, 열렬히

1) 오랜 기간 떨어져 있은 후에, 그녀의 가족들은 그녀를 반갑게 맞이했다.

2) 나는 우리가 깨진 것을 알지만, 만약 당신이 다시 합치기를 원하면 나는 반갑게 당신을 맞이할 거야.

946. Without fail (*adv.*) – 확실히, 어김없이

1) 그들은 주택 대출금을 한 달에 한번씩 30년 동안 빠짐없이 냈다.

2) 그는 지금부터는 수업시간에 맞추어 오겠다고 그의 선생님께 약속했다.

947. With the best (of) (*adv.*) – ~에 못지않게, ~ 만큼 잘

1) 그는 그들 못지않게 농구를 잘한다.

2) 그녀는 원어민 못지않게 영어를 잘 말한다.

948. Word for word (*adv.*) – 한자도 바꿈이 없이, 말 그대로

1) 그 기자는 말해지고 있는 것을 한자도 바꿈없이 그대로 적었다.

2) 나는 네가 말한 것을 그대로 기억한다.

949. Worked up (*adj.*) – 흥분한, 화난, 걱정하는

1) 그의 아내는 그가 두세 시간 집에 늦게 올 때면 항상 화낸다.

2) 그는 그가 시험에 떨어졌기 때문에 착잡해 했지만, 우리는 그에게 그것으로 세상이 끝난 것은 아니라는 것을 상기시켜 주었다.

950. Work off (*v.*) – (일이나 활동을 통해)제거하다. 풀다.

1) 그녀는 그녀의 과체중을 줄이기 위해 항상 운동을 한다.

2) 그는 화를 가라앉히고 지금은 냉정해졌다.

3) 조깅은 원치 않는 몸무게를 줄이는 뛰어난 방법이다.

951. Work on (*v.*) – 효과가 있다. 설득하다. 노력하다.

1) 그는 은퇴를 한 이래로 작고 다양한 지역 프로젝트를 위해 바쁘게 일하고 있다.

2) 대통령은 재경위원회에서 그의 조세 개혁법안을 입안하기 위한 노력으로 파악된 관망자

들을 설득하고 있다.

952. Work out (*v.*) – 해결, 개발 또는 마련하다. 조정하다. 잘되다.

1) 수개월의 논쟁 끝에, 마침내 합의를 이끌어 냈다.
2) 경영진은 모든 고용인들에게 이익이 될 새 계획을 개발했다.
3) 정부는 지난해부터 국가 경제구조에 대한 철저한 조사를 위한 새로운 접근방법을 개발하려고 시도해 오고 있다.
4) 나는 때때로 그녀가 체육관에서 운동하는 것을 본다.

953. Wrapped up in (*adj.*) – 오직 ~에만 골똘하다.

1) 나는 지금 일자리를 찾는데 골똘해 있어서 전화하지 않아서 미안해.
2) 그는 그의 마지막 과제에만 골똘하고 있어 좀처럼 밖에 나갈 시간이 없다.
3) 그녀는 오로지 그녀 자신만 생각하고 다른 어느 누구도 생각하지 않는다.

**** Wrap up (*v.*) – 포장하다. 끝내다. 옷을 따뜻하게 입다.**

1) 이거 선물이거든요, 포장해주세요.
2) 나는 한 시간 정도 후까지는 이 일을 끝내야만 집에 갈 수 있다.
3) 오늘 옷을 따뜻하게 입는 것 잊지 마라, 밖이 춥다.

954. Write down (*v.*) – 적어두다.

1) 그녀는 주소와 전화번호를 그녀의 전화번호부에 적었다.
2) 나는 속기용 구술녹음기를 조금 전에 하나 샀다. 그래서 지금은 내가 말만하면 나의 비서가 모든 것을 받아 적는다.

**** Write off (*v.*) – 장부에서 손실로 처리해 지우다. 공제하다.**

1) 서방국가들은 제3세계 국가들의 모든 차관을 공제해 주는 것을 고려하고 있다.
2) 그는 그의 빚들을 공제 받기 위해서 파산신청을 했다.

**** Write out (*v.*) – (생략함이 없이) 다 기재하다. 자세히 쓰다.**

1) 지원서에 당신의 이름을 생략하지 말고 다 쓰시오.

**** Write up (*v.*) – 보고서를 쓰다. 쓰다.**

1) 새 화재가 났을 때 기자들은 그들의 신문의 기사를 쓰느라고 바빴다.
2) 과학자들은 그들의 실험의 보고서를 썼다.
3) 나는 그 강의의 요약을 써줄 것을 부탁받았다.

Y

955. Year-around / Year-round (*adj.*) – 일 년 내내 하는(할 수 있는, 사용할 수 있는, 이용할 수 있는)

1) 실내 스케이트장은 아이스 스케이트를 연중할 수 있는 운동으로 만들었다.
2) 운동선수들은 일 년 내내 연습을 하지만, 경기는 시즌에 한다.

**** Yearlong (*adj.*) – 일 년 내내 계속되는**

1) 연중 계속되고 있는 가뭄이 거대한 산불을 야기한 중요한 원인이다.
2) 오늘날 많은 학생을 위하여 학교가 일 년 내내 운영하는 시설처럼 되어가고 있는 것 같다.

956. Year-end (*adj.*) – 연말에 작성하는, 연말의

1) 그 회사의 회계부서에서 일하는 직원들은 연말 보고서를 만들기 위해 이번 주말에 일해야만 한다.
2) 기름 값의 연말 폭등은 저소득 가정에게는 치명적인 영향을 주어왔다.
3) 많은 사람들이 망년회에서는 술을 많이 마시고, 술에 만취한 상태로 집까지 운전해 가는 경향이 있다.

957. Yearn for (*v.*) – 간절히 바라다, 그리워하다.

1) 그녀는 훌륭한 동반자를 간절히 바란다. 그녀의 외로운 삶에 기쁨을 가져다 줄 그런 사람.
2) 그는 유럽에서의 휴가를 간절히 바라고 있고, 그것이 그의 가장 큰 바램이다.

958. Yield (*v.*) – 드러내다, 밝히다.

1) 과학적인 탐험에 의해, 우주는 조금 씩 조금 씩 그것의 비밀을 드러내기 시작했다.
2) 그 왕릉 발굴은 그 왕조시대의 삶에 대한 중요한 정보를 제공했다.

저자약력

김옥경

- 미국 Ohio에 있는 Kent State University에서 심리학 학사와 동 대학원에서 교육학 석사 받음.
- Kent State University 신입생담당 어드바이저로 근무.
- 퍼스트 내셔널 뱅크 주택융자과 근무.
- 세계은행 번역담당 역임.
- 대전 우송대학교 영어 전임강사 역임.
- 청주대학교 영미어문학 / 현 어학교육원 외국인강의전담교수로 재직중.
- 자연사랑모임'한국자연의 친구들'대표.
- 1998년 미주 중앙일보 신춘문예에 논픽션 부문 가작 수상(미국 시집에 영시 게재).

Vocabulary 1250
American Style Practical English

2010년 9월 10일 개정판 인쇄
2010년 9월 17일 개정판 발행

저자 / 김옥경
발행인 / 고종식
발행처 / 우용출판사
등록일 / 1997년 11월 25일
출판등록 / 제 2001-1호
주소 / 서울특별시 마포구 망원1동 338-53
전화번호 / 02) 324-6577
팩시밀리 / 02) 324-6177

정가 / 20,000원

ISBN / 978-89-6249-042-8 13740

www.choolpansa.com